Mountains Come Out of the Sky

MW00559476

(Nick Hale/Getty Images)

Mountains Come Out of the Sky

The Illustrated History of Prog Rock

WILL ROMANO

Backbeat
Books

An Imprint of Hal Leonard Corporation

Copyright © 2010 by Will Romano

All rights reserved. No part of this book may be reproduced in any form, without written permission, except by a newspaper or magazine reviewer who wishes to quote brief passages in connection with a review.

Published in 2010 by Backbeat Books
An Imprint of Hal Leonard Corporation
7777 West Bluemound Road
Milwaukee, WI 53213

Trade Book Division Editorial Offices
33 Plymouth St., Montclair, NJ 07042

Printed in the Unites States of America

Book design by Damien Castaneda

Library of Congress Cataloging-in-Publication Data

Romano, Will, 1970-
  Mountains come out of the sky : an illustrated history of prog rock / Will Romano.
    p. cm.
  Includes bibliographical references and index.
  ISBN 978-0-87930-991-6 (pbk. : alk. paper)
  1. Progressive rock music--History and criticism. I. Title.

ML3534.R675 2010
781.66--dc22

                          2010032445

www.backbeatbooks.com

For Sharon, Molly, and Maggie

Author's Note

The majority of interviews featured in *Mountains Come Out of the Sky* were specifically conducted for inclusion in this book. In addition, I drew upon interviews I completed as a freelance music journalist on assignment for such publications as *Goldmine*, the *New York Post*, *Modern Drummer*, and *EQ*.

Author-provided artwork was gathered from various sources, including record label press materials, contemporary publications, personal music memorabilia, and original album packaging.

ix FOREWORD by Bill Bruford

1 INTRO: What Is Prog?

5 IN THE BEGINNING: The Beatles, Early Floyd,
The Moody Blues, Frank Zappa, and the Rise of the Moog

17 PINK FLOYD: When Pigs Fly

31 KING CRIMSON: Twentieth Century Schizoid Band

47 EMERSON, LAKE & PALMER: Welcome Back My Friends . . .

59 YES: Going for It All

71 GENESIS: Crymes and Misdemeanors

83 JETHRO TULL: Minstrels in the Gallery

91 COLOSSEUM AND GREENSLADE: For Those About to Rock . . .

97 THE CANTERBURY SCENE: In the Land of Grey and Pink

109 CAMEL: Dust and Dreams

115 GENTLE GIANT: On Reflection

121 PROG FOLK: Out of the Mist

135 PROGRESSIVO ITALIANO: Musica Rock Romantica

143 GERMAN PROG AND THE KRAUTROCKERS

151 SONG FOR AMERICA: Can the U.S. Export Prog?

163 TUBULAR BELLS: Exorcising Mike Oldfield

167 RUSH: Modern-Day Warriors

181 U.K.: Sunset on the Empire?

185 THE RETURN OF THE KING (CRIMSON)

195 THROWING IT ALL AWAY: Genesis, Yes, and ELP

207 MARILLION: Doin' It in "Style"

215 DREAM THEATER: The Soul of Prog?

225 PROGRESSIVITY CONTINUES INTO THE TWENTY-FIRST CENTURY

235 ACKNOWLEDGMENTS

236 BIBLIOGRAPHY

242 DISCOGRAPHY

CONTENTS

grandiose pastures/postures that led "Aqualung" into "Thick As A Brick" and hence to "Passion Play."

We'll ignore "Benefit" (Tull No. 3) — Anderson seems happy enough to do likewise according the Chrysalis info sheet — and hypothesise a situation where Tull return to "Stand Up" (Tull 2 — still with me?) and pursue a different route out of possible alternatives to arrive at "War Child," their last album.

Anderson himself goes some way to supporting this view in the following quote: " 'War Child' is like a sophisticated 'Stand Up,' inasmuch as it's made up of personable kinds of songs. It was a very refreshing

important album."

Me neither, though "Minstrel" obviously has far grander pretentions.

As Anderson takes pains to assure us, it has far more of a "direction," is "more positive," is "as different from 'War Child' as 'Stand Up' was from 'Aqualung'."

True — but the intention is clear. And it seems reasonable to assume that Jethro have withdrawn if not to square 1 at least as far as square 2 to re-explore the index of possibilities.

Which means that, at the very least, the sensitive among us can approach the current day Jethro without fear of being brutally assaulted at every twist and turn by the bombastic riffs

od Tull. Ian Anderson always been better applying not inconsiderable lyrical p wess towards reportage rat than pulpit-thumping.

Side one opens with an announcing the performance a minstrel troupe (don't be put off, spoken word is a minimum) over which derson, apparently liste from the "audience," conclu to a companion, "They're going to like this." Thence the title track, a synthesis Tull riffs and licks which w in this context, though I can why CSM thought it a con when reviewing same single. It serves to establ Tull/Anderson as the minstrel of the

Foreword

FEW OF US INVOLVED IN THE golden years of progressive rock expected the subject to be written about and discussed with quite such enthusiasm decades after the last pair of flared loon pants had been hung out to dry. Had we been able to foresee the more constrained music-scape of forty years hence, however, we nascent progsters might have better appreciated the wild amounts of freedom we were being given. A patient, long-suffering, and generous record industry was supplying us with unlimited studio time and then letting us get on with it. We just thought this was what rock music was.

Arguably, until the Beatles' 1967 *Sgt Pepper's* album, pop music was created broadly according to a fixed set of musical principles about what should happen when guided by strict notions of acceptability and the public taste. The sound track to the late-'60s counterculture had no interest in any fixed set of principles, and even less in public taste. For a brief, heady and aberrant decade, the crew ran the ship, and the captain was stowed below. In the best sense of the phrase, progressive rock didn't know what it was doing. The ship may have gone round in circles for a bit, but then it set sail for the heart of the sunrise.

The main contributors were making it up as they went along. When I was in Yes, we felt we could do anything we wanted, so long as it didn't sound like anybody else. When Atlantic Records sent their top A&R man, Tom Dowd, to London to supervise the making of *The Yes Album*, he listened quietly at the back of the studio for a while and returned to the U.S., fully aware that what was going on at Advision Studio 1 was not subject to the usual laws of pop or rock music as he understood them.

As a subject for doctoral theses and learned discussion, progressive rock has everything you need. A reasonably clearly defined beginning and end, with a peak golden period followed by a slower decline and fall, a sociopolitical context against which the music could be heard (the counterculture), and at least three major technological innovations in place to facilitate change (the long-playing vinyl record, stereo twenty-four-track recording, and FM radio). From Pink Floyd's wildly imaginative 1967 *The Piper at the Gates of Dawn* to ELP's horrific 1978 *Love Beach*, progressive rock flew, like Icarus, too near to the sun, crashed, and burned. After a period of disgrace, a 1980s neo-progressive movement took hold in the charred subsoil, to be followed by the current resurgence and reevaluation—of which Will Romano's excellent book is a part. This was the life cycle of the progressive butterfly, the perfect little art scenario—something like the Pre-Raphaelites or the Bloomsbury Group in the visual arts.

Romano has wisely enlisted many of the principal players to tell us firsthand how the story unfolded from their respective points of view. He has interviewed me on several occasions, and it's a pleasure to be considering his work instead, for a change. He makes an affable and enthusiastic tour guide, pointing out everything you need to know about the main features of the rocky outcrop affectionately known as "prog." His book, of which he can be justifiably proud, is a friendly, colorful, and thorough account of one of the last century's most enduring of musical movements by a commentator who's clearly an enthusiast. Progressive rock, then, is still with us, if limping a bit. To misquote Frank Zappa, "Prog isn't dead, it just smells funny."

Bill Bruford
Surrey, U.K. 2010

Bill Bruford, the godfather of progressive rock drumming, was at the top of his profession for four decades playing with Yes, King Crimson, Genesis, Earthworks, and many more. His taste for the unpredictable in live performance led him to collaborations with dozens of the world's top jazz and rock musicians in pursuit of the innovative, the unusual, and the unlikely. Though Bill is now retired, his life's work is well documented on CD, DVD, and in his book Bill Bruford: The Autobiography, *all available at www.billbruford.com.*

(K & K Ulf Kruger OHG/Getty Images)

WHAT IS PROG?

ONLY GLUTTONS FOR PUNISHMENT DARE TRY THEIR hands at the definition of "progressive rock," as it is almost too extensive, too elusive, too amorphous and contradictory to put down on paper. Prog rock is a bit like pornography—the lines and definition can be blurred, but you know it when you see it.

Historically, progressive rock had been forged from the musical fires lit by American blues and R&B pioneers as well the major proponents of the 1960s psychedelic movement. In part, progressive rock was a natural outgrowth of flower power and hippie/utopian sensibilities. The psychedelic bands did as much experimenting with musical form, sometimes dispensing with pop music structures and expectations (dabbling in elements of world music and free jazz), as they did with illegal and illicit substances.

With a classicist's sense of precision and ambition, "the progressives" gave shape to amorphous forms of drug-addled and hallucinogen-inspired rock music and, taking a cue from bands such as Pink Floyd and the

Genesis at Shepperton Studios, October 1973. (Pictured are vocalist/percussionist/kick drummer Peter Gabriel, left, and kit drummer/backing vocalist Phil Collins.) (Ian Dickson/Getty Images)

Beatles, approached rock music as an art form while developing along a completely different evolutionary musical branch (and occupying a different head space).

The problem is, every artist could be called progressive. The term itself becomes meaningless: Artists from Elvis to the Who to Jimi Hendrix to the Clash could be seen as being progressive in their own ways. Is a band progressive merely for evolving? Every band evolves. U2 evolved. R.E.M. evolved.

Next you say, "Okay, the music itself must be progressive, in that it moves from one mood or shape to many different ones within the span of a single song." Fine. But this statement runs into the same problem. Black Sabbath changed its music within the framework of one song (they used compositional dynamics) in the late 1960s and early 1970s. So did Led Zeppelin. And the Who. They took the listeners on a journey.

Are they progressive rock?

The textbook definition of progressive rock prescribes an artistic approach to music (which later became a *genre* of music) that developed, initially in Britain, in the late 1960s and continued into the 1970s, which sought to fuse rock with different musical styles, usually of distinctly European origin—from classical to folk. Prog rock was, generally speaking, written, performed and listened to by white, middle-class kids.

Applying the definition gets to be a bit sticky, however. Fitting music into a category leads to a hierarchy that, ironically, the progressives were against from the start. The fact is, there may be a standard description of prog rock as the major progenitors had perpetrated, but the banner of progressive rock houses encompasses many diverse artists, many of which have little in common with one another. How does King Crimson

sound like Emerson Lake and Palmer? Is Jethro Tull remotely connected to Genesis? In theory, no barriers exist in progressive rock: At its best, progressive rock is postmodernism run amok.

Some would argue that all the above-mentioned bands deal, or have dealt in some form, with keyboard technology, and touched upon European art music at some point in what is considered their most "progressive" periods.

Somewhere along the line, prog rock took on certain identifying factors that are ripe for spoofing: banks of synthesizers, concept albums, extravagant LP cover illustrations (or LP packaging), and absurd stage costumes and fashion statements (i.e., wizard hats and sequined capes)—all of which have been both parodied and explored by artists with earnestness and fervor.

"There has always been progressive music at every level," says Yes vocalist Jon Anderson. "You had progressive jazz, and some of the great classical composers of the twentieth century were considered progressive minimalists, and others, like Karlheinz Stockhausen, who were jumping into electronic areas as well."

"The concept of progressive music is pretty wholesome, you know?" says Greg Lake, bassist and vocalist for Emerson Lake and Palmer. "But really, it became very twisted. It became the easy target for the press. . . . But the essence, really, of progressive music is pretty much the essence of all of rock 'n' roll, which was to move forward and to discover new things. To try to express yourself in, I suppose the word is, an original way is not really different, in a way, than what any of the rock 'n' roll artists did during the 1950s and 1960s. Everyone tried to move his game on. What happened in the case of progressive rock that earmarked as it as a special genre was that it is a European movement, which made it kind of peculiar. The roots of progressive music were, essentially, European. At least that strain of it that we are talking about—Pink Floyd, ELP, King Crimson, that sort of thing, that took its influences a lot from European music. There was very little else to draw from the well of inspiration of rock music. By the time 1969 came, perhaps 1968, '69, it was really time to look for some new avenues of inspiration rather than drawing from blues or American jazz or country and western music, the idea occurred to draw more from European classical structures, folk also."

"I like to think of it as an expansion of rock," says Ian McDonald, cofounder of King Crimson. "As I had said many times, it's breaking out of the two guitars, bass, and drums format for a rock band. I never liked the term *progressive rock*, anyway, and I'm just using it as a reference, because progressive rock turned on itself and became more regressive. It became a

parody of itself. For me, it just meant broadening out the straight-ahead rock-band sound."

"Some thought we were soft rock," says Yes guitarist Steve Howe. "Then [Yes] got called symphonic rock, and then it was orchestrated rock, and then it was cinemagraphic rock."

"Progressive to me was always a cross between American R&B and European classical music," John Wetton (King Crimson, Family, Asia) told the author in 1995. "If you put those two together, you have the formula for great progressive rock. I defy you to name me a classic progressive rock album that doesn't have those two qualities somewhere. It must have the rhythmic pulse of the blues, but it must have the melodic European stuff."

The success of bands such as the Beatles, the Moody Blues, Procol Harum, and others was part and parcel of a larger cultural flowering that would encompass the growing and dynamic progressive rock movement, uniting a generation of musicians and listeners alike in a conversation and a common search for answers.

"There was a confluence of factors involved in the mid-1960s," notes Gong bassist Mike Howlett. "The rise of technology, economic revival after World War II, a hugely disproportionate number of youth, the Vietnam War, and the civil rights movement were all happening at the same time. The creative avant-garde found itself in a large body, for once, rather than the fringe, and suddenly at the center of popular cultural movements that inspired and encouraged one another. The other factor is the psychedelic influence and the sudden availability of LSD, which certainly expands people's creative imagination and opens people to the potential of all the power of coordinated art forms. When you combine music and fashion in a big cultural conglomeration . . . and throw some acid into the picture, you're going to get some extraordinary events and

extraordinary experiences," says Howlett. "That spurs people who make art to go further."

"What we're talking about gets back to watersheds," says John Lodge, bassist and vocalist for the Moody Blues. "You don't realize its importance at the time. If there was anything that the '60s and '70s did, it was open the conversation. Young people throughout the world were saying that we'd just had two world wars in the last forty years, perhaps it is time we open up conversations about things that can be really important to us. I think that this is really what happened, Woodstock and the Isle of Wight Festival in the U.K. It wasn't a goal: I think it was a conversation. This was really from 1967 through 1973. That, to me, was the major part of modern rock history. That is when, if there is any philosophy in rock 'n' roll, that's when it happened. That was the watershed."

The wave of British artists that would include Yes, Jethro Tull, King Crimson, Emerson Lake and Palmer, and others represented, on some level, a conservatism, as these artists accentuated one half of the postmodern/modern equation or definition of progressive rock by being apolitical and bringing structure to chaos.

Australian scribe Craig McGregor, writing in 1970, once pointed out that in order for rock 'n' roll to survive the 1960s and thrive in the 1970s, it must turn from "Dionysian frenzy" to "Apollonian order" to something resembling order and classicism.

"Instant orgasm is great," McGregor said, "but stales with repetition."

Despite cries of critics to the contrary, rock music needed prog to exist. "Progressive rock was an extension of psychedelia," says Howe. "The psychedelic bands did whatever they wanted, didn't they? But after that, there needed to be some sort of containment, some shape. I think progressive rock became that framework."

IN THE BEGINNING

The Beatles, Early Floyd, the Moody Blues, Frank Zappa, and the Rise of the Moog

"TO ME, THE FIRST PROGRESSIVE ROCK band was the Beatles," says Ian McDonald. "The dawn of so-called progressive rock, or the acorn, to me was the song 'Yesterday.' Just before the interview I pulled out my vinyl album of *Help!*, to see what year that came out. It was 1965, and I was nineteen years old, and I loved all kinds of music and I already loved the Beatles, and I had interests in jazz and classical, but I basically loved rock music and the Beatles in particular at that time. When I heard 'Yesterday,' a little lightbulb went off that told me that something new was happening right now with this because of the use of a classical string quartet. It was not the first time strings had been used on a pop record—that goes way back to Gene Pitney and Buddy Holly . . . but there was something about the use of strings in that song that . . . had classical music influence and style and to me that was the dawn of progressive rock. Of course, people went on to explore and introduce various influences and expand the scope of two guitars, bass, and drums to almost anything you can think of. That gave the rest of us permission or license to do it ourselves. The progressive era was happening just as the Beatles were breaking up, and that whole era of *Revolver* and *Sgt. Pepper's* and *Magical Mystery Tour* basically gave new bands, at that time, license to do whatever they wanted."

"The Beatles opened up the doors for everybody," says Jon Anderson.

"Dare I say the Beatles slip into [progressive rock] a little bit with *Sgt. Pepper's*," says Ian Anderson, vocalist and multi-instrumentalist for Jethro Tull. "Though somehow I can't bring myself to acknowledge that Paul McCartney, the master of the showbiz form, be let into that world inhabited by Pink Floyd and their successors to that progressive move in music."

"The Beatles led the way with *Revolver*," says Justin Hayward, guitarist and vocalist for the Moody Blues. "The Beatles are kind of responsible for a lot of musicians thinking that they . . . didn't have to fit [their music] into a three-minute format."

The Beach Boys' Brian Wilson had first heard the Beatles' *Rubber Soul* in December 1965 and it was "definitely a challenge for me," Wilson later commented. Wilson remarked at how each cut on *Rubber Soul* was stylistically "stimulating," and he soon went to work on the Beach Boys' recognized masterpiece, 1966's *Pet Sounds*, a title that not only references the animal-like experimental noises heard on the record but the fact that *Pet Sounds* was Wilson's "pet" project while the band was on tour without him.

"I was in the music business at the time, and my very first recognition of acid rock—we didn't call it progressive rock then—was, of all people, the Beach Boys and the song 'Good Vibrations' [released as a single and not included on *Pet Sounds*]," says Phillip Rauls, former Atlantic Records and Regional Promotional Manager. "They used an instrument called the theremin, and it was an electronic instrument and you could run your hand between this electronic signal and make the pitch go up and down. They used it in sci-fi and horror movies—the black-and-white B movies. That sent so many musicians back to the studio to create this music on acid."

"The whole ethos of rock 'n' roll in the early days was about pretty girls, cars, and having fun," Eric Woolfson, one half of the Alan Parsons Project, said in 2009. "The Beach Boys were the classic example of a band moving from fun surf music to phenomenally progressive stuff."

While the Beach Boys and Beatles were deadlocked in creative competition (which would result in the Beatles' *Sgt. Pepper's*—one of the pillars of progressive rock), others were gaining by leaps and bounds, topping their previous outputs. The Yardbirds, perhaps known as much for their guitarists (i.e., Eric Clapton, Jimmy Page, Jeff Beck) as their music, branched out into experimental blues-rock after their early days as a Chicago blues–styled British band that had taken up the Stones' residency at the Crawdaddy Club, owned by industry big wheel Giorgio Gomelsky.

"They started off as this English R&B band, basically," keyboardist/organist Brian Auger told the author in 2007. "Then they kind of branched out into different things, like, 'Shapes of Things' and 'For Your Love,' which was the biggie."

Songs like "For Your Love" (featuring bongos and harpsichord), written by future 10cc guitarist/vocalist Graham Gouldman (he also penned the hit "Heart Full of Soul," one of the earliest known appearances of the sitar in rock music, followed, of course, by the Beatles' "Norwegian Wood [This Bird Has Flown]" and the Rolling Stones' "Paint It Black"),

"Shapes of Things," and "Over Under Sideways Down" were atmospheric guitar workouts.

"We started playing twelve-bar blues and then we made it a bit more interesting. Probably the main person was [bassist] Paul Samwell-Smith, and I don't know where he got the idea for all of the buildups," says drummer Jim McCarty, one of the founding members of the Yardbirds—a partial reference to Charlie Parker—as well as a member of the later progressive bands Renaissance and Illusion. "We were always concentrating on making music very exciting. We would play a song, then drop it all down, and then build it up with this big crescendo on the bass and drums. When we got Jeff [Beck] in the band, he had all of these weird and wonderful sounds. He wasn't a straight blues guitar player. It was all about getting an atmosphere going that was very exciting."

Beck would, of course, continue to explore throughout the 1960s and 1970s with the Jimmy Page–penned "Beck's Bolero"—a melding of Maurice Ravel's "Boléro, ballet for orchestra" and the mid-1970s fusion sounds found on such Beck albums as *Blow by Blow* and *Wired*.

FRANK ZAPPA, PROCOL HARUM, AND THE BEATLES

"Early Soft Machine, Kevin Ayers, a band called the Wilde Flowers, with Robert Wyatt singing," said Yes/Genesis/King Crimson drummer Bill Bruford. "These bands were doing something different. I was young, but it was the first time I had heard anybody singing in 5/4. Or singing in unusual phrasing or unusual length of meter. Until then, pop songs were 'dum de dum dum de deedly dum de dum.' But Robert Wyatt used all kinds of different phrasings and unusual bar lengths and unusual chord sequences. This being in the mid-1960s. And that would be about the first time anybody

Procol Harum, 1971. *Left to right*: bassist Alan Cartwright, multi-instrumentalist Chris Copping, drummer Barrie Wilson, guitar Dave Ball; lyricist Keith Reid, and keyboardist Gary Brooker. (Courtesy of A&M Records and Chrysalis)

smelled that something weird was happening. The Beatles had a couple songs in 7/4. And there were some strange intimations in the Beatles material in '64, '65, '66."

In 1966, Frank Zappa and Mothers of Invention broke from the underground with the release of the double album *Freak Out!*—a tour de force rock album dripping with orchestral flourishes, Dixieland jazz, satire, "trivial pop" (by Zappa's own description), blues-based guitar solos, studio craft (the massive echo effects in "Who Are the Brain Police?"), incisive political criticism, sexual double entendre, barbershop harmonies, the sick buzzing of the African mouth instrument (the kazoo), animal/jungle and avant-garde noises, R&B vocal/'50s doo-wop (one of Zappa's favorite forms of music), multitracked madness (making full use of the stereo image), and strange vocal inflections and orgiastic yelping (among other things).

Songs such as "Who Are the Brain Police?," "I Ain't Got No Heart," "How Could I Be Such a Fool," "Wowie Zowie," "Help, I'm a Rock," "The Return of the Son of Monster Magnet," and "It Can't Happen Here" mix and subdivide musical genres, sometimes from one second to the next. "The Return of the Son of Monster Magnet"—what Zappa jokingly referred to as a two-movement ballet—in particular is a blue-haired society's worst nightmare coming to life. (Supposedly, the song was the result of letting hippies run rampant in the studio and recording whatever came into their minds. The result is a "bright, snappy number.")

Given that the song—and the album—ends with whacked-out chipmunk voices, one has to wonder if the entire fifteen-track package were not some elaborate practical joke on the listener. (One also has to wonder just how much the Beatles were listening to *Freak Out!* in the months before they composed the music for the studio masterpiece *Sgt. Pepper's*, which itself closes with equally and seemingly nonsensical vocals, apart from boasting other similar sonic character-

istics (e.g., the use of a kazoo in "Lovely Rita" as Zappa had used it in "Hungry Freaks, Daddy").

"The funny thing about *Freak Out!* is Frank did what he thought people wanted," says Paul Buff, a highly influential inventor/engineer during Zappa's formative years as a professional musician in the early 1960s. "He just did it in a very renegade fashion."

Moving into 1967, we see that four records were crucial to the early development of progressive rock: the Moody Blues' *Days of Future Passed*; Pink Floyd's debut, *The Piper at the Gates of Dawn*; the Beatles' recognized classic *Sgt. Pepper's Lonely Hearts Club Band*; and the single "A Whiter Shade of Pale" by Procol Harum, which was followed by an eponymous full-length release.

The Beatles had explored baroque pop with the use of ensemble strings in "Eleanor Rigby" and "Yesterday," while less than two years later, Procol Harum included elements of Bach's Suite No. 3 in D

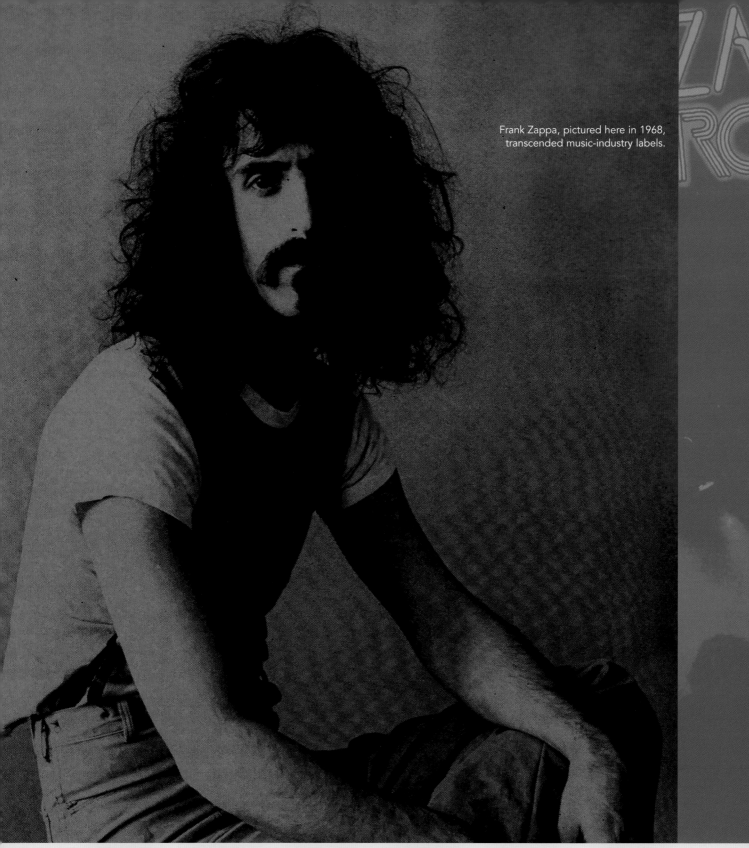

Frank Zappa, pictured here in 1968, transcended music-industry labels.

Cucumonga
(1963)

Freak Out!
(1966)

Absolutely Free
(1967)

We're Only In It For the Money (1968)

Hot Rats
(1969)

The Grand Wazoo
(1972)

Major in their number-one U.K. hit, "A Whiter Shade of Pale." Procol Harum's combination of classically inspired organ and piano lines and Robin Trower's burning blues guitar work made for an unusual, amalgamated sound.

"I was interested in some of the far more serious music of Bach, B Minor Mass and things like that," explains Procol organ player Matthew Fisher. "I was never that stuck on James Brown or Bobby Bland, you know? It was within the two that there was nevertheless a large area of overlap in our musical tastes."

Fisher describes how his musical equipment was a pivotal ingredient in making the song a classic: "All of those glissandos I play on the Hammond M-100 organ, they were just all done with one finger or one thumb," says Fisher. "If you want to do a glissando, you could do one on an M-100 just using one finger; your fingernail, even. You can't do that on the B-3. You'd break your fingers. The keys are that much heavier. The sound of the M-100, compared to the Hammond B-3, is murky. The M-100 just sounds much more like it's in a dungeon or something. It doesn't have the clarity and force that the B-3 has, and using that powerful of a tool might have been something I'd have been uncomfortable with in those days."

Months before "A Whiter Shade of Pale" shot to number one in Britain (and number five in the U.S.), the Beatles had resigned from roadwork in the summer of '66 (much like Brian Wilson)—their tour ending, appropriately enough, in the hippie utopia of San Francisco—and turned Abbey Road Studios into their very own musical sandbox and produced some of their most experimental and groundbreaking music.

"Penny Lane" and "Strawberry Fields Forever," the first sides the band released since regrouping after taking a break from one another and (generally just) being the Beatles, seem innocent enough on the surface. But dig a bit deeper, and you'll soon find creepiness and a darkness that envelop the tracks. Admittedly, the lyrical content of songs such as "Maxwell's Silver Hammer" and "Eleanor Rigby" are disturbing (if not just plain sad), but they aren't damaging psychologically.

"Strawberry Fields Forever" opens with the dreamy, wispy, soft puffing of flutes created by the Mellotron—a keyboard/gadget/monstrosity/invention, employing the same technology as the earlier Chamberlin keyboard, that, through the activation of prerecorded tape reels and a series of pulleys and pinch rollers, via the pressing of keys produces sounds of strings and other acoustic instruments, usually for a duration of roughly seven or eight seconds.

The limited functionality of the instrument gave rise to the development of a hand technique that former Moody Blues keyboardist Mike Pinder, a pioneer of the Mellotron, called an arpeggiated style of chording—a rolling of the fingers to avoid unwanted sonic gaps. Furthermore, the 'Tron also gave birth to a slew of lesser known instruments created by independent vendors who tried to improve on the design and affordability of the machine. Among them were Dave Biro, whose Birotron worked on eight-track tapes (Biro built the first one while listening to Yes's *Tales from Topographic Oceans*), and Ken Freeman, who created the String Symphonizer.

Though notoriously and frustratingly unpredictable—it was a delicate piece of equipment to start with, and fluctuations in voltage caused major problems with tuning, which was embarrassingly apparent on the road (supposedly Yes keyboardist Rick Wakeman was so incensed with the instrument's inability to stay in tune, he set one on fire)—the Mellotron was meant to beef up the sound of a rock band and turn the group into a symphonic unit of some sort.

"I remember hearing *Sgt. Pepper's* for the first time, and it is such a cliché, but when I was at college, a student in every room had the album on and was playing a different track," says 10cc's Kevin Godley. "It actually made me uncomfortable because the noises were unfamiliar. But after two days' exposure, it clicked in a mighty way. 'Fuck. This is it. Gimme a piece of this.' It was so much more significant than anything. They broke the rules because they could. They dared. And who dares wins."

"If the Beatles had never crossed that line, which they did in 1967, progressive music may never have happened," Wetton told the author in 1995. "The Beatles moved into the experimental, classical, world music [arena], and that was what gave us progressive music. Unless you have an alternative [perspective of history], that is my view of things. That's the way my life happened, anyway."

"I remember when we first heard *Sgt. Pepper's*," says Styx's original vocalist/keyboardist, Dennis DeYoung. "It was summer. Hot. That's what I remember. Nobody in the neighborhood [Chicago] had air-conditioning; it was 1967. I was with

Overnight Sensation (1973)

Apostrophe (') (1974)

Roxy & Elsewhere (1974)

Tom Nardin, who was in the band at that time, at the Panozzo brothers' [former Styx rhythm section] house, and we ran out to get the record, because the Panozzos' parents had one of those Zenith console stereos in their living room. We sat there and it was hot and we listened to it over and over. It changed everything. It changed everything."

THE BAND YOU'VE KNOWN FOR ALL THESE YEARS

Rock itself can be interpreted as a progressive idea—something that lives on the cutting edge of society and art, which is constantly being redefined. Ironically, and quite paradoxically, "progressive rock," the classic era of the late 1960s through the mid- and late 1970s, introduces not only the explosive and exploratory sounds of technology (from early electronic rhythmic devices, thanks to high-profile drummers such as Carl Palmer on Emeron, Lake and Palmer's *Brain Salad Surgery* and Graeme Edge on the Moody Blues' 1971 record *Every Good Boy Deserves Favour*, to the obvious advances in keyboard technology) but traditional music forms (classical and European folk) and (often) a pastiche compositional style and artificial constructs (concept albums), which suggests postmodernism.

This may be why progressive rock has given writers and musicolo-

gists fits for over four decades. The terminology for, the artwork chosen to represent, and the very nature of the music seem inherently contradictory—a combination of opposites. For instance, how do we categorize the Nice's "Five Bridges Suite" and "Pathetique Symphony No. 6 3rd Movement"? Or, for that matter, something like Yes's *Tales from Topographic Oceans*, Pink Floyd's *The Dark Side of the Moon*, Rick Wakeman's *The Six Wives of Henry VIII*, and Genesis's *The Lamb Lies Down on Broadway*? What about Rush's Romantic literature–inspired tone poem "Xanadu"? What do we make of music that's composed as pastiche that combines the traditional and modern, the universal and the contrived?

"It's an ironic consequence of *Sgt. Pepper's* success that an album of such hugely disparate themes and emotions, niftily shoehorned into a pseudo live performance by the inclusion of a bracketing title song and some sound effects, should have led to a rock trend—the concept album," says Justin Currie of Scotland's Beatlesesque pop-rock band Del Amitri. "Well before *Pepper*, pop musicians had been maximizing the emotional impact of sequencing and gap timings on LPs, not least the Beatles themselves from *A Hard Day's Night* onward. *Sgt. Pepper's* was the apotheosis of pop's ambition to be complex,

subtle, and in essence 'symphonic.'"[1]

It's no surprise that the Beatles spent months completing *Sgt. Pepper's* and, some reports claim, burned through upward of a hundred thousand dollars to complete the record's production process. With George Martin at the helm, no idea was too outrageous. One of the most outstanding examples of studio trickery—among tapes being sped up and slowed for songs like "When I'm Sixty-Four" and "Lucy in the Sky with Diamonds"—may not have required much money, but an awful lot of time and energy. It involved a cutting, shuffling, reshuffling, and splicing together of various taped organ, harmonium (played by George Martin, as he had done for "The Word" on *Rubber Soul*), and bass harmonica performances (which recall the wheezing and whirling effects of a calliope) to create the sonic vertigo of the fairgrounds variety for backing tracks heard in "Being for the Benefit of Mr. Kite!"

"The Beatles made it more acceptable for music to expand into other areas, like fairgrounds music," says Curved Air vocalist Sonja Kristina.

The impact of *Sgt. Pepper's* spread far and wide (the record shot to number one in the U.S. and the U.K., and has spent more than two hundred weeks on the British charts, when you include chart reentries), but not

---

[1] "The idea that *Sgt. Pepper's* is somehow a concept album is quite difficult to defend, because the title song of *Sgt. Pepper's* doesn't quite bookend the album," says Simon Warner, who teaches in the school of music at the University of Leeds in the U.K. "Let's not forget that 'A Day in the Life' ends the recording. The Beatles seem to hint at live performance during the course of the recording, but it's a kind of constructed liveness. Maybe in that sense there's a concept at work?"

A Hard Day's Night (1964)

Revolver (1965)

Revolver (1966)

Magical Mystery Tour (1967)

Abbey Road (1969)

(Opposite) *Sgt. Pepper's Lonely Hearts Club Band* (1967)

everyone got the philosophical joke. Richard Goldstein, music critic for the *New York Times*, slammed the record for its unreality, singling out the song "She's Leaving Home" as an "immense put-on" (and the writer didn't mean this philosophically, either).

"The obsession with production, coupled with a surprising shoddiness in composition, permeates the entire album," Goldstein wrote on June 18, 1967. Time has proven Mr. Goldstein wrong, one thinks, but this critique, and others like it (some that said the Beatles destroyed rock 'n' roll), kicked off the music press's long "love affair" with progressive rock.

The impact of *Sgt. Pepper's* was far greater than perhaps Goldstein— or anyone else (perhaps even the Beatles)—could have seen. "There were some good things and bad things that *Sgt. Pepper's* opened the door for," says Les Fradkin, who was a session musician in London in the late 1960s and completed many a track at Apple Studios. "The good thing is that it proved to the record industry that an album format, or something resembling a concept album format, had commercial viability, and that the studio had a sound unto itself. The bad part is that people who did not have the level of genius of the Beatles went ahead and attempted to ape *Sgt. Pepper's* and failed to match it. *Sgt. Pepper's* did something in America that was interesting: It destroyed the garage band sound. Before that you had your ? & the Mysterians and your "Little Bit O' Soul" by the Music Explosion. . . . All of those bands could function. *Sgt. Pepper's* destroyed the chance of average kids on the block to make a record like that. Traffic's 'Paper Sun' and the Rolling Stones followed."

Indeed. Songs like Traffic's "Dear Mr. Fantasy," "Withering Tree," "Heaven Is in Your Mind," "Smiling Phases," and "(Roamin' Thru the Gloamin' With) Forty Thousand Headmen" were cinematic rock tunes (with blues, soul, and folk twists) engineered by the legendary Eddie Kramer (Jimi Hendrix, Led Zeppelin), which were undoubtedly informed by *Sgt. Pepper's*.

"Mainly thanks to the Beatles, albums and experimental studio production were seen as being the cutting edge of music: as a more mature and autonomous medium for serious work," says drummer Chris Cutler (Henry Cow, Art Bears).

"Lennon and McCartney are like Adam and Eve, and the rest of us have been begot by them," says Dennis DeYoung. "What is it that we did that . . . [the Beatles] didn't do? I may have missed it, but I think they pretty much did everything. The rest of us figured out what scraps we could get onto our own plates after that."

PIPERS AT THE GATES OF ABBEY ROAD

"The Beatles were around the studios when we were making *The Piper at the Gates of Dawn* at Abbey Road," says early Pink Floyd and Syd Barrett comanager Peter Jenner. "The Beatles were down in studio three and we were in studio two. They were making *Sgt. Pepper's*. Rumor had it that both Lennon and McCartney, or one of them, were at the Roundhouse gig [Floyd played], and I dare say that they heard stuff wafting out of our studio and we heard stuff wafting out of their studio. Then we were summoned in to hear a bit of a remix session.

"We went in like schoolboys to visit our so-called idols," continues Jenner. "George Martin and George Harrison were both there, and Lennon was working away on something, fussing on 'Being for the Benefit of Mr. Kite!' I think."

It's impossible to know who was feeding what to whom—music and experimentation were simply in the air. Syd Barrett's altogether eerie, childlike, paranoid, nineteenth-century children's literature–inspired imagery, crawling with tiny people (as in a Richard Dadd painting), dominated songs such as "Astronomy Domine," "Lucifer Sam," "The Gnome," "Interstellar Overdrive," "Matilda Mother," and "Take Up Thy Stethoscope and Walk" on *The Piper at the Gates of Dawn*, which roamed corners of the mind—a mind in the prestages of disintegration and fragmentation—that not even the Beatles would enter or inspect.

The music of the period, like the nineteenth-century literature that a generation of Brits were brought up on, was a psychedelic experience in and of itself. "Lewis Carroll and . . . Edward Lear were big influences on our generation," says Jenner. "Our parents turned us on to those books because it had an impact on their childhood. Edward Lear and Lewis Carroll had a very important impact on British culture. There's something else for you to write about: Without Edward Lear and Lewis Carroll, would we have gotten *Monty Python*?"

What is creepy and perhaps disturbing is the thought that Barrett wasn't self-conscious about his music. Meaning, it's difficult to know for sure whether what we're hearing offers a small window into Barrett's psychosis or is merely the product of a playful mind.

"Syd was really singing a kind of blues, wasn't he?" asks Anthony Stern, filmmaker and friend to Barrett in life. "The music possessed an inherent moan. And, yet, 'Interstellar Overdrive' is not something that comes from suffering. It's something that was coming from wild abandonment and a love of life that pulses with the rhythm of nature or outer space."

Barrett's mind radiated scenarios most of the free world hadn't even imagined. Floyd was compelled to match these lyrical visuals with auditory colors. Barrett was probing inner space, and he and his bandmates in Floyd were attempting to reveal the results of this examination through swatches of sonic texture, the use of panning techniques to offer a panoramic "view" of the music, oddly arranged vocal noises, and strange guitar feedback and string plucks.

"When you find you can't do something technically perfect, you're almost forced, out of self-esteem and self pride, to go into something abstract," says Stern. "When you can't paint like Rembrandt or draw like Picasso, you tend to go happily into abstraction, and you can amaze people."

THE MOODY BLUES

"The record we liked most and were inspired by was an American record by a group called Cosmic Sounds, which is called *The Zodiac: Cosmic Sounds*, on Elektra, when everything you bought on Elektra was really good," says the Moody Blues' Justin Hayward. (Paul Beaver was the creative force behind the *Zodiac* project and employed the Moog for this 1967 release.) "We were playing some songs from *Days of Future Passed* onstage much earlier in 1967, and we recorded a few, including 'Nights in White Satin,' for the BBC some considerable time before our Deram [a subsidiary of Decca] recording. Although we had the idea of writing songs representing parts of the day before the release of *The Zodiac*, I would still say that this record influenced the way we recorded *Days*."

Songs such as "Nights in White Satin" and "Forever Afternoon (Tuesday?)" were written in accordance with the band's "a day in the life" stage theme. "During this transition period, we played two sets, because we did our old songs in the first set and the *Days* songs in the second," says Hayward.

Days of Future Passed is a landmark recording, marked by one of the first prominent attempts at fusing true symphonic music with rock. "That idea, actually, was Decca's,"

says Hayward. "We were just lucky to be able to have an opportunity to record. Decca wanted a demonstration record to try to help sell their stereo systems, and we didn't have a recording contract, so they approached us because we owed them money and they wanted to recoup on sessions they had paid for that had done nothing. So we got a lousy deal. But we got to record our own stuff. Peter Knight, [conductor with the London Festival Orchestra], took some of our themes, and it was very much a stereo context. Unbeknownst to them and us, it coincided with the rise of stereo radio, and the stuff was perfect for it."

"We were all planning and working toward this morning-and-afternoon concept, and someone from the label came along with Dvořák's New World Symphony," says drummer Graeme Edge. "We just said, 'Well, we don't know.' In fact, we had recorded a couple of the songs we had written for the BBC, just live onstage, to put out on the radio, because the musicians' union had restricted needle time on the air so they needed pop music that was recorded live. . . . I remember that was the first time we had heard 'Nights in White Satin' recorded. The version we were doing then was nothing like the one we wound up with."

The Moodys' symphonic approach was a new direction for the band, a far cry from the blue-eyed R&B the band had been recording in the mid-1960s.

The Moodys had even backed legendary Chicago blues artist Sonny Boy Williamson II when the harp player/singer came through Britain. (He used to call the band "Muddy Boots.") "We were playing blues all the time, and that's why 'Blues' is in the title [of the band]," says Edge, who was a member of Gerry Levene and the Avengers prior to joining the R&B Preachers, forerunner to the Moodys. "But we suddenly started to

feel a little phony, because we'd never seen a field of cotton, let alone picked cotton out of one. We weren't quite sure what a smokestack was—you know, 'Smokestack Lightnin'.'"

If the Moodys hadn't changed their musical direction, they might have wound up being an interesting footnote in the record books. "I suppose people in life always look for watershed moments, and I suppose the watershed for the Moody Blues was that we became part of the progressive rock avalanche," says bassist/vocalist John Lodge. "At the time we thought we were writing and recording our very own personal music with no regard for anyone else. We are always looking for new avenues to explore, I think."

Thanks to the production skills of producer Tony Clarke, *Days of Future Passed* was the first in a long line of Moody records that used cross-fading, a technique through which one skillfully blends a song into another, giving the sensation that the album is one continuous piece of music.

This "cinematic feel," as Clarke dubs it, produced by the cross-fading technique, was the perfect method by which to capture the feel of the band's stage show in the late 1960s.

"[Clarke] was a huge influence for two reasons," says Edge. "He was as young and enthusiastic as we were. Don't forget, he started off as a house producer for Decca, and he was the only one who was young like us. We could have been stuck with some real traditional guys, shall we call them? Part of his influence was the fact that he was open to hearing our ideas. He would say, 'I don't know what you're talking about, but we'll give it a try.'"

The rising swells of woodwind flourishes and sweeping string passages coupled with Edge's sometimes trippy/sometimes deep spoken-word poetry, studio experimentation, the layered vocal harmonies, Hayward's ability to smoothly inject emotion into his vocal delivery, Ray Thomas's breathy flute playing, sonic elements entering the stereo image at interesting points in the mix, and the use of the Mellotron create a lush (often Romantic) musical palette that would become (less the orchestral instruments) a Moody Blues hallmark across records from 1967 through 1972 such as *In Search of the Lost Chord*, *To Our Children's Children's Children*, *On the Threshold of a Dream*, *Every Good Boy Deserves Favour*, *A Question of Balance*, and *Seventh Sojourn*.

Hayward concedes that it was the Mellotron that perhaps added the most depth and dimension to the band's music. In some ways Hayward and the Moodys were lost without the Mellotron. "I had no idea how to open 'Forever Afternoon,'" says Hayward. "The Mellotron came to the rescue. Tony Clarke really loved it too, and it gave us that dimension that freed us in a way from the restrictions of thinking about counterpoint to the guitar or some sort of balance to the guitar sound and drums. I love that instrument with a passion."

Days of Future Passed was a success (reaching number twenty-seven on the British charts in early 1968). "Forever Afternoon (Tuesday?)" was a Top 20 British hit, while "Nights in White Satin" was a Top 20 British hit (and reentered both the U.S. and British charts in 1972 in the Top 10). For the next five years, the Moodys, before disappearing for a few years (only to launch a tremendous comeback in the late 1970s and early 1980s with *Octave* and *Long Distance Voyager*) would rack up hit after hit while perfecting their cross-fade/suite approach to writing and recording.

"I wish I could say there was some master plan about the Moodys," says Hayward, "but it was sort of a series of blundering coincidences and accidents that kept us going, really, through the first ten years of the band."

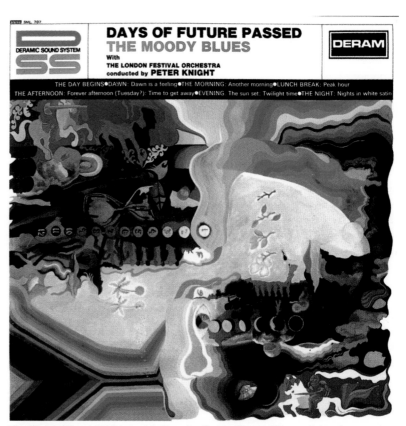

The Moody Blues' 1967 symphonic rock offering, *Days of Future Passed*.

SWITCHED ON . . .

As music was expanding, so were the tools to make that music. The imaginations of musicians grew (either organically or by some other means), and technology met the challenges of catering to creative and groundbreaking artists in the mid- and late 1960s and early 1970s.

With roots in 1950s sci-fi sound effects, the work of Louis and Bebe Barron as heard in the film *Forbidden Planet*, and electronic experimentation in avant-garde composition (though organized attempts had been made to synthesize electronic noise as early as the nineteenth century), the emerging synthesizer field turned the keyboard into a lead instrument. An entire commercial industry grew around the concepts realized by trailblazers and geniuses such as Don Buchla and, most famously, Robert Moog, on opposite ends of the country.

"Bob Moog rejected the idea of a polyphonic keyboard, because he said it was like an organ," explains Tom Rhea, an associate professor in the Department of Electronic Production and Design at Berklee College of Music, who worked at Moog in the 1970s. "The fact that it was modular and monophonic was critical, and that was a certain amount of novelty in and of itself. It forced keyboard players to rethink their art and craft, because keyboard players had been notorious, of course, for being the person in the band who comps and fills. They were not the sexy guy with the guitar at the front of the band. They were stationary and a lot of things like that. Then the monophonic expression came, and that meant the keyboardist started headlining bands."

By harnessing basic sound waveforms to produce sound effects via ring modulator and oscillator circuitry—later on the actual representations or approximations of instruments—and bending pitch in the same way an organic or acoustic instrument can, synthesizers were a viable new development for musicians. One could be a synthesizer player but not necessarily a piano player.

Church organist and electronic experimenter Paul Beaver (who was using the theremin, among other devices, for film scores) and session guitarist Bernie Krause bought an early Moog synth and became sales reps for Moog "because nobody else could teach and play the instrument," remembers Krause. "Interesting story: I was playing guitar, just kind of eking out an existence. I had read about an early model of the Moog, a test model of the synth that was used on a commercial for American Express, which was done with seven seconds of music, and the guy supposedly got paid very well. I was asking, 'Why am I working in the studio with a guitar, making sixty dollars an hour, when I could make serious money playing a few notes on the synthesizer?'"

At first Beaver and Krause met with resistance from the industry toward the Moog synthesizer. Most people didn't understand its applications let alone its implications. Some did, of course, but they were few and far between.

"Paul Beaver went around for a year in 1966 with a synthesizer showing various people what it could do," says Krause. "We couldn't even get anyone to allow us to do a demo with the synthesizer then. What led to our success was really a conspiracy of events. We set up a booth at the Monterey Pop Festival in 1967, with the last three hundred bucks that we had to our name. While record label guys—Jac Holzman, Clive Davis, [and] Mo Austin and Joe Smith at Warner Brothers and Reprise —— were vying to get artists signed to their label, these artists, in turn, saw a booth at the festival away from all of that, and we sold about ten or fifteen synthesizers. So we had gone from nothing to having sold these for

which we got a commission. These were fifteen thousand dollars a pop. The problem was that the artists were so stoned that they couldn't play them. Not only would we get the commission for the synthesizers, but later on we would get commission for dates. So we went from doing nothing to working eighty hours a week in the studio in London and New York and Los Angeles and San Francisco."

Carol Kaye, veteran session bassist with an enviable list of credits (from the Beach Boys to Jerry Goldsmith) remembers seeing Beaver use the synthesizer on dates in the 1960s.

"It was unusual to use a synthesizer on recordings," remembers Kaye. "Paul's using the synthesizer was remarkable and an omen of the future, though none of us thought that at that time; it was just 'something new.' Studios were big on trying 'new' things for a while, then discarding those ideas for newer ideas. But after a few years, I realized just how groundbreaking Paul's work was at the time."

With releases such as *Ragnarok Electronic Funk*, *In a Wild Sanctuary* and *Gandharva*, featuring saxophonist Gerry Mulligan and guitarist Mike Bloomfield (among others) and recorded in Grace Cathedral in San Francisco, Beaver & Krause used the synthesizers in an assortment of musical settings, from slight funk rock to gospel to all-out sonic experimentation.

Wendy Carlos (formerly Walter Carlos) had worked with electronics pioneer Robert Moog on developing the Moog synthesizer. With producer Rachel Elkind-Tourre, Carlos recorded the groundbreaking 1968's *Switched-On Bach*, which showed the world what a Moog synthesizer could do. There were others, of course. Dick Hyman, for instance, with his *Moog: The Electric Eclectics of* . . . record, as well as the musical team Beaver & Krause, not to mention the Doors, the Monkees, and, of course, the Beatles, who used the Moog on *Abbey Road*.

"George Harrison bought one,

but he could never figure out what the fuck he was doing," says Krause. "If it hadn't been for George Martin, the Beatles producer, who I also sold the synthesizer to and spent time [teaching it to him], it probably wouldn't have seen the light of day either. I worked with Harrison, but I didn't work with the Beatles. Martin was really the one who understood it and performed on it. He was doing electronic tape music at the BBC, back in the mid- and late 1950s, long before he met the Beatles."

Later, when the portable (somewhat affordable) Minimoog, with pitch and modulation wheels, was unveiled in 1971, keyboardists everywhere had access to amazing sounds, opening up a whole new chapter in music (and music retailing) that wouldn't be challenged until Yamaha released its DX-7 in the early 1980s with manufacturers' presets. (ARP designed their own portable, compact synth, the Odyssey line, based on the ARP 2600.) While this was great for a mass market, that thrill of discovering and customizing sounds, all the research and development a musician undertakes—something the early progressive rock synthesizer users did well—was virtually lost.

"The Minimoog and the modular Moog and ARP and whoever was doing voltage-controlled equipment where you rolled your own sound, that was a radical move," says Moog vet Tom Rhea. "Monophony was a radical move. The DX-7 represented a move toward the center. It was a regression, in a way. The Minimoog was away from the mainstream. It was in keeping with the natural flow of technology.

"The thing about the Moog is that it brought to mind instrumental music but not a particular instrument," Rhea continues. "It was like an unknown instrument. That's why it was new. Progressive rock and the synthesizer were made for each other because it required a certain amount of cerebral approach to things to even get into synthesizers."

(Michael Ochs Archives/Getty Images)

PINK
FLOYD

When Pigs Fly

LANDING ON THE MOON HAS ALWAYS BEEN A metaphor for the impossible. Some said it could never be done. We all know that the act of rocketing to our nearest satellite is no longer impossible (conspiracy theorists notwithstanding), but the expression has stuck and continues to articulate mankind's hunger to explore the unknown and touch the outer cosmos.

Proponents of progressive rock, in all its many forms, attempted to do the same within the context of the musical universe: expand the boundaries of accepted music and musical knowledge while stretching their individual abilities as performers, musicians, artists, and people to achieve works that, today, seem unimaginable and even unattainable.

Pink Floyd were one of the first important bands to experiment with rock music, offer a new way of thinking about and hearing sound, offering intonation and interpretation for the ineffable, inevitable, and incontrovertible while leaving their unique footprint on the progressive rock landscape.

A cult band that transformed themselves into a global musical phenomenon, Floyd have become simply untouchable, their lives and times the stuff of rock music legend. When, at a crucial early juncture in their development as a creative unit, they lost their charismatic front man—when even their managers thought they were doomed—the Floyd pulled themselves up by their bootstraps, recruited a new guitarist, and set out on a course that would make them the biggest rock band in the world.

When the band were at their most dispirited, they wrote, recorded, and completed an album that sat on the U.S. charts for a cumulative and unprecedented fourteen years.

Unlike other progressive rock contemporaries who attempted to re-create (sometimes in very literal terms) the sound of an orchestra, Floyd would not be seriously tempted by the lure of this particular strain of progressive music (though they did dabble in it, too), and instead explored more organic aural territory that seemed to capture the sights and sounds of the outer and inner cosmos.

The Floyd remain firmly within the genre while (largely and incredibly) escaping the stereotypical fantasy-imagery silliness, faux profundity, psychobabble, apparent pursuit of technical prowess, and (sometimes) overwrought classical tendencies that have made so many of their contemporaries victims of their own excesses.

Yet the classic Floyd lineup of bassist/vocalist Roger Waters, guitarist/vocalist David Gilmour, drummer Nick Mason, and keyboardist/vocalist Rick Wright—despite infighting, inconsolable sadness, madness, regret, guilt, and loss—changed the face of progressive rock forever and turned cult popularity into superstardom.

COSMIC BO DIDDLEY

George Roger Waters was born in Surrey, U.K., but raised in Cambridge by his mother, reportedly a strict schoolteacher (his father, Eric Fletcher Waters, died in World War II in Anzio, Italy, in February 1944, when Roger was just an infant).

Waters left Cambridge in 1962 to pursue a degree in architecture from London's Regent Street Polytechnic, where he met drummer Nick Mason, a Birmingham native, and both joined the band Sigma 6, of which future Pink Floyd keyboardist Rick Wright was already a member.

Guitarist/vocalist Syd Barrett (born Roger Keith Barrett in Birmingham in 1946), a childhood friend to Waters (and teenage buddy to his replacement, future Floyd guitarist Dave Gilmour), joined the group that eventually became Pink Floyd—a moniker Barrett had concocted by fusing the names of obscure Piedmont blues artists Pink Anderson and Floyd Council.

The four-man lineup of the Pink Floyd, as they were sometimes referred to, supplied, along with the Soft Machine and a handful of select other bands, the sonic backdrop to London's hip, underground psychedelic circuit in the latter half of the 1960s.

"A lot of what the band played were old blues songs and things, but the solos, instead of being wailing guitar solos, there was this wall of sustain and noise," says former comanager Peter Jenner. "Rick and Syd had Echoplex on their instruments, so I couldn't make out where this noise was coming from. I remember walking around the stage, trying to figure out who was playing what."

"They . . . made you stop and say, 'What the fuck is that?'" says keyboardist Billy Ritchie, formerly of the influential British progressive rock bands 1-2-3 and Clouds. "I couldn't even judge Rick Wright as a player: He was concentrating on using [keyboards] as a sound instrument. It was all very original. I'd never heard anything like it."

At the close of 1966, Floyd secured a deal with EMI for five thousand pounds (to the dismay of some in the underground scene who thought the band had "sold out") and treated the studios at Abbey Road as their own sonic playground while recording 1967's groundbreaking *Piper at the Gates of Dawn* with producer Norman Smith (who'd worked with the Beatles but had admitted to never being a big fan of Floyd).

The Piper at the Gates of Dawn was a Top 10 British hit, but even before its release, the Floyd were already showing signs of busting loose of the constraints of the underground music scene and becoming their own band. The songs "Arnold Layne" and "See Emily Play" were Top 20 and Top 10 British hits, respectively, in the spring and early summer of 1967, but Floyd were soon to be known as an album-oriented band—and later an FM radio sensation—interested, it would seem, more in the idea of presenting the album as a complete artistic statement than as merely a collection of possible hits.

"Pink Floyd were, straight off the bat, a band that could deliver a catchy hit single but had this other urgent desire to experiment with kaleidoscopes of sound," muses Jethro Tull front man Ian Anderson.

"Floyd was really the first rock band signed to EMI that was considered an album act," says Jenner. "From then on, they had the freedom to extend themselves artistically."

Fronted by the charismatic, good-looking, dark and mysterious rock poet Barrett, Floyd, while spinning music that was itself a mind-altering experience (awash in waves of noise, seemingly less compositional than textural), were plugged into the pulse of the psychedelic circuit.

"I think Syd went from someone who would go for a jolly walk down the street into a music shop to buy some guitar strings, to someone who was suddenly a pop star and was asked the meaning of life," Jenner says. "He was not political or philosophical in that way, even though he was seen as some sort of leader of an underground movement."

But as a leader of the underground, he was also subject (and vulnerable) to the same kinds of experiences (and vices) as everyone else in the scene. That involved overindulgence of hallucinogens, which may or may not have been the cause of his mood swings, general despondency, and stubbornness regarding the band's creative direction. For example, Barrett legendarily walked out on a Floyd performance on the *Top of the Pops* television program (the last of three appearances the band were making on the show).

"Syd simply didn't have the same motivations as other people," says filmmaker Anthony Stern, who befriended Barrett in the 1960s and included Floyd's "Interstellar Overdrive," featuring Barrett, in his 1968 documentary, *San Francisco: Film*. "He just wanted to play his music. It was like that [1962] film *The Loneliness of the Long Distance Runner*, in which this rebellious young working-class lad stops about fifteen yards before the finish line during the big race. 'If it matters so much to you, you can win. I don't care.' Syd simply felt like he shouldn't conform and play to what other people's expected game is."

"Syd wrote very quickly," says Jenner. "That was another problem. We always said, 'Come on, Syd. Write us another hit.' I think that was part of the pressures that did him in."

Barrett vacationed in Spain, taking some time off from writing and the band, but he returned, it appeared, even more damaged than when he left, some say. He'd become paralyzed onstage, staring like a deer in the headlights, or else detuning his guitar while on the bandstand, as if sabotaging the band in midperformance. Barrett was slowly withdrawing from the world, seemingly

becoming lost in his own mind.

Some speculate that Barrett was simply ingesting too many drugs to be effective as a performer—and that those drugs may have triggered a latent predisposition to some form of mental illness. (It should be stated that Barrett was never diagnosed, then, or later in his life, with a mental illness.)

"Syd's mistake, I suppose, was he became greedy for the [LSD] experience," says Stern. "It was a bit like a guru or someone who . . . forces himself to stay in this high level of Samadhi, a highly evolved state. Normal bodily systems break down. . . . The brain is not made for that."

The band had long since stopped asking why this was all happening and had begun formulating plans to quietly phase out Barrett but continue to work with him as a songwriter, much in the way Brian Wilson operated with the Beach Boys.

The combination of an acid overload, the impact of losing his position in the band, the agonizing regret of recording for a commercial entity such as EMI before he really had a chance to take Floyd into other musical dimensions, and, some say, his inability to move past the death of his father, Max, when he was just fifteen years old, may have pushed Barrett over the edge.

"What the drugs did was bring out what was there and amplify it and exaggerate it," says Jenner.

"I think it's fair to say that his mind would have been destroyed one way or another fairly soon," says Stern. "If it wasn't LSD, it would have been something else."

SET THE CONTROLS FOR THE HEART OF THE SUN

Guitarist David Gilmour, a friend of Barrett, was at the ready and joined as the band's fifth member for a little while. But this setup was awkward and uncomfortable. Barrett was not pleased with Gilmour's presence, and the new guitarist felt out of place for a time.

However, it soon became apparent how valuable—and necessary—Gilmour was. Barrett had finally gone off the deep end, and Gilmour was the perfect replacement.

"The first time I had heard Dave play, he mimicked Jimi Hendrix and then Syd," says Jenner. "Dave is a wonderful guitar player, but earlier on, he was an incredible mimic. He now plays David Gilmour, but when he started, he played other people."

Gilmour would evolve and combine the best instincts and aspects of blues-oriented guitarists of the day: Perhaps a bit like Eric Clapton and B. B. King, Gilmour proves that it's the emphasis and emotional impact of each note played that counts, not the speed by which those notes are delivered that gives music its power.

If Barrett was the spacey conceptualist, then Gilmour was, by comparison, the better technician; much more tied to the traditional blues-rock mythos of singing guitarist as a shamanic figure with the ability to extract base and complex emotions from the instrument.

Barrett would make one more appearance with Floyd on the band's 1968 LP, *A Saucerful of Secrets*, which contains only one Barrett-penned track, the closer, "Jugband Blues."

"I don't know if you've ever heard his song, 'Vegetable Man,' but that's one he wrote around that time, and it's a description of who he was," says Jenner. "It wasn't used by the band, I think, because it was too much for them. They just couldn't handle where the song was coming from."

Despite the exclusion of "Vegetable Man" and another song titled "Scream Thy Last Scream," the Floyd were progressing at an incredible rate without Barrett's input, creating music that had a psychological punch. "Let There Be More Light" certainly plays into the paranoia and perceived paranoia of a hallucinogen-scrubbed mind (catch the reference to "Lucy in the Sky with Diamonds").

The chiming, metallic pings of vibraphone, Mason's incessant boxy patterns (guided by the listless vocals), ghostly organ tones, and the constant, repetitive nature of the opening riff make "Set the Controls for the Heart of the Sun" (the title taken from a Michael Moorcock sci-fi novel called *The Fireclown*, aka *The Winds of Limbo*) is something akin to sonic tantra, a distant cousin to a hypnotic one-chord Delta blues.

Other songs offer a magic window into the band's craft and psyche, such as the chilling, kazoo-laced anti-war ditty "Corporal Clegg" (its message on the psychological effects of war would be a subject Waters would dive into with more regularity and depth later in the 1970s); "A Saucerful of Secrets," a horror show of noise, featuring piano bashing, oscilloscopic-like sonic whirlies, and organ drones that hint at a funeral procession; and Wright's melancholic Mellotron-enhanced avant-pop tune "See-Saw."

The closer, Barrett's "Jugband Blues," begins with folky guitar (with what sounds like recorder) and the line "I'm almost obliged to you for making it clear that I'm not here." It then descends into auditory madness, with horn players seemingly operating of their own accord and playing separately, barely (if at all) listening to one another. Then the chaos cuts off. It simply ends. An acoustic passage follows, as if nothing that came before it really mattered.

It's difficult to know whether the song represents Barrett's self-awareness or his confusion, or if it is a kind of sly yet scathing indictment of his bandmates for slowly pushing him out of the band. Whatever its meaning, "Jugband Blues" is disjointed and disturbing and can be interpreted as a kind of waking dream, a nightmare, really, and an eerie conclusion to

Barrett's work with the Floyd. Even more strangely, the song was a Top 10 British hit—and Barrett's final act as a member of Pink Floyd.

MORE, UMMAGUMMA

After Barrett faded away, Floyd began searching for a new course. With the release of albums like *More*, *Ummagumma*, and *Atom Heart Mother*, the Floyd were no longer chasing dreams of psychedelia in an attempt to hang onto Syd's music and memory. These are not the strongest Floyd efforts, but they show a band attempting to define itself.

More (recorded as a sound track for Barbet Schroeder's 1969 film of the same title) runs the gamut of natural sounds, jazz, world music, whooshing gong overtones, semi-acoustic folk-rock ballads, and blues-informed guitar dirt and became a Top 10 British hit in June 1969.

The stoic, paranoia-laced musical step toward the band's future beloved space-age prog rock was further solidified by 1969's double album, *Ummagumma* (the title taken from a slang expression for sex), which contains live material (the entire first disc), band collaborations, and solo spotlights.[2]

Mason has called the live material appearing on *Ummagumma* "antiquated," and he was half right. Songs like Barrett's "Astronomy Domine" (which at times approaches the raucousness of the Who), "Set the Controls for the Heart of the Sun," the gothic "Careful with That Axe, Eugene" (released as a single in 1968), and "*A Saucerful of Secrets*" are from the band's past, but they also possess a primal and mystical quality that rivals their psychedelic studio counterparts.

The second LP features five compositions by the four Floyd protagonists: Wright's four-part keyboard

suite "Sysyphus" (sometimes brilliant, sometimes gothic, sometimes ponderous), reflecting his classical training and jazz soul; Waters's gentle acoustic "Grantchester Meadows" and "Several Species of Small Furry Animals Gathered Together in a Cave and Grooving with a Pict" (a collage of vocal effects, echoes, and tape loops that ends with a reference to Hendrix's "The Wind Cries Mary"); Gilmour's "The Narrow Way," a precursor to the blues-based cosmic prog of *The Dark Side of the Moon*; and Mason's multitracked experimental-sound-effect-and-percussion solo, "The Grand Vizier's Garden Party."

Ummagumma, a Top 5 hit in Britain, demonstrates how far ahead of other bands Floyd was: By highlighting the talents of the individual members of the band, Floyd had, essentially, handed Emerson Lake and Palmer—which had yet to be formed—a blueprint for their 1977 double LP, *Works Volume 1*.

ATOM HEART MOTHER

After scoring music for Italian film director Michelangelo Antonioni's 1970 movie/faux documentary on the counterculture, *Zabriskie Point*, Floyd recorded 1970's *Atom Heart Mother*, featuring the orchestral, choir-based side-long epic title song, written in collaboration with interactive sound installation/electronic/TV and film composer Ron Geesin (who had collaborated with Waters on the 1970 sound track *Music from the Body*).

Ironically, the more interesting parts—the brass, choir, and cello bits—belong to Geesin. That they do is not much of a surprise: The band's constant touring was beginning to tire them—and this listlessness shows a bit on *Atom Heart Mother*.

The second side recalls the second disc of *Ummagumma*, with Gilmour, Waters, and Wright penning a song apiece. Mason collaborated on the inane elongated closer, "Alan's Psychedelic Breakfast: Rise and

---

[2] Prior to the release of *Ummagumma*, Floyd had composed two long pieces, "The Man" and "The Journey," for a live performance dubbed "The Massed Gadgets of Auximenies—More Furious Madness from Pink Floyd," which contained bits that were used in other capacities.

Shine, Sunny Side Up, Morning Glory," based on Floyd roadie Alan Stiles' inner dialogue regarding breakfast choices.

The song features the wonderful snap-crackle-pop of preparing and then eating a morning meal complete with coffee, scrambled eggs, toast, "flakes," bacon, and (who could forget?) marmalade. Stiles's activity gives way to a pleasant though quasi-silly pastoral rock hymnal.

It's a strange ending to a record that simply feels (at times) unnecessary, and one that seems to do little to advance the band's overall direction. In some ways *Atom Heart Mother* was even more disjointed than *Ummagumma*, but the album would, incredibly, become a number-one hit in the U.K. (the band's first to do so) and break within the Top 60 in the U.S.

Floyd seemed to be at a crossroads: They were achieving success, but they were clearly on the down slope artistically. What was their next move, and would they continue to experiment with sound effects and orchestration? Would they do something else entirely?

MEDDLE

By early 1971, Floyd were quite bored—and fed up—with their live set (too many older numbers were being requested by audiences) and disenchanted by the succession of film work and imperfect releases such as *Ummagumma* and *Atom Heart Mother*.

But seemingly out of nowhere came a breakthrough: The band exploded with creativity and began writing material for a 1971 record that would eventually be titled *Meddle*.

Certainly, Barrett is still ingrained in the band's music, in songs like "Echoes" and "One of These Days." But, on the whole, here was a simpler, much more powerful Floyd, sometimes building tracks via small musical increments, behind the strength of Mason's straightforward rock grooves and Gilmour's soaring

and scintillating blues-rock riffs.

For the opening "One of These Days," Waters and Gilmour play complementary bass riffs (fed through a Binson Echorec, an Italian-made delay unit), which fit together like pieces of a sonic puzzle. Nick Mason sounds like a *Sesame Street* character when he belts out, around the 3:38 mark, "One of these days I am going to cut you into little pieces," seemingly changing the complexion of the song from midtempo, groove-based rocker to anthem for a serial killer. (The song was, quite appropriately, made up of little pieces and hard edits were concealed by Mason's sonic cymbal swells.)

More sonic expansion follows: Gilmour's "A Pillow of Winds," featuring the soon-to-be-classic double-tracked vocal effect, is a piece of music that falls somewhere between British folk, church, psychedelia, and blues.

"Fearless," a song about conquering impossible odds, features a football crowd singing Rodgers and Hammerstein's "You'll Never Walk Alone" (from the musical *Carousel*, based on Hungarian writer Ferenc Molnár's 1909 play *Liliom*).

The carefree "San Tropez" (a track that originally featured Gilmour on bass and Waters on guitar), as its title suggests, feels very much like a prewar bluesy jazz jam evoking bygone ditties of the French Riviera, sun, and sand.

The country blues number "Seamus" features Gilmour's dog of the same name (and is spiritually and musically somewhere between Memphis, '40s Chicago, the Mississippi Delta, and Great Britain's motor city, Birmingham).

Finally, a twenty-three-and-a-half-minute "Echoes," which takes up the entire second side of the original LP, is as much a song about Darwinism (and instinctual knowledge) as human connectedness. The song's impressionistic sounds recall music of a distant past while conjur-

ing images of futuristic worlds, foretelling of music to be made for upcoming releases such as 1973's *The Dark Side of the Moon* and 1975's *Wish You Were Here*.

"They could spend literally hours on just a few measures of one song," says producer Mike Butcher, who engineered some of the *Meddle* sessions at Morgan Studios. "I can remember one session where they just sat around for hours waiting to be inspired, but nothing was coming. It was a bit like a *Monty Python* skit: One of them would have an idea, present it to the band, and then someone would say, 'No, no. We can't do that.' And that idea was dead."

"There was a point where we sat about not knowing what to do," Rick Wright said in a 1972 interview.[3] "Then *Meddle* came, and since then we've been quite excited about what we've been doing."

"Somebody like Pink Floyd went into the studio and what comes out is material that's different than they had imagined," says Butcher.

Meddle helped to establish Floyd's massive appeal (it soared to number three in Britain in November 1971; number seventy in the States) and clearly set the stage for succeeding records.

But with popularity came inner turmoil—the kind that would eventually tear the band apart in later years. With increasing regularity, Waters became the point man (and on *Meddle* he either wrote or cowrote every song). But Gilmour was clearly one of the most talented musicians in the band (along with Wright, largely because of his restraint). Whose instincts were better? Who would, and could, step back for the sake of the song? Who would or could inject himself into a situation for the better? Inevitably, heads would butt—and they did.

"The friction between Roger Waters and the rest of the band was

3 Disc and Music Echo, February 5, 1972.

Infinite appeal: Floyd's 1969 expansive double record, *Ummagumma*, reflects the scope of the band's cosmic groove.

definitely going on at that time," adds Roger Quested, head engineer for the *Meddle* sessions at Morgan. "I suppose I had the same sense of humor as Roger, and when he was doing vocals, I was encouraged by the rest of the band to give him a ribbing over his singing."

"They were surprised that anyone had talked to Roger that way," confirms Butcher. "*Meddle* was really Roger Waters's album as far as I am concerned. It really establishes what he would be doing later on. He was very much the boss, as far as I could see, on that album. He would be sitting at the console next to the engineer, when he wasn't playing, and would be active, like a producer would, moving faders up and down. You could see that what Roger was doing was accepted by the band. Or, at least, it seemed to be accepted by the band."

RELICS

By the early 1970s, Floyd was the center of all kinds of activity: In 1971, they had released a career retrospective via EMI/Starline, titled *Relics*, which, like its name, has been rendered outdated. But in its time, it proved useful for its inclusion of the two early Barrett-era singles, "Arnold Layne" and "See Emily Play."

More importantly, Floyd had begun writing and recording music for *The Dark Side of the Moon* (and performing it onstage), had created music for film and ballet, and were the subject of a concert film: Adrian Maben's *Pink Floyd Live at Pompeii*, filmed in October 1971 with the aid of twenty-four-track recording equipment.

Pompeii, a cinematic experience *Melody Maker* said "gels beautifully," features the band performing in an empty ancient Roman amphitheater, as well as studio footage of Floyd recording music for the upcoming *The Dark Side of the Moon*.

Though the film wouldn't be released until 1974, in retrospect, seeing Floyd in this setting, hearing the nearly fully formed musical ideas emanating from Waters, Gilmour, and Wright lends credence to the theory that *The Dark Side of the Moon* was a totally inspired project. It was obvious something big was coming, but just how big no one could have guessed.

SHOOTING FOR THE MOON

The Dark Side of the Moon—a title inspired by Barrett (as in a description of the predicament and location in which his Pink Floyd bandmates had left him)—is the brilliant culmination of everything that had come before it, while reflecting the artistic growth of the post-Barrett Floyd.

The Dark Side of the Moon is as much an examination of the twentieth-century British psyche, the everyday stresses applied to that psyche, as a descent into madness and an examination of the temporal nature of time and space, sanity versus insanity, and the movement toward materialism—not spirituality—in modern society.

It's also a combination of polar opposites: the "eternal" sun (representing birth and the boundless potential of youth) and the symbolism and mysterious pull of its lunar companion (i.e., aging, dementia, and death). It's hard to imagine one without the other. In fact, in astrological, astronomical, and biological terms, it's impossible.

Waters seized upon the conceptual void left by David Gilmour's lack of lyrical contributions to *Dark Side* and was clearly on a mission to rid the band of its spaced-out lyrics in order to make a more universal record. Waters distills Barrett's bizarre, LSD-induced insights into universally understood terms and concepts of isolation, death, fear, hope, war/conflict, existential angst, love, and dementia, which beckon the listener to question his or her own sanity.

The record opens with "Speak to Me," which features a looped kick-drum pattern (approximating a heartbeat), random voices speaking about madness, the ticking sounds of clocks (at various speeds), cash register rings, the cries of singer Clare Torry, backward chords, hair-raising laughter, and the rhythmic pulses of what sounds like a jackhammer (garnered via manipulation of two EMS VCS-3 Synthi-AK synths). It's a maelstrom of sights and sounds previewing for the listener all that he or she will experi-

SYD SHINES ON

After he was nudged out of Pink Floyd, Barrett was comanaged by Peter Jenner and Andrew King, who were hot to revive the troubled troubadour's career. Though Barrett attempted to make recordings (on some of which he was backed by the Soft Machine) in 1968, after his exit from Floyd, sessions were wayward and sporadic. This material wouldn't see the light of day until 1970's *The Madcap Laughs*, and that was only with the help of David Gilmour and Roger Waters.

"I have very mixed views about Syd's solo work," says Jenner. "I think it's a shadow of what it once was. I've always used the analogy of a trolley bus not making a sound and coming out of a thick fog. People in the street are not able to see the top of it. Then when it finally got to its stop or destination you would see it only to watch it disappear into the fog again. I kept hearing bits of Syd and then it would disappear and then a bit more would come out and then disappear into the fog again."

Barrett had turned up for a 1969 session during the making of former Soft Machine bassist and Barrett fan Kevin Ayers's *Joy of a Toy*, though this session, too had been lost to the mists of time. (Syd's guitar work was ultimately shelved as being too psychedelic for Ayers's pop direction, and the track with Barrett's handiwork, "Religious Experience," wouldn't be unearthed and released until *Toy* was remastered and reissued on CD in 2003 by producer Mark Powell.)

Toward the end of 1970, Syd continued to write painful, disturbing, and Lewis Carroll–inspired childlike songs such as "Effervescing Elephant," "Rats," "Gigolo Aunt," "Baby Lemonade," and "Two of a Kind," which appear on his second album (produced by Gilmour and Wright), titled simply *Barrett*.

Barrett's material would crop up periodically on official and bootlegged releases alike, such as on 1988's *The Peel Sessions*, 1989's *Opel*, 1994's *Crazy Diamond* boxed set, 2004's *The Radio One Sessions* (an extended version of the *Peel Sessions* disc), and 2009's *Rhamadam*.

In July 2006, Syd Barrett died from complications of diabetes. The myths and legends surrounding his life, work, and mental state continue to grow to this day.

"There are pop musicians who have taken a lot from Syd," says friend and filmmaker Anthony Stern. "Syd will become more famous in his death than in his life. It will be unstoppable."

Syd Barrett, *The Madcap Laughs* (1970): "Syd was very difficult," remembers David Gilmour. "The guy was in trouble."

ence throughout the course of the long player.

As "Speak to Me" ends, it slides into "Breathe"—a meditation on the value of slowing down life in order to appreciate what's around us.

"On the Run" follows, marked by Mason's sixteenth-note hi-hat pattern and the VCS-3. The hypnotic, sequenced wave is joined by maniacal laughter, a plane crash, a helicopter buzz, and briskly moving footsteps, among other noises, seemingly symbolizing the everyday events and phobias that make up the business and busy-ness of life.

The following song, "Time," with lead vocals by Gilmour and Wright, is alight with ringing alarm clocks (the same heard at the opening of the record), as if issuing us a wake-up call. (Mason's chasmic rototom performance echoes the infinity of space, adding weight and significance to the message.)

"I suddenly thought at twenty-nine," Waters said, "'Hang on, it's happening, it has been right from the beginning, and there isn't suddenly a line when the training stops and life starts. . . .' The idea of 'Time' is similar to 'Breathe.' To be here now, this is it."

"Breathe Reprise," which is essentially the last verse of "Breathe" deferred, concerns our fears regarding the Great Beyond. Rick Wright's stark jazzy and classical chord sequence and Gilmour's slowhanded slide guitar lend "The Great Gig in the Sky," a sonic exploration of the dying experience, its signature uneasy and mysterious atmosphere.

What puts the song over the top, however, is the agonized gospelesque

screams performed by Clare Torry, a relatively unknown singer/EMI songwriter highly recommended by engineer Alan Parsons. This sonic stardust conjures a deathbed scene, a confessional, and, finally, a spirit rising.

Side two of the original LP opens with the rhythmic audio montage of "Money," a song that rattles with the ringing of cash registers, ripped paper, automatic telephonic call-switching system clicks, and the jingle-jangle of coin bags.

"Money" is shaped around Waters's funky and quirky 7/4 bass riff, and features memorable sax work by Dick Parry. "It's a really nice solo, but it's not an easy one," says saxophonist Mel Collins, who toured with Waters in the mid-1980s and in 2000. "Roger even told me it was edited. It jumps from a high note to a low note. I know Roger was a stickler about the solo: He wanted me to play it note for note. Now I know why I was drinking a bottle and a half of Bacardi a day."

"Us and Them," a song that was originally written for (and then rejected by) Michelangelo Antonioni (for *Zabriskie Point*), focuses on the subjects of war, racism, and the mental armor we use to shield ourselves from empathizing with others.

Wright's evocative hymnal and jazzy chords are at once hair-raising, calming, and utterly impersonal, underscoring the theme of the song. Complementing this mood is Gilmour's almost unaffected vocals and Parry's breathy sax work.

"Any Colour You Like," the shimmering instrumental interlude between "Us and Them" and "Brain Damage," is elevated by effervescing sonic burbles

from the VCS-3 synth and Wright's organ and Gilmour's shivering "Badge"-like guitar effects, and dovetails nicely into "Brain Damage," a song written partly about Barrett.

Its gospel choir, maniacal laughter, and caterwauling guitar tones (mixed in such a way as to give the listener a sense of space and sonic depth) offer the listener a hi-fi theater-of-the-mind experience.

The record closes with "Eclipse," a written homage to everything we experience in life, warning us that all things must pass. The song and the album conclude on the heartbeat pattern heard at the record's opening.

Waters has always maintained that the ending sends a positive message, perhaps because of the new life we sense regarding the album's closing beating heart. But the song—and indeed the entire record—is much deeper lyrically and slams our psyches with the undeniable notion that death is final and inevitable and that we only have one chance to get it right.

CHART SUCCESS

The Dark Side of the Moon took over six months to record, and once it was finished, even the band knew there was something special about it. Simply, the record changed the band forever: It stayed on the Billboard album chart for fourteen years in America (six in the U.K.) and has sold well over forty million copies worldwide.

"It's always baffled me," said Gilmour in 1984. "When we made it, we knew it was the best we'd done. But we hadn't even gone gold before then."

Branded by the iconic cover image of white light being refracted

A Saucerful of Secrets (1968)

Meddle (1971)

The Dark Side of the Moon (1973)

Animals (1977)

The Final Cut (1983)

A Momentary Lapse of Reason (1987)

through a prism (hinting at the kinds of hidden truths inherent in the music), *The Dark Side of the Moon* is perhaps the very pinnacle—and a surprisingly anomaly—of the progressive rock movement: It took the overbloated idea of the concept record and made it palatable to everyone.

"Roger and Dave, and Rick, too, had done an incredible job of keeping the band going," says Peter Jenner. "It's an incredible achievement. They said to me, 'You can't see it without Syd, can you?' I said, 'No, I can't.' I couldn't and I was wrong. *The Dark Side of the Moon* was an enormous success. I have to give them huge respect and admiration for what they did and went on to accomplish."

WISH YOU WERE HERE

Prior to recording their *Dark Side* follow-up, Floyd had embarked on an experimental project—*Household Objects*—for which the band restrained themselves from using commercial instruments, instead deciding to tinker with found, ordinary household devices, to make rhythm, noise, and, ultimately (they'd hoped), music.

But after weeks of fruitless labor, the band abandoned the idea when Waters had another brainstorm for a new concept album based on the subject of absence.

The new album, eventually titled *Wish You Were Here*, was as much homage to Barrett as a reflection on the record business, the rock 'n' roll lifestyle, and the general physical and mental exhaustion the band had been experiencing the last couple of years.

For Waters that meant his sharp sarcasm, pent-up anger, bitterness, and sly wit would no longer be tempered by stoicism and timeless, lofty

concepts. What comes through on *Wish You Were Here* is genuine emotion—whether it's anger or sadness—on tracks like "Welcome to the Machine," "Have a Cigar," "Wish You Were Here" (about Barrett's mental fire being extinguished), and the nine-part suite "Shine On You Crazy Diamond" (lamenting Barrett's past genius and loss of mental lucidity).

There was no denying Pink Floyd's current status: They were rock royalty and sales heroes as far as the record company was concerned. But success never sat well with Waters, and it's interesting that the band's emerging front man would seemingly manifest the same sorts of feelings Barrett had years earlier.

"The 'machine' is self perpetuating," Waters said, "because its fuel consists of dreams. . . . It's for that reason that people throw themselves into it. . . . And the dream is that when you're successful, when you're a star, you'll be fine. . . . That's the dream, and as everybody knows, it's an empty one."[4]

"I don't envy someone who's successful," says filmmaker Anthony Stern. "Being a successful artist is really simple: You just learn to play the publicity machine. But to be a great artist, you have to turn your back on all of that."

It's somewhat ironic that so much of Wish You Were Here—an album that many fans cite as the band's best (and a multimillion-unit seller in its own right)—should be dedicated to the doomed underground poet.

The lyrical undercurrent of "Shine On You Crazy Diamond," Parts I through V (Parts VI through IX are instrumental and a Rick Wright tour de force), is a strange mixture of detached reportage, pep talk, sadness,

and black humor, ruminating on Barrett's mental state. (Gilmour's bold and beautiful serpentine blues riffs, with his signature light touch of the whammy bar—not to mention the chimey yet monolithic arpeggio cutting through the thin, soupy sonic fog of Moog and glockenspiel—made the song a legendary live staple.)

Dripping with sarcasm, "Have a Cigar" is an ingenuously constructed song (sung by band friend, folkie/prog-folk songwriter Roy Harper) exposing the mindless—and endless—spiel and spin of slithering record industry types attempting to worm their way into the very core of big sellers like Floyd.

Poetically, the song collapses upon itself, shrinking in the mix to transistor radio sound quality (a commentary on the band's acceptance of its own commercialism?). As the transistor radio seems to fade, we pick up another signal: Someone is flipping through radio stations (a commentary on homing in on some kind of artistic clarity?) until the scratchy and distant sound of a twelve-string (in the right channel) is met by a clearer, panned-slightly-to-the-left-channel six-string acoustic guitar just before Gilmour sings the now-famous/infamous line, "So, so you think you can tell . . ."

Essentially, "Wish You Were Here" undercuts whatever optimism comes through in "Shine On You Crazy Diamond": That Barrett is lost inside his own head and can't be helped is a foregone conclusion. He was a formidable general in his day, but now he—and perhaps the writer of the song—are hopeless, just a casualty of the war/life.

In an eerie coincidence, rumor had it that while the band was mixing the song "Shine On You Crazy Diamond," Barrett ambled into the studio at Abbey Road. He hadn't been invited and at first no one even recognized the rather rotund man with shaved head and eyebrows, murmuring something about wanting to lay down

---

[4] The cover imagery for *Wish You Were Here* was further commentary on the business: The front shows two men entering a business agreement, one poor chap burning up the instant he's shaken hands on the deal. The Magritte-esque back cover shows a semi-invisible label executive holding up a see-through record (indicating music as commodity?) with his shoe resting on a well-worn suitcase plastered with *The Dark Side of the Moon* stickers, echoing the them of the band's on-the-go lifestyle.

guitar tracks. Waters spotted him and pointed him out to the others.

The band was shocked and saddened at this bit of ungodly synchronicity. (Reportedly, Waters was reduced to tears when Barrett began speaking.) They were speechless.

After this strange encounter, Barrett retreated into what was probably his first love, painting, and, as has been reported, never saw his former Floyd bandmates again.

ANIMALS

While Floyd clearly still owed a tremendous debt to Barrett (if, for nothing else, the concept of madness and the strain of madness being shoved under Waters's nose as a viable theme for rock records), the band increasingly became a vehicle for Waters's repressed anger, misanthropy, and childhood scars.

This was never more apparent than on the next three albums released by the band—1977's *Animals*, 1979's *The Wall*, and 1983's *The Final Cut*.

At its most basic, *Animals*, written nearly entirely by Waters (perhaps informed by George Orwell), divides the human race into three classifications: pigs (the privileged and ruling classes), dogs (the rebels, mavericks, hunters), and sheep (everyday people just trying to get through their lives). By personifying animals, it forces us to see human behavior and archetypal human personality traits more objectively.

At its most complex, *Animals* is a descent into the human (and British) psyche and subconscious motivations that decries the power of "the man," the inner workings of a democratic Western society, its inherent contradictions, and the ills that plague it.

Animals opens with a Dylanesque folky acoustic strumming and Waters's nasally vocal twang for the song "Pigs on the Wing (Part One)," and is followed by the Gilmour-sung meditation on disillusionment titled "Dogs" (featuring

some of the guitarist's best work on the album), "Pigs (Three Different Ones)" (snorting beasts of the title noisily announce the entrance of the song about decadence), "Sheep" (animal-on-animal violence and the great masses being kept in line through fear), and "Pigs On the Wing (Part Two)" (the companion piece to the opener, which may refer to ultimately accepting your station in life).

These large-as-life themes were expanded to gigantic proportions for the record's accompanying visuals: A fifty-foot swine, designed by the German company Balloon Fabrik, was tied to the smokestacks of the Battersea Power Station while snapshots were taken for the LP's cover.

Reportedly, the dirigible was accidentally loosed over Hyde Park and touched down (or crashed) a farm in Chilham. That same pig, filled with helium, was used for the band's live show—just one of the many extravagant props that the band used for their live productions, which also included a giant octopus, a dual-mirror wheel to cast blinding beams of light, one large bespectacled school-teacher marionette, a ditched plane, and other spectacles.

In many ways, *Animals* was the start of it all—the supersize Floyd show. From here on in, fans would come to expect the mind-blowing lengths to which Pink Floyd would go to entertain a crowd in the 1970s and the early part of the 1980s.

THE WALL

Floyd performed, on and off, for the first six months of 1977 in support of *Animals*. Gigging in arenas in North America and Europe, Waters became irritated first by the impersonal nature of the venues (calling them "oppressive") and then by the audiences themselves. (Waters famously spat on a rowdy fan in Montreal at Olympic Stadium.)

Waters once again reflected on the affairs of his life and gleaned a

new subject for a concept record, *The Wall*, centered on an aging, emotionally numb, and detached rocker named Pink, who's fallen prey to his fears, perhaps much like Waters. Building a barrier between himself and the outside world appears to be one way for Pink to protect himself.

"I started thinking, 'What is this wall and what's it made from?'" Waters told *Guitar World*. "Then the idea started to occur to me that the individual bricks might be from different aspects of the history of my life and other people's lives."

We journey through Pink's haunted psyche, experiencing the trauma and lurid details of his birth, cruel school headmasters, the death of Pink's father in the war, a smothering mother (who attempts to shelter her son, to a fault), the icy effects of the Cold War, an adulterous wife, the slow spiral toward madness, and an acknowledgement of the pain the rock star has caused those around him by being emotionally unavailable in songs such as "Comfortably Numb," "Another Brick in the Wall (Part I)," "Mother," "Goodbye Cruel World," "Goodbye Blue Sky," "The Trial," "Young Lust," and "Empty Spaces."

In later years Gilmour, embittered by legal wrangling with Waters, called *The Wall* a "catalog of people Roger blames for his own failings in life . . ."

Perhaps. But, interestingly, some of Gilmour's most memorable and biting guitar work appears on *The Wall*—from the famous, towering blues-based solo in "Comfortably Numb' to the glassy, heavily compressed funky rhythm guitar of "Another Brick in the Wall (Part II)" (featuring the voices of a chorus of children recorded in the stairwells of the Arts High School in North London) and the fingerpicking style he employs in "Goodbye Blue Sky."

While it's difficult to argue that the band's twenty-six-song double album was evidence of Floyd curtailing their self-indulgent tendencies, the individual songs that appear on *The Wall* are bite-size bits (no "Echoes" here) that, by virtue of being so, defined mainstream music. *The Wall* went to number one in the U.S. in 1980 and number three in Britain.

STAGING *THE WALL*

Transferring Waters's jaundiced dream to the stage required a construction crew: A crane was needed to erect a thirty-five-foot high wall (which was nearly 160 feet across) of white cardboard bricks.

The wall separating the band from the audience, a stage design concept created by illustrator Gerald Scarfe, had built-in holes so concertgoers could see the band. By show's end, the wall would come crashing down and the band would be on full display.

"*The Wall* blew my mind," says Trans-Siberian Orchestra mastermind Paul O'Neill. "The whole concept of putting the bricks up little by little during the show so that by the mid of show, the stage is walled off and then you hear someone say, 'Is there anybody out there?' It was brilliant. They were always pushing the envelope. It has withstood the ultimate critic—time."

OUTSIDE *THE WALL*: *THE FINAL CUT* AND BEYOND

The effect of *The Wall*—both musically and visually—is immeasurable and spawned the semi-animated movie adaptation, 1982's *Pink Floyd: The Wall*, directed by Alan Parker, starring Boomtown Rats front man and future Live Aid organizer Bob Geldof.

In 1983, Floyd released *The Final Cut*, a semi-symphonic final studio record helmed by Waters (who wrote all the music), and yet another concept album, largely exploring the same thematic territory as *Wish You Were Here*, *Animals*, and *The Wall*. In this installment, Waters takes cynical aim at the military, organized religion, and the very societal fabric of England.

The Final Cut is merely an extension of the barrier—the wall—Waters had erected the previous few albums. There are some genuine magical musical moments here (e.g., "Paranoid Eyes," "The Hero's Return"), but too much of it feels like retread, as if Waters were wallowing in his own misery, sometimes to the point of melodrama. In addition, the R&B-tinged rocker "Not Now John" and the cautionary tale of societal conformity "Your Possible Pasts," both Top 10 U.S. hits, wouldn't have been out of place on *The Wall*.

All of this only served to further heighten the tension between Waters and his remaining bandmates, who were had already waved good-bye to keyboardist Wright, who'd been ousted prior to the recording of *The Final Cut*.

It appears Waters began thinking of Floyd as the vehicle for his own personal reflection and pain—the other members were there to help orchestrate and bring his grand (and sour) ideas to life. Nothing more. Nothing less.

Unsurprisingly, given the band's morale, Floyd didn't tour *The Final Cut*, and in 1985, Waters announced he was leaving the band, having already released a 1984 solo record, *The Pros and Cons of Hitchhiking*.

(Gilmour countered with his own solo album, *About Face*, his second, the same year.)

For all intents and purposes, the band was no more—reportedly never to be a whole again. This didn't stop fans from continuing to flood the record stores to buy Floyd albums or gobble up anything even remotely tied to the band.

Floyd's mystique had grown to enormous proportions in their absence—more than anyone could have known. By the mid-1980s, Floyd laser shows were cropping up at various venues, such as New York City's Hayden Planetarium at the American Museum of Natural History, playing to the stoner crowd and the average Floyd fanatic hungry for the band's marriage of dazzling light displays and aural atmospherics.

Still, the band members kept their distance and continued to work separately until Gilmour and Mason decided to reassemble the band, without Waters, and even extended an invite to the bassist's nemesis and erstwhile Pinky, Wright.

Waters was furious, even calling the events that transpired "the Floyd fraud." A bitter war of the words in the press and legal battle ensued. Waters sued his former mates over the rights to the name but lost, and the Gilmour version of the band released *A Momentary Lapse of Reason* in 1987, which went on to sell millions, making Floyd one of the biggest comeback stories in music of the decade. (Waters had released his 1987 solo album *Radio K.A.O.S.* earlier in the year, but it was soon overshadowed.)

Floyd was a virtual inspiration for any "dinosaur" act that's ever been written off as dead: The revamped and rejuvenated band played sold-out shows (multiple nights in a single city in some cases) across three continents, wowing audiences with classic material, syncopated laser light displays, one flying bed, and a giant inflatable pig. (Waters owned the rights to the pig

The Piper at the Gates of Dawn (1967)

Wish You Were Here (1975)

The Wall (1979)

Live at Pompeii: The Director's Cut (DVD, 2003)

A faceless label executive: Welcome to the machine.

and, to avoid legal action, Gilmour and Mason attached testicles to the monster swine.)

"David Gilmour, over the years, polished and honed Pink Floyd," says Jethro Tull's Ian Anderson. "They've played to their strengths. Particularly Gilmour, who had that really shiny veneer of excellent skillful guitar playing, which made Pink Floyd, then and now, one of the most important bands of all time."

The double live *Delicate Sound of Thunder* followed in 1988, capitalizing on the band's recent success and world tour. Two years later

Floyd emerged with Rick Wright as a formal member and the number-one U.S. record, *The Division Bell*—Gilmour's first real foray as the leader into conceptual rock, on the subject of communication (which might even address the rift between him and Waters in "Lost for Words").

Nineteen ninety-five's live *P.U.L.S.E.* followed. Waters was reportedly invited to perform with Floyd in England on the night the band was filming for the accompanying video release of *P.U.L.S.E.*, but he declined.

Ten years went by, Floyd was a memory, and then the impossible: Waters, Gilmour, Wright, and Mason reunited for a four-song set at the Live 8

ALAN PARSONS: TALES OF IMAGINATION

The Alan Parsons Project (APP), formed in 1975 by engineer/producer Alan Parsons (who was then best known for his work with Pink Floyd on the band's 1973 hi-fi breakthrough, *The Dark Side of the Moon*), and master songwriter Eric Woolfson, dented the U.S. Top 40 from the mid-1970s through the mid-1980s with such orchestrated, progressive pop songs as "(The System of) Doctor Tarr and Professor Fether," "I Wouldn't Want to be Like You," "Games People Play," "Eye in the Sky," and "Don't Answer Me."

Unlike other studiocentric outfits such as Mandalaband and the art-pop band 10cc, APP married a four-on-the-floor techno-dance feel with odd time signatures and expansive symphonic elements, producing deceptively complex tunes that, at their core, were very melodic.

"Alan and I met at Abbey Road [Studios]," said Woolfson before his untimely death in December 2009. "He was working in one studio and I was working in another, and we were very similar heights as far as our size. We saw eye to eye, literally, so we got [to] talking and I was impressed with this guy. He was very modest, despite the fact that he was working with some of the biggest artists of the day."

Woolfson eventually came to manage Parsons and finally work with him in the Alan Parsons Project. With Parsons and Woolfson at the helm, and a stable of first-rate session musicians (including members of bands such as Pilot, Ambrosia, and Curved Air), APP had the potential to metamorphose into whatever the two protagonists had envisioned the music to be—and they dared to dream in wide-screen.

APP, as Pink Floyd had before them, became known for their aural visions, beginning with 1976's *Tales of*

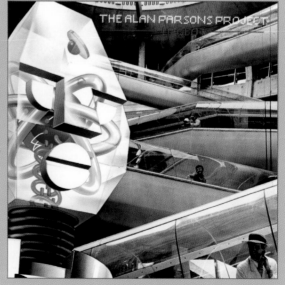

I Robot (1977)

Tales of Mystery and Imagination: Edgar Allan Poe (1976)

Pyramid (1978)

Eye in the Sky (1982)

concert to end global poverty in Hyde Park in 2005. The band acknowledged the debt they owed Syd Barrett, and on they went with their set.

The moment was surreal—and also shortlived. Rumors of the band coming back together were quickly quashed. Gilmour went on to release *On an Island* in 2006 (his first solo album since 1984's *About Face*). Mason's name crops up on reissues from time to time (from such disparate acts as Robert Wyatt, Gong, and the Damned), and Wright appeared on *On an Island*.

In the spring of 2006, Gilmour hit the road (with Wright on keyboards), spawning the double album *Live in Gdansk*, as Waters and Mason teamed up for a competing tour. The divided halves of Floyd, though trolling around separately, each performed *The Dark Side of the Moon*, stirring rumors once again of a band reunion. Sadly, it was never to be: Wright died in September 2008.

Some still hold out hope that the two prodigious songwriters of Floyd—Gilmour and Waters—can sit across a table and discuss life, love, and their hopes and fears and get down to recording new material once and for all.

"As I've said, I respect the band a lot for what they've accomplished," explains Peter Jenner, "but the only thing I can't respect is the way they can't bury the hatchets and do another record about growing old, [about] the disillusionment of age, which I think would be great, because a lot of their fans are growing old as well. Not all are, but a lot of us are. And we'd like to see it happen."

So much of Pink Floyd's history is steeped in achieving the unthinkable: In the summer of 2010, Gilmour and Waters reunited onstage in England for a benefit show. At press time, the pair had promised to perform together again on Waters' solo tour later in the year, stoking speculation of a Floyd resurgence. Can Waters and Gilmour perform one more minor miracle?

Mystery and Imagination, based on short stories and poems of Edgar Allan Poe—a literary figure Woolfson had been fascinated with as a child growing up in Glasgow, Scotland, in large part due to filmmaker Roger Corman's cinematic interpretation of the author's timeless and terrifying stories.

"I remember being petrified that Pink Floyd would get hold of the idea," Woolfson said. "We called everything by fake song titles . . . so that nobody would know what the real subject matter was."

Parsons and Woolfson used anything and everything at their disposal to experiment with sound, including sampled noises, various stringed instruments, and orchestras.

"I remember when we were recording in Kingsway Hall in London, which has a marvelous sound, and the underground trains, when they'd pass, would give you a terrible rumble, which sometimes necessitated a retake," Woolfson said. "We were in the middle of recording a section of 'The Fall of the House of Usher' and in comes this fantastic rumble. That sound was mixed in as a subsonic effect. We couldn't have picked a better place to record."

Despite APP's reputation as a synth-based studio band, Parsons and Woolfson were bound and determined to skirt the use of synthesizers in favor of more organic sonic elements.

"For the first two albums, I kind of almost avoided synths," says Parsons. "It was really odd that I got the title of electronic synth wizard."

When released, *Tales of Mystery and Imagination* was a Top 40 hit in the U.S., and entered the British charts in the Top 60. Its success was enough to convince Woolfson and Parsons that APP was a viable project, and they continued to release Top 10 U.S. albums such as 1977's *I Robot* (based on the Isaac Asimov book *I, Robot*) and 1982's *Eye in the Sky*, and Top 20 hits like 1980's *Turn of a Friendly Card* (inspired by Woolfson's and Parson's time in the gaming Mecca Monaco) and 1984's *Ammonia Avenue*.

In many cases, the varied sound textures and overall atmosphere of the records gave the productions an uncommon and often subtle sonic richness. "To be a producer/engineer like Alan is really a talent," said Woolfson. "It only just hit me when I began managing him."

Other audiophile dreams included 1978's *Pyramid* (which bears conceptual and musical links to Floyd's *The Dark Side of the Moon*), 1979's *Eve* (on the psychological impact of the fairer sex's stranglehold on the male psyche), 1985's *Vulture Culture*, 1986's *Stereotomy*, and 1987's *Gaudi*—boasting such musical attributes as symphonic pomp and Györgi Ligeti–style choral clusters.

"If there was anything unusual, we went for it," Woolfson said. "Alan's approach was, you didn't just play one line on one instrument. You'd play a line and then about another half dozen different things with it, and then he cherry-picked what combinations worked. Alan had layers of sound on top of layers, which was his technique. I used to joke, 'Nature abhors a vacuum and so does Alan Parsons.' If there was a space, he wanted to fill it with something."

(Ian Dickson/Getty Images)

KING CRIMSON

Twentieth Century Schizoid Band

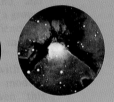

IF THERE'S ONE GROUP THAT EXEMPLIFIES THE
progressive rock era—its willingness to change the parameters of accepted
rock, its constant search for new inspiration—it's King Crimson.

Given the impact of the band's debut, *In the Court of the Crimson
King*, one could argue that Crimson single-handedly had more to do with
creating the entire genre of prog rock than any other band in Britain.

"King Crimson emerged at a particular moment when there was a
cultural effervescence that really carried anyone and everyone along with
it," says Greg Lake, bassist and vocalist for the band in the early days.
"King Crimson emerged at that very moment when the cork popped."

As if reaching us on some subconscious level, the musical and lyrical elements of the early King Crimson seemed to crystallize and codi-
fy what is now defined as prog rock, despite the changes in musical
direction and personnel, in an attempt to remain fresh while maintaining a discernible identity.

"People seemed to have latched onto Crimson lyricist Pete
Sinfield's style, this kind of purple prose," says founding member Ian
McDonald, the band's wind player and Mellotronist. "It seems lyric writers
needed to work in this kind of wordy style, using medieval imagery of knights

and dragons and things, in order to call themselves progressive."

Musicians from soon-to-be-highly-influential bands looked up to Crimson—people such as Steve Hackett from Genesis and Peter Banks and Bill Bruford of Yes (the latter would join Crimson in the early 1970s).

"We thought we were pretty hot stuff until Crimson came along," says Yes's original guitarist Peter Banks. "They were so much better than us that we literally said, 'We have to rehearse a lot more.'"

BEGINNINGS

Crimson has it roots in Bournemouth-area bands, most notably the trio, Giles, Giles and Fripp (featuring bassist Peter Giles sharing vocal duties with his brother, drummer Michael Giles, and guitarist/piano player Robert Fripp), which recorded *The Cheerful Insanity of . . .* for Decca's Deram sublabel in 1968.

Multi-instrumentalist Ian McDonald and then-girlfriend and former Fairport Convention vocalist Judy Dyble placed an ad in the popular music weekly *Melody Maker* for "Musicians Wanted," in the hopes of forming a band. "Giles, Giles and Fripp had put an album out, but that hadn't done anything, really," says McDonald. "Peter Giles answered the ad, saying, 'Why don't you come see us. We're a three-piece band.' And it went from there.'"

The chemistry seemed to be right, and the quintet cut recordings at Brondesbury Road, in London, on Peter Giles's two-track in the band's flat (issued as *The Brondesbury Tapes 1968* on CD in 2001). "It was quite primitive, but nonetheless we got some quite nice recordings done," says McDonald.

After the sessions, Dyble left, but not before cutting an early version of "I Talk to the Wind," which would later appear on Crimson's *A Young Person's Guide to King Crimson* in 1975. (Material from this time period

would be used as the basis for songs on the band's debut as well as for 1970's *In the Wake of Poseidon*, 1971's *Islands*, and even Peter Sinfield's 1973 solo record, *Still*.)

McDonald, who had appeared on one official Giles, Giles and Fripp release, a single for "Thursday Morning" (the final chapter of "The Saga of Rodney Toadey" from *The Cheerful Insanity of . . .*), remained and the band pressed on.

"We wanted to move to another level, and that basically meant getting a front man for the Giles brothers," says McDonald.

That front man turned out to be vocalist Greg Lake, a friend of Fripp from the Bournemouth area, a onetime member of the Gods and Shy Limbs, who'd apply cross-picking technique to the bass guitar that he'd learned from instructor Don Strike (the same music teacher Fripp went to).

"When Greg took over the lead vocal and the bass, that's when we had King Crimson," says McDonald. "I brought my pal Peter Sinfield in, although he and the band had already met, and he became the lyricist and somewhat of a mentor and visionary while handling the lighting and PA."

Once Lake and Sinfield were onboard, bassist Peter Giles was sent packing (though he'd reappear with Crimson on *In the Wake of Poseidon*). "We needed a front man, a lead singer," says McDonald. "Between Giles, Giles, Fripp, and myself there really wasn't a strong front man or singer. That was [Greg's] job. He just happened to play bass as well. Pete was arguably the more accomplished bass player . . . but we had to make the change."

It was an odd assortment of people, but it worked. "There are some strange characters," says Pete Sinfield. "I'm a sort of this funny mixture of clown and harlequin and incredibly emotional queen-of-the-night sort of person. I'm an only child, very shy; my mother was bisexual, and I have a

bohemian background. Three of them [Fripp, Lake, Giles] came from the Bournemouth area—a very middle-class area of southern England. But Greg's parents were very, very poor.

"I remember Greg talking to me one time about his upbringing," Sinfield continues. "He lived in a pre-fab, cheap housing unit. He said he used to see the people next door to him with peaches in these throwaway tins. Greg said he never had peaches in his house. That put a certain sort of drive into him that he was going to rise above all of this and have peaches for his tea."

"That was my childhood, poverty, basically," says Lake. "But when I became about twelve years old, one Christmas my mother and father asked me what I wanted and I said that I'd like to have a guitar. They bought me this cheap guitar on the condition that I took lessons. I did, and I met Robert Fripp in the process."

"Ian McDonald is this blue person most of the time with these emotionally cheerful spots," resumes Sinfield. "The interesting thing about Ian is that his parents shoved him off because they didn't quite know what to do with him."

"It's true," says McDonald. "I was in a military band from the age of sixteen to twenty-one. I had trouble from my father, especially through my school years. I didn't do well in school and got kicked out. Finally, my parents put me away in the army when I was a teen, because they didn't know what to do with me. I spent one year at the Royal Military School of Music and basically learned to read music and a certain amount of orchestration and also used tuned percussion."

Unraveling Fripp is a book in and of itself. For one thing, Fripp has attempted to eschew the blues-based electric rock guitar tradition by drawing not only from American jazz and blues but European folk and art-music/classical traditions. It's why his guitar playing sounds and feels different from, say, Peter Green's or Eric

Clapton's. Geniuses both. But Fripp's talents lay elsewhere. Even his thought processes seem to be different.

"I remember going to his flat, way back in 1969, and I saw all of these paperback books, because he's a big reader, like me, but every one of them had its own plastic bag," says Sinfield. "I prefer a well-thumbed library book. But if you put those two personalities together, it's an interesting combination, because you get the precision of Robert and the funky, who-gives-a-shit thing from me."

"I knew Fripp pretty well," says Yes's Banks. "Fripp used to come and watch [Yes] play at the Marquee [before Crimson started]. He later moved into the apartment house I was in, that used to be the Yes apartment in Fulham in London. So many musicians lived in that place—50A Munster Road. He seemed a bit like a schoolteacher. Not exactly patronizing but highly intelligent. I don't know anybody else quite like him. What I would say about him is that when we would ever have a discussion, he could never be wrong. He had a great knack of convincing you that he was right."

"Bob was amazing," adds onetime Crimson drummer Andrew McCulloch. "He was left-handed but taught himself to play right-handed. He was always a very studious worker."

Fripp once described himself as the grandson of a miner who died at fifty-nine, and the son of a father who told him to "leave school at sixteen to help feed his brothers and sisters."[5]

This could *not* have been easy for young Bob Fripp. Anyone who has grown up in a family with a similar dynamic knows it's about sacrifice and maturation—traits omitted by some of Fripp's detractors.

"Robert is a lovely man," says David Enthoven, the "E" in E. G., Crimson's former management company. "Much misunderstood man. But I had a lot of fun with him. Got drunk with him. I'm still pleased to call him a friend."

"Robert has a reputation of being quite prickly, but that reputation comes from the music press—and he's prickly with the music press, because he sees them as rather irrelevant to what he does," says Porcupine Tree founder Steven Wilson, who remixed and remastered some of the Crimson catalog.

PUTTING IT TOGETHER

Prior to joining the erstwhile Giles, Giles and Fripp, Sinfield and McDonald had worked together with future band roadie Dik Fraser on bass. (Sinfield and McDonald had written material, including "The Court of the Crimson King," from which the band got its name.)

Few rock bands had such a close relationship with lyricists. Keith Reid with Procol Harum, Robert Hunter with the Grateful Dead, and Pete Brown with Cream were perhaps the most high-profile examples.

"I must have been amusing and/or valuable to them," says Sinfield. "It became increasingly so, because this was a bunch of professional, almost cynical, musicians. King Crimson were great players: They really should have been jazzers, but what they lacked, without blowing my trumpet too much, was imagination."

"The original King Crimson agreed on more or less everything on musical terms," says McDonald. "You always hear of stories of bands bickering and people trying to get their little bit on the record . . . but we never really had any of that. We were all in the same place, which was pretty great. We all knew what the band was. It was unspoken."

MOVING OUT

Crimson moved out of their Brondesbury rehearsal space and hit Fulham Road in London, where they set up shop. The band performed its first show at the Speakeasy in London in April 1969, and continued on playing the London scene, eventually earning a residency at the Marquee.

Their Hyde Park performance, supporting the Rolling Stones, in July 1969, was held before half a million people, and solidified the band's appeal while increasing their visibility. "[Yes] never played with them, luckily," says Banks, who saw Crimson at their Speakeasy gig. "They were much better than us."

"I saw [Crimson's] early gigs in London and I went down there with Bill [Bruford], and we just stood there," says bassist Ray Bennett, later of Flash, featuring Peter Banks. "He was saying something to the effect of, 'This is what I wanted [Yes] to sound like.'"

Former Pink Floyd comanagers Peter Jenner and Andrew King were promoters of the Hyde Park shows and remember how Crimson accelerated to the front of the line and got such a primo gig opening for the Stones.

"David Enthoven managed them and wanted to get them on the bill [at Hyde Park]," remembers Jenner. "Andrew [King] and I thought everyone wanted to be on the bill with the Stones and that we could make a lot of money for it. We said to David, 'It'll cost you a lot. . . .' So he sent over an envelope with a lot of money in it and I was so embarrassed that we sent it back to him. . . . He has never forgotten that."

"Absolutely 100 percent true," says Enthoven. "Pete Jenner and I have been firm friends ever since. Jenner is a man of great integrity."

As it turns out, Crimson didn't need to bribe, beg, steal, or borrow. The band's live performances were growing in popularity, intensity, and power. "We had a residency at the Marquee, and we played there once a week and that was how our reputation started to grow," says McDonald. "We used to get a good crowd. But when we did Hyde Park, opening for the Stones, and then played the Marquee after that show, the place was absolutely jammed. Steve Hackett, who I knew

[5] Liner notes, Robert Fripp, *Absent Lovers Live in Montreal 1984*.

Drummer Michael Giles, *left*, and Ian McDonald recording the *McDonald and Giles* album at Island Studios, 1970. (Courtesy of Virgin Records)

"At paranoia's poison door": the iconic schizoid face of Crimson's 1969 debut.

even before he joined Genesis, was amazed at what we were doing. He noticed that it wasn't all just trashing and noise. There was a lot of delicate music as well."

The Crimsos were beginning to trust each other, and even went as far as switching instruments with one another on occasion. "You could play almost anything that came to mind and know that the other players would be with you, hearing and supporting it," says McDonald. "Even to the point where, perversely, they

would sort of leave you out there on the edge by yourself."

"With Crimson, performances were a matter of interreaction," says Lake. "That's when, as a bass player, if I play particularly passionately, I fire up the drummer, force him to play better. Or it's when he does a drum fill that forces you to play a bass lick that you just wouldn't have thought of."

"One night at the Whisky a Go Go in Los Angeles, the improvisation descended into silence," says McDonald. "Then it became a game of chicken as far as who was going to break the silence first. The audience didn't know what was going on."

Crimson's slowly unfurling,

Mellotron-drenched interpretation of Gustav Holst's "Mars" from the *Planets* suite was a major live piece. "It started off very quietly with the snare drum tapping out this 5/4 rhythm over the course of seven or eight minutes," says McDonald. "It built up until it became this wall of noise, very dark, very heavy."

The tape-based beast, the Mellotron, often gave the band its eerie and powerful sound by achieving a huge crescendo of approximated string (and other) noises. "Keeping Mellotrons in tune and recording them was a masochist exercise," remembers Sinfield. "It was impossible, really. I only ever heard '*The Court of the Crimson King*' in tune twice in sixty gigs, I think, whether it was outdoors or indoors."

SCHIZOID MEN

For the band's debut, the quartet and Sinfield had initially tapped producer Tony Clarke, mostly due to his experience recording the Mellotron with the Moody Blues. But after reels of recorded tapes resulted in very little usable material, Crimson decided to produce their debut themselves. It was a risk, and Enthoven and partner John Gaydon went into debt to finance the damn thing.

So obsessed were management with getting a finished product that Enthoven talked Wessex Studios into allowing the band to use the facilities for free on the promise that the money would be paid back when the band secured a record deal.

"That was a dangerous thing to do," says Enthoven. "It was complete madness. We took huge risks—mortgaged the house and whatever."

The proof, as they say, is in the pudding. *In the Court of the Crimson King* is arguably not only one of the most important records in the history of progressive rock but in rock music in general.

Even before the music begins, the record opens with a mysterious hum— a mechanical sound that evokes space travel. "That abstract wind sort of sound is the pipe organ," says McDonald. "I put my arms across the keyboard and rolled my forearm up and down over it, overloading the wind organ that was pumping air, making this wheezing, gasping sound."

John Landis, director of the movie *An American Werewolf in London*, once remarked about the classic Universal monster movie *The Wolf Man*, saying that the setting was disorienting: It could be Western or Central or Eastern Europe, motivating viewers to ask, 'Where are we? What century is this?'

"Now that you mention it, [21st Century] Schizoid Man' does set up an atmosphere of, 'Where are we?'" says McDonald. "Of, 'I'm not quite sure of what this is. Is that sound mechanical or natural?'"

Despite its links to the past (and future), "Schizoid Man" was written squarely in the present. Fripp, perhaps jokingly, once stated during an early live Crimson performance (in San Francisco in December 1969) that Spiro Agnew, the disgraced vice president under U.S. president Richard Nixon dubbed a "traveling salesman for the administration," was the model for the "21st Century Man."[6]

"To be fair, at the time, it was just a very good singable line—'21st Century Schizoid Man'—because it was percussive," says Sinfield. "Plus, using 'twenty-first century' gave it a modern, slightly depressing edge, and the lyrics were written to be like flashes from the news."

The simultaneous staccato phrasings played by alto sax, electric guitar, bass, and drums (and the pregnant pauses that follow each rhythmic grouping) in the section subtitled "Mirrors," dangle on the edge of nothing—they feel like incomplete musical lines or thoughts. The song has us on the edge of our seats as drummer Giles swings through jagged rhythmic edges.

"Mike had the great technique of a jazz drummer," says McDonald. "If you listen to the recorded version of 'Schizoid Man,' that middle section, it swings like crazy even though it's in an odd time."

The song was cut in one take. "We were well rehearsed," says McDonald. "We had to be tight on that one in order for it to work."

After the uproarious ending of "21st Century Schizoid Man," the wind instruments heard at the opening of "I Talk to the Wind" seem a peaceful respite. Yet, despite its pleasant atmosphere, "I Talk to the Wind" is just as thought-provoking as "Schizoid Man," ultimately meditating on the insignificance and impermanence of the human race.

Lake's breathy vocal delivery is underscored by McDonald's multi-tracked clarinets (recalling a British dance hall/Beatles vibe) and breezy flute solo, the latter of which converses nicely with Giles's light, jazzy touch.

"It's difficult to have a flute in a rock context, but it helps to reinforce the theme—the wind," says McDonald.

"Epitaph," the last song on the original side one of the album, is as prophetic as it is biting, as if the speaker from "I Talk to the Wind" had finally sobered and wonders if his world can be saved. "Epitaph" does little to quiet the confusion, musically and lyrically: It is at once orchestral and military—featuring thundering classical percussion on one hand and tribal-like war patterns on the other, musically translating the lyrical imagery of the rolling wheels of Sinfield's apocalyptic war machine.

"Epitaph" is a world spinning out of control, drawing the conclusion about our society's technological achievement: What we do best is wage war, our signature invention. Immediately we make a connection between Simon & Garfunkel's "Sounds of Silence," an antiwar anthem inspired

[6] Http://www.senate.gov/artandhistory/history/common/generic/VP_Spiro_Agnew.htm)

by the tumultuous times of the 1960s (post-JFK assassination) and the line in "Epitaph" concerning the wall on which the prophets wrote.

"The whole album was quite political, because I am a political animal," says Sinfield. "We were living in very political times in '67 and '68, and the record was recorded in '69, and we were all influenced by various things happening in the world, like Vietnam."

"Every song Peter wrote about was about the generation gap, the Establishment, and how people in power were in control of other people's lives," says McDonald. "As the record says, 'An Observation by King Crimson.' It's observing what's happening politically and socially."

"I started off with some stanzas of Byronesque poetry, even based on the poem [containing the lines] 'The Assyrian Came down like a wolf on the fold/ And his cohorts were gleaming purple and gold ["The Destruction of Sennacherib"]," says Sinfield. "That is very gothic, and if you look it up, it is influenced by iambic pentameter [poetic rhythm]: 'The wall on which the prophets wrote is cracking at the seams/ Upon the instruments of death . . .' I had an idea to put music to it and Ian went, 'I like that. I can do that.' He took it away and did it very well."

The brass setting on the Mellotron elevates the level of gloom, alluding to the monolithic rhythmic march of "Mars." "There's a finality to it," says McDonald. "Some people have likened that middle section where the Mellotron goes soaring up to the mushroom cloud of an atomic bomb. I don't think we came up with the term *doom rock*, but it is a very doomy song, in a very real sense."

Though it took quite some time to arrange and write, "Epitaph" may well be the perfect King Crimson song. "I will never forget the day when we recorded 'Epitaph,'" says Lake. "We were looking for a solo for it, and Ian McDonald said, 'I have an idea for this.' We all looked at him and we

thought he'd come out with some sort of sax solo or something. He said, 'Low clarinet.' [Laughs] Just take a listen to the record again. I mean, it comes to the solo and you hear clarinet, you know? This low, dirgy, grim [clarinet]. What an idea. Perfect."

IN THE COURT

The original side two of *In the Court of the Crimson King* opens with the dreamy "Moonchild, Including the Dream and the Illusion," a deep album cut that some might remember from its appearance in Vincent Gallo's 1998 film, *Buffalo 66.*

If there is any filler on the band's debut, it's the studio improvisation "Moonchild." However, it does serve two great purposes: Most of the rest of the record concerns itself with politics and current affairs of the day, and "Moonchild" seems like a psychedelic, slightly Japanese, and necessary mental tune-out or time-off that McDonald describes as a "willow-pattern" painting in musical terms.

"Improvisation was an essential part of what King Crimson was," says McDonald. "There's little evidence of that on the first album other than the filler improv in 'Moonchild,' which has vibes, drums, and guitar. Greg didn't play on it, but his vocals were used—panned half-right in the stereo image, which he was never too happy about."

"Moonchild" clears the palate for the main course: "The Court of the Crimson King (Including the Return of the Fire Witch and the Dance of the Puppets)." With a towering refrain, spilling-over-the-bar line drum fills, and conspiratorial lyrics, "The Court" is, next to "Schizoid Man," the band's most well known song.

"Originally, it was sort of Dylanesque," says Sinfield, going on to sing in a rapid delivery evocative of Dylan: "'On soft grey mornings widows cry . . .' It will ruin it for you forever now if I keep singing it this way."

"There's a syncopated bass figure used in 'The Court' that was inspired

by Otis Redding's 'I Can't Turn You Loose,'" says McDonald. "I actually worked that into the Mellotron part of the chorus of the song. It's not exactly the same notes, but it's the same rhythmically."

The iconic flute solo in the tune picks up on the Eastern music vibe presented in the previous song, "Moonchild." "The end of the flute solo is borrowed from 'Scheherezade' [Symphonic Suite, Op. 35] by [Nikolai] Rimsky-Korsakov. I put it at the end of the flute solo, and people expect it when it comes now if I'm ever performing it live."

Crimson taps into a baroque vibe by using a Baldwin harpsichord, adding a traditional touch. "It was so essential, in my mind, that I couldn't imagine 'The Court' without it," says McDonald. "It's the sound that accompanies the line Greg sings, 'The cracked brass bells will ring.' It also comes in at the end of the flute solo with a kind of splayed-out arpeggio to bring the song back to E minor for the verses."

SECOND ENDING

Just when you think the song has come to a close, it wheezes back to life for a screeching Hammond organ and all-out Mellotron cacophonous vamp, complete with roundhouse drum fills skating across the stereo image from left to right.

"The part that opens the second ending is myself and Mike sitting side by side playing the little pipe organ used earlier in the record," says McDonald. "It was like, 'All right, let's do a completely mad version of the chorus.' It's interesting because we are playing the chords in a new key. It's a bit like a Picardy third, I suppose. Same sort of idea. That device helps to refresh the ear and keep interest."

The song doesn't so much end abruptly as get sucked into the center of the sonic image, creating a kind of vortex, calling to mind an object being beamed up into an alien spacecraft.

"Yeah," says McDonald. "Or

something swirling down the drain. Either way you want to look at it."

CRIMSON KING

Sinfield's use of medieval images such as puppets, the purple piper, the keeper of the city keys, a pilgrim's door, the black queen, and on and on, are like pieces in some cosmic chess game. Authority, and perhaps an evil one at that, grinds the wheels of fate, just as a grand court jester (juggler) unleashes orchestrated madness with a simple hand gesture. His lyrics present the duality and dilemma of the Western world, the divide between the elites and the common people.

"'The Court of the Crimson King' is asking, 'Are we the devil's playthings?'" says McDonald. "It's not necessarily promoting anything demonic. It's a question of control."

"Those lyrics are why I used to be called pretentious," says Sinfield. "[The Crimson songs] were rock songs—you weren't supposed to talk about the history of the world, the fact that we're doomed to repeat it. It was influenced by some of the more gothic poets like Byron and Tennyson, the time of empire. Bob Dylan and others were doing similar things, and I thought I'd have a go at it with a slightly different style."

CHEMISTRY

A lot has been made of the chemistry of the band. But it seems its inherent destructive quality ran just as strong. Was *In the Court of the Crimson King* a reflection of the world as much as of the band and its ability to conjure some sort of dark, mysterious force? Did the mischievous Sinfield create a controversial name (and reinforce it through overt and subliminal lyrical symbolism) only to enlist us in some fiendish parlor game for his own amusement?

"We were not promoting any kind of devil worship or anything like that," cautions McDonald. "What we were doing was basically reflecting or illustrating the world as it is. Or the

way things were heading."

Some remain skeptical and unconvinced and think that Crimson may have been controlled by the very same forces they were singing about. "Robert Fripp and the King Crimson creed was and is a complex creature that somehow personifies the world as I see it today," says Gordon Haskell, who would join Crimson and was Fripp's band member in the pre-Crimson R&B group League of Gentlemen. "I have to decide once and for all if [Fripp] was playing his part in the creation of our present society or merely foretelling it."

UNCANNY MASTERPIECE

In the Court of the Crimson King, an observation by King Crimson, was released in October 1969 and shot to number five on the British charts, into the Top 30 U.S. Famously, Pete Townshend announced to the world (in a full-page ad that ran in *ZigZag* magazine) that Crimson's debut was an "uncanny masterpiece" and "fucking incredible."

Fripp attributed the band's successes to what he called the "good fairy." How else to explain the band's amazing run of luck? "Well, *something* was happening," says Sinfield. "It was sort of a fluke."

"I would say that what we got was the correct album at the end of the day," says Enthoven. "I remember I took the record to Chris Blackwell at Island and he said it wasn't his cup of tea but he totally understood it." (Island released the record in Britain.) "The most interesting thing was taking it to Ahmet Ertegun [at Atlantic], who you would have thought would have hated it, but he loved it." (Atlantic released it in America.)

But just like the sucking vortex concluding the band's debut, things began to slide down the drain quickly. Within months of the release of Crimson's debut, the whole thing appeared to be breaking apart. Even the illustrator of the record's iconic image

(the "paranoid man"), Barry Godber, died not long after the record appeared.

In a stunning move, toward the end of a 1969 U.S. tour, McDonald and Giles announced that they had had enough and wanted to quit the band. "Mike and Ian didn't like flying," says Lake. "At the time, we were on a tour of the United States . . . and we got to San Francisco and they had decided that they didn't want to do it. They didn't want to tour; they were far happier in the studio just making records."

"There seems to be something about Crimson and people leaving, and I suppose I was the first culprit," says McDonald, who moved to New York in the 1970s and later found success with the arena rock band Foreigner. "It was my first tour and I was very homesick. I had trouble dealing with the very quick rise and acceptance the band was experiencing. I didn't even really realize the implications of leaving and how important the band was."

IN THE WAKE OF MCDONALD AND GILES

Following their Crimson experience, McDonald and Giles partnered for an oft-overlooked gem of progressive rock/pop, 1971's *McDonald and Giles*, featuring Steve Winwood on piano and organ, and bassist Peter Giles, with words by Peter Sinfield for the twenty-one-minute epic "Birdman."

Crimson pressed on with Fripp, Lake, and Sinfield at the helm of a new lineup, which included prodigal bassist Peter Giles, Mike Giles (who was reduced to session drummer), saxophonist/flautist Mel Collins (formerly of the band Circus), jazz pianist/composer Keith Tippett, second vocalist Gordon Haskell (that's him on "Cadence and Cascade").

Crimson's 1970 sophomore effort, *In the Wake of Poseidon* (the title of which was a kind of in-joke referring to the tidal wave of uncertainty that nearly consumed Crimson in the aftermath of the original band's

Bruford, circa '74.

breakup), contains memorable material (e.g., "Pictures of a City (Including 42nd at Treadmill)," the three-part "Peace," "Cat Food," and "Cadence and Cascade," the latter two, despite the LP credits, written largely by McDonald and Sinfield), but it feels like a watered-down review of the debut album.

Perhaps the band was unsure of itself and straining to hold on to a formula. And just when the band appeared to be at its most vulnerable, Crimson was delivered what could have been their knockout blow: Before the end of the recording sessions, Lake announced he was leaving to join Nice keyboardist Keith Emerson in forming a new group.

"Robert wanted to carry on with King Crimson," says Lake. "I said to him, 'Look, if one guy was going to leave, maybe you can replace one guy, but two guys is too fundamental.' To me, that was the end of the band. It's hard to talk about what-ifs. I don't know what would have happened had the band stuck together. I suspect the band would have gone on. It would have continued to make good music. The people in it were fantastic."

Incredibly, *Poseidon* scored a higher position on the British charts than the band's debut (climbing to number four and within the Top 40 in the U.S.), but more changes were to come.

LIZARD

Crimson had been reduced to a studio band by the time Sinfield and Fripp were fixing to record the band's third and perhaps most bizarre record, *Lizard*—a horn-driven, EMS VSC-3 synth-seduced, oscillator-inflected, musique concrète–inspired, bizzaro prog record from the darkest corners of the duo's collective mind.

"Robert and I spent an awful lot of time making that record," says Sinfield. "We didn't have anything else to do, really. It was really the two of us with a bunch of musicians coming in and out."

Idle hands, as they say. Couple the strange musical elements with the loose album concept of masks and disguises, and *Lizard* is revealed to be slightly demented. In "The Battle of Glass Tears," one section of the side-long title track (Fripp's first foray into long-form composition), chaos ensues: Collins's sax is slowly panned from right to left, and soon, sax fills both channels. Mellotron, cornet (played by Mark Charig), guitar, drums, bass, and acoustic piano intermingle in a free-for-all and in call and response. It's madness.

Even "Prince Rupert Awakes" (the opening section of "Lizard"), sung by Yes's Jon Anderson, which could be one of the sweetest melodies Crimson ever recorded, is subverted by reverse guitar riffs, avant-jazz sonic stabs, strange lyrical devices, and the Mellotron's demonic sonic webbing.

"'Prince Rupert' was really about Charles II and the Roundheads," says Sinfield. "[Charles II] had this thing about having these little gas toys that would explode when hitting the floor. I'd collect these odd facts and try to put them together in a kind of collage."

Throughout the record there's a constant tension between dark and light, and scattered references to the twelve Jungian archetypes, represented and reinforced by Gini Barris's opulent, medieval, illuminated-manuscript-style LP cover artwork. (It's possible to interpret the cover as a seditious commentary on sacred texts, which only completes the artistic package and reflects the depth of its perversity.)

"Fripp might have had [musical designs] in his mind's eye all the time," says Haskell, the band's singer and bassist after Lake left. "He might have been wiser to share that vision with the rest of us, so that we could be more cooperative and understanding. One has to praise the individual players. Chaos is achieved with the record, and in places it was chaos."

"I found it a very daunting task recording with Crimson," says drummer Andrew McCulloch. "You would play something and Bob [Fripp] would say, 'Right. This is King Crimson. Now you don't play what normal people would play under these conditions. Think about it.' It was a big leap for me."

ISLANDS

By the band's next studio album, 1971's *Islands*, the lineup had changed

In the Wake of Poseidon (1970)

Lizard (1970)

Islands (1971)

Earthbound (1972)

Larks' Tongues in Aspic (1973)

Red (1974)

The original four-piece lineup in 1969. Left to right: Lake, Giles, Fripp, and McDonald (Courtesy of Rolling Stone London edition/Discipline Global Mobile)

again: Haskell, who left in a huff over creative and financial reasons he says, and McCulloch were gone, and in came vocalist/bassist Boz Burrell (later of Bad Company) and drummer Ian Wallace, who joined forces with Fripp, Mel Collins, and Sinfield.

Songs such as "Sailor's Tale," "The Letters" (which evolved from the Giles, Giles and Fripp song "Why Don't You Just Drop In"), "Ladies of the Road," the title track, "Prelude: Song of the Gulls" (parroting another GG&F track, "Suite No. 1"), and "Formentera Lady" were perhaps more consistent than the material on *Lizard*, but not as explorative.

"The band were influenced by jazz, really," Ian Wallace told the author in a 2003 interview. "We were leaning toward John Coltrane and Miles Davis and even free jazz. We allowed ourselves to go anywhere we wanted."

As the music became more elastic, tension grew within the ranks. Fripp and Sinfield weren't seeing eye to eye on the band's musical and lyrical direction: Fripp even began questioning Sinfield's passion for the music.

"The famous falling-out between Robert and me was really because we

had a new band, new musicians, and I wanted the sound to be more Mediterranean and Robert wanted it to be more urban and aggressive and gritty," says Sinfield.

"Robert had decided that he could no longer work with Peter," said Wallace. "He came to the other three of us and said, 'It is either me or him.' That was it, you know?"

Sinfield was out. (He later recorded a solo record, 1973's jazzy-orchestral *Still*, featuring past, current, and then-future members of Crimson.) It seems *Islands* was the appropriate title for a record, which, in 1971, reflected the division between the band's members.

After a 1971 U.S. tour, Crimson reconvened for a rehearsal/writing session. "[W]e did a tour of the United States, the first [this band did] of the U.S., and it went really well," Wallace remembered. "Robert said, 'I want this band to be an equal split; I want equal input creatively and writing-wise.'"

"We came back from an American tour and we had six weeks off before the next tour of America," says Collins. "The idea, Robert said, was that we would write and come up with some

material [for] the next album. I had written a few bits and pieces. Some ideas. When we got back into rehearsals, Robert just sat on his stool and refused to play anything I had written. He said, 'It's not Crimson.'"

"Mel just ran from the room," remembered Wallace. "He had just been blasted down. I was just so exasperated at that point, I stood up and put my sticks on the drums and said, 'I'm outta here.'"

"To be honest, the thing with Fripp just destroyed me," Collins says. "I had left the rehearsal room in tears. I said something to Robert like, 'Thank you, Robert. You've done it again.' So the band was no longer."

"David Enthoven, the manager, called us up and said, 'We have a two-month tour of the States starting in February, we've got contractual obligations, would you just do this?'" Wallace said. "We did and we really enjoyed ourselves. We actually got to one point where it was like, 'This is really good. We want to continue.' But Robert had already made his plans to get Bill [Bruford] and John [Wetton] and that was it."

Multi-instrumentalist
McDonald was key
to Crimson's early
success. (Courtesy
of Ian McDonald)

BRUFORD/WETTON/ MUIR CROSS ERA

Save for a release of the live *Earthbound*, documenting (though with poor sound quality) the exploits of the Burrell-Collins-Wallace lineup, the dark years were over, and a new creative age was to begin.

King Crimson Mach III, very much like the original Crimson, operated on an improvisational basis (especially during live performances), delivering avant–hard rock throughout the early and mid-'70s.

Drummer Bill Bruford had held the drum throne in the supergroup Yes just prior to joining Crimson. That Yes's *Close to the Edge* had eaten a lot of time and tedious studio work only served to frustrate Bruford, a notoriously restless musician who was more interested in musical spontaneity than musical calculation. Crimson called.

John Wetton had been known as the hot bass player in England ever since his days with Mogul Thrash and Family, and a brief stint with Renaissance (three shows).

"I've known Robert since I was fifteen years old," Wetton said in a 1995 interview the author conducted. "I was one of those musicians who had technique that was beyond my comprehension. I could play and I guess it was somewhere around [1972] that I bumped into Robert Fripp. We talked about forming a band. It was going to be King Crimson Three."

The final third of the rhythm section was filled by Jamie Muir. An avant-garde percussionist, Muir was prone to performing outlandish stage acts (he'd bite down on blood capsules to great vampiric effect) while banging on found instruments and noisemakers of all sorts. He commanded strange atonal percussive blasts, helping to direct and transform this new King Crimson from minor-key, jazz-oriented band to experimental heavy metal outfit.

David Cross, violinist and Mellotron player, provided a key-

boardist foil for Fripp's guitar. Cross was one of some half dozen important rock violinists working at the time. "Crimson was a very natural place to be because there weren't any boundaries beyond our own lack of vision," says Cross, who claims to have picked up the violin at age seven, because his father was an accomplished piano player. ("In Freudian terms, it was probably a decision not to get into a major competition with my father," explains the violinist.)

The last component of this new Crimson was lyricist Richard Palmer-James, who'd been a school friend of Wetton in their preteen days. He was likely tapped because no one else in the band could write lyrics or was interested in doing so.

Perhaps in a strange way, the potential and promise of the 1970–'72 Crimson was finally fulfilled. As dense as some of the material was from 1972–'75, there was a transparency in the songwriting.

"The period with Ian Wallace and Boz Burrell was quite difficult," says Enthoven. "That [band] was more dope-driven, where the Fripp, Bruford, and Wetton band was really music-driven. Some nights it was really great, and some nights it was shite. But for me that was an exciting period, because it really became experimental music."

It was this lineup that produced one of the milestones of Crimson's career and, indeed, the entire 1970s progressive era: *Larks' Tongues in Aspic* (a title suggested by Muir), featuring "Book of Saturday," the passionate and melancholy "Exiles" (some of the most beautiful work the band had done up to that point), the Middle Eastern/West African–informed "The Talking Drum," "Easy Money," and the two-part title track (Part One being a Asian-music-tinged sleeper; Part Two, an art-metal, Stravinsky-esque workout in 10/8.)

The album is littered with uncredited laughs (one spurt of laughter is obviously sped up, sounding like a tiny demon cackling), snippets of

film dialogue, recurring musical themes, the sound of insect buzzing, and animal noises, as if there were some subtext running through the music. Did these fine Englishmen really harbor dark, deep visions?

"In King Crimson, we did outrageous things with . . . the rhythmic intensity," Bruford said. "Of what the instruments were supposed to do, or not supposed to do. What harmony [we] were supposed to have or not supposed to have."

On its surface, the music behaves much like jazz, but it is not jazz in tonality. It is more "jazz" in its spirit and free-form approach. Fripp has admitted that he expanded his musical palate at this point in time to bring in European classical influences and psychedelic blues.[7]

"In King Crimson's case, I think a lot of it was coming from Stravinsky," says Fred Frith of Henry Cow, a contemporary of King Crimson. "You can hear actual lifts of *Rite of Spring* in ["Larks' Tongues in Aspic, Part Two"]. The rhythm section is actually playing a passage directly taken from *Rite*. I use it when I'm talking about rock and classical music to my students."

STARLESS AND BIBLE BLACK

In early 1973, Crimson Mach III claimed its first casualty: Muir experienced a spiritual transformation and decided to quit the band. He went on to lead a monastic life as a Buddhist monk throughout the '70s and resurfaced in the London experimental music scene, most specifically playing with avant-garde jazz guitarist Derek Bailey and much later, in the 1990s, with former Crimson drummer Michael Giles.

Muir's exit couldn't have come at a worse time: Crimson was set to record its next album, eventually titled *Starless and Bible Black*, a title reportedly inspired by Dylan

[7] Fripp diary, March 11, 2001.

Thomas's play *Under Milk Wood*.

"I remember playing a piece for [Bruford] on a record by [British pianist] Stan Tracey," says explains former Yes man Peter Banks. "The album was *Jazz Suite: Inspired by Dylan Thomas's 'Under Milk Wood'* [recorded in 1965], and the second track was called 'Starless and Bible Black.' I remember Bill going, 'Oh, that's beautiful.' It's still one of my favorite pieces of all time. Years later I noticed there was a King Crimson album called *Starless and Bible Black.*"

Short on material, Crimson pulled from their live performances at the time. (The instrumental "Fracture," for instance, a centerpiece of the second side of the original LP, was recorded in Amsterdam's Concertgebouw, with the crowd noise surgically removed.)

Two studio tracks, "The Great Deceiver" (with its multitracked guitar madness) and "Lament," make up some of the strongest material of the entire early- to mid-1970s Crimson material. The former, referencing a journey Fripp made to the Vatican and the commercialization he witnessed there, comes rushing at you like a folk-metal Eastern European gypsy sonic tidal wave.

"The process was always very democratic in terms of writing," explains David Cross. "Everybody in the band was a very powerful, creative musician with a lot to offer. The best stuff, to me, was when there was a lot of give and take, whether that was in terms of formal ideas that people actually brought in, or whether it was less formal in terms of the improvisation and allowing someone to speak musically."

"Lament" is tragicomedy. The first verse tells of an artist who once dreamed of a time when his words would flow out like poetry and his music would touch people. (The musical concept was underscored by Cross's lamenting violin work and Mellotron strings, framing the song as a kind of mock rhapsody.)

By the second verse, the "bubble's burst," and the aging musician confesses to his romantic partner that his life has not turned out the way he thought it would, as the music dissipates into an aggressive 7/8 groove, which underscores the musician's disorientation.

The following "Trio" and "We'll Let You Know," both improvisational, were recorded live in Glasgow, and both dispense with a normal song structure.

"The main reason it's called 'Trio' is because there are only three of us playing," says David Cross. "Bill didn't play on that. . . . On that particular night he just folded his arms and didn't play, which is, of course, as big a contribution as anything. Also, the term *trio* is a kind of dance in 3/4—a minuet. It's the contrasting section to a piece of music, and I think that contrast, which is what a minuet was always used for, was in our minds at the time."

"The Night Watch" (based on Rembrandt's seventeenth-century painting *Company of Frans Banning Cocq and Willem van Ruytenburch*, also known as *The Night Watch*) is one of the most starkly beautiful songs in the Crimson canon (check the violin and guitar playing in unison starting at approximately 0:47, after a provocative wash of cymbals take us back through the mists of time). It, too, was recorded live (appropriately, in Amsterdam), with vocals later overdubbed in the studio.

Despite the twentieth-century electrified raucousness, the music seems to hold on to some baroque tradition, preserving it, as a curator of an art gallery would.

"There seemed to be a sense that anybody trying to create, particularly at that point, had a sense that whatever came to the fore that was new needed to incorporate what had gone before, as well," says Cross. "The desire to make a connection with one's roots is important."

"The Mincer," which closes side one of the original LP, is an amorphous squeaker that doesn't so much

end as run out of time. (Supposedly, the band ran out of tape, and we can hear the instability of the medium as the tape spools to an end. Crimson were definitely crowding the canvas.)

"Fracture," the eleven-minute closer, begins softly and creeps up in volume as we hear Fripp performing what seems to be the famous Don Strike cross-picking style. The slow, twisted guitar figures and the later, low-volume guitar dribblings sound like something more akin to a polka than to rock.

Wetton is locked in with Bruford, even as he seems poised to usurp the entire rhythm section and Fripp's guitar work. Bruford is both chaotic and controlled, playing gongs, thunder sheets, cowbells, and glockenspiel, among other percussive equipment.

Cross says he drew on his backgrounds in meditation and theater for the band's nightly improvisations. "The drama training was very useful," Cross says. "In drama [class] we had been doing stuff like method acting, which was emotional recall. . . . While I was in Crimson, I was trying to induce a certain state of mind without the use of any artificial drugs. [You'd get] yourself into a place where [you'd feel] things rather than think about them. That was a useful place to be when trying to make music."

CROSS TO BEAR

Crimson was a dream come true for a while, but as an American tour wore on in 1974, it became apparent that Cross was no longer meshing well with the volume and ethos of King Crimson—the violinist was simply overmatched by the growing swell of noise coming off the drums and guitar and bass amps. Both Fripp and Cross were wondering if Crimson was the venue for a violin player. Crimson Mach III had claimed another victim.

"I was having lots of difficulties of not being able to hear myself properly and problems with tuning," Cross says. "I don't think I was able to deliver as much as I'd hoped I might."

Ironically, the tour ended in Central Park, New York, on July 1, a show Wetton says still holds special meaning for him: "If ever there was a blueprint for a concert for me, that was it," said Wetton. "It was everything. It was just perfect for me."

Of the performance, Fripp has said that he registered a tingling down his spine for the first time since the 1969.[8]

Crimson were clearly on the verge of something, and where they were headed would provide prog metal bands, even Crimson itself, influence and fertile musical ground for decades to come.

RED

Unfortunately for the members of Crimson, Fripp was going through a spiritual transformation in 1974 (similar to the one Jamie Muir had two years prior), in which he, as he described it, needed to lose his ego to truly be self-aware. He experienced his spiritual eureka moment upon reading the teachings of British scientist/mystic/author/spiritual teacher and World War I veteran John Godolphin (J. G.) Bennett, a pupil of George Ivanovich Gurdjieff, a Greek-Armenian panspiritual teacher, author, philosopher, and musician whose doctrine was alight with Zoroastrianism, Buddhism, Eastern Orthodox Christianity, the Kabbalah, Sufism, and more.[9]

Embattled by little financial success in the band, fried from constant personnel changes since the band's inception, and faced with yet another record to produce (the soon-to-be-recorded *Red*), by the mid-1970s, Fripp needed to recharge his spiritual batteries. He withdrew and enrolled in the International Academy of Continuous Education, far from the music industry.

"I think that was the best thing he could have done to sort himself out, in a way," says sax man Mel Collins. "It straightened Robert out a bit. I couldn't tell you in a million years what was at the root of the issues, but I think a lot of it had to do with ego and insecurity . . . and his control [issues]. It becomes impossible to work with that kind of situation."

Fripp hadn't completely divorced himself from his musical life. He reconvened with the band—now a power trio of sorts—at Olympic Studios to record Crimson's final album of the 1970s, *Red*.

One would hesitate to call *Red* a reunion album, but it does shuttle various elements of Crimson past into the present. David Cross, as well as earlier members of Crimson's line-up—Ian McDonald, Mel Collins (who happened to be doing a session with Humble Pie at Olympic at the time), cornet player Mark Charig, and oboist Robin Miller—appear.

From the very opening of *Red*, we're kicked in the teeth by the aggressive instrumental "Red," featuring Fripp's escalating lead line and an ominous uncredited cello playing. Next is the dynamic "Fallen Angel" (a succinct cradle-to-grave account of an urban gang member's life and death), then "One More Red Nightmare" (featuring Bruford's thrashing of an upside-down, trashy 20-inch Zilco crash cymbal), "Providence" (a live track from the band's previous tour featuring Cross on violin), and the twelve-minute-plus "Starless," a song of immense power and emotion, acting like something of a culmination of the band's jazz-metal art-rock.

"I think *Red* is the best of the next wave of Crimson," says McDonald. "Robert defined the band and found his voice, as far as I'm con-

cerned, guitar-wise."

Red may be considered the pinnacle of the band's artistic achievements in the 1970s, but it was not an easy record to make. Convinced that he could not truly understand or know anything about the world around him—or even have an opinion of it—Fripp was led by humility and inaction throughout the sessions for *Red*. It was Wetton and Bruford who helped bring the album to the finish line.

"At the time we were recording [*Red*], Robert Fripp said he wanted to take a backseat, because he wasn't sure where this [band] was going," Wetton said. "Bill Bruford and myself knew *exactly* where it was going. We . . . took the front seat on it and pushed for that very up-front, [Zileo]-cymbal, in-your-face guitar [sound]. Yeah, definitely. *We* did that. You can hear it from the first track. This band is not fucking about."

Each of the tunes is bursting and bristling with conceptual brilliance, from Foxx fuzz- and wah-inflected bass burps and winding low-end leads to 13/8 patterns and wild odd-time alto sax solos, Collins's delicate soprano sax puffing (and McDonald's screaming, abstract sax work), bold and brassy bebop-meets-big-band horn blowing, and grinding, industrial-strength six-string assaults tempered by fleeting measures of acoustic guitar counterpoint overdubbing. (Check the guitar melody reprised by Mel Collins on soprano sax near the end of "Starless," bringing the piece to a heartbreaking and rousing conclusion.)

"It was balls-to-the-wall progressive rock," Wetton offered. "It was shit-hard rock 'n' roll. It was heavy metal, really."

Excited by the prospect of having an original Crimson member among the ranks, Bruford and Wetton were pushing for McDonald to rejoin and travel with the band on tour. McDonald agreed, but before the release of *Red*, news broke that Fripp had disbanded Crimson. The band, as *New Musical*

---

[8] *The Great Deceiver* book liner notes: Robert Fripp diary July 1, 1974; *Red: 40th Anniversary Series* liner notes by Sid Smith.

[9] Http://www.gurdjieff.org

[10] *NME*, Sept. 28, 1974; *Record Mirror*, Oct. 5, 1974.

CRIMSON

**OURT OF THE CRIM-
NG** (Island): This comes
ng Crimson's new album
a doom-laden two-sided
h a sound that owes a lot
Moody Blues and Procol

vocal and backing sound
chorus—it has a great
hat really hits you. As a
has a big over-awing at-

ly it will help sell the

OUT TOMORROW

KING CRIMSON: In The Court Of The Crimson King (Island): First LP from the group heralded by those who know to be the most exciting discovery of the year. Get over the most horrific cover of the year, and you'll find the pundits are not wrong.

A brilliant mixture of melody and freakout, fast and slow, atmospheric and electric, all heightened by the words of Peter Sinfield.

Shades of the Moody Blues about the feel of the title track and "Wind" but suddenly you're ripped out of serenity by almost schizophrenic cacophony! Impossible to select a track as this must be heard as a complete entity. It will sell and sell, and

FRIPP: major talent

establish King Crimson as a major talent.****

TRACKS: 21st Century Schizoid Man; Mirrors; I Talk To The Wind; Epitaph (March For No Reason, Tomorrow And Tomorrow); Moonchild (The Dream, The Illusion); The Court Of The Crimson King (The Return Of The Fire Witch, The Dance Of The Puppets).

SINCE for the moment I'm still here, may I predict a Number One album for the most popular oldies of them all—**King Crimson?** I don't say they're very good or very different—the LP is all soft/loud contrasts and rubbish lyrics. Even on stage they look and sound pretentious. But I'm sure these elderly purveyors of trend music will make number one. **DISC.**

NEW MUSICAL EXPRESS On sale, Friday, week ending October 18, 1969

← KING CRIMSON AT LAST

KING CRIMSON: IN THE COURT OF THE CRIMSON KING (Island stereo ILPS 9111; 37s 5d)

LONG-AWAITED first album from the remarkable King Crimson, a group which manages to provoke either loathing or fanatical devotion but which is undoubtedly capable of building for itself a sizeable reputation.

This stunningly-packaged LP provides a varied selection of King Crimson's style, although it lacks some of the drive of the stage performances that have made their name. Nevertheless as a first album it is extremely good.

Many influences and shades of various groups can be detected in their work but the total effect as they veer into improvisations that take from pop, jazz and classics is totally original and always captivating.

21st Century Schizoid Man, side one opener, is among the best numbers on stage with an almost vicious presentation and a snarling vocal from **Ian McDonald**. On record it loses some of its bite but McDonald's muzzy far off vocal adds drama to some brilliant instrumentation. I Talk To The Wind on the same side is softer King Crimson; a pretty ballad.

On side two, the 12-minute Moonchild, including The Dream and The Illusion, is another side of the group again — an atmospheric, freaky just-a-shade-too-long piece which draws on jazz and classics.

The 8-minute closer The Court Of The Crimson King, constructed with a fine ear for drama, is a powerful item that builds and falls with devastating effect.

King Crimson, on this showing, have it in them to be huge. **N.L.**

Other titles: **Epitaph,** including **March For No Reason** and **Tomorrow And Tomorrow.**

★

**G CRIMSON:
The Court Of
Crimson King "**

a Mellotron, it
ike one. I like it,
al, nice production,
ty.

he Moody Blues, it
very much like
ng Crimson, I've
them. I don't know
be a hit but it's

remind me of the
t but they're not
ressive
P.P. ARNOLD

MELODY MAKER, October 25.

KING CRIMSON: "In The Court Of The Crimson King " (Island). This eagerly-awaited first album is no disappointment, and confirms their reputation as one of the most important new groups for some time. It gives little idea of their true power on stage, but still packs tremendous impact, especially the brutally exciting "21st Century Schizoid Man" and the eerie title track, with its frightening mellotron sounds. It's not all high power stuff, though — there's some nice flute from Ian McDonald on the beautiful "I Talk To The Wind" and "Moonchild" is pretty, though too long. The vocals are clear and controlled and the instrumental work can hardly be faulted. This is one you should try to hear.

King display

IMHOFS, in New Oxford Street, are running a large window display of King Crimson's album "In The Court of The Crimson King" this week. In its first week, Island report sales of more than 17,000 for the album, excluding copies exported to the Continent.

MUSIC BUSINESS WEEKLY

KING CRIMSON: The Court Of The Crimson King — Parts I and II (Island).

One of the most advanced and far-sighted groups on the underground scene, King Crimson has come up with a musical montage that defies description on a few lines. It's a pop epic, embracing all manner of styles and ideas, with a lyric that's sheer fantasy. Not commercial? Well, not altogether perhaps, though it does have a catchy chorus. But please do try to hear this pop extravaganza — it's great! **N.M.E**

Express and *Record Mirror* had reported as early as September 1974, had "ceased to exist"[10], as Fripp had declared Crimson "over for ever and ever."

"Fripp basically asked me if I wanted to go out [with the band on tour], and I don't know if he was asking me to rejoin or come on the road," says McDonald. "I've always thought there may have been a little bit of revenge in there. John felt very disappointed that a tour never happened. This was a similar situation to what had happened with the original King Crimson band. In that case, I was the one who spoiled it. I think maybe [Fripp] wanted me to say I would come back and then he promptly folded the band. That is just my hunch."

"[Robert] was starting to get disillusioned," Wetton said.

"I think John Wetton felt the group was poised for, I have to use the words, 'big time,'" adds McDonald. "He felt the group was . . . for the first time on the verge of being widely known."

"As he did with us and as he did with the John Wetton–Bill Bruford outfit, I think [Fripp] got to a point where he couldn't see the wood for the trees," Collins says.

The live record, *USA*, was culled from a performance in Asbury Park, New Jersey, in late June 1974 (and features overdubbed tracks by Roxy Music/Curved Air keyboardist/violinist Eddie Jobson) and appeared in 1975. A best-of compilation, *A Young Person's Guide to King Crimson*, was released in 1976. The initials R.I.P. were printed near the bottom of the back cover of USA.

SMALL, INTELLIGENT HIGHLY MOBILE UNIT

Fripp's Bennett/Gurdjieff minimalist philosophy of becoming a "small, intelligent highly mobile unit" correctly foretold a sea change in the industry and the rise of punk—it

appeared he collapsed Crimson just in time for this legendary band to retain its integrity, and even gain a fan or two in the intervening years.

In 1974, by his own admission, Fripp had a "terrifying vision of the future"[11] and his response was to run from a world in flux. (Fripp would tangle with his label and management company throughout the 1980s until eventually winning back the rights to his music. He runs the independent record label Discipline Global Mobile, dedicated largely to issuing and reissuing Crimson studio and live material.)

From roughly 1975 to 1980, Fripp did sessions with Brian Eno, Keith Tippett, and David Bowie, and produced Peter Gabriel, among other projects. The once and future King C guitarist would resurrect Crimson again in the 1980s, and totally revamp the style, feel, and look of the band. It would be a far more disciplined, mature, and open Fripp who took to the stages of the world in the early and mid-1980s.

Wetton signed on as Roxy Music's touring bassist and later as a member of Uriah Heep. Just two-plus short years after Crimson's demise, Jobson would work with both Wetton and Bruford in the British prog/jazz-rock supergroup U.K. In the early '80s, Wetton formed Asia with Yes's Steve Howe, ELP's Carl Palmer, and Yes/Buggles keyboardist Geoff Downes.

Bruford was a hired gun for several years after Crimson, keeping busy with Gong, National Health, Genesis (as a touring drummer), and Pavlov's Dog. He formed his own instrumental rock/fusion band Bruford and the aforementioned U.K. before rejoining the '80s Crimson.

Ian McDonald went on to form the arena rock band Foreigner and, in later years, the 21st Century Schizoid Band—dedicated to reinterpreting Crimson material—with Mel Collins (who continued band and session work throughout the 1970s, most notably with Camel, Bryan Ferry, and Eric Clapton), guitarist/vocalist Jakko

Jakszyk, and Crimson exiles/brothers bassist Peter Giles and drummer Michael Giles. (Michael Giles was replaced by former Crimsonite Ian Wallace, who reinvented his former band's music with his Crimson Jazz Trio up to his death in 2007.)

RED RESURGENCE

In the 1990s, amid the grunge and alternative rock "revolutions," Tool named Crimson as an obvious influence and Kurt Cobain cited *Red* as one of his favorite records

"All of a sudden, American kids were talking about this band King Crimson," Bruford told the author in 1994.

It seemed a natural segue for Crimson to return, and Bruford happily and willfully rejoined the musical beast. "It's a six-piece band," Bruford said. "It's recording a major album in October [eventually titled *THRAK* and released through Virgin] and it will be out in 1995. It sounds great, I must say. Two guitar players, two [Chapman] Stick players, two drummers. Double trio. So, each one of these trios can function on its own."

The double trio included bassist Tony Levin (who also played Stick), drummer (and former Mr. Mister member) Pat Mastelotto, Trey Gunn (who played Stick, bass, and, later, touch guitars made by California-based luthier Mark Warr), guitarist/vocalist Adrian Belew, Bruford, and Fripp.

Though the double trio split (Bruford and Gunn are no longer members, but Mastelotto, Belew, Levin, Fripp, and a new addition, a second drummer, Porcupine Tree's Gavin Harrison, has come aboard), the unusual and adventurous musical spirit of Crimson survives into the twenty-first century.

"There's a little phrase that comes around when we play together," says Mastelotto, "and it goes something like this: 'If you've heard it or played it, don't do it.' That came directly from Robert. That's a philosophy a musician can use."

[11] Liner notes reissue *Exposure*, 2006.

(Ian Dickson/Getty Images)

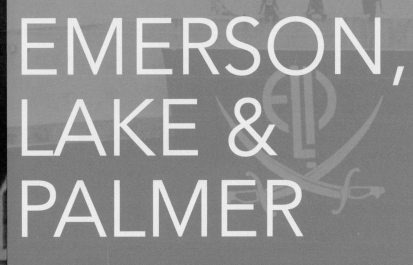

EMERSON, LAKE & PALMER

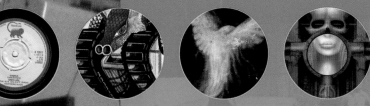

Welcome Back My Friends . . .

MANY FANS OF PROGRESSIVE ROCK CLAIM YES WERE THE soul of the genre: If this is so, then Emerson Lake and Palmer were certainly the power, the glory, the spectacle—the so-called first supergroup of prog rock.

As soon as news hit that Keith Emerson, the keyboardist for the Nice; Greg Lake, the bassist/vocalist of King Crimson; and Carl Palmer, the drummer for the Crazy World of Arthur Brown and Atomic Rooster, had joined forces as ELP, the press had dubbed the band a supergroup—before they'd played a single note.

The band was "supersize" in everything: ELP were superfast and boasted superhuman virtuosity, superegos, and a super pedigree. Perhaps sensing the weight and responsibility of such a mantle being handed to them, Emerson Lake and Palmer performed as though they had something to prove to themselves and the world.

The band's shows were some of the most bombastic in prog rock history, full of pyrotechnic physical prowess and stage production: Whether it was Palmer's blazing, Buddy Rich–inspired drum solos; live cannons being fired onstage; Emerson's humongous modular synthesizer unit (a literal wall of sound equipment, augmented by stacks of Leslie cabinets, used to generate ungodly noises);

or a rotating, "flying" piano, ELP never let up—or disappointed.

EMERLIST DAVJACK

It was Emerson's work with the Nice that fostered the kind of musical climate that allowed ELP to not only survive but thrive.

After attempting to hold down a nine-to-five job, Emerson, a native of Todmorden, Lancashire, England, who'd marveled at his dad's musical abilities, gave up the notion of having a normal job (and life) and followed his heart in becoming a musician. By the mid-1960s, he had already begun gigging in London.

"Keith and I were together in what was originally a blues band that turned into a Booker T. and the M.G.s/Stax Records type of musical situation, called Gary Farr & the T-Bones," says former Nice bandmate Lee Jackson. "We became very good friends, which we are still to this day. I was living in his flat, and he came over one Saturday saying he had been offered to put a band together for this ex-Ikette [Patricia Cole/P. P. Arnold], who just had a hit record at the time ['The First Cut Is The Deepest']."

"We started to put ideas together, never realizing we'd actually do anything with them," continues Jackson, who handled bass and vocal duties for the Nice. "It was jazz, but we were also messing around with a bit of classical stuff. Similar to what Jacques Loussier—the French jazz musician who played classical pieces—was doing."

That's when Andrew Loog Oldham, the founder of Immediate Records and onetime Rolling Stones manager, became aware of Jackson's band. "He told us, 'Pat is going back to America and I want to take you guys in and make you a band on your own, and we're going to make an album,'" relates Jackson.

The Nice, then a four-piece (including Emerson, Jackson, drummer Brian Davison, and guitarist Davy O'List), were signed to Immediate and released two songs: "Rondo," an inter-

Emerson, Lake & Palmer, 1977. (Courtesy of Atlantic Records)

ELP: s/t (1970)

pretation of Dave Brubeck's "Blue Rondo à la Turk," a fusion of jazz and classical world music from 1959's *Time Out*, containing references to Leo Janáček's Sinfonietta (later to reappear in "Knife-Edge" by ELP) and (possibly) Bach's famous Toccata and Fugue (which was also played by Jackson and Emerson in the T-Bones); and "America," the Leonard Bernstein/Stephen Sondheim song from the original musical *West Side Story*, which was recorded and performed as a protest to the Vietnam War. (Emerson, controversially, even burned the American flag onstage at an infamous performance at the Royal Albert Hall in the late 1960s.)

"I remember I made contact with Emerson just shortly after he [started to play] 'Rondo,'" says Dave Brubeck. "I asked him why he played his version of 'Blue Rondo' in 4/4 [instead of 9/8], and, you know, it's easier for some people to relate to music in common time."

The band's debut, *The Thoughts of Emerlist Davjack*, followed and was released in 1967, prog rock's pivotal year. Though the Nice may have been under the radar, compared to other groundbreaking acts of the day (including the Moody Blues, Pink Floyd, and Procol Harum), that only meant the band required more time to perfect its approach.

But all the ingredients for future progressive rock success were present in *Emerlist*: space-age tinkling of the Hammond organ ("The Flower King of Flies"), Beach Boys–influenced vocals (the title track), sonic experimentation (e.g., in "Tantalizing Maggie," for which Emerson plucks piano wires; and "Cry of Eugene," which features O'List's ghostly feedback, approximating the sound of Mellotron strings), innovative reinterpretation ("Rondo"), and production savvy ("Azirial"). It's a rich stew. Heck, even the title of the record is a mass of jumbled-up names of the band members.

The Nice became known for moving from one genre to another—classical, jazz, and rock—with impunity.

"Classical music sacred me," admits Emerson. "I didn't think I was good enough to play it, although I used it in quotes to accentuate a solo and then play whole pieces to the extent that it woke up the classical repertoire."

The Nice continued to evolve, but there was one drag: Guitarist

O'List wasn't adding that much. In fact, the case can be made that he was detracting from the band's progress. Ultimately, O'List was asked to leave. (More about that in a moment.)

"[Keith] was always envious of all the guitarists because they could move around the stage, while he was stuck to what was ostensibly a piece of furniture," says Jackson. "Once his mother came to a gig and she brought Pledge furniture polish, and he said, 'For God's sake, Mother.' She only did that once. But we pulled his leg about that for months."

The Nice became an organ trio as much by circumstance as by design, forging ahead much in the same way Roger Waters and Floyd did without Syd Barrett. Simply put, O'List was a deeply troubled young man, and Emerson's motives for developing the band weren't sinister.

Some speculate that O'List was angered and even depressed that Emerson was stealing the spotlight. After all, Emerson was using and abusing his Hammond—rocking it, tipping it over, causing a distorted, metallic wash by disrupting the organ's reverb chamber, and even stabbing knives—a gift from Motörhead's Lemmy Kilmister, then a Nice roadie—into the organ to sustain notes as he violated his instrument. He was a showstopper.

By 1969 the Nice had released an album called, simply, *Nice* (titled *Everything as Nice as Mother Makes It* in the U.S.), featuring a live version of "Rondo (69)," a reworked "Azrael Revisited," a cover of Tim Hardin's "How Can We Hang On to a Dream" (appearing as "Hang On to a Dream"), and an extended version of Dylan's "She Belongs to Me."

Within a year, the symphonic *Five Bridges* appeared, featuring the band with the Sinfonia of London on the title track suite—a commissioned piece that marked the Nice's first major all-original epic, ruminating on the five (now seven) bridges spanning the Tyne in Newcastle.

Though no one knew it at the time, "Five Bridges Suite" was the band's swan song. Emerson was beginning to get stir-crazy with the Nice. He felt he needed new vistas for musical inspiration—things the Nice didn't seem to be providing him.

Enter King Crimson's Greg Lake. "Coincidentally, King Crimson were playing at Bill Graham's Fillmore West [mid-December 1969] and we were supporting the Chambers Brothers, and on the same bill was the Nice with Keith Emerson, and we happened to have been staying in the same hotel," remembers Lake. "In the bar at night we all met up and Keith asked, 'How is it going?' I said, 'Well, it's going great but the band is breaking up.' And he said, 'Strange you should say that. I think the Nice is breaking up. To be honest, I think I've taken it as far as I can. I don't think there's anything else I can do. I think I'm going to move on.' So we began discussing forming a band. Keith said, 'I like the idea of a three-piece band.' So we decided then to look for a drummer."

Lake had contacted Mitch Mitchell from the Jimi Hendrix Experience, which had just recently broken up. "We talked with Mitch and he was very nice, and a great drummer," says Lake. "At one point we were going to meet with Jimi, and we were going to get together and have a jam to see if it was possible to form a band between the four of us."

But it never happened. The dream band, a Nice-Crimson-Experience amalgam, didn't materialize, and instead Robert Stigwood, who had managed Cream and the Bee Gees, called Emerson and Lake, asking if drummer Carl Palmer, of Atomic Rooster and formerly of the Crazy World of Arthur Brown, could come down for an audition.

It seems Palmer was primed to work with Emerson, given his experience playing with organist Vincent Crane, with whom he'd worked in the Crazy World of Arthur Brown and Atomic Rooster.

"It was a natural evolution to put those three guys together," explains Lake's Crimson bandmate Ian McDonald. "I know Greg always had big ideas and he always used to think big. I think he pulled it off with ELP."

ELP DEBUT

Though ELP had performed live previously, it was the band's appearance at the Isle of Wight Festival, dubbed the "British Woodstock," held before six hundred thousand spectators in late August 1970, that stands as the supergroup's official unveiling.

"At the time, British groups ruled the world," says Justin Hayward of the Moody Blues, who also made an appearance at the festival. "They would continue to do so for the next three or four years."

It was obvious from the Isle of Wight (and from ELP's self-titled debut, which was soon to follow) that this band was not fooling about. The press were stunned, and fans eagerly awaited the band's first release, which is now a classic of the genre.

The opener, "The Barbarian," is an artistic proclamation as much as a description of a rock band that would take no prisoners. Based in large part on Béla Bartók's "Allegro Barbaro," "The Barbarian" lent a dark, Eastern European folk feel to the record that melded surprisingly well with this keyboard-led heavy metal.

The fuzz-bass, Palmer's rapid brushwork, and the song's overall disturbing tonality makes it difficult to listen to without thinking of saber rattling, spilled blood and guts, and war. This is ELP: barbarian rockers at the gate poised to conquer Rome (i.e. the record industry), hinting at the musical pillage and plunder yet to come.

"Emerson was unbelievable," says Eddy Offord, who engineered ELP's debut. "He's probably one of the greatest keyboard players in that style who's ever been. . . . The [Minimoog] synthesizer had just come out, and I think we had the first one at our studio [Advision]. No musician could run it. The solo you hear

The "Hendrix of the Hammond":
Emo abusing his keyboard.
(Jorgen Angel/Getty Images)

at the end of 'Lucky Man,' I believe, is the first take. I mean, Emerson just blew it up and that was the end of that. It was over in a few minutes. There were controls on the thing, one called portamento, which allowed you to slip or glide through a series of notes so you could make these really strange noises— '*weeahweeahweee*'—that were unlike anything anybody had ever heard. Keith used this for 'Lucky Man.'"

"If you listen to 'Lucky Man' and you ask somebody who wasn't watching what Emerson was doing, he'd say, 'What the heck is this guy playing?'" says Tom Rhea. Rhea wrote the first owner's manual for the synthesizer in 1970, and even spent time with Emerson, educating him on the synth's capabilities. "Never in a million years would I think someone would say, 'Yeah, it's some kind of keyboard.' The sound itself was so powerful and monophonic, and what Emerson and Moog did was help make keyboards, or synths, lead instruments in the way that guitars and saxophones

were. The keyboardist didn't have to be relegated to the back of the band, laying down foundation."

"What made me love Emerson Lake and Palmer were two things," says Styx's Dennis DeYoung. "I loved the fact that a keyboard player could be looked at as a guitar player. But beyond that, it was 'Lucky Man.' Because 'Lucky Man' is almost like an English Renaissance song, and it's a great song, whether the synthesizer sweep is in it or not. So, the cake was the song, the synthesizer was the frosting. That is what made it progressive rock."

Before long, the very name Emerson was synonymous with Moog, and vice versa. "I was fortunate to have Bob Moog available for my music, although I did buy my modular system for thirty thousand pounds," says Emerson.

"I remember Keith had to raise money to buy his first Moog synthesizer," says onetime manager David Enthoven, formerly of E. G.

Management. "I was thinking, 'Christ, how am I going to pay for it? How is this thing going to work on the road? How are we going to get it around and maintain it?' The Mellotrons were a big enough problem. The first synth he got was like a huge plug board, basically. Keith managed to get sounds out of it, but when it broke down, it was a nightmare. The Moog was the show."

"The modular Moog was just astounding," adds keyboardist Danny Brill, who saw ELP on their first U.S. tour in 1971. "Our jaws dropped when Emerson played it. Most people hadn't heard anything like it."

By the end of 1970, ELP's debut had reached the British Top 4 and went Top 20 in the U.S. in 1971. While critics failed to see the value in what ELP was doing (legendary BBC DJ John Peel famously called the band's grand unveiling at the Isle of Wight Festival a "waste of talent and electricity"), they were gearing up for a new album and a world tour, which would soon change everything.

TARKUS

The band's second studio record, *Tarkus*, broke all the rules. Fans and even critics point to "Tarkus"—a twenty-one-minute, side-long composition—as Emerson's ultimate work; an off-the-rails, atonal sonic attack full of rhythmic fury.

Inspired by European art music, the composition was Emerson's most ambitious to date and was given shape by Palmer's 10/8 practice rhythm, which matched a left-hand ostinato piano pattern Emerson had been working with. In his memoirs, *Pictures of an Exhibitionist*, Emerson explained that he wanted to create "a vast sheet of sound that defies conventional structures" and had a "free-floating sense of time signature and key."

When the keyboard whiz explained to Lake that this was a direction he wanted to pursue with ELP, the singer/guitarist scoffed. Lake felt the music . . . well, he felt there was no music. In short, he hated the song and thought it lacked form.

A disagreement over the song arose and was so big it nearly caused a huge rift, threatening to tear apart the band (Emerson threatened to quit). Lake, of course, would come to love the song and he'd stamp his musical style on it with a few straight-ahead rock moments, such as "Mass" and "Battlefield." In the end, "Tarkus" stands as one of progressive rock's masterstrokes.

"'Tarkus' was a departure from the regular rock format and a testing ground for furtherance in ELP," says Emerson. "There was no real reference in 'Tarkus' to any existing musical composition. Although I was inspired by [Alberto] Ginastera's bravado orchestrations at points in my career, there's nothing in there from him."

Despite *Tarkus*'s successes (the album charted in the Top 10 on both sides of the Atlantic, going to number one in the U.K.), critics were calling ELP's performances flashy, melodra-matic, overblown, or worse.

Certainly a survival instinct took hold for ELP at some point, and it's no surprise that Emerson struck back with a virulent musical poison such as "Tarkus."

The packaging completed the band's extreme musical vision. Just as ELP was pushing boundaries with its music, chasing uptight critics out of theaters, cover artist William Neal, who had been working for a design firm C.C.S. Associates, dreamed up his own sort of nightmare—a biomechanical miracle. A half-tank/half-beast creation—an "armordillo" complete with tire treads and long-barrel gun—informed by Roger Dean's cover art for Afro-beat band Osibisa's self-titled debut, which features a mammoth with butterfly wings.

"There's no doubt that the drawing of the armadillo tank that became [the cover of] *Tarkus* took the band, and indeed most folk who saw it, by surprise," says Neal. "After their first album, ELP hadn't a clue which way to go visually. It just so happened that, in an idle way, like you do on the phone sometimes, I had scribbled this little armadillo tank on a cover sheet for an LP presentation to the band. It shouldn't have even been there. Keith Emerson saw it and right away said this could work with some of his musical pieces. Tarkus was reworked, of course, and beefed up, and we did the same reconstruction with the other creatures too."

The inside gate depicts the genesis of Tarkus, his utter destruction of rival monsters, and the one chink in his armor, exploited by the manticore, a half-man, half-lion beast with a scorpion's tail. Before long, the image of Neal's manticore—and by association the mean S.O.B. Tarkus—became iconography representing not only ELP but the entire prog rock genre.

PICTURES AT AN EXHIBITION

Recorded by Eddy Offord prior to the release of, but issued after, *Tarkus*,

Tarkus, 1971. Illustrator William Neal's frightening "armordillo".

Pictures at an Exhibition was cut on an eight-track machine live at Newcastle City Hall in March 1971.

Originally slated to be the band's sophomore effort, *Pictures*, which includes "Nutrocker" (originally recorded as "The Nut Rocker" by B. Bumble and the Stingers in 1962), was held back. Sensing the premise of the record was a bit too reminiscent of the Nice's previous work, ELP decided against releasing it as the band's sophomore effort.

Pictures at an Exhibition opened a new world for ELP—and its listeners. Inspired by the death of close friend Viktor Hartmann (whose work was exhibited at the Russian Academy of Arts after his death), Modest Mussorgsky wrote *Pictures at an Exhibition* for piano, illustrating ten "scenes," steeped in Russian and pre-Christian Slavic myth, which were later orchestrated by Maurice Ravel (the form in which most people of the twenty-first century know it).

"I think the fact that we are European, we are not American, we're not going to fall heavily on the blues and jazz," Carl Palmer says. "We had to kind of develop our own musical environment."

Transferring the symphonic version of *Pictures* to a three-piece band (the piano piece would have been difficult enough in its own way) brings into sharp focus just how skilled ELP had become at navigating all of the

Pictures at an Exhibition (1972)

subtle shifts of tempo and moods.

"When you try to interpret *Pictures at an Exhibition*, a piece of classical music with three people, trust me when I tell you, you really have to plan it carefully—otherwise it sounds like shit," says Lake.

While ELP went at the work with wild abandon, the grand spirit of the original is intact. But some didn't hear it that way. The tension between the classical music establishment and ELP's so-called bastardizations of great works would dog the band for the rest of its career.

"The interesting fact about *Pictures at an Exhibition* was that as soon as the ELP version became a hit, the sales of the formal versions, the orchestral version, climbed," says Lake. "At the time they thought it was just a quirk. They paid no more attention to it. But still, even to this day, there's a type of blindness in the classical world, really, and I think it's a type of defense mechanism in order to protect their ailing world, which is, in my opinion, totally the wrong way to go. They should be taking down the walls, opening up the doors to allow people to do interpretations of classical works . . . rather than say, 'This is not the formal version, this is not the exact score, fuck it, we don't want to be involved.' What they should be saying is, 'Look, this is interesting and may open the door to a lot of classical music to people, who would not have heard it before.'"

In order to engage the audience, Lake added lyrics to the instrumental pieces, causing mortification among some purists. Yet the clarity and beauty of Lake's vocals have yielded some of the most moving moments of the entire performance and of Lake's career.

"All I can tell you is, the moment you start applying lyrics and vocals to classical music, you are almost condemned to becoming crass, you know?" Lake says. "It almost inevitably sounds awful and contrived and banal and all of those terrible things. So to make it sound credible and appropriate and sympathetic was quite an undertaking."

Lake succeeded, and the soaring "Great Gates of Kiev" is monumental; at once an oppressive piece of music speaking to the sadness, the cry of Mother Russia (which accounts for most of the minor keys used) and the hope of a better world (the uplifting majors), a better life—and a better afterlife.

"While I was coming up with these lyrics and vocals, I was listening to, I'll be honest with you, the Red Army Choir," says Lake. "That's really how I got into that style, because I thought, you know, 'How am I going to do this?' I looked to Russian influences, really, which are quite dark in a way. I also wanted the effect of walking through a gallery. I then began to think that the pictures in this gallery are emotional pictures with a Russian sentiment, a Russian harmonic structure. I guess I felt that the Russian people had suffered and that was an element I wanted to capture.

"I think at the end of it all, I held out this feeling of hope," Lake continues. "That's why I sing, 'Death is life,' at the end of the piece. I didn't want to end on 'Death is death,' you know? It's kind of bittersweet. The music at the end is tremendously uplifting, and yet the underlying sentiment, the underlying reality of Russia, is tragic."

TRILOGY

ELP's official third studio album, appropriately titled *Trilogy*, falls comfortably into the formula but is also one of the most enjoyable and consistent records of the band's career.

Whereas *Tarkus* and *Pictures* were balls-out affairs, partly or mostly centered on a central theme, *Trilogy* is scattered and pulls back on the intensity and musical innovation.

For starters, there's the intelligent, largely acoustic ballad "From the Beginning," which follows in the footprints of "Lucky Man"; "Abaddon's Bolero," based on Ravel's "Boléro" (here in 4/4 time, not 6/8), which seems an almost obligatory nod to the classical (though some might reckon pseudoclassical) world; the bluesy "Living Sin"; and "The Sheriff," a lighthearted tune in the spirit of "Are You Ready, Eddy?" and "Jeremy Bender," which adds a ragtime piano at the song's conclusion—actually a multitracked Steinway grand piano running at slightly different speeds. ELP's adaptation of Aaron Copland's "Hoedown" (from his *Rodeo* ballet), while reminiscent of the Nice's take on Brubeck's "Rondo," is performed with alacrity—and was played even faster in concert. The opener, "The Endless Enigma (Part One)," quotes Tchaikovsky's *Pathétique* (before chirping along in an odd time), and is followed by "Fugue" (which, as does any fugue, dives into counterpoint) and the trumpeting fanfare of "The Endless Enigma (Part Two)."

BRAIN SALAD SURGERY

Brain Salad Surgery was a departure for ELP. It was the record that separated them from most of the rest of the progressive rock crowd, allowing them to ascend to at least the same artistic level as King Crimson and pitting them toe-to-toe with their chief rivals, Yes, at the retail counter. Thus it is all the more strange that the album was the first to be made without the guidance of coproducer/engineer Offord.

"At that time, there was so much tugging and pulling going on between Yes and ELP," says Offord, who'd worked with both bands simultaneously. "I had reached a point that I had to

Carl Palmer's humongous drum setup reflected his aggressive orchestral approach. (Richard McCaffrey/Getty Images)

decide who I was going to work with. They were just jealous of each other and the fact that I was working with both bands. Finally, Yes talked me into going out on the road with them [for the *Close to the Edge* tour] to help reproduce the studio material live. I was almost becoming a sixth member of Yes. So I had a decision to make, and I decided not to work with ELP."

Pity, really. *Brain Salad Surgery* is the band's greatest work, musically, sonically, compositionally, and technologically. ELP was ahead of the curve in many respects with the album, and, arguably, went to heights that neither they nor anyone else would ever achieve again.

The album opens with a rousing rendition of "Jerusalem," a cover of a Hubert Parry composition based on the William Blake poem (an excerpt from his *Milton: A Poem in 2 Books*),

which appeared in 1916. It's been orchestrated both by Parry and Edward Elgar and falls roughly within the period of the so-called English classical renaissance of the late nineteenth and early twentieth centuries. This was not Bach, Bartók, or Janáček. "Jerusalem" is, through and through, a nod to English classical music.

"Jerusalem" is as universally accepted and revered a song as you're going to find in the U.K., satiating the public's need for hymns and national song.

"I'd always heard talk of it becoming some sort of English national anthem," says Jeremy Dibble, professor of music at the University of Durham and author of *C. Hubert H. Parry: His Life and Music*. "You'd often read that England had no real classical music of its own. The cry went up in the second half of the nineteenth century: 'If we are a civilized culture, we

should have this art music, too.'"

"Rather than follow my contemporaries into Americana, I've stuck to my English heritage for main inspiration," says Emerson. "Although I do allow myself some moments of departure."

ELP continued to break through barriers: Emerson wrote an electronic music piece, a rearrangement of the fourth movement of Ginastera's Piano Concerto no. 1, rife with Moog protosynths.

To match the sci-fi nature of the music, Palmer had an electrical engineer, Nick Rose, design synthetic, or electronic, drums, which, along with Emerson's synth freakouts, littered the tune in sonic explosions. Palmer's new percussion arrangement was also full of bursts of tuned percussion, timpani, and tubular bells.

"What happened was, Carl would trigger sounds from the drum kit,

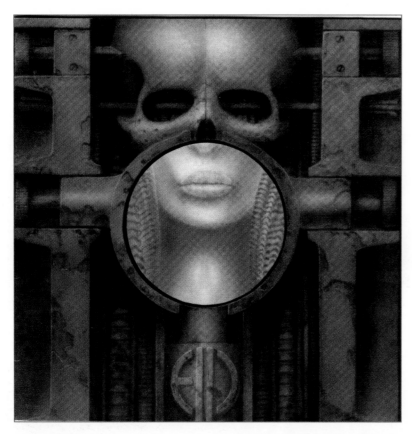

Rise of the machines: ELP's
1973 milestone recording,
Brain Salad Surgery.

using a pickup and preamp that would be placed inside the drum," remembers engineer Paul Northfield. "It was in the very early days of drum synthesis, but this allowed Carl to be a bit more cutting-edge as a drummer."

"I did use electronics a lot with ELP," Palmer told the author in 2006, adding that he could trigger repeated rhythmic patterns as well as turn them off via a remote foot switch. "[On] *Brain Salad Surgery*, the track called 'Toccata' had electric drum sounds going off. Everyone thought they were keyboards. Nobody knew it was the drums and nobody wanted to, so I just played it down and let it go. There were all these electronic drums making all of these horrendous sounds, you know? They are kind of dated. But at the time, they worked."

Despite the raucous noise it makes, "Toccata" nearly didn't see the light of day. Briefly, Emerson insisted that the Ginastera piece be included on the record, but the band had yet to get clearance for it, mainly because

Ginastera's agents refused to allow the music to be used on a rock record.

The band was running out of time—they had an album to finish, and why hadn't Emerson taken care of this bit of housecleaning earlier? Emerson hopped a flight to Switzerland, hoping to convince the Argentinean composer to change his mind.

"I remember Keith coming back from going to see Ginastera in Switzerland, in Geneva, and Ginastera told Keith when the played him ELP's version, he said it was '*diabolique*,'" says Northfield. "Keith took that to mean it was terrible. But Keith had misinterpreted what he said. When Ginastera's words were properly translated, Keith understood that Ginastera was saying that the piece was 'evil' and conveyed the essence of his piece, not that he disliked it. Ginastera was so impressed that he endorsed the song on the original LP liner notes."

Then there are the three compositions, known collectively as Karn Evil 9, that are simply ELP's shining moment.

Initially, Emerson had envisioned the pieces as links in a sci-fi story, dubbed "Ganton 9," that told (or foretold) of a planet on which sin, decadence, and organic life (and emotion) had been outlawed.

Lake invited Crimson lyricist Peter Sinfield to add his literary touch to the musical proceedings. Once they were twisted into Karn Evil 9 (Sinfield had heard Emerson's musical ideas and thought some of it sounded like a carnival, hence the title), the pieces began to take shape. A rarity in the ELP world: suddenly the lyrics were as memorable as the music.

Sinfield's bizarro wordplays from Crimson's *Lizard* daze seemed to have evolved (or devolved?) into full-blown wacko-loon for two of the three Karn Evil 9 "Impression"s. (The second "Impression" is instrumental.) Sinfield simply unleashes a kind of lyrical Circus of Weird, which resulted in many legendary lines, such as, "Welcome back my friends to the show that never ends," "supersonic fighting cocks," and "a stripper in a till," which speak to the overarching concept of artificiality.

The multidimensional lyrics met the challenge of complementing Emerson's layered arrangements. Within that period of just a few years Emerson had honed his songwriting skills to better orchestrate for a rock band and better execute music he'd heard in his head. Emerson's ability to change moods in a piece with the use of so few notes is chilling.

"Karn Evil 9, Third Impression," the perfect finale to the record and, despite Emerson's protests, bookends with, and comments on, the opening tune, "Jerusalem."

If "Jerusalem" speaks of natural, sexual potency and, ironically, building a spiritual nation through vigilance, then "Third Impression" (which uses warlike/erotic imagery similar to that in "Jerusalem") describes mankind in an epic struggle, apocalyptic in nature, with a monster of his own creation—artificial intelligence.

"Third Impression" is a nightmare scenario that leaves little hope. At least in Stanley Kubrick's *2001*, we're presented with a spaceship's operating systems computer—HAL 9000—that was confrontational but with purpose (to test humanity). ELP's computer serves no such purpose. It's here to conquer mankind, not see it prosper and evolve.

As if we needed further reinforcement, the "Third Impression"—and hence the record—concludes with the Moog synthesizer rattling and beeping notes, first very slowly and then in rapid gunfire manner. It seems unstoppable—and inhuman. The machines *have* taken over.

Brain Salad Surgery was to become a near-perfect progressive rock album, but throughout the production process, hurdles had to be overcome. For one thing, the original title of the album (*Whip Some Skull on Ya*—a euphemism for fellatio) was rejected by Atlantic Records, distributor of ELP's then–newly established Manticore label. It wasn't until Mario Medious, Manticore label president, hijacked the line "Just need a little brain salad surgery/ Got to cure this insecurity" from Dr. John's "Right Place, Wrong Time" that the title was approved. What does "brain salad surgery" mean, you might ask? Same as "whip some skull on ya."

Then there was the iconic cover image that almost wasn't. The band agreed to use two pieces of artwork already completed by H. R. Giger (then a relative unknown outside of Zurich, Switzerland, as this was years before his popular book *Necronomicon* and his involvement in design for Ridley Scott's hit sci-fi/horror movie *Alien*). Both were original paintings

using airbrush and freehand techniques in the same vein as his now-famous, as Giger describes it, "surrealistic biomechanical dreamscapes."

Giger's scaly, reptilian creatures and images were simpatico with ELP's detailed and gothic musical scope, that cyborgization of the free and precise, of the acoustic and electronic—and certainly in tune with one of the record's themes of humanity's epic struggle with computer technology and artificial intelligence.

The trouble was, one of the paintings prominently featured the puckered lips of a beautiful alien woman (Giger says it was based on his wife Li) moving toward the tip of a penis, presumably to perform some emergency brain salad surgery. (The other Giger painting, which was used on the front cover, featured a human skull being crushed by an elaborate torture device.)

Predictably, Atlantic Records were horrified by what they believed was a pornographic painting, and said the phallic imagery had to be removed in order to get the album into stores. Giger was reluctant but eventually agreed to airbrush the extraneous extremity and camouflage it so it appeared to be a "shaft" of light.

"It was quite graphic," says Northfield. "If you look at a center label on an English copy of the record you can still see it pretty clearly."

The record cover, like some of the earlier ELP efforts by William Neal, was a work of art and major feat of printing. The front was cut into two interconnecting flaps, forming the abovementioned skull-vice image (with a central circular portal allowing us to peek at those luscious lips). When the flaps are opened, the image of Li is fully revealed and the LP can then be removed from its inside pocket.

Imagine arguing with a record company about a penis. Imagine wanting to have a penis on your cover about to be "operated on." Never let it be said that ELP lacks a sense of humor.

Brain Salad Surgery appeared in

the fall of 1973 and went Top 5 in Britain (it climbed to number eleven in the States) just as ELP played to enormous crowds in sporting arenas across the globe into 1974.

No one rolled like ELP: Thirty-six tons of equipment included Palmer's two-ton stainless-steel drum kit (containing nine Paiste cymbals, two gongs, a 134-pound church bell, timpani, tubular bells, and more); Emerson's eight abused Moog synths (including the monstrous modular rig) and a grand piano (among other keyboards); and Lake's mini arsenal of guitars and one Persian rug, an item for which Lake was mocked by the press and public at large. Lake's defense for allowing himself such self-indulgence? He says he was electrocuted once in Germany via a vocal microphone, which allegedly blacked him out. When he was conscious again, he'd asked the ELP road crew to put down a rubber mat to ground the electrical cords. When Lake saw that the mat did little to beautify his stage area, he then requested carpeting be put down over it. Figuring Lake's tastes ran to the expensive, the crew came up with his now-infamous rug, reputed to have cost six thousand pounds.

"I think with Greg it was a bit like Elvis buying Graceland," says Pete Sinfield. "Interesting psychological probe there, of someone who grew up poor and developed lavish tastes."

WORKS

In 1974, taking a break from recording, ELP turned its attention to running the Manticore label, releasing the extravagant live triple album and Top 5 U.S. hit, *Welcome Back, My Friends, to the Show That Never Ends—Ladies and Gentlemen, Emerson Lake & Palmer*, which documented the band's recent international sweep and featured sprawling versions of "Tarkus" and "Take a Pebble" (not to mention the three "Impressions") and a faster-than-a-speeding-bullet rendition of "Hoedown." Manticore also released studio albums by recent label signings, the Italian prog rock acts Premiata Forneria Marconi (PFM) and Banco del Mutuo Soccorso.

After the world tour, ELP affairs took a backseat. By 1975, the trio were working separately: Palmer was being educated at the Guildhall School of Music & Drama in orchestral percussion; Emerson was busy laying down "Honky Tonk Train Blues" (composed by the Chicago-born boogie-woogie pianist Meade "Lux" Lewis) with big-band swing arrangement for a twenty-piece jazz orchestra by Alan Cohen (which became a U.K. Top 21 hit); and Lake recorded a pair of Christmas tunes (both cowritten with Sinfield) which were released as the single "I Believe in Father Christmas," backed with the English fairgrounds tune "Humbug," the former becoming a kind of evergreen, a "Somewhere Over the Rainbow" for the prog rock crowd.

"The Christmas song was written not as a single, not as a pop song, but as a serious commentary on what's happened to us over the years," says Lake, who calls the Christian holiday "a time of correction," referencing the Christmas truce during the World War I. "Christmas was really just the vehicle that Pete [Sinfield] and I chose to show how cynical people have become. Christmas used to be goodwill amongst all men, peace on earth. How has it descended into nothing more or less than a marketing opportunity?"

Once it became obvious that the three members of ELP could only do so much without the momentum of the band to carry them, they decided to regroup, rather than record solo records, and pour their energies back into writing new material.

The last time the band had recorded in the studio together was 1973—three years prior. Lake said ELP took time off from recording to find a proper direction to go in as a band. They did. Having exhausted, they believed, the technological options available to them, they turned their gaze toward symphonic music.

The project that emerged involved the Orchestra de l'Opéra de Paris for what would become a double LP showcasing each member's individual talents as a musician, and their talents collectively, dubbed *Works, Volume I*.

Each member was allowed one side of an LP to develop his own material, and the fourth side would be relegated to band compositions.

Coproduced and cowritten by Sinfield, Lake's "side" is part Neil Diamond, part Mediterannean romance, part blues-bump parody (with strings attached). "Lend Your Love to Me Tonight," "Nobody Loves You Like I Do," and "Hallowed Be Thy Name" (featuring Emerson, Palmer, and a ninety-plus-piece orchestra) are largely forgettable, although "C'est la Vie" and "Closer to Believing" (which Lake says took him and Sinfield two months to write) leave a positive impression.

You always hear about composers interpreting and intersplicing key aspects of their lives and influences into their master works. "Piano Concerto No. 1," orchestrated by John Mayer (who conducted the London Philharmonic Orchestra), is a slice of Emerson's psyche, musical heritage, and personal life, the first time since the Nice's "Five Bridges Suite" that he tackled an orchestral arrangement.

"Everything in my piano concerto comes from my heart and is entirely original," says Emerson. "There's not one line in it [about which] anyone can say, 'He ripped that off.' I was fortunate at the time to have a beautiful nine-foot Steinway grand piano in my barn studio. I just looked out over the countryside, with birds singing, and composed. The last movement— 'Toccata Con Fuoco'—was written about my house burning down."

The most musically diverse portion of *Works, Volume 1* is turned in by Palmer, who was never particularly known for his songwriting. Here, however, classical, funk, and jazz-rock fusion meld nicely, sometimes within the same song.

Putting his percussion education to good use, Palmer interprets Bach's "Two Part Invention in D Minor" partly on vibraphone (a new skill Palmer perfected courtesy of his lessons with James Blade, who also appears on the track on marimba); the second movement of Sergey Prokofiev's *Scythian Suite*, dubbed "The Enemy God Dances with the Black Spirits"; a new orchestral version of his drumming showpiece "Tank"; and (as if picking up on the California session/fusion vibe breaking into the mainstream at the time) "L.A. Nights" (cowritten by Emerson, featuring Joe Walsh of Eagles fame on guitar), most of which was recorded nearly two years prior.

While the three solo sides have their moments, one thing is certain: ELP operated more efficiently and (for the most part) creatively as a team. The opening track of the

The Nice: Elegy (1971)

Trilogy (1972)

Welcome Back, My Friends, to the Show that Never Ends – Ladies and Gentlemen, Emerson, Lake & Palmer (1974)

The Atlantic Years (1992)

The Return of the Manticore (1993)

fourth, and final, side, the band's version of Aaron Copland's "Fanfare for the Common Man," features the then-new multitiered keyboard, the Yamaha GX-1 polyphonic synthesizer (which Emerson uses for the horn and woodwind textures in the tune).

"Fanfare" reached number two on the British charts, but the song nearly didn't happen. Copland was not thrilled when he caught wind of the fact that a rock band was interpreting his work.

What's surprising—and this will shock classical music aficionados—is that Emerson was accomplishing something similar to what Copland had with his compositions: bringing different forms of art to the masses. Copland was a populist, and perhaps ELP were too, despite their elitist reputations. But Copland either failed to see the value in having a rock band record his music, or denied there was a connection between his populist bent and Emerson's sensibilities.

"The band sent Copland the music to ask permission, and he said something along the lines of, 'If I was able to stop you, I would,'" remembers Sinfield.

Copland's response was certainly radically different from Ginastera's, but that didn't stop ELP. They pressed on, regardless of whether the composer had given his blessing or not. Crazy: Rock audiences were introduced to Copland, as *Works, Volume I* became a Top 20 U.S. hit in 1977. But this did little to calm Copland, who apparently could hold quite a grudge.

More than a decade later, when Emerson and Palmer joined forces with Robert Berry to form the band 3, Copland reps refused to let the band televise a performance of "Fanfare for the Common Man" at Atlantic Records' fortieth anniversary concert bash at Madison Square Garden in May 1988.

Adding insult to injury, the *Works* tour of 1977 was perhaps a bridge too far. ELP, instead of using

symphonies in the towns they were touring, decided to travel with a sixty-plus-piece orchestra, which drained the band financially, despite the fact that they were selling out arenas.

The band refers to the nights when the orchestra and band were in synchronicity as being magic, but ELP eventually had to break free of the strings and continue touring as a three-piece to cut their losses.

Some of the reviews for the tour were predictable. The *New York Times* called out ELP for its inflated stage performance, puking up the same tired old criticisms of pretentiousness regarding progressive rock and its vulgarity in mixing classical and amplified music.

Manticore's Mario Medious succinctly summed up ELP's struggle when he said in 1977: "The band know they're not going to make any money out of it, even playing baseball stadiums, but they feel it's their music, their lifework they're presenting."

Works, Volume 2 appeared in November 1977, showing yet another side of the band. Composed largely of older recorded material, some dating as far back as the *Brain Salad Surgery* sessions of 1973 (e.g., "Tiger in a Spotlight," "Brain Salad Surgery"), and including the popular "Honky Tonk Train Blues" and "I Believe in Father Christmas," *Works, Volume 2* is a mixed bag of musical influences as far ranging as early jazz, folk ballads, and vocal standard.

It was downhill from there. Nineteen seventy-eight's *Love Beach* did little to rejuvenate the band's image. Who could blame the public? The very name *Love Beach* is synonymous with prog rock going commercial—and going totally lame in the process. Atlantic Records in America even agreed to slip a Manticore-approved, ELP "tour gear" merchandise catalog into the LP sleeve, further solidifying the image of a band that had "sold out."

Despite some bright spots ("Canario" by Joaquín Rodrigo and

one or two catchy MOR rock love songs), *Love Beach* is a hybrid of pop and classically influenced rock; unleashed in a punk-infused world, it seemed to prove all the critics right: ELP were tired, boring, and strangely provincial. Even the sprawling, dramatic package of the *Works, Volume 1* double album (and to an extent its successor, the single LP *Works, Volume 2*) had been more focused, and even seemed to convince the general audience that the band was still pushing ahead in *some* acceptable creative direction.

In Concert was the last *legitimate* record released by ELP in the 1970s. Recorded at Olympic Stadium in Montreal during the *Works* tour of 1977, it appeared in 1979, featuring songs "Peter Gunn," "Knife Edge," the third movement of Emerson's "Piano Concerto No. 1," "The Enemy God," "C'est La Vie," and a spine-tingling version of "*Pictures at an Exhibition*," in which Lake's voice soars above busy instrumentation during "The Great Gates of Kiev." By 1980, the band had broken up: A rather inadequate greatest hits was issued shortly thereafter.

Palmer once said that he would have liked the band to have gone out on a high not a low note. ELP spawned a few spin-off bands and finally re-formed in the 1990s.

Despite what Palmer called a "dreadful" record, 1994's *In the Hot Seat*, ELP were again relevant. Their catalog had just been reissued, remastered, or otherwise beefed up for CD format. *In Concert* was expanded and rereleased under the title *Works Live*, and was joined by a slew of best-ofs, an interactive King Biscuit concert CD package, and two boxed sets (*The Atlantic Years* and *The Return of the Manticore*, with the latter featuring fine liner notes by longtime friend and music writer Chris Welch) were spreading the gospel.

Perhaps Palmer got his wish after all: ELP didn't end on a low note—the band never really stopped. ELP is a state of mind; the show that never ends.

(Peter Still/Getty Images)

YES

Going for It All

BRILLIANT. INNOVATIVE. MYSTICAL.
Dysfunctional. Accessible. Enigmatic.

Rarely has a rock band (let alone a *progressive* one) embodied so many contradictory musical traits and remained intact (in one form or another) across a span of over five decades. Yes are truly one-of-a-kind and are arguably the most popular and enduring of the progressive rock bands established in the late 1960s.

Images of the band remain imprinted in our minds—Rick Wakeman's sequined cape; dry ice fogging up the stage as the band performed one of their most beloved epics, "Close to the Edge"; the block-serpentine letters coiling around one another to form the band logo; guitarist Steve Howe's chunky Gibson ES-175 . . . Classic.

Jon Anderson and bassist Chris Squire founded Yes in 1968. The two met at a Soho nightclub in London, called La Chasse, and discovered they shared a mutual love of the Beatles and Simon & Garfunkel. They began writing material together, recruiting drummer Bill Bruford (found through an ad in *Melody Maker*), guitarist Peter Banks, and classically trained organ player Tony Kaye.

"Jon Anderson and I were talking about what we liked as far as music, and by then I had also became a big Simon & Garfunkel fan, so I was keen on their vocal harmonies," says Squire. "I was also being influenced by what was going on at London's Marquee club, which had become my local venue for music."

Bruford's love of jazz and jazz drummers like Art Blakey and Max Roach is evident in the angular approach the rhythmatist takes to percussion. Bruford told this writer that he "happened to be in London in 1968, which was a very fertile time in music. I watched Mitch Mitchell trying to be Elvin Jones with Jimi Hendrix in a local pub in Beckenham, and I think I wanted to be Max Roach with Yes. It sounds childish—we were only eighteen."

Because of Squire's background in the church choir, he brought his knowledge of harmony to the Yes creative melting pot. "I was singing in a choir even before I started to play bass," Squire says. "I was aware of musical structure—how the top-line melody interacted with the bass line. I think it was quite common for a lot of people of my age to be in a church choir when they were kids."

Squire and Banks, the latter a self-taught guitar player and an emotional and musical free spirit, were both in the bands the Syn, and Mabel Greer's Toyshop (though Banks eventually left the band). Anderson had previously been in a band called the Warriors (which also included drummer Ian Wallace). Hammond organ player Tony Kaye was playing in various bands, most notably Johnny Taylor's Star Combo, and Bruford had, mostly notably, briefly joined Savoy Brown for a few gigs.

"As Mabel Greer's Toyshop we kept playing at the Marquee," says Banks. "God bless the Marquee. If it hadn't been for [that club], a lot of those bands would never have existed."

"The musicians in Yes had already spent about ten years in other bands, so we weren't young spring chickens when the band started," says Jon Anderson. "We were all in our midtwenties. We were convinced that we were making a very different approach to music than most people."

This was evident on some of the more mature numbers the band performed and recorded. It seems the elements that made each member great were synthesized and combined to create a sound that the band would develop for the next five decades—three-part harmonies, Anderson's soaring vocals, Squire's aggressive bass playing, guitar acrobatics, and effective, mood-changing keyboard texturing.

Yes's eponymous debut hit the shelves in the fall of 1969 with memorable psychedelic pop rock songs such as "Beyond and Before," "Harold Lang" (which sounds as though it may have had an impact on a young band named Genesis and, in particular, its singer, Peter Gabriel), a jazzy seven-minute cover version of the Byrds' "I See You" (one of the best examples of the band's harmonies at work that slips into a bit of classical-jazz-rock during the quiet portion of Banks's extended solo), the Beatles' "Every Little Thing" (check the "Day Tripper" guitar riff that Banks slyly slips into the song), "Beyond and Before" (cowritten by Mabel Greer's Toyshop guitarist Clive Bailey), "Looking Around," and "Survival."

"The only thing I can think about Yes was, because no one really cared [about what we were doing], there was nobody to tell us what we could and couldn't do," says Banks. "Socially we weren't rebelling against anything at all. It was the tail end of the '60s, and at that time, the whole hippie movement was becoming more

political. Certainly in America there were protests against Vietnam, and some of that was mirrored over here in London. There was certainly no political motivation of any kind in a band like Yes. Musical motivation, yes, but social and political, no."

Jon Anderson's idea to fuse an orchestra with Yes's psychedelic pop rock sound achieved mixed results on the band's sophomore record, *Time and a Word*. (Deep Purple and the Nice had already utilized orchestras as well.)

Despite the bright spots, and mainly because of the lows, *Time and a Word* marked the end of the line for Peter Banks. Though his guitar playing served a complementary function within the band (his solos oftentime elevated songs), he never completely saw eye to eye with the other members. His sometimes erratic approach (from the band's point of view) didn't always suit a prepared musical program.

"I've always have been an improviser," says Banks. "That was one of the problems. I would throw something in from left field. It was difficult particularly for Jon, because he would expect a certain organization. I would put in a guitar lick that just wouldn't fit. I can understand. I was asked to leave. We did have disagreements, particularly at rehearsals, but that was the thing that worked well for the band. We were all different people and came from different social backgrounds and different musical backgrounds, and through some strange chemistry, the music pulled itself together."

Eventually the band recruited Tomorrow guitarist Steve Howe, who was as much influenced by Chuck Berry as Chet Atkins; the countrified, stratospheric boogie of Jimmy Bryant (whom some had dubbed the most precise and fastest guitarist on the planet); and pedal steeler Wesley "Speedy" West.

Tomorrow had generated a buzz with their song "My White Bicycle," something of a British psychedelic anthem/relic. Howe had also previously played with the Syndicats, the In Crowd, and Bodast (as well as chief songwriters for the band, Dave Curtiss and Clive Maldoon, of "Sepheryn"/"Ray of Light" fame), and had worked as a guitarist for R&B/soul singer P. P. Arnold and with Delaney & Bonnie in 1969.

"Ducking and diving and darting around the musical possibilities seem to have come from early musical influences," says Steve Howe. "I had already been playing the guitar before I had heard the Les Paul records he'd made with Mary Ford, and I had heard the Tennessee Ernie Ford records, with brilliant guitar playing by Jimmie Bryant and Speedy West *before* I picked up the guitar."

The impact of these artists is obvious: "Cactus Boogie" displays Howe's countrified soul, and the "cracked whip" heard in "Diary of a Man Who Vanished" from the guitarist's 1979 solo record, *The Steve Howe Album*, is clearly influenced by Tennessee Ernie Ford's "cracked whip" in the song "Mule Train.' (In Ford's case, the crack was created by his voice; in Howe's it was "Howe hitting a metal tea tray with a drumstick, adding tape delay, then compressing with a Urei 1176 while adding EMT plate reverb," says recording engineer Gregg Jackman.)

The band's first record with the new guitarist, christened, appropriately enough, *The Yes Album*, was a declaration: This was a new band, with a new direction, building on an established sound, which would, essentially, give the band a career.

The Yes Album showed Yes in a different, perhaps better, light. Though Emerson Lake and Palmer were headed for superstardom (they were already considered a supergroup before they played their first gig), Yes appeared to be gaining ground on them as well as on similar acts, such as Jethro Tull and even their idols, King Crimson.

"We felt secretively competitive

[with] King Crimson," says Howe. "Obviously, ELP was closer to our field of play and, obviously, there was respect for what they did: Rick and Keith Emerson . . . in a way, you had to think of them in the same breath. But we soon realized that, hang on, we owned a little bit of acreage somewhere in the plot of what was called the English resurgence, or what I call post-psychedelia. There was a nice spaciness about us, and we were kind of finding our feet in a whole new world."

"The funny thing was, at the time, when I was involved [with] Yes I was also involved with Emerson Lake and Palmer," says producer Eddy Offord. "I was spending a lot of time with both bands. No one wanted me to work with the other band. So Yes said, 'You have to get away from ELP,' and ELP said, 'You have to get away from Yes.' Everyone was just trying to outdo everyone else to see who could be more adventurous, more cutting-edge and . . . who could go the furthest. Both of them certainly had one eye on what everyone else was doing to see if you they could do it better."

The impact of Howe was felt almost immediately. In the opening bars of the first track on *The Yes Album*, "Yours Is No Disgrace," Howe wrings every ounce of twang and squeezes out a brassy, slightly wah-inflected metallic tone (via an early flanger device) from his rig and his trusty Gibson ES-175.

"Yours Is No Disgrace" marks one of the longest songs to appear on a Yes recording to date—over nine and a half minutes, foreshadowing larger pieces of the band's future repertoire, prominently featuring the Moog synthesizer, most notably in the opening instrumental section where it states the main theme.

Recorded live at the Lyceum Theatre in London in July 1970, "The Clap," a solo acoustic piece marked by a ragtime fingerpicking style, is yet another facet of Howe and

Yes s/t (1969).

the band. The title "The Clap" is said to be a misnomer (it was meant to be simply "Clap," a tribute to the birth of Howe's son, Dylan). Amazing how one word can completely change the meaning of a title.

"Starship Trooper," a title inspired by Robert Heinlein's 1959 sci-fi book *Starship Troopers*, though it has little (if anything) to do with the book's story line. However, there do seem to be a few threads running through the song. It appears, once again, that the lyrics capture Anderson's journey to the divine (within him and without), wrapped in personal memory, the wisdom of astral traveling, new-age sentiment, and UFO imagery.

"I remember Jon was a very nervous singer," says Offord. "Yes would build up a song, and poor Jon had to sing his little part over this masterpiece. The guy was quaking in his boots, you know? He was always nervous, and we would always try to find ways for him to relax. In the beginning he was more nervous about his lack of musical education, but I think as time went by, and [as he] built an alliance with Steve, who provided more of the musical things, he become more confident."

The Yes Album was a breakthrough for Yes, reaching number seven on the British charts in April 1971 (it became a Top 40 hit in the U.S. in 1972). Still, *The Yes Album* was a mixed bag of originality and recycled ideas (e.g., Howe repositioned "Nether Street," a song he cowrote as a member of Bodast, as "Würm"—the transcendent climax of "Starship Trooper).

One suspects, too, that the songwriting credits have as much to do with "democracy" in labor as with the need for each of the key composers in the band to seek sole credit for something, even partial bits. (Who could argue that the "Life Seeker" section of "Starship Trooper" wasn't straight out of the spiritual playbook of Anderson? Or that the harmonized voices of "Disillusion," from the same song, weren't influenced by Squire's love of Simon & Garfunkel and his church choir experience as a boy?)

As cynical as it sounds, this is what fueled the competition within the band and pushed Yes to greatness. The individual spotlighting of talent (which would reach its pinnacle by the next Yes record, *Fragile*) could very well be one of the key components of prog rock. Besides, featuring a solo guitar piece such as "The Clap," regardless of the brilliance of the writing and performance, is not the best way to prove to the world that you're a cohesive unit. It's to show off. Fans said thank goodness.

There would be more of that with the band's *Fragile* album, an even bigger success. "*The Yes Album* came out, and that did very well," says Howe. "It encouraged us to be experimental again and just go for it. The challenge was to be extremely original and competent on *Fragile*. The recording techniques—and Eddy Offord was brilliant at that time— were very advanced, and we felt that we were at the cutting edge of what you could do at that time."

Yes was constantly in motion. This fact, coupled with a general frustration that Tony Kaye had to be dragged kicking and screaming into using the emerging technology of synthesizers (though he had indeed used

a Moog on *The Yes Album*), caused the band to decide to dump the organist in favor of a more flamboyant and flashy player, Rick Wakeman of the Strawbs, who'd studied at the Royal College of Music and was not only committed to using synthesizers but had begun making a name for himself doing just that.

"Tony Kaye was mostly playing B-3 and not much else, and not wanting to do much else," confirms Offord. "Yes then found Rick, who could kind of become an orchestra electronically."

Yes was synthesizing all sorts of influences, beginning with the opening tune of *Fragile*, "Roundabout" (which features the immortal lines "In and around the lake/ Mountains come out of the sky and they stand there," inspired by the band's travels through the U.K. countryside): Very likely the song that introduced a generation of Americans (and others) to Yes, it is a fine example of the band's individuality coming through while supporting a tune.

"When I moved to acoustic guitars with Yes on 'Roundabout,' I proved to myself that I wasn't going to be pinned down as a guitarist," says Howe. "I knew that I wasn't going to be a blues guitarist and nothing else, let's say. I'd hedgehop."

"Roundabout"'s reverse piano fade-in, followed by Howe's bright harmonics, was a foreboding and unusual entrance into a world of rugged and mysterious musical terrain. "Jon came into the studio one day and said, 'I want to hear this kind of "meeeoooohwrr" sound,'" says Offord. "We talked about different backward sounds, and we finally settled on a backward piano. So what we did was turn the tape over and record the piano forward, and stop at exactly the right time so it coincided with the first note of Steve's guitar. It all kind of blended together. It was a physical tape manipulation, rather than putting it into the sampler and hitting

the button."

If Yes were established as five guys, of varying degrees of musical knowledge and influences, spotlighting individual talent, then *Fragile* was the clear culmination of the band's original mission that was left unfulfilled by *The Yes Album*.

Not only did each member have his moment in the sun within each song, but on *Fragile* each member had the focus placed squarely on him: Wakeman performed a multikeyboard interpretation of an excerpt of the third movement of Brahms's Symphony no. 4 in E Minor for a solo titled "Cans and Brahms"; Bruford supplies a snaky sixteen-bar rhythmic workout (at thirty-five seconds it almost seems like a cheeky comment on the royalties he'd receive from the song) with "Five Percent for Nothing"; Howe unveils his classical/Spanish acoustic guitar concert piece "Mood for a Day" (if "Clap" has almost a Robert Johnson– or Big Bill Broonzy–style American ragtime/rootsy feel, then "Mood for a Day" is in the classical Andrés Segovia vein, with just a hint of folk/country, a characteristic that comes to the surface with more prominence in the version from 1973's triple live LP *Yessongs*); Squire performs a groundbreaking bass-guitar composition, "The Fish (Schindleria Praematurus)" ("Bill Bruford nicknamed me the Fish because I used to spend a long time in the bathroom when we used to share hotel rooms together," says Squire. "He would say, 'Get out of the bath. You're like a fish in there.'"); and Anderson pieces together a multitracked acoustic and vocal collage called "We Have Heaven" (which repeats at the end of the record as stray, uncredited audio, much in the same way *Sgt. Pepper's* and *Abbey Road* close.)

The cynical would quip that the band was being rushed into putting together a record, and that a record with four long pieces and lots of short solo ones was all they could muster in a short time period, or that individual members, feeling that much of the writing was being done by Squire and

Anderson, simply wanted a piece of the pie for themselves (i.e., a bigger share of the writing credits and hence royalties).

Even if any of this were true, Yes were taking a huge risk in presenting themselves in this manner. They were, after all, still very much a rock band, and a rock band that very clearly wanted the world to know that five strong musical personalities existed within the unit.

"It was remarkable that *Fragile* does exactly that," Howe said in 2005. "I don't think we'll ever have another record like that, which I think is a terrible waste, because in fact, I never wanted Yes to get into a mold with making records. . . . That technique of featuring the band and the individual all on one record was probably why we were so happy."

Completing the package and forging a relationship that would last for the better part of the rest of the 1970s, artist Roger Dean was tapped to provide the cover illustration for *Fragile*. (Dean would go on to illustrate the band's subsequent records—*Close to the Edge*; *Yessongs*, which proudly displayed the artist's work in double trifold, multipaneled splendor; *Tales from Topographic Oceans*; and *Yesterdays*, as well as quite a few Yes member solo records. Dean also designed the band's iconic logo and, with brother Martyn, Yes's live stage sets.

There was no forethought on the part of either the band, the artist, or Atlantic to link Yes's music with a specific artist or artist's work with the intent of building a lasting bond. Dean just happened to be available with an image of a flying reptile/dirigible/spacecraft orbiting the earth that seemed to speak to the escapist elements inherent in Yes's music.

"The apotheosis of album art came with Roger Dean," says Mark Wilkinson, himself an illustrator who has designed covers for albums by neo-prog band Marillion and former lead singer Fish. "How important his work was to Yes and prog music in

general is difficult to say. The band had already established themselves as brilliant musicians long before Roger worked for them, but he certainly enhanced the experience for their fans in the same way as Hipgnosis did for Floyd. I dare say some people bought Yes albums because of the cover art. Dare I also say that, to that extent, he was one of the first cover artists to rival the band in importance, certainly as far as marketing was concerned for the record company."

Fragile was Yes's breakthrough moment: In Britain it went to number seven in December 1971 (the second Yes studio record to fill that slot in eight months) and it entered the Top 5 in the U.S. in 1972. (A three-plus-minute edited version of "Roundabout" appeared as a single, backed with "Long Distance Runaround," suddenly making the eight-and-a-half-minute track radio-friendly.)

"No one ever said, 'Let's make a single,'" says Offord. "It was just another Yes song. Then, in America, they cut it down, and that was important because it was the first real radio play that the band ever had, and it helped break them in America."

"People would come up to us and say that the music you've just done from *Fragile*, this will be played in ten years," says Anderson. "[We'd] say, 'This will only last a couple of years, if that.' Not thinking that if you spend enough time on certain kinds of music, it will last the test of time."

CLOSE TO THE EDGE

With the success of *Fragile*, Yes were in the unenviable position of having to follow up a bona fide hit. Wanting to push themselves harder and further than they had gone, Yes cued themselves up for what would become (in the minds of many) their masterpiece.

Once the bond was formed between Dean and Yes, it is difficult, in retrospect, to divorce the images from the music. The cover of *Close to the Edge* at first blush seems criminal-

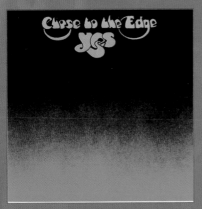

Yes's masterpiece: *Close to the Edge* (1972).

ly underdecorated; in retrospect, it is quite fitting of the nineteen-minute title song. The LP cover appears to be a slice of some unknown forest preserve. The forest, olive, and deep greens fade into one another, matching the array of natural noises blending and quelling in a maddening rush of white noise at the opening of "Close to the Edge."

The image, and other Dean illustrations, combined with the heady music operates much on the same level as medieval iconography, which was intent on bringing forth a vision of heaven through meditation. (Anyone who has seen Yes in concert performing "Close to the Edge" and other similar long-form compositions can attest to the music's liturgical qualities. It instills a kind of sensitivity in the listener, a heightened state of mind.)

It's no surprise then, to find that the jumping-off point for the conceptual themes in the nineteen-minute title song, was Hermann Hesse's novel *Siddhartha*, which, in basic terms, documented the spiritual enlightenment of the title character in his development toward becoming the supreme Buddha and founder of Buddhism.

"Around this time, I was thinking about our success and asking, 'Why me?'" says Anderson. "Why me out of all of those people who were trying to make it in London? Why would I get that chance of success? I'm getting success and I have money in the bank and it kind of freaked me out . . . to the point of wondering, 'Okay, If I'm supposed to be doing something, I better get on with it.' We can't sit around. This could all disappear tomorrow. When I was twenty-six, twenty-seven years old, I was a lunatic: I couldn't sleep for the enjoyment and excitement that I've been given a chance to be a musician in this life. So I started reading, and Hermann Hesse was a very big experience for me, and I'd want to put it into lyrical form and express what I was feeling."

When *Close to the Edge* was released, it shot to number four in Britain and number three in the U.S., having been heralded as the band's greatest work to date. Indeed. The influence and importance of *Close to the Edge* are immeasurable. *Close to the Edge* lives up to its name: It sees the band at its creative pinnacle, the peak of its power, lassoing all of its creative energies, while having the restraint not to see it fall off a cliff.

But the record also leaves a sobering legacy. Frustrated by the pace of the recording, Bruford quit the band and took a job with rivals King Crimson, leaving Yes to bring in drummer Alan White, who'd worked with John Lennon and George Harrison, reconfiguring the complexion of the band once again. (White was always a steady but solid and hard-hitting drummer in contrast to Bruford's more jazzy touch.)

"Bill was very much a purist when it came to music," says Offord. "So we would lay down a basic track—drums, bass, guitar, maybe, or organ or something, and it sounded really good. Jon was always the one who wanted to push more the classical side. So he wanted to add this and that. 'Oh, let's try this. . . .' 'Let's try that.' And it was a tendency for it to become too, especially from Bill's point of view, overdubbed and too much going on that you lost the original basis of the band. I remember Jon said one day, 'This sounds pretty good. We'll put this in the background and

it'll be great.' Then Bill said, 'Why don't you put the entire record in the background and be done with it.' He was sick of his parts being covered up by all of this nonsense."

Said Bruford himself in a 2001 interview I conducted: "I left Yes for the money. I knew I was going to get paid too much. That is when the problems start. Once you get paid, what follows next is repetition."

TALES

Close to the Edge threw down the gauntlet. The band's next studio effort, the four-song double album *Tales from Topographic Oceans*, was more outrageous, more adventurous, and perhaps full of more vagaries than any of Yes's previous albums combined.

"Jon [wrote] a lot of the stuff on *Tales* based on dreams," says Howe. "If [people] want to bitch about the lyrics, they can look at any song and say, 'What's it all mean?' If they do, they're kind of missing the point, you know?"

The plan was for Yes to work out in the country, in a pastoral and idyllic setting, to record the expansive compositions. Getting sidetracked was the first of many obstacles the band confronted during the production of *Tales*.

"The band and I had discussed putting an environment together that was conducive to creating and maybe being in a farmhouse somewhere, getting away from London," says Offord. "A lot of bands were doing it at that time; going somewhere to create in a nice environment."

But manager Brian Lane convinced the band to remain within the vicinity of London and set up camp at Morgan Studios in Willesden, where it was believed the band (management and coproducer) could have the best of both worlds while tapping the cutting-edge recording technology available to them at Morgan.

"I remember we recorded that album on the first ever twenty-four-track, two-inch tape machine ever to

come into England," says Squire. "The machine had an attendant army of engineers at all times, because it was always breaking down. When you're trying to make an album like *Topographic Oceans* and the recording machine is breaking down, or something was going wrong with it, or going out of phase, it didn't help us [laughs] get to where we needed to go. There was a lot of blind faith, I guess, that was employed to get through that record."

Yes were breaking through barriers in every conceivable way for the recording of *Tales*. Eddy Offord: "One day Jon came into the studio and said, 'When I am at home and singing in my bathroom, it sounds good. But I come into here into the studio and I can't seem to achieve the same sound.'"

"I was managing Morgan at that point," says engineer and audio maven Roger Quested. "The way I remember it, Jon Anderson actually said he wanted to sound as though he was in his bathroom; he wanted that effect. So Yes got the roadies to build a kind of booth— plywood, lumber, tiles and all—in the middle of the bathroom. You wouldn't do that kind of thing at Abbey Road. Accommodating the client like that. Yes booked the studio for about four or five months or something."

"I don't know how long we were in the studio, but I think it was closer to two or three [months]," says Squire. "Rather than what should have been six or seven. I was doing sixteen-hour days, seven days a week for a long time on that. I was hardly getting any sleep at all and driving a half hour home every night and half an hour back every day as well. It was like . . . it was a bit of a potboiler. Let me tell you, that was a very frustrating time."

"I think it was hard because it was a double album, and it took forever," says Offord. "And I guess maybe the division was [apparent] in the band and Rick was kind of more outcast and everyone was frustrated. In retrospect, there were some good parts of the

The much misunderstood *Tales from Topographic Oceans* (1973).

Yesterdays (1974) : a compilation.

album; I think maybe the band remember it as being a time of turmoil."

It was a painful birth, but the results were stunning. The very first song, "The Revealing Science of God," encapsulates many of the melodic themes appearing throughout the record as well as Yes's musical grandeur—from harmony vocals and constant tempo changes to an evocative lead melody (played by Wakeman on Minimoog) and an uncluttered sense of sonic and rhythmic interplay, perhaps unparalleled in Yes's history up to that point.

The record became a number-one hit in Britain, having been released at the tail end of 1973. (It was released in the States in early 1974, where it went to number six.) But as with the band's last epic recording, *Close to the Edge*,

Tales took its toll on the band. Wakeman, who was never thrilled by the prospect and general concept of *Tales*, and who was feeling underutilized as a songwriter, quit soon after a tour to support the album. People either love *Tales* or hate it, he said in a 2003 interview, "and I don't love it."

The record *did* garner critical praise (*Time* applauded Yes for its effort). However, on the whole, *Tales* is remembered today, perhaps unjustly, for its perceived faults. (Some fans and critics were even confused by the cover: was it ripped from the pages of Erich von Däniken's best-selling book on ancient

astronauts, *Chariots of the Gods*? Was the scene depicting an underwater world, a sunken Atlantis, or outer space?) Some critics cite *Tales* as the

Yes band photo circa 1971. *Middle row*, Bill Bruford, Jon Anderson, and Steve Howe; *back left*, Rick Wakeman; and *bottom front*, Chris Squire. (Photo courtesy of Premier Talent)

beginning of the end of prog's heyday.

"When Yes wrote 'Roundabout' or 'All Good People,' I couldn't have liked them more," says legendary Styx front man Dennis DeYoung. "But when they were on the 'bottom of the ocean' [Tales from *Topographic Oceans*], I went, 'What was that?' Let's face it: I like Yes musically. But at sixty years old, I still don't know what any of their songs are about."

WAKEMAN ON ICE

Wakeman had gone, but he'd already established himself as a successful solo artist when he was a member of Yes. Prior to the release of *Tales*, in 1973, Wakeman rolled out that rare beast of the rock music world, the instrumental concept record, with his *The Six Wives of King Henry VIII* (a Top 30 U.S. hit).

Assisted by his former mates in the Strawbs, then-current (and former) Yes members Bruford, White, Squire, and Howe, along with an arsenal of keyboards, Wakeman tackled a rather dark period of English royal history with tongue-in-cheek aplomb. Only Wakeman, with his sardonic humor, could have thought up the inclusion in the liner notes of the birth, divorce, and execution/death dates of Henry's unfortunate wives.

The Six Wives is a bit of a tone poem, as the keyboardist attempted to translate a historical character's identity through music, much in the same way Strauss interpreted Nietzsche through "Also Sprach Zarathustra" and Elgar based Variations on an Original Theme, Op. 36 (casually known as the Enigma Variations) on thirteen different (untold) personalities in the composer's life.

Wakeman's "King Arthur on Ice" tour (in support of his *The Myths and Legends of King Arthur and The Knights of the Round Table* record on A&M) is often used as an example of prog rock's excess and ridiculousness, but critics fail to point out that that *the joke wasn't lost on Wakeman*. This writer believes (to this day) that

Wakeman's earlier concept records and subsequent tours (*Journey to the Centre of the Earth*, a record that soared to the top of the U.K. Albums chart on the very day the keyboardist officially announced he'd quit Yes; *Myths and Legends; The Six Wives of Henry VIII*) operate on two levels: Firstly, they excite the imagination and inspire a romanticism with European iconography; secondly, a subtle undercurrent of satire pervades these early solo releases, so much so that they could be interpreted as a virtual aural/orchestral equivalent of a *Monty Python* movie.

Unlike some of his prog rock brethren, Wakeman seemed self-conscious enough to realize that his epic productions could be shot through with sly humor without lapsing into comedy rock or self-parody. You *could* take the music and production at face value, one would suppose, and thus *it would be* parody, but it seems Wakeman beat critics to the punch. Some may disagree, but this author believes Wakeman possesses a sense of the absurdity of life, and that some of his most extravagant musical ideas were simply an outgrowth of this.

"There's a wittiness about Rick, and there's a certain amount of tongue-in-cheekness about his production and presentation, and this fact that, 'I can, so I will,'" says post-production guru Simon Heyworth. "You know, 'It will cost a lot of money and I don't care.' There is something endearing about that in a way."

RELAYER

To fill the keyboardist chair left vacant by Wakeman (though no one could truly replace him), Yes tapped Swiss master Patrick Moraz, one of the early users of the Minimoog synth, who had followed Keith Emerson as the keyboardist in Lee Jackson and Brian Davison's post-Nice band Refugee, turning heads with such grand works as "The Grand Canyon Suite" (not the Ferde Grofé

Relayer (1974). Yes's experimental, jazz-fusion excursion.

classic piece but original music with Moraz blowing a thirteen-foot Alpine horn) and "Credo," from the band's self-titled Charisma label debut.

Moraz's classical training, solid progressive rock background (prior to Refugee, he worked with his own psychedelic band, Mainhorse), and experimental streak were the perfect fit for a band that, after such major works as *Close to the Edge* and *Tales from Topographic Oceans*, was looking to feed their ambition and broaden their musical scope.

An accident when he was a teen, in which he broke a finger, side-tracked Moraz from being a concert pianist. "I was told by my teachers that I would never play again," says Moraz. "That was devastating but I trained my left hand for six months and became ambidextrous."

The classical world's loss was prog rock's gain. Lee Jackson remembers a young Moraz and his monumental talent: "The Nice were making what we would now call a video and getting ready to perform a concert in Basel in Switzerland in 1969," says Jackson. "We were filming by day. We did the concerts and November 2, 1969, I remember was Keith Emerson's birthday. We're in a hotel having a bit of a party with some of the young ladies of the town who had attached themselves to our entourage and Keith gets on the piano, as he's wont to do, in the hotel lounge, and we see this man in a straight suit with a briefcase, and he's standing by the piano, watching Keith. He says, 'Excuse me. Could I trade fours with you?' We're thinking, 'Who is this? He's gonna trade fours with Emerson?' He sits down and Keith went [whirlwind of noise to depict fast playing]. Then this guy goes [whirling, ascending noise, the response to Emerson's riffing]. We went, 'Oh, shit.' At that point we realized that this guy knew what he was doing, you know? . . .They were playing duets and it was fantastic. I got his card. That was Patrick Moraz."

Yes manager Brian Lane called Moraz for an audition/jam session with the band in the countryside of Devon at what would later become Steve Howe's barnyard studio. Yes had auditioned other keyboardists, including Aphrodite's Child's Vangelis (Evangelos Odyssey Papathanassiou), but no one had yet emerged to fill the spot.

When Moraz arrived for the rehearsal, he found Vangelis's rig already set up. He listened to the Yes members jamming and improvised counterpoint melodies to the band's songs. Yes were immediately impressed.

"After the exchange, they started to play the first few bars of what became 'Soundchaser,'" says Moraz. "Chris and Jon said, 'Why don't you come up with an introduction for the song?' I invented it there and then. I showed it to them and explained it to Chris and Alan, because only the bass and drums enter the introduction with the keyboards. I know that my keyboard section of that introduction is the one that's on the record. Eddy

Offord had designed an unbelievable array of recording technology for a mobile studio."

From the outset, the band's upcoming record, eventually called *Relayer*, was shaping up to be another adventure in sound and rock composition. *Tales from Topographic Oceans* was so structured, the band needed something of a musical cold shower and had decided to head in a different musical direction—more into jazz and electronic/avant-garde music.

"*Relayer* was a bit of jazz-rock album for Yes," says Squire. "We tried a number of different things, and maybe that's a key to longevity—not being afraid to try a slightly different direction, or not accepting that you are capable of doing one thing, really."

When *Relayer* was released in late 1974, featuring the twenty-two-minute epic "The Gates of Delirium", it continued Yes's hot streak, going to number four in Britain and number five in the U.S. Critics, predictably, called *Relayer* pretentious. But pretentious or not, Yes had done the near-impossible: Though music was in an era of experimentation, the band had dared to go where few rock bands had before, and had scored major hits with both *Tales* and *Relayer*.

GOING FOR THE ONE

Thinking the time was ripe for the individual members to strike out on their own, Howe, Anderson, White, Squire, and Moraz released solo records—*Beginnings* (featuring members of the band Gryphon, who had toured with Yes), *Olias of Sunhillow*, *Ramshackled*, *Fish Out of Water*, and *The Story of I*,

respectively. Simply put, it was an explosion of music—much too much music for one band to record.

It's no surprise that glimmers of Yes poked through at various moments on these individual member records, proving that solo stardom was not truly in the cards for the Yes men. Nonetheless, the records, along with retrospective compilation *Yesterdays*, all did respectfully well at the retail counter, with Anderson's *Olias* scoring a Top 10 British hit.

Despite the successes, in retrospect, the middle 1970s were lost years for Yes, just as they were for ELP. Though the band did live shows during this time, no studio records were forthcoming from Yes for nearly three years. (It was longer for ELP.) When the band reconvened to begin writing and recording their next studio album, *Going for the One*, punk was just beginning to make rumblings in British pop culture. Yes couldn't have been more unhip.

What's more, trouble was brewing: Some of the members were displeased with Moraz and his rock star behavior. It soon became evident that Moraz needed to leave. But as to why, ask the members of the band and you'll receive a different response.

"After *Relayer*, when we started to work on *Going for the One*, he wanted to take Yes into a very jazzy area," says Howe. "We told him, 'Get lost. This is not a jazz band. Go away.'"

"Patrick at that time hadn't come to the studio, and he was out and about," says Anderson. "You'd think that you wouldn't have to tell anybody to be there at rehearsal. That's when

Yes: Fragile (1972)

Rick Wakeman's The Six Wives of Henry VIII (1973)

Yes: Tormato (1978)

Yes: Drama (1980)

Yes: 90125 (1983)

Yes: Union (1991)

you come to realize that you have the wrong guy. So it was time to change."

It must be said that Moraz offered something new to the band, for good or bad, and his contributions to *Relayer* made it one of the strangest and perhaps most underrated records of the Yes catalog.

One story was circulating in the press that Wakeman had rejoined Yes prior to the firing of Moraz.

The band parked at Montreux, Switzerland's Mountain Studios with an eye toward producing the new record themselves, flying without sound engineering wingman Eddy Offord. Yes had something to prove. *Going for the One* was a rebirth. Gone were the side-long epics so prevalent on the band's three previous studio albums, replaced (largely) with shorter songs. (The band dropped the idea of presenting Roger Dean–like sci-fi spacescapes to represent their music, in favor of modern, photographic shapes of skyscrapers designed by Hipgnosis, featuring a kind of twentieth-century Adam, pre–original sin, lost and in these monumental technological structures, facing this new-day Eden and confronting himself in the process.)

Just as *Relayer* was the perfect platform for the Moraz version of Yes, it's hard to imagine *Going for the One* without Wakeman.

Going for the One landed in the number-one spot in Britain, and reached the Top 10 in the U.S. But there was bad news right around the corner that even the liturgical experience of writing, playing, and recording "Awaken" couldn't purge.

The band's next record, *Tormato*, long seen as Yes's creative low point, was the end of the band in more ways than one, with repercussions that would span two decades. Aside from "Future Times," "Rejoice," "Release, Release" (which almost seems like a commentary on reactionary music, such as punk), and, to a degree, "On the Silent Wings of Freedom," most of the tracks seem limp, though not total-ly devoid of subtlety and complexity.

Spiritual wisdom imparted to audiences with previous releases seemed to dry up by 1978. Anderson and the band seemed to sink into New Age, semi-Druid-ish mystique (examine the original inner LP sleeve for graphic designs of sacred stone circles and "tors," or hills, dotting the British countryside and connected by magic lei-lines).

"Arriving UFO," for instance, takes the experience of finding answers in the vastness of the cosmos a little too literally. (And who could forget the chunks of splattered tomato splashed across the front cover—a silly and messy pun on the title? If this was an attempt at a practical joke, we didn't get it.) Even Howe admits that the band was unfocused and that "maybe we lost our way a little bit with *Tormato*."

The lyrical obfuscation that made Yes so mysterious was all but gone, no matter how well intentioned ("Don't Kill the Whale" and the aforementioned "UFO"). Maybe it's because *Tormato* doesn't know what it wants to be: a straight-ahead rock record; a slab of faux–New Age enlightenment; a tongue-in-cheek satire; a techno rock experiment (featuring keyboard devices such as the relatively brand-new eight-track-tape-driven Birotron). In the past, fusing these concepts and different musical modes wouldn't have been a problem. But with *Tormato*, something doesn't quite gel.

By the time Yes were ready to record their next album, to be titled *Drama*, Wakeman and Anderson were having serious doubts about the future of the band and where the music was going. They were also feeling like hamsters in a track, gearing up for yet another record and another tour to follow it. During the sessions, Wakeman and Anderson decided to get off the ride.

The three remaining members—Howe, Squire, and White—recruited the pop duo the Buggles—Trevor Horn and keyboardist Geoff Downes,

Going for the One (1977). Yes's return to greatness?

who had just scored a major hit with "Video Killed the Radio Star."

Some of the material, polished and reworked, from abandoned recording sessions (post-*Tormato*, released as *The Golden Age*) wound up on *Drama*.

"The Buggles were experimenting in their own way," says Howe. "'I think the song "Tempus Fugit,"' Trevor said to me the other day, 'was remarkable.' You know what is remarkable about it is that we hadn't even met Trevor and Geoff when we had recorded that. They overdubbed on top of it. At least, that's how Trevor remembers it."

"Tempus Fugit" may have been one of the only bright spots of the record, and Howe refers to *Drama* as one of the "heaviest albums Yes had done," but a lot of it feels like patch-work.

Drama charted, and the band went on the road with Horn and Downes (who later joined Howe in the pop-prog supergroup Asia) to support the record, but Yes had wheezed its last breath. Like their prog rock comrades ELP, the Yes behemoth appeared to be dead and gone. Or so some thought. . . .

Yes would return with a number-one U.S. hit called "Owner of a Lonely Heart" and surprise everyone, while transforming themselves from prog rock "dinosaur" to studio prog-pop band for the tech-savvy 1980s.

(Andrew Putler/Getty Images)

GENESIS

Crymes and Misdemeanors

DRAWN TOGETHER BY THEIR SHARED EXPERIENCE
at Charterhouse (one of the most prestigious boarding
schools in England, located in Godalming, Surrey), vocalist
Peter Gabriel, East Hoathly keyboardist/pianist Anthony
Banks, West London guitarist Anthony Phillips, and
Guildford guitarist/bassist Michael Rutherford created their
own environment: a virtual music scene, isolated from the
rest of the country and most other musicians.

Two competing school bands, the Anon and the Garden
Wall, joined forces and become one group that combined the
talents of future Genesis members Rutherford, Phillips,
Gabriel, and Banks, along with those of drummer Chris
Stewart (who later became a successful travel writer). The quintet's combined
efforts produced a demo, "She Is Beautiful" (sometimes referred to as "She's So
Beautiful") that caught the attention of producer and Charterhouse alumnus

Jonathan King, who'd recently had a Top 5 British hit with "Everybody's Gone to the Moon," in 1965.

King heard the demo and was immediately attracted to Gabriel's voice, in which he heard a rare soul, passion, and "smokiness," as he describes it. He agreed to work with the band, dubbing them Genesis.

"I thought they had great talent but were too self-indulgent," says King, who'd invited a fledgling Genesis to record more demos. "When I discovered them, they were not as good musically as they thought they were. So I used to trim and cut them down . . . and pointed them in a certain direction—more acoustic than pop, giving them Bee Gees albums to listen to and, something they don't mention all the time, all the Crosby, Stills and Nash early stuff."

Genesis recorded "The Silent Sun" and "A Winter's Tale" while formulating plans for an LP, which would become the band's 1969 debut, *From Genesis to Revelation* (a concept album based on stories and characters from the Bible).

Despite King's best effort and Genesis's enthusiasm, *From Genesis to Revelation* didn't do much of anything to excite the public. Undeterred, the band continued to write new material, having been spurred on by the adventurous sounds coming from the Moody Blues and King Crimson in the late 1960s. Genesis saw the way forward: ambitious music that rocked.

When their business relationship with King had run its course, the band began to look seriously at finding a new label. They soon came to the attention of the Famous Charisma label. "We were the first band signed by Tony Stratton-Smith—everybody called him Strat—to his Charisma label," says Mark Ashton, drummer for Rare Bird. "It was Graham Field, the organist who formed Rare Bird, and the band's producer, John Anthony, who really introduced Genesis to Strat, who had been managing the Nice. Genesis became one

of the first bands signed to Charisma, and the rest, as they say . . ."

With yet another new drummer, John Mayhew, Genesis recorded 1970's *Trespass*, featuring the band's patented organ and dual twelve-string guitar sonic tapestry (harkening back to the sound of Crosby, Stills and Nash) on material the band had been working on the previous year, including the menacing nine-minute track "The Knife," the band's first major feat as songwriters.

Trespass lives up to its title. The explosive seven-minute multidimensional opener "Looking for Someone" is followed by "White Mountain," "Visions of Heaven," and "Stagnation" (a song that developed from an earlier piece called "Movement"), the last of which features the band's signature hypnotic twelve-string acoustic picking, Gabriel's sweet flute playing, and a Banks warbling organ solo.

These were incredibly mature songs for young musicians, and Genesis were demonstrating that they could inhabit a progressive rock territory similar to that of Procol Harum, the Nice, Traffic, and even Yes and King Crimson—resting somewhere between English nineteenth-century renaissance, European folk music, American gospel, twentieth-century art music, and some as-yet-unnamed rock subgenre.

Keyboardist Banks admits that the closer (and future live favorite) "The Knife" was written with the Nice in mind.

The song also inspired LP cover illustrator Paul Whitehead, whose pen-and-ink drawings Gabriel had seen in a gallery, to complete one of his most memorable works. "When I did that cover, they had written four of the songs already," says Whitehead. "They were all very romantic. So we came up with the idea of doing a cover with a king and queen looking out at their kingdom, and Cupid peeking at them from behind the curtain. I started working on it, I got

halfway through it, and I got a call from Peter [Gabriel], who said, 'We're going to have to scrap that idea.' They had decided to use a song called 'The Knife' on the record and said that the cover I'd done didn't go with the song, you know? I was like, 'No way. I've done all of this work and they are just going to scrap it.' I said, 'Can't we find some alternatives?' Peter said, 'If you can think of something that works with what you've done, fine.' I had all kinds of ideas, such as spilling a bottle of ink over it, burning it, and doing different things to it that would corrupt the image."

Nothing was really working for Whitehead. But a visit to an art exhibition in London triggered an idea. "There was an Italian artist showing his work," says Whitehead. "His thing was slashing the canvas with a razor blade. 'Bingo.' I said to the band, 'Why don't we get a knife, the knife you're talking about, and slash the canvas and take a photograph of that.' They said, 'You wouldn't slash the canvas.' I said, 'You're damn right I would.' For me, it was the solution, because I didn't want to do the work again."

Completed by the appropriate visual, *Trespass* is one of the band's strongest packages. However, the world saw it a bit differently. *Trespass* didn't connect with a mass audience in Britain, where it failed to chart, and it wasn't even on the radar in the U.S. It soon sank without much notice.

This could have been a crushing blow for young musicians, but Genesis, along with labelmates Van der Graaf Generator, were Tony Stratton-Smith's favorite bands, his pet projects, one might say. Regardless of the shifting winds of pop music, he was going to see to it that they did not fail, even if it pooling all his resources.

"I think our band financed Charisma, basically," says Ashton, whose Rare Bird had scored a Top 30 hit in the U.K. with "Sympathy." "It was a small concern for a couple of years. Strat branched out, Genesis start-

Genesis, 1977. *Left to right*: Steve Hackett, Tony Banks, Chester Thompson, Mike Rutherford, and Phil Collins. (Photo courtesy of Atco)

From Genesis to Revelation (1969)

ed to do better, although it took Genesis a few albums to get on their feet."

"I think Strat felt strongly about the serious nature of rock as an art form," says Chris Adams, front man/guitarist/vocalist of the Scottish band String Driven Thing, also signed to Charisma. "Back then, the U.K. was like the R&D department for rock, and labels like Charisma had one aim: to break a band in the States. Apart from credibility, this meant huge financial rewards. And after Van der Graaf Generator split up [in 1972, for the first time], Genesis were definitely protected. They were the ones who could deliver that payload."

It seems Stat was unshakably loyal in his devotion to Genesis. Charisma backed the band through thick and thin, and even as Genesis made personnel changes. Sensing their rhythm section wasn't strong enough, the band had to make a hard decision.

Mayhew went quietly.

Enter Chiswick, London, native Phil Collins, a child drummer prodigy, who began playing when he was five years old and had played a bit

part in *A Hard Day's Night*.

Collins was a member of the pop rock band Flaming Youth and was certainly more aggressive and versatile than Mayhew. And Collins had confidence. Having arrived early at Gabriel's parents' house, he was asked to wait outside, have a swim in the pool. As he did, Collins listened to all the mistakes the other drummers were making and used them to his advantage. He aced the audition.

The second personnel change was completely shocking to the band. Largely due to his dislike of touring and general stage fright, guitarist Phillips wanted to bow out. No one saw it coming. "Ant" was so strong a musical personality and here he was, unable to continue because of an irrational phobia.

Ant was more than a guitar player—he was a friend from school. How would they replace him?

Gabriel and the band, leafing through the *Melody Maker*, came upon an ad placed by a musician that read, in part, "determined to strive beyond existing stagnant music

forms." The wording resonated with Genesis, and they soon called the the twenty-one-year-old London-based guitarist for an audition.

That guitarist, Steve Hackett, dazzled them not only with his technical playing but, more than anything else, with his ability to manipulate sound. Through the use of Hackett's guitar effects, Genesis heard the future, and asked him to join.

Without wasting time, the band were on the road and began to work on material for their next record, *Nursery Cryme*, which pushed Genesis into escapism and the world of British absurdity/fantasy.

The impact Hackett and Collins had on the band is felt immediately on *Nursery Cryme*: Collins demonstrates a basher's verve and a jazzer's dexterity, and even makes his lead singing debut

Nursery Cryme (1971): Phil Collins's and Steve Hackett's Genesis debut.

on "For Absent Friends."

Hackett is at once a monster and an ensemble player. The magic in Hackett's playing has always been his natural resources: He had the chops to cut anyone's head off if the song called for it, but his real contribution to the music was his ability to use sonic textures—Hackett would become known for his use of the Rose Morris MXR Phase 90 pedal—to converse with Banks's organ lines and Gabriel's melodic vocals, to help direct the band into virtually unexplored musical areas.

As such, the band recorded a tune they had been kicking around for some time, called "The Musical Box" (containing a reference to "Old King Cole," a traditional Celtic nursery rhyme), which was shaped by the unusual way Rutherford tuned his twelve-string acoustic, with high and low strings harmonizing, lending the song its air of "carousel."

"Seven Stones"; "Harold the Barrel" (based on an inane sequence of events leading up to the main character willfully and literally going out on a ledge); the comedic sci-fi drama about photosynthetic serial killers, "The Return of the Giant Hogweed" (the fuzzed-out guitar riffing is something akin to heavy-metal baroque, courtesy of Hackett's string pull-offs and hammering, years before Eddie Van Halen had thought of doing something similar); and "The Fountain of Salmacis" (based on the myth of Hermaphroditus, who was transformed into a hermaphrodite) are stirring and groundbreaking.

These were some of Genesis's most dynamic songs, not only compositionally but sonically, thanks to producer John Anthony. Whether owing to a cymbal wash that's utterly consumed by monolithic Mellotron tones, generating aural visions of spraying waterfalls; or voices tucked into neat little corners in the mix, cropping up in unusual places, the music has depth, giving perspective to and underscoring Gabriel's mythological lyrics.

Paul Whitehead remembers the band's creative process for *Nursery Cryme*. "The record company had a house down in the country in Crowborough where the band used to go and rehearse and write and so on," says Whitehead. "I got invited down a couple of times in the middle of the creative process. You know, 'Come on down and stay for a couple of days and you can figure out what's going on.' Well, what would happen is you'd get up in morning and Peter Gabriel had written lyrics. 'What do you think of these?' Everybody would look at it and would write the music from that. Or vice versa: They had the music written and Peter would write the lyrics. Being a part of the process, I gave the band the titles for *Trespass*, *Nursery Cryme*, and *Foxtrot*. They were stuck for titles."

One of the things Genesis understood, as did King Crimson and Yes, was the power of their LP covers' imagery to help complete an artistic package. Gazing at Victorian illustrations and fairy-tale books with Gabriel to stir up ideas for *Nursery Cryme*, Whitehead came up with a concept that would represent the music and Gabriel's unique and strange take on folk tales. "The cover was obviously *Alice in Wonderland*–inspired, an old English Victorian story, set on a croquet field," says Whitehead. "But instead of croquet balls, we'd use rolling heads. "

Nursery Cryme was a powerful work from a band that included two new members, but greater work lay ahead. This is obvious from the opening bars of the band's next record, 1972's *Foxtrot*: We are transported to a different place and time as soon as we hear the phantasmagoric Mellotron strings of "Watcher of the Skies," streaming at us like the vivid colors of a Dario Argento horror film, capturing the "sights" and sounds of the song's sci-fi lyrical theme.

When the Mellotron cloud lifts, giving way to a 6/4 rhythm, the song builds slowly in volume and intensity, coaxing Collins, Rutherford, and Hackett to pound away at the unusual staccato pattern.

This jiggery-pokery rhythm is made even more unusual by the fact that it distorts and shifts at different points throughout the song. Hackett once told the author that he couldn't remember a time that Genesis—or anyone else—played it correctly all

the way through onstage.

Gaining confidence as a unit, the band began to branch out. It's interesting to note that, like some of their peers, Genesis were starting to spotlight individual members of the band, as Yes had done in 1972 with *Fragile*. With *Foxtrot*, Hackett matched Steve Howe's "Mood for a Day" with the nylon-stringed classical work "Horizons."

Other tunes, such as "Get 'Em Out by Friday" and "Can-Utility and the Coastliners" are but warm-ups for the main event: the twenty-three-minute epic "Supper's Ready."

"Supper's Ready" has long been a subject of debate for fans who seek to interpret its meaning. Essentially, the song is a retelling of the entire Bible, from Eden to the birth of the Antichrist. Perhaps more importantly, it also describes a vision of the rapturous end of the world and the second coming of Christ, resting thematically somewhere between the earlier *From Genesis to the Revelation* and the band's then-upcoming record *The Lamb Lies Down on Broadway*.

Yet the imagery is so disjointed, if not idiosyncratic, it's difficult to tie together all of the references, which point to innocent, world-weary characters. Perhaps it's a search for love, a search for God, a search for God's love and a new spiritual center? A new Jerusalem, as the song tells us?

Ultimately, the song is absurdist humor, operating as a kind of lobotomy—surgically peeling back layers of the twentieth-century English psyche. Still, whatever the true intent and meaning of the song, "Supper's Ready" was to Genesis what "Tarkus" was to Emerson Lake and Palmer: an expansive musical journey through the chicanery of madness and personal expression.

To bring the music alive onstage, Gabriel began dressing in outrageous costumes. Genesis shows were replete with Kabuki-inspired garb, giant sunflowers, elements of show-puppet theater and mime, bat wings, Day-Glo

makeup burning brightly in a dark hall with the help of UV/infrared rays, dry-ice fog, an old-man mask (donned during "The Musical Box," representing the aging reptile Henry Hamilton-Smythe, whose disembodied spirit is given to flesh in the song), and a fox head and a red dress, à la Paul Whitehead's iconic character from the LP cover artwork for *Foxtrot*, which shocked not only audience members but the band the first time it was worn.

"You have to bear in mind that prog rock is very much a musical form that came out of the U.K. alongside surreal British humor like *Monty Python*," says Ian Anderson, whose band Jethro Tull had been known for its own theatrics. "It's impossible for Peter Gabriel to be onstage with Genesis, dressed as a giant sunflower, without having some kind of sense of humor."

Appropriately, the band released a live record, titled *Genesis Live*, in 1973, capturing the energy and majesty of their stage show. Despite the many boxed sets and live CDs the band has released since then, *Live* remains a standard, featuring powerful renditions of "Watcher of the Skies," "Get 'Em Out By Friday," "The Musical Box," "The Return of the Giant Hogweed," and "The Knife," recorded in Leicester and Manchester.

"Genesis had an incredible work ethic in terms of writing and collaborating and rehearsing and jamming," says Gregg Bendian, drummer for the Musical Box, a Genesis-licensed tribute band that performs note for note and rebuilds bit by bit the stage presentation of the band's classic 1970s performances. "They lived it. You don't get that music by showing up and making forty-five minutes of music to fulfill a contract."

SELLING ENGLAND BY THE POUND
Instead of compromising and Americanizing their music, Genesis looked inward to develop a more absurd, England-centric prog rock.

Selling England by the Pound (1973)

Their next studio record, 1973's *Selling England by the Pound*, was something akin to a string of subdued and subliminal *Monty Python* skits—very English, right down to the manicured landscape featured in Betty Swanwick's cover artwork. (Gabriel's voice even mutates into different British accents in "The Battle for Epping Forest," a metaphor for the struggle between the forces of light and darkness, and a mixture of styles, from synth prog rock to R&B, church hymn, Caribbean, and African.)

Despite tackling weighty subjects (e.g., war, bemoaning the loss of England's onetime glory), *Selling England by the Pound* never lets the listener take the music too seriously (a by-product of the absurdity and extravagance of the humor, perhaps?).

Opening the record, Gabriel sings a capella in "Dancing with the Moonlit Knight"—a twitchy, twinkling tune mourning the passing of England's great nation and speaking to the erosion of modern culture (as far as the writer can decipher), alluding to the mythical Grail and Arthurian legends, in which wood and wire mesh in some form of music that's neither baroque folk-classical nor rock.

As the song progresses, acoustic and electric guitars are chased by piano, organ, Gabriel's vocal baaing and baying, and Collins's military march rhythms until the floor and the sky open, like all heaven and hell broke loose.

Pound delivered the band's first British hit, "I Know What I Like (in Your Wardrobe)," which narrowly missed the Top 20, as well as "More Fool Me" (on which Collins makes another appearance as a lead singer) and "The Cinema Show" (a track, along with "Firth of Fifth," that has been kept in Genesis's live repertoire for decades). The latter is remarkable both because the synthesizer instrumental section of the song was written in 7/8, and also because Banks plays a minimal amount of notes to achieve his point. Genesis were getting better at what they do, formulating a genuine style that had been established on *Nursery Cryme* and *Foxtrot*.

"Peter Gabriel was wearing these bizarre uniforms, and they didn't make radio-friendly records, and I would get kicked out of radio stations trying to promote the records," says Phillip Rauls, an Atlantic Records radio promotion man. "They were like, 'Are you crazy? We can't play these guys. This music is like opera with a drumbeat.'"

"I was born in 1960, and I didn't see Emerson Lake and Palmer, Yes, Crimson, but I did listen to them," says onetime King Crimson bassist/Warr guitarist Trey Gunn. "But not Genesis, for some reason. I think where I was geographically located, which was in Texas, for some reason, Genesis never really was big there."

"Exactly," says Rauls. "It was very homophobic times, too. If you liked that band, you were a fag because of Peter Gabriel's stage getups. Once you got beyond that, a lot of disc jockeys didn't say the name of the artist for fear that their radio station would be associated with this phobia that long-haired, dope-smoking communist subversives were taking over."

There really wasn't anything subversive about Genesis, aside from the fact that their music and career lay outside the mainstream. However, that would change with 1974's concept double album, a milestone in Genesis's recording history, titled *The Lamb Lies*

Peter Gabriel's stage prowling and elaborate costumes injected a rare theatricality into Genesis's early live performances. Also pictured are, *left to right*: Hackett, Rutherford, and Collins. (John Lynn Kirk/Getty Images)

Down on Broadway, which alternately confused and inspired listeners with its dreamlike tale of schizophrenia.

THE LAMB LIES DOWN ON BROADWAY

Some consider *The Lamb* to be the absolute pinnacle of Genesis's progres-

sive rock period and the entire British progressive movement, due to its impressionistic characteristics. Brian Eno contributes his ambient touches—Enossification—to the band's expansive sound with a VCS-3 synthesizer to manipulate Gabriel's voice.

Yet, the importance (or lack thereof) and relevance of the musical and conceptual elements of the double record have been the cause of a continuous, raging debate.

Arguably, no other rock band, progressive or otherwise, had sounded like Genesis, particularly on the last few records, as was certainly the case

The Lamb Lies Down on Broadway (1974)

with *The Lamb*. The music simply occupied its own space and time.

"What you *don't* mean by 'having its own time,' presumably," said Hackett, "is it had its own time, because it was 1975 or something."

Correct, Mr. Hackett. The sounds we heard on *The Lamb* are simply devoid of many (if any) sonic markers that would keep it in one era.

Gabriel explained the basic premise of the plot to an audience at the Shrine Auditorium in Los Angeles in 1975: "It tells of how a large black cloud descends into Times Square, straddles out across Forty-second Street, turns into wool, and sucks in Manhattan island. Our hero, named Rael, crawls out of the subways of New York and is sucked into the wool to regain consciousness underground. This is the story of Rael."

Are we experiencing a dream sequence? Is Broadway a euphemism for a new Jerusalem? Is it a metaphor for the loss of innocence? Or was Gabriel making a political commentary on the affairs of the dual nature of the religious-secular state of Israel?

When Genesis toured *The Lamb* initially, they confused audiences who were expecting to hear the band's old "hits" and instead got a recital of new material complete with stage costumes (so elaborate it became difficult at certain points in the show for Gabriel to even sing in front of a microphone), pyrotechnics, and slide shows. It was a multimedia event, with moving parts that never quite worked correctly. But perhaps this didn't matter.

"I saw a band live in Italy and they did a version of *The Lamb Lies Down on Broadway*," Hackett said. "I [was thinking] how good the music sounded. Being able to sit out front instead of [being] onstage—when you're onstage you're not getting the full balance. You're getting this compromise, which comes down to [an] observation that Dik Fraser made. Dik was one of the guys who worked with Genesis many years ago. He was saying to me,

'A band onstage never knows when it's really *doing* it.' 'How was it for you, darling?' You know . . ."

"When I met Phil Collins I know he was a Weather Report fan and I a Genesis fan," says former Weather Report bassist Alphonso Johnson, who was pivotal in stabilizing the band's live lineup, and who had appeared on Collins's solo debut, *Face Value*. "I told him that I saw the band perform *The Lamb Lies Down on Broadway* in Philadelphia and I was maybe one of fifteen African-American people in the crowd. That concert, along with Pink Floyd's *The Wall*, changed the way I perceived music and how it can affect an audience."

Toward the end of the American tour for *The Lamb* in the late fall of 1974, as if it were a shock to anyone, Gabriel announced he was leaving the band. "It's difficult to respond to intuition and impulse and yet work within the long-term planning of the band's career," Gabriel said of his exit in a statement to the press.

It was assumed, because Gabriel was such a lightning rod for attention, that the singer was the creative force behind the band. The press, as did so many others, virtually wrote Genesis off.

"At the time we were running around with Greenslade, Genesis was just bubbling over and their management put a huge amount effort and money to getting into the States and launching them," says drummer Andrew McCulloch (Greenslade, King Crimson, Manfred Mann), who did rehearsal sessions with Gabriel after the singer left Genesis. "Greenslade liked what they were doing. But when Peter Gabriel left, we all thought, 'Well, they're in trouble now,' because Peter had incredible charisma. We thought they were finished."

Determined to prove to the world (and themselves) otherwise, a Gabriel-less band thrust full speed ahead.

The first order of business? Finding a new singer . . .

PHIL COLLINS, FRONT AND CENTER

"I witnessed the auditions for the new singer for Genesis," says Stephen W. Tayler, an engineer at Trident Studios in London, where Genesis's post-Gabriel studio record, *A Trick of the Tail*, was cut. "It just so happened that I was . . . assisting in the engineering process, helping out the engineers at a couple of sessions for what would become *A Trick of the Tail*. They were in the studio for quite some time recording the backing tracks. They had no idea who was going to be the vocalist. I got the feeling that Phil was kind of going, 'Please, can I have a go.'

"The band brought in a number of singers, and the only one I remember specifically by name was Bernie Frost, who had been a session guy and would appear often in the studio doing backing vocals for people. I believe he was a very important component to Status Quo's vocal studio sound," continues Tayler. "I remember some other singers just being awful. They sang, I believe, to the backing track of a song called 'Squonk.' Then, I remember the moment the band actually [let] Phil have a go . . ."

"Phil really half nominated himself," adds producer David Hentschel, laughing. "I think he felt he could do it, but there needed to be a push to convince the other guys."

The band was reticent to bring Collins from behind the kit to handle the lead vocal duties, despite the fact that the drummer had sung minimal lead and frequent backing vocals for the band on tour and studio efforts.

"Phil's voice, particularly in the upper ranges, was not dissimilar [to] Peter's, and so not a lot of people realized that he sang," says Hentschel. "The timbre of the voice, if you like, was similar."

"We were hanging around together playing in Brand X [Collins's jazz-rock side project with Robin Lumley,

John Goodsall, and Percy Jones]," said Bill Bruford, whom Collins had admired from his Yes days. "We were playing some dates together—I was playing percussion to his drum set. Phil was just talking about the problem he had with Genesis. That they were auditioning singers and he, Phil, thought that they were all hopeless and he thought he could do a better job, anyway. But if he went up front, he'd be worried—like any drummer would be—that the music would fall apart. I said, 'Why don't you go out front and I'll play the drums on tour or something.' He knew my style and he knew I could play the music. So he'd be comfortable that the music wouldn't fall apart behind."

Suddenly it became a real possibility. And once the band had heard Collins sing, they knew they had what they were looking for, right in their midst.

Genesis may have had dramatic musical interactions in the past, but nothing approached this "British prog on steroids" feel before. *A Trick of the Tail* reached number three on the U.K. charts. *Melody Maker* readers even voted it their favorite album of 1976, beating out Led Zep's *Presence*, Steely Dan's *Royal Scam*, Queen's *A Night at the Opera*, Dylan's *Desire*, Jon Anderson's solo record *Olias of Sunhillow*, Floyd's *Wish You Were Here*, and Peter Frampton's enduring live record, *Frampton Comes Alive*.

"People had always behaved toward the group as if Peter was Genesis," Collins remembered. "We made one album without him and suddenly it wasn't a problem."

With Bruford backing them, the band embarked on an international tour to support *A Trick of the Tail* in 1976. The tour, the first without Gabriel, unveiled the new band to the world just as it presented two English drumming powerhouses.

Collins soon grew into his own man as a Genesis singer (and studio drummer), having dispensed with Gabriel's "mysterious traveler" per-

sona in favor of his own, as he put it, "bloke next door" stage presence, which carries him through to today.

Collins and Genesis were changing rapidly. Even the decision to bring in Bruford, whom the band perceived as a kind of star, proved to be perhaps, in the end, musically a bit of a challenge.

Bruford came from a different world. On one side of the stage was the stoic Tony Banks, whose studied and dexterous approach to keyboards were perhaps the antithesis of what Bruford wished to be as a musician. There were moments one felt that Bruford (with Hackett) might tear it up, even for a few brief measures, to derail the music and release it from the strict confines of song structure. Occasionally, it happened, most notably with "The Cinema Show" and in the nightly Collins-Bruford drumming duet. This uncommon tension is what made the band an exciting, if somewhat frustrating, live band, both for the fans and for some of the musicians.

"We did that for about nine months or something and at the end, I said, 'Job done,'" said Bruford. "I didn't have any emotional input; I was just like a hired studio gun, except I was touring with the band. So I wanted to move on. But I think it got the band over a tricky moment."

WIND & WUTHERING

For its next studio album, the band again tapped producer David Hentschel.

Unlike *A Trick of the Tail*, *Wind & Wuthering* wasn't created in mass confusion and disarray. In fact, it was the opposite of such, becoming (arguably), what some fans consider Genesis's most focused album.

Genesis came totally prepared to record, and it shows. Melodic ideas and variation on those melodic ideas are developed, stated, repeated, and restated in changed form, throughout the course of *Wind & Wuthering*, lending the record a sense of cohesive-

ness from one song to the next.

Wind & Wuthering is not a concept album, but musically, it's the tightest Genesis had ever been in the studio. "That may have to do with the way it was recorded," says Hentschel. "It was the first album we recorded where we went abroad. We went over to Holland in this little studio [Relight Studios] in the middle of nowhere. The idea being that we would be completely isolated from telephones, people dropping in, and distractions, basically. That was quite a novel idea in those days. We just stayed in a little hotel down the road from the studio and basically were totally immersed in the music. The whole thing was recorded in about two weeks. Then we came back to London and finished off some vocal overdubs and a few little bits and pieces, probably for a week. Then spent two weeks mixing it. So the whole thing was very focused, really."

The proof is in the pudding. "Eleventh Earl of Mar" captures the same wispy musical atmosphere of "The Fountain of Salmacis" while presenting a luminescence all its own, complete with bass synth tones that percolate under the high-register melodic lead line.

When a wash of Collins's hi-hat and Banks's Mellotron scrubs the sonic foreground, we enter into a completely different world, one of concrete rock grooves and Hammond organ. We're later swept away by a chorus of acoustic guitars (of different string qualities) and the gentle flicking of a kalimba, which send us through a musical and mystical fog as dense as the mist shrouding the field in the cover artwork (by Hipgnosis). It's hard to think of a more gentle and "open" Genesis passage that's as musically layered.

"I think the density of the track is something that comes from having multiple writers on a majority of the tunes," says Hentschel. "Even when it came to the overdub stage, one person is adding his take to the song. That adds to the complexity or depth of the track. Everyone's a contributor, basically. It makes for a very interesting end result."

The second song, the ten-minute Banks-penned "One for the Vine," is an epic meditation on entitlement, the ruling classes, and their "divine right" to lead—and how this illusion is shattered.

"One for the Vine" is a great example of why Genesis is a "progressive" band: Aside from the fact that not much else in the rock universe sounds like it (try assigning a genre to the yo-yo-ing sonic interplay between Banks's piano and Hackett's whiny guitar tone), the track develops from one musical idea to the next without a hitch. (Banks's keyboard lines also become more complicated as the tune progresses, as if he were storing his energy for the later stanzas of the song.) The song is really seven rolled up into one, and yet it's as smooth as a three-minute pop tune.

"*Wind & Wuthering* is generally perceived as their finest hour," says Hentschel. "It might be the purest representation of what Genesis was about as a band. There are longer tracks, generally, and the tracks develop. The whole album has a very distinct atmosphere that sets it apart from many of the other records they recorded."

Despite this accomplishment, Hackett was dissatisfied with the song choice: He's even cited the song "Pigeons" and his own "Please Don't Touch" (which wound up on one of his solo records of the same title) as better candidates than the music that was chosen for the final track listing.

It's no surprise that Hackett, increasingly frustrated, and who'd tasted solo success with his 1975 record *Voyage of the Acolyte* (a Top 30 British hit), decided to leave Genesis during the mix stages of the 1977 live double record, *Seconds Out*.

Hackett would continue following his own experimental-muso path, pushing his personal limits with such releases as the hard-won acoustic album *Bay of Pigs*, *Please Don't Touch!* (featuring Kansas's Steve Walsh and Phil Ehart), the stylistically diverse *Spectral Mornings* (containing bits of reggae/Caribbean, classical, and old-timey Americana à la U.K.'s 1970s dance hall/jazz big band, the popular Pasadena Roof Orchestra), *Cured* (prominently featuring keyboardist Nick Magnus and Hackett's brother John, as well as keyboard technology and an ever-present LinnDrum rhythm machine), *Highly Strung* (containing the U.K. hit "Cell 151"), *Till We Have Faces* (a veritable smorgasbord of musical styles, from classical—as in the burst of Bach's Brandenburg Concerto felt in "Myopia"—to Latin/Brazilian double and Japanese pattern drumming), and *Defector*.

Hackett was one of the few progressive rock guitarists who could be inspired by C. S. Lewis and speak of wizards and goblins while maintaining an audience willing to overlook these transgressions because of the music's beautiful melodic core.

"Steve gets away with it for two reasons," says former Hackett keyboardist Nick Magnus. "Firstly, the lyrics are more sophisticated than [on] average, being more like poetry than prose. A certain amount of interpre-

tation and imagination is required on the part of the listener. With tasteful use of metaphors, euphemisms and ambiguity, the hobbits and virgins aren't rubbed directly in your face. Though some may be disappointed about that. Secondly, the music has that unique Hackett personality. Many contemporary prog bands that do the 'fantasy' thing tend to follow the same old formulae, and consequently sound not only cheesy, but the same as each other."

Hackett later formed the dual-guitar supergroup GTR with Yes's Steve Howe, tapping guitar synthesizer technology (something Hackett had began experimenting with in his solo material), and released its self-titled debut record in 1986.

"When you listen to Hackett's solo material, you really hear what an important part of the band's sound he was," says Laser's Edge record label founder Ken Golden. "Of course, Genesis moved on and wrote different material when he left. So, if I had to guess, if Hackett was still in the band, I think it would have carried on in the style of *Wind & Wuthering* and maybe had a few more radio-friendly songs like 'Your Own Special Way.' But I think they would have hung onto that basic sound, for a while at least."

Now a trio (augmented in live situations by Zappa alumnus drum Chester Thompson, and studio and jazz-rock ace guitarist/bassist Daryl Stuermer, both of whom made contact with the band through bassist Alphonso Johnson), Genesis were trimming away the musical fat, as it were.

Collins emerged as *the* singer of the

Trespass (1970)

Live (1973)

Voyage of the Acolyte (1975)

A Trick of the Tail (1976)

Seconds Out (1977)

Duke (1980)

Foxtrot
(1972)

1980s, and Rutherford slowly got over his trepidation about having to "replace" Hackett and mastered the art of being a lead guitarist, while Banks went with the flow, cutting down his epics to bite-size pieces. As a collective unit, the band also warmed up to elements of R&B and soul—some of Collins's favorite styles of music—introducing them into the Genesis lexicon.

Nineteen seventy-eight's appropriately titled . . . And Then There Were Three was the beginning of the band's evolution away from progressive rock. Though songs such as "Down and Out" and Banks's "Burning Rope" hark back to Genesis's early 1970s material, the old days were gone.

"A lot of people say . . . And Then

There Were Three was when the band were starting to go commercial or trying to write three-minute songs," says Hentschel. "It was a conscious decision to do that. The record company said, 'Let's have a few shorter songs.' I think it worked very well, actually."

The record spawned the romantic single "Follow You, Follow Me," a Top 30 U.K. hit (Top 30 in the U.S.), which reached a new demographic of fan.

Subsequent studio albums such as *Duke*, *Abacab*, *Genesis*, and *Invisible Touch* brought even bigger changes and would simultaneously expand and rip apart the Genesis fan base in ways that no one could have foreseen. Genesis would become one of the hottest pop bands of the 1980s, selling millions of records. Suddenly,

women were interested in this band called Genesis; they were no longer the exclusively cultural property of hairy, outcast male college students.

Genesis: *Nursery Cryme* (1971)

(Richard E. Aaron/Getty Images)

JETHRO TULL

Minstrels in the Gallery

JETHRO TULL HAD BEEN WORKING IN FOLK MUSIC IN ONE
form or another since the band's inception. Tull mainstay and front man Ian
Anderson had been messing around with guitar and harmonica from an early
age, having been seduced by Elvis and the country blues of Sonny Terry and
Brownie McGhee.

"I soon discovered that the blues scale had a quality that marked it out very
much from the church music and folk music that I grew up with in Scotland," says
Anderson, who was born in Fife, Scotland, but later moved to Blackpool, England.
"The rogue element of that blues scale was certainly a revelation to me as a . . .
teenager learning to play guitar and set me off down that route of working on music
that was in part improvisational and based on the blues scale."

Anderson realized he could stand apart from the crowd by abandoning the
guitar and learning to play an eclectic instrument like the flute. The wind
instrument was a symbol of Anderson's rebellion. And before long, his wheezing, aggressive flute style—a combination of bluesy licks and impromptu vocal-
izations informed by the style of Rahsaan Roland Kirk—would become his,
and his internationally successful band Jethro Tull's, trademark.

Prior to forming Jethro Tull, Anderson was the front man of the John Evan's
Smash (so called "because the one piece of expensive equipment that the band needed was a Hammond organ," says onetime band booker and Tull manager Terry Ellis,

"and they didn't have the money to buy one. John Evans's mother had put up the money for the deposit, and in order to thank her, they called the band after her son. But it was Ian's band.")

Tull came together when club owners began searching for blues acts and asked Ellis and his partner, Chris Wright, of the Ellis-Wright booking agency based in London, if they had any bands the venues could put on their calendars.

Wright had seen the Smash in Manchester and remembered that they sprinkled in blues tunes among their R&B/soul repertoire. He contacted Anderson to see if there was interest in pursuing a career as a blues musician. There was, but there was one hitch: Unlike many of the blues bands of the era, the Smash didn't have a showstopping guitarist.

Meanwhile, Anderson's friend Mick Abrahams, who had been in the Luton-based outfit McGregor's Engine with future Tull drummer Clive Bunker, was watching his band fall apart around him. The band's bassist, Andy Pyle, later of the Kinks and Wishbone Ash, announced he was leaving, and it appeared as though the band was finished.

"Andy had gone off to get a drink or something, and literally three or four minutes later Clive went into the toilet, so I was left in the dressing room on my own," remembers Mick Abrahams. "In walk Ian Anderson and bassist Glenn Cornick, and they said, 'We've listened to you play and our band needs a kind of guitar player like you, because our guitar player is leaving. . . . We have quite a lot of work lined up. Would you be interested in joining us?' I had already heard the band and thought they were quite good. I said, 'Well, my band has just folded up, so, yeah.'"

Abrahams trekked to Lippinsonham, just outside Blackpool in northwestern England, and rehearsed in an old church. Soon after rehearsals, the band moved their base to Luton, which was nearer to London.

In the move, some members fell away (including drummer Barriemore Barlow and Evan, both of whom would become part of the Tull story again) as the band was being booked under a variance of names: John Evan's Smash, John Evan Blues Band, the John Evan Soul/Blues Band, Navy Blue, Ian Anderson's Blues Band, Ian Anderson's Bag of Blues, Ian Anderson's Bag of Nails.

"I even suggested 'Ian Anderson's Bag of Shit,' but that didn't go down too well," says Abrahams with a laugh. "Lastly, a booker in the [Ellis-Wright] office had just done a thesis in history, and one of the people whose name . . . he'd come across was a guy called Jethro Tull."

"Jethro Tull was a nineteenth-century agriculturalist, an inventor of the seed drill and also a musician, and we all said, 'Why not?'" explains Ellis. "It was certainly better than a lot of the other names we'd tried."

"But after that, everyone thought we were a bunch of druggies, out of our heads, because of the agricultural angle," says Abrahams. "But we were the furthest thing removed from that. I don't think anybody in the band was a heavy drinker, even. But of course we played a very odd form of blues."

Thanks to some fancy financial maneuvering by Ellis, Tull had the support it needed in order to make a name for itself with its eclectic blues style and Anderson's wild-eyed stage persona. In the 1970s, Anderson's stage dress would become more elaborate, with a slight taste of the satirical, as the front man became notorious for his codpiece, earring, Mephisto beard, and knee-high boots, placing him somewhere between court jester, American hobo, wannabe pirate and English nobility, not to mention his Pan-like one-legged, flute-playing balancing act, which was the perfect counterpart for the amalgam of dirty blues, Renaissance, Elizabethan, and medieval musical flourishes the band would eventually incorporate into their folk-rock style.

A typo had the band originally recording under the moniker Jethro Toe for the MGM label (for the single "Sunshine Day"/"Aeroplane"). That was of little consequence: The band, featuring Anderson, Abrahams, Cornick, and new drummer Bunker, soon struck a deal with Island in 1968. The label released Tull's full-length debut, *This Was*.

This Was is a rich blend of styles, featuring songs such as the traditional and guitar showpiece "Catsquirrel"; "Dharma for One"; the Delta-by-way-of-British-blues "A Song for Jeffrey" (based, as are all of Anderson's "Jeffrey" songs, on future Tull bassist and fashion plate Jeffrey Hammond-Hammond); "Some Day the Sun Won't Shine for You"; Abrahams's swingin' blues "Move on Alone"; and a cover of the Roland Kirk tune "Serenade to a Cuckoo."

"After we appeared at the Sunbury Jazz and Blues Festival and released the record, we just started to tear shit up," says Abrahams. *This Was* reached number ten in Britain.

"I remember standing at the side the stage during some shows and just thinking, 'My God. They are so good,'" says Ellis, who plays sleigh bells on, "A Christmas Song," which has since been added as a bonus track to the CD version of *This Was*. "It was a good feeling to know I was working and representing people of enormous talent."

But despite the album's success, trouble was brewing behind the scenes. Abrahams was not very happy with the creative direction the band was taking, nor was Anderson (or presumably Ellis) content with Abrahams's desire for Tull to remain a hard blues-based rock band. Friction was inevitable.

"When they first started, it was kind of Ian and Mick's band," says Ellis. "So you had two focal points, because Ian was the singer and flute player, and Mick was the guitar player—and a hell of a guitar player. Really, really good. When Ian began writing his own songs, that took the focus away from Mick. So Mick got more and more unhappy.

Everybody knew that they would have to kick Mick out, because he was making life unbearable for them."

"I had a falling-out with Ian and it was a bit of an emotional time," says Abrahams, who formed the legendary blues band Blodwyn Pig. "Ian went in the direction he did and was right to do it, and I went in the direction I did, and was right to do it. Never the twain should meet."

"If you look at the bands that were playing the same circuit, and playing the same rooms above pubs that we were, a band like Fleetwood Mac," says Ellis, "they were a blues band, but they progressed. Ian just didn't want to play the same kind of music anymore."

"By 1969 our music had become more eclectic with the departure of Mick Abrahams," says Anderson. "Jethro Tull became an eclectic band by the summer of 1968 when I was writing the next lot of songs that became the second Jethro Tull album [*Stand Up*]. Then, of course, things like balalaikas, bouzoukis, and mandolins had come into the mix alongside some keyboards and a more eclectic view of the musical world. It made Jethro Tull stand out from the crowd, somewhat, because we had our own various elements of world music influences and classical music creeping into the thing at that point. We were certainly not just a blues band by the end of 1968."

In the wake of Abrahams's exit, future Black Sabbath guitarist Tony Iommi temporarily filled in, though he never played a live date. (Iommi appears in the Rolling Stones' "documentary" *Rock and Roll Circus*, but only mimes to backing tracks.) Along with Iommi, reportedly, Roxy Music/Nice guitarist Davy O'List also was tapped for a very brief time. Neither really worked out.

"We auditioned for guitarists, and Tony Iommi had come to the audition and he got the gig," remembers Ellis. "But then he wasn't comfortable with the whole Jethro Tull setting. He just couldn't get into the art rock."

A guitarist by the name of Martin Lancelot Barre had appeared during the auditions but was turned away when Tull invited Iommi to join. "Ian remembered Martin, and he was the guy who had almost made it, but not quite," says Ellis. "You know, 'Come back and all is forgiven.'"

Barre, a guitarist of great taste, passion, and (in a rare combination) restraint, was (and has always seemed to be) a musician without a giant ego, which has allowed the wild-eyed minstrel of the gallery Anderson to lead his merry musical circus through whatever artsy adventures took his fancy.

The band released the popular singles "Love Story" and "Living in the Past," a flute-heavy slice of pop-jazz in 5/4, and their sophomore effort, the aforementioned *Stand Up*, featuring "A New Day Yesterday," "Nothing Is Easy," a version of Bach's "Bourée in E Minor," and "Fat Man."

After Island rejected the band's single "Sweet Dream," Ellis and Wright decided to form their own record label specifically to release Tull's single, naming the record company Chrysalis (a name created by joining the two words "Chris-Ellis"), which would be the home of Tull for the next three decades.

"I think Jethro Tull was important to Chrysalis, and Chrysalis was important to the development of Jethro Tull," says Ellis. "Jethro Tull was certainly a unique musical talent that enhanced the reputation of the company, but Chrysalis was cutting-edge and Ian could feel comfortable in being involved with it."

Tull would continue to appear on Island, and in 1970 *Benefit*, the band's third album, emerged featuring former bandmate John Evan on piano and organ, adding still more texture to Tull's gradually growing and layered sound.

Benefit skillfully negotiates blues, folk, jazz, and hard rock throughout songs such as "With You There to Help Me"; "Teacher"; "Nothing to Say"; "To Cry You a Song"; "Sossity: You're a Woman," which, at points, plays like a Bach lute suite with nasal-ly vocals pressed on top; "Son" "A Time for Everything?"; "For Michael Collins, Jeffery and Me" (about the astronaut who orbited the moon as Neil Armstrong and Buzz Aldrin took giant leaps to the lunar surface); and "Play in Time."

While critics would later despise Anderson for forgetting his blues roots, evolving into something more than a blues singer and flautist seemed the only logical choice for him to make as an artist.

"The more progressive bands at the time—Yes, the Nice, and King Crimson—stood pretty much outside the world of blues, for the most part," says Anderson. "They certainly gave me the feeling that I could afford, in a more eclectic and folky way, to follow those rather braver musical directions than to be another middle-class English white blues band. Whilst it's served Eric Clapton over the years, it wasn't really what I felt either equipped to do or wished to do, since I am not African American or American. I think it was a bit like me trying to play some Chinese Mandarin music. It just doesn't fly, really."

"THE MOTHER OF ALL CONCEPT RECORDS"

It wouldn't be until 1971's *Aqualung* that Anderson and Tull fully developed their folk-minstrelsy approach and dove headlong into orchestral accompaniment, with songs such as "Wond'ring Aloud"; "Cheap Day Return"; "Mother Goose"; "Slipstream"; the religious fearmongering of "Wind-Up" (which addressees the concept of discovering the divine through spirituality, not dogma); and the gothic and ghoulish "My God," a scathing indictment of organized religion's power grab, which Anderson calls "an anguished cry, a song of anger derived from my first experiences challenging religion as it was taught to me when I was fourteen years old."

Anderson has always fought the notion that *Aqualung* is a concept record. "I kept saying, 'It has a title track and is dressed up with a nice, cohesive album title, album artwork, and text on the album cover and so forth'," says Anderson, "and two or three songs, you could say, hang together loosely on the subject of organized religion. But most of the songs on the record have nothing to do with the others. So it could not possibly be a concept album. However, people persisted in referring to it as a concept album at the time, and some still do."

While we can't rightly call *Aqualung* autobiographical or even 100 percent conceptual, it seems to be the first serious attempt by Anderson to organize a grand personal and political artistic statement. "*Aqualung*" is one of the rare cases in rock that raises our consciousness while not preaching to an audience, and yet makes us simultaneously grossed out and sympathetic toward a social plight. We, in a strange way, see ourselves in *Aqualung* (the subject of the title song, which features lyrics penned by Anderson's first wife, Jennie).

"When I sing the song '*Aqualung*' onstage, I hope homelessness is something that doesn't leave the forefront of my mind," says Anderson, who calls the song a "fleshed-out social documentary." "The day that I'm automatically singing the words and not thinking about them is the day I should stop singing them."

Anderson may not have thought of *Aqualung* as a concept record, but the follow-up, he says, was intended to be "the mother of all concept albums."

In pre–*Spinal Tap* splendor, Tull served up 1972's *Thick as a Brick*, a satirical, album-long suite presented with straight-faced conviction. The original LP design replicated a provincial newspaper, *The St. Cleve Chronicle*, complete with a dozen pages (with "below the fold" flaps tucked into the gate), upon which an award-winning epic poem by a fictional child literary genius, twelve-year-old Gerald "Little Milton" Bostock, was printed.

However, according to the news report on the "front page," Bostock was stripped of the stipend given to him by the Society for Literary Advancement and Gestation (SLAG) due to the disturbing nature of the poem.

Conveniently, the poem serves as the album's lyrics, containing concepts as varied as young men coming of age in British society, governmental manipulation of young minds, and pre-Christian British paganism.

"When Jethro Tull made the album *Thick as a Brick*," says Anderson, "it was with tongues firmly in cheeks. *Thick as a Brick* is a spoof album, and it is not to be taken seriously."

Anderson had spent some time apart from the music press after the release of *Aqualung*, declining requests for interviews. So it's ironic (or is it appropriate?) that he created his own alternate world (one he had complete control of) and distributed this newspaper (which even includes a review of the record) to fans as if ignoring the reality of critical commentary and inevitable prejudice by members of the British music press and, perhaps, even the public at large.

The record is all over the map, bouncing from jazz (Anderson plays sax, violin, and trumpet on the record, though he now calls brass instruments "rather rude and shocking") to some strange mixture of Celtic/Eastern European gypsy/Middle Eastern scales to orchestral percussion timbres; symphonic themes; baroque rock; a mess of odd times, military marches, and melodies; medieval-tinged lute passages; and Celtic and Old English–styled folk.

Musical concepts repeat (sometimes with variation), while the interaction between drummer Barriemore Barlow (who makes his first appearance on a Tull record), bassist Hammond-Hammond, flautist Anderson, guitarist Barre, and keyboardist Evan is fluid, making the music dense without being tedious or boring.

Thick as a Brick went to number one in the U.S., to the Top 5 in the U.K., and motivated Chrysalis to release the highly acclaimed best-of package, *Living in the Past*, in fall of 1972.

It seems Anderson and the boys just couldn't get enough of a good thing. Next, Tull aimed for a proper concept album that wasn't overtly satirical like *Thick*, but would continue in a similar vein of absurd English humor.

The band had recorded three sides of what was planned to be a double album, but circumstances conspired to keep the record from ever seeing the light of day. "It floundered in the process of making it, mainly because of illness and production problems," says Anderson. "We were working in France and abandoned that idea, and started from square one. We came back to London and wrote and recorded an album in a relatively short space of time."

The time crunch and the band's misfortune helped to produce a cynical and darker record, titled *A Passion Play*, centering on the subjects of life, death, and rebirth, following (as far as we can surmise) the journey of character Ronnie Pilgrim's soul. (The "passion play's" four acts are listed in a mock theater program, which was printed in the original LP.)

It's rock as art, clearly steering away from Anderson's own onetime admission that popular music is *muzak*. Whatever your opinion of *A Passion Play*, it demands dissection and analysis, and is another example of rock music having evolved.

Though *A Passion Play* was not as successful as *Thick as a Brick* (it has too many shifting tempos and moods, and as soon as we are introduced to one musical idea, it doesn't last long enough to be fully developed and allow for the music to breathe and groove), the album is as extreme an artistic statement as Tull would ever make.

"It's always fun—and I have to stress the word *fun*—to get into areas that are a bit unusual and a bit untrodden, bits of turf that other people haven't gone near," says Anderson. "I find that enjoyable to do because you know straight away from the title and the subject material onward you are kind of doing something that other folks haven't done, or that they may have done but perhaps not in the field of contemporary pop or rock music."

"The *Passion Play* was the first tour I'd ever seen of the band," says guitarist Guy Manning (Manning, Parallel or 90 Degrees, the Tangent). "They played in the U.K. two nights, doing *A Passion Play*, but the album hadn't come out yet. I just thought it was the most marvelous thing I had ever heard. I didn't want it to end. It was a very complicated, full presentation. It started out with a white dot pulsating on a screen. Then you saw a ballerina get up off the floor and start dancing around, and she starts to run down a corridor and dive through a window, smashing the window and the glass as the band jumps out from behind the amplifiers with a pyrotechnic puff of smoke. We felt that this was brilliant, and would put Tull right to the top of their game."

Not everyone agreed. Critics hated the indecipherable plot and (what they deemed) unnecessary elaborate multimedia stage production, which included a live-action film shown during the concert, based on the album's calculatedly mad interlude, titled "The Story of the Hare Who Lost His Spectacles," narrated by John Evan, who donned devil horns.

Evan's—or we should say, Satan's—sophistication, the Lewis Carroll–like fantasy setting, the incidental string arrangement, a prancing giant newt (and other human-sized creatures), and dancing ballerinas are more creepy than amusing, instilling a fear in us as though we've left our own bodies and have entered into a kind of hell—the exact state of mind some critics surmised they were in after witnessing the stage production of *A Passion Play*.

Because of the horrid reviews, Tull threatened to stay off the road permanently, reportedly to work on a feature-length film dubbed *War Child* (though Anderson later stated that this was a story concocted to, in part, help garner front-page news in the music magazines

Grabbing a (cod)piece of the prog-rock action: Ian Anderson of Jethro Tull. (Michael Ochs Archives/Getty Images)

and secure some time off from a killer work schedule). Anderson and the band were committed to the music and, on more than one occasion, called it the best work they'd done up to that point.

"We waited for the write-ups in the papers, and we were looking at the *New Musical Express*, the *Melody Maker*, *Sounds* in the U.K. and it was absolutely slated," says Manning. "We thought, 'We were there. How could this be? We were there.' That was a moment in time when the journalistic world had been turned, in my opinion. No longer did journalists have to be deferent to an artistic temperament. They said whatever they thought. Even

if they didn't think it, they would say it if it was provocative."

Rolling Stone magazine called *A Passion Play* "vapid," "all play and no passion," and "tedious nonsense." In a particularly damning review, *Melody Maker* quipped that the album "rattles with emptiness." Due to its opinion-leader status in the U.K., *Melody Maker* reviews were sent over the wires and replicated by newspapers on both sides of the Atlantic.

"It's rather downbeat and not very satisfying," says Anderson of *A Passion Play* after all these years. "It has its moments, but it's missing the kind of rather careless humor, the careless sort of silliness of *Thick as a Brick*. It remains the firm favorite of the most dedicated and obsessive of Jethro Tull fans. It is something of a badge of honor if you have managed to listen to *A Passion Play* twice all the way through. You deserve a purple heart and elevation to a record listener's hall of fame, or something. That kind of marks the end of that period for Jethro Tull."

What followed was 1974's *Warchild*, a major turning point in the band's career. While some of the progressive elements of the previous three albums were present, *Warchild*, undoubtedly, was the result of the critical reaction to *A Passion Play*, and the streak of conceptual (or near-conceptual) rock the band had been writing and recording since *Aqualung*.

Though the band made use of British folk motifs and symphonic arrangements by David Palmer, who'd studied at both the Royal Military School of Music and the Royal Academy of Music (and who brought to the band the scholarly world of classical and medieval music as well as musical history and theory), the songs were more accessible and shorter than they'd been in the past three years. Featuring "Skating Away (on the Thin Ice of the New Day)" and "Bungle in the Jungle," *Warchild*, having drawn on material from the ill-fated, pre–*Passion Play* double album, boasted FM radio hits and reached number two on the *Billboard* album chart in America.

"We happened to be considered progressive rock with a couple of our more convoluted and intricate pieces of music of the time," says Anderson. "It was the right thing for the time, but by 1974, it wasn't. We kind of went back to doing generally shorter songs with more traditional shape and form."

"I think *A Passion Play* was one too many," says Ellis. "Ian had done the over-the-top concept album with *Thick as a Brick*, and that was enough. Then he went back to writing songs."

Tull didn't completely refrain from self-indulgence: Nineteen seventy-five's baroque/hard rock/orchestral/folk album, *Minstrel in the Gallery*, plays like a medieval *Sgt. Pepper's*. It's really an Anderson autobiography, covering his loves, lusts, pains, regrets, shortcomings, and beliefs (such as those put forth in "Cold Wind to Valhalla"—an admission by Anderson that he's no hero, in this or any time—and the nearly seventeen-minute suite "Baker St. Muse," regarding Anderson feeling like an ordinary citizen, being squeezed by the tax man, rejected by a woman, pissed off at the press).

Yet, very much like the Fab Four, who had cloaked themselves as the Lonely Hearts Club Band, Anderson was masked by the persona of a traveling minstrel.

"I think the thing to keep in mind about the *Minstrel in the Gallery* album is that it's rather like *Aqualung*: an album of contrasts," says Anderson, who sequestered himself for a month between December 1974 and January 1975 to write the material for the record. "It is not on the same level or harping on about the same things. But *Minstrel in the Gallery* is an album of dynamic changes marked by the use of small orchestral ensembles and a lot of acoustic instruments. I think *Aqualung* and *Minstrel*, though separated by four of five years, share a bond."

With *Minstrel*, Tull had morphed into something more reminiscent of Fairport Convention, Renaissance, and Steeleye Span than King Crimson. The band would pursue this direction with more frequency and depth with 1976's *Too Old to Rock 'n' Roll, Too Young to Die!* (even though it was very much a concept record, recounting the exploits of an older greaser/a never-has-been veteran rocker who gains notoriety by appearing on a TV quiz show) and 1977's *Songs from the Wood*, a strange hybrid of classical and Celtic, and the pinnacle of this particular artistic vein. *Songs from the Wood* truly feels as though it comes from nowhere. Perhaps it does. In order to write this material, Anderson had settled into a state of mind he'd rarely visited, let alone lived, in his earlier years. Living in the English countryside with his new wife, Shona Learoyd, who was expecting the couple's first child at the time, gave Anderson new perspective on life.

Nothing in the Tull catalog matches the musical balance achieved with *Songs from the Wood*, which compiles hard-rock licks, traditional folk odd tempos, church music in the counterpoint style of Giovanni Pierluigi Palestrina, baroque trills, moments of lush orchestration (most of which were written by David Palmer), medieval minstrelsy, Renaissance dance tunes, thunderous drums (the kind found in Scottish folk music), electric blues guitar riffs, and pagan imagery that speaks directly to the past.

What we have in *Songs from the Wood* is practically a history of British popular music over the last thousand years, including the unexpected

Aqualung (1971)

A Passion Play (1973)

Songs from the Wood (1977)

A (1980)

Crest of a Knave (1987)

Roots to Branches (1995)

British holiday hit from December 1976, "Ring Out, Solstice Bells" (mostly played in 7/8 time).

"I think Ian looked back to his Scottish upbringing and Scottish folk songs," Martin Barre told the author in 2003. "We were not a unit, and we never have been. And we aren't now. We are very much five different thinking people with very different tastes in music. . . .We get on well enough musically to throw ideas around . . . and produce something that's very much [enjoyed by] all of us."

"Ian is a very sophisticated mind and a formidable intellect," says Dee (formerly David) Palmer (Palmer underwent a sex-change operation in 2004). "He could read a book and give a lecture on it the next day. The development of our style, from 1968 to 1980, was a slow but measured tread of development. In his quiet moments he used to turn things over in his mind. For instance, he never had the time for Zappa. But then suddenly he did. Captain Beefheart went on the road with us and changed his mind. When he spoke with them, he realized that they were just as intelligent as he was. At that time, in the '70s, when we all were still quite young, we were still on that learning curve. Ian would take things on and they would become part of him."

"I play only by ear: I don't read music," says Anderson. "I don't have any formal musical training whatsoever. I learned from David Palmer some things that I couldn't put a name to or couldn't quite put my finger on, and that's important."

Nineteen seventy-eight's *Heavy Horses* wasn't as dense as *Songs from the Wood*, nor was it as intense. In an era of revolving disco balls and punk's fuck-all energy, the appearance of Anderson and the boys in the photograph on the back cover of the LP, all decked out tuxes, lounging around in a carpeted room of the finest wood, leisurely sipping wine from dainty glasses, coupled with the fact that the album had been dedicated to the various indigenous breeds of hors-

es and ponies of Britain, made *Heavy Horses* the furthest thing from hip an album by a rock band could be in the late 1970s. One wonders if this were not all some form of joke again—the band's jab at themselves for being comfortable middle-class rockers.

"He and I had some words over some of, well, what I called the 'country' material," says Ellis. "*Heavy Horses*, specifically. I was not happy about that. My thoughts are, 'You're a musician, you're writer. I understand you need inspiration.' Ian, at a certain point, did what most people in England do: He went out to the country and bought a house, and that became his inspiration. I said to him, 'I don't think a kid in the projects in Detroit can relate to hunting foxes, Ian.'"

Though Tull wouldn't seriously pursue this direction again, such exchanges only served to show the divide between Anderson, his management, and his own band. Ellis didn't last long beyond the release of *Heavy Horses*—and neither did the band's progressive rock and prog folk tendencies, which were quickly evaporating in any case. The coffin was nailed shut when Tull's resident symphonic arranger, Palmer, exited.

"I've never discussed it with him . . . but I wonder whether or not with the benefit now of thirty years of hindsight, Ian ever wondered whether we could have carried on in the direction we were going and let us develop organically, rather than making oblique changes," says Palmer. "It's kind of like taking the petro engine out of a motor car and installing rubber bands and winding it up to see if it works."

In retrospect, the release of 1978's double album, *Bursting Out: Jethro Tull Live*, a fine blend of material, was the last hurrah for dense, folk-baroque rock music.

As Tull flung themselves headlong into the 1980s, the musical complexion of the band had transformed itself into a streamlined, harder-edged rock outfit to meet the demands of the time and Anderson's need for change.

What followed was strong material, just not the kind that fans had expected from Tull throughout the 1970s. Releases like 1979's *Stormwatch* and 1980's *A* (originally intended to be an Anderson solo record), which features Curved Air/Zappa/U.K. alumnus violinist/keyboardist Eddie Jobson, as well as 1982's *Broadsword and the Beast*, 1987's *Crest of a Knave*, 1989's *Rock Island*, 1991's *Catfish Rising*, and 1995's *Roots to Branches* (among others), reflected a part of the band's past prog glories, but essentially, their greatest contribution to the longevity of the band was laying the groundwork for a revamped sound (i.e., distorted heavy blues-rock guitar, aggressive flute, and powerhouse drums) that carries on to this day.

It seems "prog rock" was but one avenue Jethro Tull explored in its long and storied career. "At that time, we were creating what was our contribution to progressive rock, mainly *Thick as a Brick* and *A Passion Play*, we were just full of fun about it," says Anderson. "Yet the very parochial Englishness of the successful music of that period did fail to get across, I think, because the cultural references weren't there. The Italians took to heart this grand sort [of] serious nature to the music. I think that was probably the case in a few other countries as well. Japan, for instance. For us, it was a big fun time. It was not as serious or anal as it is considered to be these days. I think we should all try to remember that."

Minstrel in the Gallery (1975)

(Michael Ochs Archives/Getty Images)

COLOSSEUM AND GREENSLADE

For Those About to Rock . . .

COLOSSEUM—STEEPED IN THE BRITISH BLUES SCENE OF THE
1960s, with members who'd played with iconic names such as Graham Bond
Organisation, Alexis Korner's Blues Incorporated, John Mayall's Blues Breakers,
Georgie Fame and the Blue Flames—were one of the major forerunners to the
British jazz-rock movement, having evolved into one of the most groundbreaking
British underground bands of the late 1960s to mix blues, jazz, rock, and classical.

"The interesting thing is," says Colosseum drummer and founder Jon
Hiseman, "that in hindsight what we were doing kind of led to what people call
a progressive scene. We never really thought about it."

Hiseman was fascinated by jazz as a youngster—having studied New
Orleans through New York bebop—and turned his passion into professional
work, performing in the British jazz scene of the 1960s.

"I played a lot in the British jazz scene and got heavily involved in the new
wave of semi-free-form jazz, and then I got into rhythm and blues, because I
could earn money at that," says Hiseman, who'd played with John Mayall as well
as Graham Bond Organisation, replacing Ginger Baker, who was off to form
Cream with another former Bond alumnus, Jack Bruce. "So here I am in the
rhythm and blues scene, but my whole upbringing was actually elsewhere, and
then I turned professional because Graham Bond asked me to join him. Now, of
course, Graham Bond had been the leading jazz alto saxophone player in the

U.K. before he switched to play organ and sing, and Dick Heckstall-Smith, who was in his band, was one of the leading jazz saxophonists in England before he made the switch over to play blues. Jack Bruce and Ginger Baker, who had been in Graham Bond's band for three years before I joined it, both come out of the jazz business."

Fellow Colosseum members Dave Greenslade (keyboards), Tony Reeves (bass), and Heckstall-Smith were jazzmen at heart who logged serious miles with blues and R&B bands.

"At thirteen or fourteen I met Jon Hiseman and Tony Reeves at a local youth club that was connected to the church, and we started to play," says Greenslade. "That's just what we did. We were all interested in Duke Ellington, Modern Jazz Quartet, Dave Brubeck, and the British jazz scene, places like Ronnie Scott's. We'd go to hear people whenever we could. We loved jazz, really, and started playing the youth-club circuit, and they'd have these talent competitions, which we always used to win."

Greenslade gigged with a semi-pro band called the Westminster Five, took up residence in Morocco while playing in a band there, came back to England, joined Chris Farlowe and the Thunderbirds and then R&B/soul singer Geno Washington's Ram Jam Band.

Tony Reeves had been playing with John Mayall prior to Colosseum and, like Heckstall-Smith, had been let go by the British blues maven. "You're still a musical virgin unless you've been sacked by Mayall," says Reeves.

"John Mayall was a sacker," says Hiseman. "He used to change his personnel quite frequently, and he did it by firing people. The only three people I'm aware of that he never fired were myself, Eric Clapton, and Peter Green. We left."

It was during his stint with John Mayall that Hiseman decided to get his old gang together to form a new band. "John gave the band three weeks off or something, when he took a holiday in America," says Hiseman. "During that time Barbara [Thompson, now Hiseman's wife] and I went to Rome. This was in the autumn of 1968. We had been away for three weeks and it was our last couple of days in Rome and we walked up to the Forum and up to Palatine Hill and we stood overlooking the Coliseum and I turned to Barbara and said to her, 'I'll go back to London, and I'm going to form my own band, and I am going to call it Colosseum.' . . . Barbara said, 'Go for it.'"

"I was playing with Geno Washington's band," says Greenslade. "After eighteen months, I got a call from Jon Hiseman—I hadn't seen him for quite a while. He said, 'I've had it with all of these characters in the music business. I want to form a band.' He said, 'We have no idea what we are going to earn, and we have no idea what we are going to play.' But I said yes straightaway and left Geno and that comfortable income to go to a drafty church hall in Elephant and Castle in London, with Tony Reeves, Dick Heckstall-Smith, Jon Hiseman, and myself as the core of Colosseum."

"When we came to form Colosseum, first of all I picked like-minded people," says Hiseman, who also hired guitarist Jim Roche, who left after only six weeks. Hiseman replaced him with James Litherland.

The band's debut, *Those Who Are About to Die Salute You* (released through Philips's Fontana label) runs the gamut from blues to classical to jazz to hard rock, covering the shufflin' "Walking in the Park" (written by Graham Bond, previously performed and recorded with Heckstall-Smith and Hiseman), and squeezing out the jazzy baroque instrumental "Beware the Ides of March" and the funky R&B ditty "Debut," featuring a mini drum solo restating the jittery saxophone and Hammond L-100 organ melody lines.

"Basically what you had in Colosseum was jazz improvisation on top of what were blues sequences with shuffle or eighth-note feels," says Hiseman. "In a way, the whole ethos, the dialogue that takes place in jazz between the drummer and the soloist . . . I retained that dialogue."

From the word go, Colosseum were on tour, and their road work helped the band achieve a measure of success: *Those Who Are About to Die Salute You* reached number fifteen on the British albums chart, and the band's greatest work was still ahead of them.

Colosseum's sophomore effort, *Valentyne Suite*, released through Philips's new progressive rock sublabel Vertigo, was on the leading edge of British experimental popular music at the time. (Colosseum did, in fact, sign with manager Gerry Bron, and the band's debut was licensed to Philips's Fontana.)

"I told Gerry, 'I would like to re-sign Colosseum [to Philips],'" says Olav Wyper, who was general manager at Philips and spearheaded the launch of Vertigo (and later RCA's progressive rock sublabel Neon). "He said, 'Why? They will be back on Fontana and sell only a few hundred albums.' I said, 'No, they will be among the first bands released on a new label. It's going to be called Vertigo.' He agreed to that."

Before launching, the label nicked the classic Hitchcock *Vertigo* spiral as its signature image (you'll find it on any Vertigo LP, some of which are now quite collectible), the kinetic properties of which made a bold statement about the dizzyingly diverse and sometimes experimental nature of the acts they signed, such as Black Sabbath (originally Earth), psychedelic folk band Dando Shaft, Rod Stewart, Manfred Mann's Chapter Three, Uriah Heep, Jade Warrior, Gentle Giant, and others. "I was articulating what the music could do—changing your perspective," says Wyper.

The dynamic in Colosseum was beginning to shift before the recording of the next studio album, 1970's *Daughter of Time*. Tony Reeves had given his notice and left, and the band had recruited singer Chris Farlowe, who had scored a number-one hit in 1966 hit with his version of the Rolling Stones' "Out of Time" for Immediate Records.

"It was the classic [reason], really: musical differences," says Reeves. "You only have to listen to Colosseum now. Chris Farlowe is singing. That's a different trip. Mind you, he's an incredible singer, but that is not what Colosseum was about. It's never a bad thing to move on and go into new things."

Reeves may have missed a good one. For the recording of *Daughter of Time*, Colosseum had the opportunity to slow the process down a bit—to spend more time with the material before committing to it, something they couldn't do previously. However, Hiseman admits this may not have been all a good thing. "Our biggest problem was that we had gigs every night of the week," says Hiseman. "We literally would arrive in the studio at night, work until about four in the morning, roll out the equipment, and start up the motorway to get the next gig. I think we spent very little time making the first two records. We finally put our foot down and said, 'This is ridiculous.' *Daughter of Time* was a new venture for us, because it was the first time the band recorded material in the studio that was not played onstage. We never did much stuff from *Daughter of Time* onstage. It was the only true studio album we ever made."

The band's sound did change slightly, and even though the record doesn't carry the same musical impact as the previous albums, *Daughter of Time* makes for a curiously diverse and inspired affair. It seems that not only truth, but music, is the daughter of time.

Check out David "Clem" Clempson's wah-inflected and screaming blues-laced guitar work in "Three Score and Ten, Amen" and "Down Hill and Shadows," as well as Hiseman's double-kick-drum solo in "The Time Machine." While some might comment that these were prime examples of musicians "overplaying," these tracks also capture Colosseum at their most passionate.

Other highlights include the symphonic "The Time Lament," the rousing and edgy title track "Bring Out Your Dead" (listen to Greenslade on the organ and Clem on guitar playing simultaneous licks as Hiseman pounds out a beat per musical note), and the Jack Bruce/Peter Brown song "Theme for an Imaginary Western" (also recorded by, among others, Greenslade, Mountain, and Bruce himself).

"Theme for an Imaginary Western" may have served multiple purposes: It's an allegory of the life English musicians had lived in the 1960s (specifically in and around London). Some musicians left London for the world stage to find fame, fortune, and romance (and sex), and others didn't. The writer won't speculate on Brown's or Bruce's motivations for writing the song (though it may be a thinly veiled criticism of the American music industry and its impact on British musicians).

"The funny thing is that song, Cream didn't want to do it," Mountain guitarist/vocalist Leslie West recalls. "Jack Bruce wrote that song when he was in Cream and . . . Jack said that Eric [Clapton] thought the chords were a little complicated for a regular blues [song] . . . so he just kept it. He did it on his *Songs for a Tailor* album, and when we started Mountain, we were looking for material. . . ."

Colosseum also covered another Bruce/Brown song, "Rope Ladder to the Moon," which appears on *Colosseum Live*—the band's final album of the 1970s and their first for Bron's Bronze label, based on recorded performances, most from a March 18 concert at Manchester University, and the rest from a show in Brighton. (Bronze would continue to release Colosseum material even after the band had broken up.)

"We never bothered to listen to the tapes, because we all assumed they were terrible," says Hiseman. "We thought it was a lifeless, dull night. We went on to record another three or four nights. But when we listened to the tapes, takes that we thought were fan-

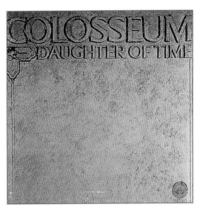
Daughter of Time (1970)

tastic were completely over-the-top. It was all too thick. Everybody was trying to play too much. It was a steam train coming at you all the time. But when we listened to the first two gigs, the first one, in Manchester, sounded fantastic."

Despite the fact that Colosseum were working more than ever, the band's days were numbered. Lacking material for another studio record, having ambition but no time to truly realize their musical visions as they were constantly on the road, doing a Scandinavian tour without singer Chris Farlowe, and watching guitarist Clempson take a job with Humble Pie's Steve Marriott spelled the end. By November 1971, Colosseum were on the precipice of ruin.

"Jon couldn't face rounds of auditions for guitar players, and quite frankly, I don't think I could have either," says Greenslade.

By the time the band was winding down, progressive rock could, and oftentimes did, satisfy fans' need for gritty, musician-friendly music. Though jazz-rock fusion was just starting to get its legs in a major way in the late 1960s and early 1970s with Tony Williams, Brian Auger, Miles Davis, Herbie Hancock, John McLaughlin's Mahavishnu Orchestra, fusion as a genre wouldn't be codified as a commercial force, realistically, until later in the decade of the 1970s. Colosseum didn't stay together long enough to capitalize on the genre's success, which was reaching new commercial heights with Weather Report and Return to Forever.

The band continued to work for over half a year after the release of the *Live* record, but no new material had emerged, except for one piece—a very long and complicated song that Heckstall-Smith recorded for his solo album *A Story Ended*, called "The Pirate's Dream."

"'The Pirate's Dream' really broke the band up, in a way, because it was a bridge too far and nobody had the stomach for it in the end," Hiseman says.

The members of Colosseum went their own ways: Hiseman established Tempest (with young guitarist Allan Holdsworth riding shotgun) with the express purpose of writing shorter (more accessible) rock and blues-based songs, only to reform Colosseum (in a way) as a funky fusion band under the banner of Colosseum II (featuring guitarist Gary Moore) and releasing groundbreaking electronic and jazz-rock material such as *Wardance* and *Strange New Flesh*. Heckstall-Smith set out on a solo career, Clempson replaced Peter Frampton in Humble Pie and Farlowe jettisoned to Atomic Rooster.

Perhaps most significantly, Dave Greenslade, half of the creative driving force of Colosseum (Heckstall-Smith being the other half), and Tony Reeves (who would go on to join Curved Air later in the 1970s) formed the band Greenslade.

"Really, if you listen to the stuff David wrote on *Daughter of Time*, that's the beginning of Greenslade," says Hiseman. "Dave wanted to go on to write more of what he had done for *Daughter of Time*, right around the

time synthesizers were starting to come in. So he went off and established Greenslade, which was a true prog rock group, really."

"Whatever the style of music was in Greenslade, it really is just what happens when you put Dave Greenslade, [keyboardist and vocalist] Dave Lawson, Andrew McCulloch, and Tony Reeves together," says Gregg Jackman, who engineered some of the early Greenslade material. "I don't suppose there was any intention of making it 'like' anything. The 'prog rock' label is likely to be put onto any music that uses rock instruments but more chords than you'll find in the average church hymn."

"Next thing we knew, we had a deal with [Warner Brothers]," says Greenslade.

Right off the bat, the band appeared to have a couple of problems: How do you have a rock band without a guitar player (even Greg Lake played guitar, not just bass, when complementing keyboard wizard Emerson), and how does a band coordinate two keyboardists without each occupying or stealing the other's sonic frequencies?

David Greenslade had always been a big Mellotron, Hammond organ, and piano (and electric piano) man, whereas Lawson was a pioneer of analog synthesizers. What's more, on some of the band's recorded material, especially those written exclusively by Greenslade or Lawson, there would only be one keyboardist featured. Problem solved.

Greenslade were a balanced outfit, with an equal division of labor, two keyboardists who were polar opposites, an extraordinary drummer, and a versatile (and tasteful) bassist. In short, the band

was a tight-knit friendly group, and one that fits squarely in the "prog rock" genre. This might sound like a backhanded compliment, but Greenslade, in the early and mid-1970s, crystallized the British prog rock movement with such albums as their self-titled debut and the sophomore effort *Bedside Manners Are Extra*.

Greenslade and *Bedside Manners Are Extra* are simply archetypal prog rock records. While this may be an ignoble prize, at least the guys were around before and while this music was becoming a so-called genre. For all intents and purposes, Germany's Triumvirat were as much a "British" progressive rock band as ELP and Jethro Tull.

The band's debut as well as *Bedside Manners Are Extra* (both released in 1973) presented a number of unforgettable and definitive tracks that delve into sci-fi concepts, inject a bit of tongue-in-cheek humor, and mix musical styles. The albums were even packaged with the requisite Roger Dean album covers (featuring a green-skinned, crimson-eyed, multiarmed humanoid creature, part extraterrestrial, part Hindu avatar). "I worked with Roger Dean at one of our rehearsals," says Greenslade. "On the back of a menu at a local pub, I sketched out an idea for a symbol, and that became the first cover. I wish I still had [the menu]. It was so popular, that cover, that I thought, 'Well, we have ourselves a brand image.' I've used it on everything after that."

By 1974's *Spyglass Guest*, the band had added Colosseum alumnus Clempson (the guitarist joined Greenslade, as he did Colosseum, for the band's third studio record).

Those Who Are About to Die Salute You (1969)

Valentyne Suite (1969)

Live (1970)

Greenslade (1973)

Bedside Manners Are Extra (1973)

Spyglass Guest (1974)

Drummer McCulloch, with rolling fills up the yin-yang, simply plays like a muthafucka on the record, delivering arguably his greatest recorded performances this side of Crimson's *Lizard*.

Thanks in part to McCulloch's command and kick-ass rhythmic approach, *Spyglass Guest* pushes Greenslade into similar jazz-rock fusion territory explored by, say, drummer/bandleader Billy Cobham and guitar master Jeff Beck. It suits Greenslade, as if this were the true reason the band had come into being.

While debate rages as to whether Greenslade was merely created in the mold of established rock bands such as Genesis, Yes, and Emerson Lake and Palmer, *Spyglass Guest* is the record—for better or worse—on which the band grew into its sound.

The one problem that plagued Greenslade was raising enough money on tour to become a viable unit. As well as the band got along—their courtesy for one another is almost boring—they weren't drawing the huge crowds of rivals and contemporaries Jethro Tull and Floyd.

"Running a band is expensive," says McCulloch. "It doesn't make money as it is, unless it is hugely successful."

Despite having a Top 40 record in *Spyglass Guest* in Britain (it hit number 34 in September '74), the band was toughing it out on the road come spring of 1975. They released one more studio record, *Time and Tide*, but the end was near. "The band was going through the point where Greenslade was off to do his own thing, and we had finished our contract with Warner Brothers, and we really didn't want to do that again," says McCulloch. "We really didn't think we would go any further than we had already gone. We asked, 'How is it going to get any better if we sign on for another five years?' Dave Greenslade was trying to get more into films, and Dave Lawson was not a great traveler— he didn't like being away a lot. We all had our reasons."

Through the end of the 1970s,

After Greenslade, bassist Tony Reeves joined the progressive rock band Curved Air, fronted by sex symbol/vocalist Sonja Kristina. (Erica Echenberg/Getty Images)

Dave Greenslade went on to release solo records, including *Cactus Choir* (featuring Reeves) and the double album *The Pentateuch of the Cosmogony*, a collaboration with fantasy illustrator/arranger/keyboardist Patrick Woodroffe (Phil Collins makes an appearance). The latter was a cross-media affair (it was both a book and double album), and its story about the creation and destruction of a planet has relevance for the twenty-first century.

After Greenslade split, many of the members found work in diverse musical fields. Greenslade stayed busy doing TV work ("I was working for the BBC, doing three series at a time," he says) and returned to recording rock music in the 1990s, looking to literature as inspiration, once again, when he recorded 1994's *Terry Pratchett's From the Discworld*, based on Pratchett's fiction novel series.

After his stints with Greenslade, Roy Harper, and Stackridge, Dave Lawson found his way to film work, most notably playing on composer John Williams's scores for the original *Superman* and *Star Wars* films (that's Lawson on ARP 2600 conjuring the sounds of an "electric tuba" for the famous Tatooine cantina scene). He became one of the leading authorities on synthesizers in the U.K. session scene and appears as a programmer on Yes's 1983 comeback record, *90125*.

Reeves, the perennial musical Renaissance man, surprisingly, found himself out of work after Greenslade split, but soon recovered. "I got to call for an audition for Curved Air," he says. "I passed."

THE CANTERBURY SCENE

In the Land of Grey and Pink

THE CANTERBURY SCENE BRIDGED psychedelia, British jazz, and what would become known as "progressive rock" through absurdist humor, healthy doses of virtuosic interplay, equal reverence for James Brown and Ornette Coleman, and a fearless sense of musical exploration.

Since the list of available musicians willing to play an often uncompromising jazz-based, avant-progressive style was relatively short, many alternatively minded artists of this Kent-based scene gravitated toward one another, establishing legendary branches of the Canterbury sound's musical family tree.

"The people who played at Canterbury made this particular noise and had a particular brain pattern, I think," adds bassist/vocalist Richard Sinclair, who was born in Canterbury but, as of this writing, lives Italy, and formed the Wilde Flowers and Caravan. "Parts of England created different styles of music. [Canterbury] is the major religious center and is the [home of] the Church of England . . . and because of that there exist certain harmonics that make a certain noise."

Ground zero for the Canterbury Scene, the Wilde Flowers (formed in 1963) culled (at various times) the talents of drummer and future cult figure Robert Wyatt, rhythm guitarist Richard Sinclair, vocalist Kevin Ayers, bassist Hugh Hopper and brother saxophonist/guitarist Brian Hopper, guitarist Pye Hastings, and drummer Richard Coughlan.

The Wilde Flowers gave rise to perhaps the most important Canterbury scene bands: the Soft Machine and Caravan, who in turn spawned such notable groups as Gong and Matching Mole.

Rampant inbreeding led to a kind of hothouse artistic weirdness, initially. But as scene musicians began to branch out to work with others, the music press (and the artists themselves, in some cases) tagged anyone involved with one of the original groups as belonging to the Canterbury scene simply by association.

"Of course, the term *Canterbury* . . . encompasses musicians who have never been near Canterbury in their lives, or ever been in England," bassist Hugh Hopper told the author in an interview before his death in 2009. "In fact, there was never very much happening in Canterbury itself—it was, and still is, a small conservative town. We had to leave it and move to London to make it."

"The Soft Machine was more jazzy and out there," adds Steve Hillage (Gong, Arzachel, Khan). "Gong were song-oriented. But some of the use of chords and melodies were quite similar. You'd hear the influence of early twentieth century French classical music, like Debussy. And, for myself, having gone to Canterbury University, it was a kind of real thing to me."

SOFT MACHINE

One of the most important bands of the Canterbury progressive music scene was the Soft Machine, formed by Wyatt, Australian guitarist Daevid Allen (who had lived with Wyatt and his mother, Honor, in Kent), Ayers, and organist Mike Ratledge.

Having taken its name from a 1966 William Burroughs novel, *The Soft Machine* (though they also performed under the moniker Mister Head), the Softs pushed their music toward the experimental and improvisational, shared bills with Pink Floyd, and created the psychedelic sound tracks to locked-door LSD parties (or "happenings") at London's Marquee Club, securing their status as one of the more innovative underground bands of the day (and even gaining a following in France).

In 1967, the band released its first single, "Love Makes Sweet Music," backed with "Feelin', Reelin', Squealin'.'" But before the Softs could even record a full-length, changes (a constant of Soft Machine's history) were occurring. Allen, whose visa to remain in the U.K. had expired, was denied reentry to Britain and was forced to remain in France.

The guitarist, of course, would go on to form the internationally and intergalactically known Gong, as Wyatt, Ratledge, and Ayers (then managed by the *Animals'* Chas Chandler, who was also looking after Jimi Hendrix) pressed on, recording Soft Machine's debut for ABC/Probe (a U.S.-only release), boasting such weird and wonderful tracks as "So Boot if at All," "Joy of a Toy," "Hope for Happiness," "Why Are We Sleeping?" "We Did It Again," and "Lullabye Letter."

The band's early music is unlike anything else in the Soft Machine catalog. Inventive and organic experimentation is expressed in hypnotic minimalism, incessant, cathartic clouds of cymbal crashes, backward sound effects, blue-eyed soul, Indian spiritual chant, blues, penetrating (and even horrifying) early proto-prog fuzz organ solos (Ratledge's Lowrey organ pumped through guitar amplification), a hint of jazz-rock fusion, and psychedelic/avant pop.

"When I was roadieing for the Soft Machine in '67, while Kevin was still on bass, the first few live gigs I heard I was knocked out," said Hugh Hopper. "The band was seriously loud, and Ratledge's fuzz organ solos could take the skin off your head. They sounded like a trapped wasp."

Growing tensions and creative differences split the band (a situation which may have been instigated by the appearance of future Police guitarist Andy Summers), and Ayers left to pursue a solo career, one that has been full of musical eccentricities, beginning with *Joy of a Toy* in 1969.

Ayers was replaced by bassist Hopper, who contributed significantly to the band's sophomore effort, *Volume Two*, which underscores the band's absurdist bent while boasting a grittier, jazz-rock pastiche compositional style, as displayed in "Pataphysical Introduction (Pt. 1)" (inspired by the French surrealist writer Alfred Jarry's concept of "the science of imaginary solutions"), "Dedicated to You, but You Weren't Listening," "Hibou, Anemone and Bear," "Dada Was Here," "Fire Engine Passing with Bells Clanging," and "Thank You, Pierrot Lunaire."

Hopper collaborated closely with Wyatt, who wrote many of the lyrics to the bassist's music. "Mainly, my joining meant that [Mike] Ratledge had more say in the music," Hopper said in 2007. "He was not a psychedelic rocker/poet like Daevid Allen or Kevin Ayers, and [he] saw his chance to move the music more to jazz/experimental and contemporary classical, his own fields of interest."

As the title of the song "A Concise British Alphabet" suggests, the Soft Machine were intent on rewriting or reinventing the very language of rock music—and, specifically, British rock music—by fusing sweet pop (and often dissonant) melodies, Indian-style chants, free sonic expression, and polyrhythmic meters.

"Well, we were definitely not trying to sound like everyone else," Hopper said. "There were a million guitar bands doing all the usual covers, and we had wider interests than just rock or just jazz."

"FACELIFT" &
ROCK BOTTOM

By 1969, Soft Machine had expanded its lineup to include Lyn Dobson on soprano sax and flute as well as most of the front line of the British jazz pianist Keith Tippett's band: cornet/trumpet player Mark Charig, trombonist Nick Evans, and alto saxophonist Elton Dean, who'd become one of the most beloved members of the Softs.

"Elton was, at heart, a jazzer," said Hopper, "and deep down a free jazzer. We had already been involved in stuff like that several yeas earlier, before Soft Machine—the trio Robert and I played in with Daevid Allen in 1963 had a lot of free playing. So Elton probably nudged us in that direction a bit."

What could be the band's crowning achievement, *Third*—a double album with one song per side—blurs the lines between composition, production, and improvisation. The opening track, "Facelift," composed by Hopper, was spliced together from performances the band gave at shows in Birmingham and Croydon in early 1970, and features Ratledge's most disturbing organ solo caught on tape to date.

Third also features "Slightly All the Time" written by Ratledge, Wyatt's "Moon in June" (which Wyatt performed virtually alone), and Ratledge's "Out-Bloody-Rageous," the opening for which was created via backward tape loops of organ and electric piano. (*Third*, like the work of the author that inspired the band's name, plays with narrative flow, cutting up the body, or bodies, of work to create a collage of sound and vision.)

After winning critical praise and scoring a Top 20 British hit in July

1970 with *Third*, Wyatt, Dean, Ratledge, and Hopper recorded *Four* in the autumn of 1970 in Olympic Studios in London, moving further from psychedelic pop and headlong into horn-drenched jazz and organ-based jazz rock with the addition of former Delivery band member Roy Babbington on double bass. (Swinging, simultaneous, and knotty melodic lines intertwine in songs such as "Teeth," "Kings and Queens," and Hopper's four-part suite "Virtually.")

Despite the record going Top 40 in the U.K., and the band's musical direction becoming more defined, Wyatt sensed that the Softs were no longer headed down the path on which they'd started. He exited, not having written a single song on *Four*.

Like Ayers before him, Wyatt would have a long career as a quirky prog-pop songwriter, one that he had already undertaken as a member of Soft Machine. (Wyatt had recorded his first solo album, *End of an Ear*, for CBS in summer 1970.)

However, after appearing on Keith Tippett's Centipede's *Septober Energy* in 1971, Ayers's *Whatevershebringswesing* (in the same year), and his own band Matching Mole's 1972 self-titled debut and *Little Red Record* (which took its name from the English pronunciation of the French translation for Soft Machine), Wyatt fell out a third-story window (in an alcohol-induced stupor at a party in London in 1973) and was paralyzed from the waist down. His 1974 album, *Rock Bottom*, recorded in the wake of the accident, is regarded as a classic of the progressive pop and rock genres.

Wyatt, now something of a cult hero, continues to write, perform, and record his own material to this day. "I've always felt that Robert was my intellectual superior," says Daevid Allen. "Robert loves the feeling of something at the point of dropping, like a tree that had been chopped but has yet to fall. He loved the feeling of the tipping point, because of the ten-

sion, and captured that feeling in his drumming as well. Robert simply was the most original, powerful influence in Soft Machine."

"DARK SWING"

With Wyatt's exit, Soft Machine moved further left of center with the addition of Aussie drummer Phil Howard, a free jazzer with the intensity of Elvin Jones and aggressiveness of Tony Williams.

Despite the undeniable brutality of Howard's bashing and the detectable glee in Dean's lyrical sax playing, Hopper and Ratledge were not altogether keen on the band's new direction and wished to return to a more structured musical repertoire.

Inevitably, Howard was given the axe, but not before he completed tracks for the band's next studio record, *Fifth*. (You can hear the Howard version of Soft Machine in all its fury performing renditions of "All White," "As If," "Out-Bloody-Rageous," and the Howard drum feature "Dark Swing" on live recordings from 1971, compiled for the Moonjune Records 2009 release, *Drop*.)

Nucleus drummer John Marshall, who had initially been asked to replace Wyatt (but was busy with Jack Bruce), was tapped. This time Marshall accepted, finishing the remaining drum tracks for *Fifth*.

But the personnel change, which proved too much for Dean (he left), presented an opportunity for keyboardist/saxophonist/oboist Karl Jenkins, who joined. However, because of Jenkins's authoritative and compositional style, Hopper began to regret bringing him in. After recording 1973's *Six*, Hopper, too, left, and the following album, 1974's *Seven*, features yet another lineup boasting bassist Roy Babbington, Ratledge, Marshall, and Jenkins.

BUNDLES

After being dropped by CBS, Soft Machine regrouped and hooked up with Allan Holdsworth (Tempest, Nucleus), one of the most talked-about young guitarists in England. The band signed to EMI's Harvest label and released *Bundles*, a true departure from the previous few records.

"The music was entirely a reflection of the people involved," said John Marshall in a 2006 interview with the author. "We wanted someone who would bring his own approach to the music, and the hope was that it would perhaps take the music in different directions. Whoever joined was not expected to conform to a strict template or replicate what had gone before. The most extreme example of that was when Allan Holdsworth joined—we completely changed the repertoire and ditched practically all the previous stuff."

But before *Bundles* was even released, Holdsworth accepted an offer to play with New Tony Williams Lifetime, and recommended guitarist John Etheridge as his replacement.

"Things were quite different in those days, and the guys they tried out were just not suitable for Soft Machine," says Etheridge. "I felt quite strongly that I could do it. If not for Allan, they wouldn't have known me, and they would have gotten a saxophonist, not a guitarist, I'm sure. Luckily, thank God, Allan left my number and they got in touch with me."

Etheridge played gigs in Europe immediately following the release of *Bundles*, and continued in Soft Machine's new direction: guitar-driven jazz-rock fusion band. By 1976, perhaps sensing that Jenkins was controlling the ship ("Karl Jenkins actually ran the band," Etheridge says, "and that created tensions with Ratledge and John Marshall to a certain extent") and that guitar solos were the rule of the day, original member Ratledge split, appearing only as a guest on 1976's studio album, *Softs*.

"[Ratledge] wanted to leave for ages," says Etheridge. "He never enjoyed life on the road. I had talked

to Hugh Hopper, and he said that Mike never enjoyed the road from the very beginning. When Mike left, he was the last original member. That was quite an issue, I think. I will say this: He wrote some wonderful songs that really had some magic to them. There's a live version of 'The Man Who Waved at Trains' [originally appearing on *Bundles*] floating around out there, and it is a lovely tune. He really had something."

ALIVE & WELL

Alive & Well: Recorded in Paris, which featured Steve Cook on bass and Fairport Convention violinist Ric Sanders, appeared in 1978, and 1981's *The Land of Cockayne*, an effort Etheridge refers to as a "Karl Jenkins project that had the Soft Machine name on it," showed signs of the band on the skids.

With few gigs rolling in, and the members pushing themselves in many different directions, the protagonists decided to go their separate ways. "Generally speaking, the band played to big audiences, and at the same time, the atmosphere in the band was not that great, to be honest," says Etheridge. "It was always was like that; always personality problems in the Soft Machine."

"Soft Machine, like every band, was made up of very different characters at all stages of its life," said Hopper (whom Etheridge once referred to as the "soul" of the band). "We all had positive and negative qualities that influenced the music."

"Soft Machine could have done so much more if there had been proper cohesion inside the group, probably if there had been a leader," adds Etheridge. "Plus, the management was just dreadful. Critics said we were not the 'real' Soft Machine. While I think there's continuity from *Third* straight through to an album like *Softs*, in a way, the critics were right: We were not the original Soft Machine. We were something different. And that made all the difference."

LEGACY

Musicians from different eras of the band's history, including Holdsworth, Hugh Hopper, John Marshall, and Elton Dean, joined forces to establish Soft Machine Legacy in 2004 (a cause championed by Moonjune Records head Leonardo Pavkovic).

After getting the project off the ground, Holdsworth left and, in a turn reminiscent of the mid-1970s, Etheridge took his friend's slot. This new lineup produced Legacy's 2006's self-titled debut and *Live in Zaandam*, as well as a concert DVD filmed in Paris.

In early 2006, Elton Dean passed away, and the band brought in saxophonist/flautist Theo Travis, who was featured on Legacy's 2007 studio record, *Steam*. Travis's "Ambientronics" brought yet another dimension to the Soft Machine sound.

" 'Ambientronics' is a mixture of delays, an octave pedal, and a looping device, whereby I play a line and spontaneously record it and send the sound you're playing down an octave or two," explains Travis. "It creates a kind of matrix, a layering of rhythmic and harmonic ideas."

Sadly, in 2008, Hopper died, leaving Etheridge and Marshall as the only surviving musicians in Legacy whose histories stretch back to the 1970s. As of this writing, Legacy had tapped onetime Softs bassist Babbington and were continuing to tour and record; labels such as Moonjune and Cuneiform commission, reissue, and unearth Softs material.

CARAVAN

Though Soft Machine were the darlings of the underground in the late 1960s and early 1970s, Caravan—whose founding members were formerly in the Wilde Flowers—began to build excitement not only owing to its previous associations, but because of its lighthearted humor (sometimes based on double entendre), tireless hard work (the band did nothing but rehearse and live in tents at Graveney, outside Canterbury, for six months before they

Early Soft Machine. *Left to right*: Kevin Ayers, Robert Wyatt, and Mike Ratledge.

Kevin Ayers:
Joy of a Toy (1969)

received a record contract), and ability to write classically inspired works that were witty and unpretentious.

Right out of the gate, guitarist Pye Hastings, bassist/vocalist Richard Sinclair, keyboardist David Sinclair (Richard's cousin), and drummer Richard Coughlan proved they were different from their Canterbury compatriots with their 1968 self-titled debut on Verve—a record that blended tricky time signatures, sweet melodies, driving (at times militaristic) rhythms, and Brit folk and jazz chord voicings in songs such as "Place of My Own," "Love Song with Flute," "Policeman," "Magic Man," "Ride," and "Where But for Caravan Would I?"

"I think the first record was a kind of mess," says Richard Sinclair. "But an interesting mess. It was good mixture when Caravan started. We all had the same goal: to make our music, write it ourselves, and make a living from it."

Though Caravan's deal with Verve led to nothing (MGM, Verve's parent label, ceased operations in the U.K.), the band was soon picked up by Decca (on their sub Deram) at the urging of producer David Hitchcock.

Produced by the band and Terry King (their manager), Caravan's sophomore record, the suggestive 1970 effort *If I Could Do It All Over Again, I'd Do It All Over You*, boasts songs that would become cult classics: the fourteen-minute extended classical-jazz-blues track "Can't Be Long Now/Francoise/For Richard/Warlock," the title track (a semi-Latin/pep-rally pop song marked by grinding organ tones and contrapuntal vocal melodies), the heartbreakingly whimsical "And I Wish I Were Stoned/Don't Worry," and the dreamy ten-minute suite "With an Ear to the Ground You Can Make It/Martinian/Only Cox/Reprise."

Though their records had yet to chart, the band's hard work was about to pay off: They were turning the heads of promoters and club owners, who were keen on booking them, and were ready to unleash 1971's seminal *In the Land of Grey and Pink*.

Featuring Richard Sinclair's "Golf Girl" (a personal song wrapped in satirical lyrical layers), the sword-and-sorcery-laced "Winter Wine," and the side-long, nearly twenty-three-minute epic "Nine Feet Underground," composed largely by

David Sinclair (the latter two as surreal and inviting as the two-toned landscape of Anne Marie Anderson's cover image), *In the Land of Grey and Pink* is seen as the band's best work.

"*In the Land of Grey and Pink* came from a real extreme [sentiment]," says Richard Sinclair. "[David] had had enough of writing, because he had done so much on the first two records. Dave was really bursting with music and really needed to get this composition out, so he wrote twenty minutes' worth. We now have 'Nine Feet Underground' because of it."

Despite the creative outlet, it wasn't long before David Sinclair left Caravan to join Robert Wyatt in Matching Mole, which was (in a strange way) more pop-oriented than Caravan. Caravan then released 1972's blues- and jazz fusion–based *Waterloo*

Lily, featuring keyboardist/piano player Steve Miller, who'd been fronting his own band, Delivery (with his younger brother, guitarist Phil Miller, and saxophonist Lol Coxhill, both of whom appear on *Waterloo Lily*).

"I'd met Steve because I began playing with Phil Miller, and the band needed a keyboard player and Steve was blues- and jazz-oriented," says Sinclair. "It was something I've never done—play pop music from jazz and blues. The music on *Waterloo Lily* was generated, really, as a collage of the band members' playing styles."

Despite the fact that Caravan were taking chances (Hastings even dared to have orchestration on the record), Miller decided that Caravan was not for him, and Richard Sinclair, wishing the band's musical path had evolved into something with more of a jazz edge, also split (within only days of Miller's untimely exit) in July 1972.

GROWING PLUMP

Caravan may have been broken, but the group was picking up the pieces (and very nicely). Determined to continue through further personnel shifts, Caravan eventually boasted a lineup that included bassist John G. Perry, Peter Geoffrey Richardson on viola and, ironically enough, returning hero David Sinclair. It was this configuration that produced 1973's *For Girls Who Grow Plump in the Night*.

It was as if Caravan hadn't missed a beat. With the addition of more synthesizers, (the ARP 2600, specifically) Caravan's music not only retained its established inane wit ("The Dog, the Dog, He's At It Again") but further pushed into progressive jazz/folk/classical territory with songs such as the opening track "Memory Lain, Hugh/Headloss," "Hoedown," the knotty "C'thlu Thlu," and the odd-tempo rousing rocker "L'Auberge Du Sanglier/A Hunting We Shall Go/Pengola/Backwards," the final section of which is a Mike Ratledge composition.

For Girls Who Grow Plump in the Night rests alongside *In the Land of Grey and Pink* in terms of its dynamism and interactivity. Caravan were simply locked in, and they capitalized on this creative cohesiveness by recording the live orchestral effort *Caravan & the New Symphonia* in 1974 (containing new material and songs from *For Girls Who Grow Plump in the Night*, which translate very well to this symphonic setting), and following it with the somewhat unfocused (but still intriguing) *Cunning Stunts* in 1975, a record that broke into the Top 50 in the U.K.—the first Caravan record to do so.

Though *Cunning Stunts* was a minor hit, it was, ironically, Caravan's last studio album to appear on Decca—a troublesome situation that kicked off an unfortunate series of events that sent the band into a bit of a creative tailspin.

While the follow-up, 1976's *Blind Dog at St. Dunstan's* (on BTM Records), just missed the Top 50 on the British charts, the trend of collecting uneven tracks into an album—a trend that (in retrospect) appeared to take shape as early as *Cunning Stunts*—was starting to take full effect. Dave Sinclair left once again and Jan Schelhaas, a future member of Camel, took over the keyboard reins.

In this configuration, the band's sound morphed into something a bit more compromised: It was far too involved to be pop and much too middle-of-the-road to be considered "progressive."

"Pye had always been pushing for that popular rock approach," says Sinclair. "He was not like his brother [Jimmy], who is a real jazzer and had played with the BBC Orchestra. I suppose you can say [Pye] was influenced by Kevin Ayers—someone who taught him to play guitar."

Caravan continued into the late 1970s and the 1980s with records such as *Better by Far* and *Back to Front*. Reuniting in the early 1990s—with Richard Sinclair, Pye Hastings,

Richard Coughlan, and David Sinclair—the band decided to have another go at it, though (of course) more lineup changes were to follow.

To their credit, Caravan managed a studio record, 1995's *The Battle of Hastings*, and have continued into the twenty-first century, most notably with an appearance at the Northeast prog rock festival NEARfest in 2002. A CD and accompanying DVD, *A Night's Tale: Live in the USA*, commemorating the experience are available.

HATFIELD AND THE NORTH, NATIONAL HEALTH

After his departure from Caravan, keyboardist Steve Miller worked with Lol Coxhill in Coxhill/Miller, and bassist/singer Richard Sinclair eventually formed Hatfield and the North (a name taken from an English motorway sign) with Phil Miller, keyboardist/composer Dave Stewart of the late-1960s/early-1970s classical rock band Egg, and former Gong and Delivery drummer Pip Pyle.

"I was really ready to leave Caravan when David Sinclair left, because he was the only chance to make [the band] move in a Hatfield-type direction," says Sinclair.

Via Virgin Records, the Hats released their jazzy and absurd 1974 self-titled debut (which is largely composed of interconnecting suites and musical interludes and features Robert Wyatt, in wordless duet with Richard Sinclair, on Phil Miller's entrancing "Calyx") and followed it up with 1975's *The Rotters' Club*, on which Dave Stewart, who'd penned complex songs such as "Lobster in Cleavage Probe" and "Son of 'There's No Place Like Homerton'" for the debut, comes into his own.

"It was a proper creative entity," says Phil Miller. "I think *The Rotters' Club* is the summation of that, actually. With *The Rotters' Club*, we worked far harder to learn the music by heart. We always rehearsed, whether there was a gig or not, and worked on original music. Dave [Stewart] became more involved in the writing and started composing music specifically with players in the band in mind."

Hatfield and the North folded not long after the release of *The Rotters' Club* as Phil Miller (later of his own band In Cahoots) went on to join National Health in 1975 with Stewart, drummer Pyle, Gilgamesh guitarist Phil Lee, bassist/vocalist Mont Campbell (formerly of Egg), and second keyboardist Alan Gowen, who'd been in Gilgamesh as well as Sunship with one-time Crimson percussionist Jamie Muir. (Interestingly, King Crimson and Yes drummer Bill Bruford was the original drummer for National Health until 1976.)

Through various personnel changes, National Health released three records of highly composed and expertly performed jazz- and art-rock material: 1977's self-titled debut, *Of Queues & Cures*, and *D.S. al Coda*. (*Playtime*, featuring a four-member lineup led by Gowen, including Henry Cow bassist John Greaves, appeared in 2001 on Cuneiform Records.)

"I'm not being humble here, but I only wrote one piece for National Health, and that didn't compare to what Dave and Alan [Gowen] wrote," says Miller. "I thought they were the cornerstone of why National Health was such a formidable beast. Alan, who unfortunately died too young in 1981 from leukemia, was a fantastic writer, and his contributions were superb. They were not impossible, but they were demanding pieces in the chord progressions and lead voicings."

Meanwhile, Sinclair had a bit of fun with the irreverently titled *Sinclair and the South* before eventually joining Andy Latimer, Andy Ward, and Pete Bardens in Camel.

"People say, 'Don't you think that the Canterbury Scene is a bit of a hoax, a myth, that it really doesn't exist apart from people trying to link various musicians?'" asks Sinclair. "I'm not sure about that. But I've tried to catalog everything I've done under 'C'—Camel and Caravan. [laughs] It's easier for people to find the music bin."

GONG: THE SPACE WHISPERERS

No longer permitted in the U.K. because his visa troubles, former Soft Machine guitarist Daevid Allen made a life for himself along the Mediterranean in the late 1960s.

"I was no stranger to Paris, as I had been there earlier in the 1960s and stayed at the Beat Hotel—a kind of vortex for writers and artists of the day—where I met Beat author William Burroughs and writer/painter Brion Gysin," says Allen. "It was intellectually challenging, and almost all of my ideas were revolutionized by living there for about six or seven months."

After a brief stopover in Majorca (more like he was run out of the country by authorities for suspicion of political insurgency), Allen returned to Paris, and Gong began in earnest in 1969.

"I was lucky enough to be an active participant in the cultural revolution in England, and I saw similar things in France, as well, with the student riots of May 1968," says Allen, who was heavily influenced by Pink Floyd's Syd Barrett (and what he calls, his "glissando guitar" playing). "By contrast, in France, there was this huge tension building up—and I was on the side of the students, of course—and it was the same cultural energy as Britain, but expressed in different ways. It was a really interesting education for me, because it represented this kind of yin and yang."

RADIO GNOME INVISIBLE

Allen strived to make music that could create a transcendent experience, a spiritual change in the world, and attempted to do so through writing songs.

In the fall of 1969, flanked by partner and vocalist Gilli Smyth, saxophonist/flautist Didier Malherbe (whom Allen had met on Majorca when the former was living in a goat herder's cave), and percussionist Rachid Houari, Allen recorded 1970's *Magick Brother*, a record full of cosmic guitar effects, Smyth's patented "space whisper," and memorable but laconic rockers, introducing us to the songwriter's knack for spinning whimsical mythological tales.

Nineteen seventy-one's *Camembert Electrique* and *Continental Circus* (the sound track to a 1971 documentary of the same title on the subject of motorcycle racing—one of a few sound tracks for French cinema Gong had recorded at the time) continued in this direction, defining and giving shape to the musical, conceptual, and mythological maelstrom that was swirling around Allen's head since before Gong was officially formed.

"The very idea of Gong—even the title—really came from Bali," says Allen. "Being Australian I related to the Balinese culture, and I saw the symbol of a gong—it's round, you hit it, and it rings for a long time—as almost like the spiritual ohm, which encompassed everything."

It was in 1973 that Allen introduced the so-called Radio Gnome trilogy (a concept that was addressed on *Camembert Electrique*), which encompasses 1973's *Flying Teapot* and *Angel's Egg*, and 1974's *You* (all of which were released through the fledgling Virgin Records).

The trilogy attempted to offer an alternative reality (a competing mystical religion of sorts, based on the global myth of the hero's journey) while combining elements of the artistic and political movements Allen most admired: surrealistic humor (of the sort similar to Alfred Jarry's political satire, *Ubu Roi*, which sparked riots in the streets of Paris in the late nineteenth century), the anti-musical performance-based Fluxus movement, and outright anarchical (though peaceful) protest.

Allen, a Beatnik and former communist turned hippie, created Planet

Gong (a largely invisible "world" inhabited by Zero the Hero, Pot Head Pixies, Yoni the witch, a magic earring, and octave doctors, which sends the people of Earth—and anyone else tuned in—positive energies and secret transmissions) as a way to subvert the accepted form of reality and offer another mental and spiritual pathway.

"I think the idea of Gong and the concept of the hero myth is about self-discovery," says bassist Mike Howlett, who came to London in 1970 from Sydney, Australia. "I think it goes along with this idea that the music—the very act of making music—can communicate something to us. The world that communicates with us, which may be an inner or an outer world, is Planet Gong."

"I've always seen Gong as a mystery school," says Allen, who briefly left the band after *Flying Teapot*, disenchanted by the business (or lack thereof) of Gong but was lured back by the band's Virgin deal. "I try to leave the concept wide open as I can, because everybody has their own spiritual path."

Gong was—and still is, judging by Allen's space-pixie stage outfits—one hell of a doozy. They've succeeded in creating their own universe, a farcical sci-fi, acid-induced world in which even the musicians in the band have been christened (by Allen) with alter egos—a kind of yin and yang.

"Didier Malherbe [sax and wind instruments] had the most beautiful name of all: Bloomdido Bad de Grasse," says keyboardist Tim Blake (aka Mr. Hi T. Moonweed), who'd written music for the Radio Gnome trilogy. "I don't think I ever called the man Didier. The sound engineer had the best name of all: the Switch Doctor. In fact, 'Switch Doctor' was the name of the first electronic tape collage experiments [Allen] did in the mid-1960s. He had worked with tape loops with Terry Riley in the early '60s as well."

Gong's music, particularly on

Angel's Egg (arguably the band's most "progressive" record) and *You*, seems to revolve in its own orbit. There's very little in the progressive rock world to compare with this musical amalgam of technically proficient runs (featuring voices doubling vibraphone tones), seductive "space whisper" effects, and billowing (and sweaty bebop) sax lines receding into a matrix of backward tape noises, spiraling spacecraft-blastoff synth sounds (enhanced by Blake's use of "ping-ponging" tape echo delays), gamelan-like bells, Terry Riley/La Monte Young–like ethnic minimalism, Hindu-ish hypnotic chants, and jazz- and blues-informed guitar riffs.

These sounds were as much a result of each individual band member's input as the dynamism of the band as a whole, which included Allen, Smyth, Malherbe, classically trained drummer/percussionist Pierre Moerlen, guitarist Steve Hillage, keyboardist Blake, and bassist Howlett.

"For *Angel's Egg*, we recorded with the Manor Mobile equipment in a forest in France in a chateau [Paviullon du Hay], and everybody seemed to be high on acid," says recording engineer Simon Heyworth. "It was a hippie commune type of environment—band members were living together—and this may have contributed to the kind of telepathic music being made."

"In a sense, Gong followed the construct of the hero myth," says Howlett, who joined the band in 1973. "Any time a group of musicians are strings on a greater instrument that are played by a higher consciousness, that's called the Octave Doctor. That's a very Jungian thing—the collective unconscious that's greater than the sum of the parts. If the musicians surrender to that, they have the possibility of making remarkable music. I think that occurred on 'Isle of Everywhere,' from *You*, for instance, where the basic tracks were done in one take. We were locked into this cycle of time changes that moved

from 4/4 to 7/8 to 6/8 to 4/4 and so on. Each eight-bar section would move up a minor third, and when we'd dropped a full octave, we'd drop a beat, changing the time signature."

"From the very first time I had jammed with Didier [Malherbe], even before I joined Gong, when I was on tour with Kevin Ayers, an electrical charge went off," says Hillage. "It all felt very natural. I didn't so much get the call to play with Gong as *heard* the call."

PIERRE MOERLEN'S GONG

Perhaps out of disappointment that *You* wasn't the commercial barn burner some expected (judging by Virgin's advertising push), or because the music business (and all of its vices) was beginning to wear on the band, or because he felt Gong could not top the musical chemistry they'd achieved on *Angel's Egg* and *You* (or maybe because he simply felt the band had accomplished its initial mission), Allen walked away from Gong for the second time in 1975, seemingly abandoning the mythology—and the faith—forever.

In his wake, most of the members dissipated: Hillage launched a solo career (which garnered such multigenre classics as 1975's *Fish Rising*, which very well could have been a Gong record, as Virgin was pushing Hillage to become top Pot Head Pixie in Allen's stead; 1976's *L*, produced by Todd Rundgren; and 1977's *Motivation Radio*. Hillage continues to work in the ambient/electronica field with his project System 7.

Mike Howlett went on to become a record producer and took up the Gong mantle (along with Malherbe, Hillage, and keyboardist and Hillage partner Miquette Giraudy, who appeared on *You*) for 1975's *Shamal* (produced by Nick Mason).

Pierre Moerlen followed in their footsteps and headed up his own version of Gong, which continued recording through the 1970s, 1980s, and even into

"There was a time in the early '70s, in France, when Magma and Gong were the two big bands," says Gong guitarist/producer Steve Hillage. "We were yin to their yang: their 'dark planet' concept was the opposite of our musical vision." (GAB Archive/Getty Images)

Gong: *You*
(1974)

the 1990s, with releases such as *Expresso, Gazeuse!, Expresso II, Downwind, Time is the Key*, and *Breakthrough*.

"Pierre went off into that sort of perfectionist jazz-rock thing—a bit like my old band, Soft Machine, did—and he obviously wanted to put all the studying in classical percussion he did at the Conservatoire Régional de Strasbourg somewhere," says Allen. "You know the old saying: Trust in God but tie up your camels first.' . . . I think you need to tie the camels. That is, you really need to know how to play. But then you have to leave enough space empty and let the wind carry you."

THE OCTAVE DOCTORS RETURN

To the delight of true believers everywhere, Allen would periodically continue activities under the Gong banner or some approximation of such (he recorded and gigged with Planet Gong and then New York Gong with members of the band that would

become Material—Bill Laswell, Michael Beinhorn, and Fred Maher) with such releases as 1980's *About Time*, 1989's *Gongmaison*, the 1992 official Gong release *Shapeshifter* (episode four of the Radio Gnome series), 2000's *Zero to Infinity* (part five of the series), 2004's *Acid Motherhood*, and 2006's *I Am Your Egg*.

Veteran members of Gong have been gigging together since 2006, but it wasn't until 2009, with the appearance of *2032* (the year, according to Gong mythology, that the Octave Doctors return and Pot Head Pixies spread joy of the new age across the globe), that a full-blown reunited band—featuring Allen, long-time partner Smyth, Howlett, Malherbe, Hillage, Giraudy, and new members drummer Chris Taylor and saxophonist/flautist Theo Travis—made its biggest post-'70s splash. (Moerlen, sadly, died in 2005, and personal and creative issues have kept pioneering synth man and sometime Hawkwind

member Tim Blake away.)

"We were sort of sucked back into it—back into the energy," says Hillage, who produced and mixed *2032* for the band's indie label, G-Wave Records. "Daevid had a big burst of energy and came up with another episode of the story."

Allen's strangely alluring musical vision has not lost its impact and has been championed by the trippy/electronica band Massive Attack (and Gong were invited to open their Meltdown festival in June 2008 in London). Radio Gnome and the music of the trilogy have left a lasting impression on prog rock and listeners in general—even if the Gongmeister thinks otherwise.

"Everyone says, 'Daevid, when you pop your cork, no one will be able to replace you,'" Allen says. "Well, I don't believe that. When there's a vacuum, it gets filled. It may not be the same thing as [it] was before, but it allows energy to continue."

Soft Machine: *Volume One* (1968)

Soft Machine: *Volume Two* (1969)

Soft Machine: *Third* (1970)

Khan: *Space Shanty* (1972)

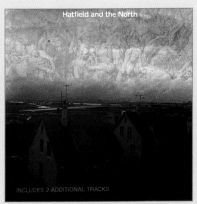

Hatfield and the North: s/t (1974)

Gong: *2032* (2009)

Caravan: *If I Could Do It All Over Again, I'd Do It All Over You* (1970)

Caravan: *In the Land of Grey and Pink* (1971)

Kevin Ayers: *The Confessions of Dr. Dream and Other Stories* (1974)

(Estate Of Keith Morris/Getty Images)

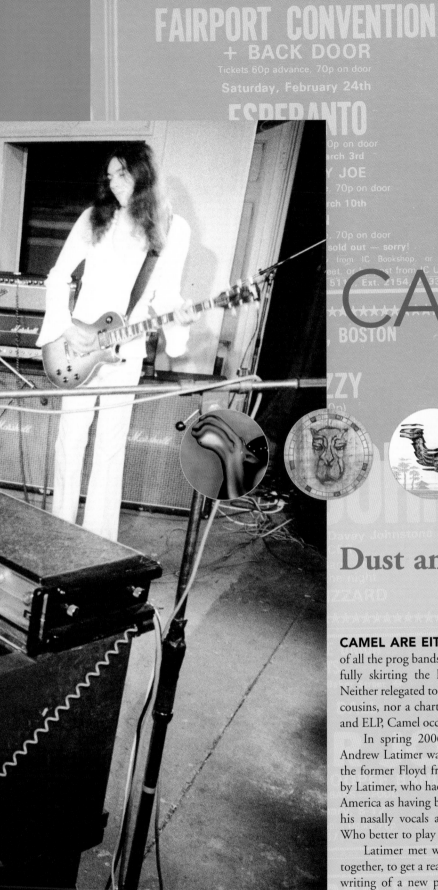

CAMEL

Dust and Dreams

CAMEL ARE EITHER ONE OF THE MOST HAPLESS of all the prog bands or easily the best example of a band successfully skirting the laws commonly governing the music biz. Neither relegated to cult-band status, like their Canterbury scene cousins, nor a chart-topping success story, like Pink Floyd, Yes, and ELP, Camel occupy a strange musical territory all their own.

In spring 2006, Camel guitarist, mainstay, and founder Andrew Latimer was invited to perform with Roger Waters for the former Floyd front man's world tour. Waters was intrigued by Latimer, who had been known around England, Europe, and America as having been influenced by David Gilmour, owing to his nasally vocals and passionate, blues-inflected guitar solos. Who better to play classic Floyd material?

Latimer met with Waters and the two agreed to perform together, to get a read on each other's musical temperature. "The writing of a new project is progressing well, but as you have heard, there's been a few distractions," Latimer wrote in an e-mail to fans and interested parties. "Hearing from Andy Fairweather Low and consequently meeting Roger was an extremely enjoyable experience. It all happened very quickly, and before I knew what was happening, I was playing

Camel, 1977, mimicking Floyd's *Ummagumma*? *Left to right:* Andy Ward, Pete Bardens, Andy Latimer, and Richard Sinclair. (Courtesy of Deram)

Rain Dances (1977)

'Comfortably Numb' at full blast somewhere in London.

"The band sounded great, and then . . . Roger asked me to belt out 'Breathe.' Singing softly, I could manage it, but needing to belt it out was a whole other story. I did a fairly croaky rendition but the cruncher was 'Wish You Were Here.' Roger, forever the quintessential Englishman, smiled and said, 'Bit high for you?' We talked for quite a while. What a nice chap he is, very easy to talk to. I felt like I'd known him for ages."

As run Latimer's and Camel's luck, though, the guitarist didn't get the gig.

But had it come off, it would have been a hard-core prog fan's wet dream—a unification of pupil and teacher; vindication for all the years Camel had flown just below the radar. Yet the circumstance is of just the sort to which Camel fans have grown accustomed and have accepted as another round in the band's good fight.

"We're considered progressive by default, really," Latimer told the author in 2003. "I don't mind. I am quite pleased, although I don't really think of us as a progressive band. Camel was a band that maybe did more instrumental music than most. That was what it was. It's kind of interesting to me, because I always thought that people like Yes and King Crimson and ELP were much more obscure than Camel. They were probably better players and consequently got into much more complicated material, which made it even more obscure, less accessible."

Still, jazz- and Latin-tinged rhythms did show shades of experimentation. Unfortunately, the market wasn't ready for another Santana-ish or a half-baked, sometimes-focused, emerging progressive band with psychedelic lean-

ings. Camel's self-titled debut only sold five thousand units, a quantity too low for MCA to justify keeping them on their artist roster. When MCA declined to pick up the contractual option for a second record, Camel roamed free for weeks until manager Geoff Jukes signed them to his own Gama Records, a deal that led to a contract with Decca.

In November 1973, the band settled into Basing Street Studios to record *Mirage*. Producer David Hitchcock had been exposed to the more absurdist strain of British prog, having recently finished sessions with Caravan (1972's *Waterloo Lily*) and Genesis (*Foxtrot*). While Camel displayed no real sense of overarching irony, Hitchcock nonetheless seemed to tap the band's ability for more expansive songwriting (e.g., Latimer's nine-plus-minute Genesis-style epic "Nimrodel/the Procession/the White Rider," inspired by J.R.R. Tolkien's *The Lord of the Rings*.)

Having spent the better part of the previous year and a half on the road with Barclay James Harvest and Wishbone Ash, Camel had a better idea of what worked and what didn't, and were familiar enough with their own songs to nail transitions and even take chances in the studio.

After playing their new material to generally receptive crowds, Camel released *Mirage* in March to a bit of controversy. The cover design was intentionally created to ape the graphics used on Camel-brand cigarettes. Sensing an opportunity, the band's management struck a sponsorship deal with the European branch of Camel cigarettes. The crossover marketing plan included such campaigns as five-pack minis featuring the record's track listing. Despite the European division of Camel taking to the idea, their American counterpart wanted nothing to do with the rock band.

"When we first did it, the European company of Camel loved the idea," Latimer said. "They thought we would just gain a whole bunch of new audiences. Of course, America, at that stage, wanted Camel to be a respectable cigarette that only a healthy gentleman or rugged guy might smoke. They didn't want teenagers, or anything to do with pop music. So they put a stop on this right away."

Nonetheless, by November '74, *Mirage* had entered the *Billboard* album chart at number 149, and on the strength of the material, the band was getting calls for gigs throughout Europe and was booked for a short tour of the States.

The follow-up, *Music Inspired by the Snow Goose* (a concept album based on the short novel *The Snow Goose*, by author Paul Gallico), "was still in its infancy," Latimer remembered. "We had just finished writing it and we weren't 100 percent happy with it. We had recorded some parts and had gone off and done this mammoth tour. It was only supposed to be a six-week tour, but I think it turned into a three-month tour, backing Wishbone Ash and doing about fifty states. It was a mind-boggling thing for a band like us. It was our first time in America. We were opening for people like Kiss, Steppenwolf, MC5, Ted Nugent—a lot of strange people. Every time we did something like 'Mystic Queen' or a slower ballad, people would shout out, 'Fuckin' rock 'n' roll.' So we started to tailor our set to include some fast numbers."

Camel heeded the feedback the American audiences were handing the band and incorporated changes to their Snow Goose songs.

In a surprising move, Camel dispended with vocals and went for broke, creating an album-long, virtually instrumental suite.

"The record company freaked out when they first heard the record because it was just one piece of instrumental music," Latimer remembered. "They were saying, 'Hey, how can we sell this shit? How can DJs play it on the radio?' There weren't even grooves in between the tracks. . . ."

Nonetheless, Camel defended their creative vision, and their steadfast resolve proved to be correct. *The Snow Goose* stayed one, long instrumental suite and, ironically, tracks such as "Flight of a Snow Goose" and "Rhayader" were released as a single in May '75, the band's first "sides" for Decca. Despite Gallico's efforts to clamp down on the band's usage of the title *The Snow Goose* (Camel eventually inserted the phrase *Music Inspired by . . .* to avoid a legal mess), the album entered the British charts and went to number twenty-two. And, despite the label's resistance, the LP broke overseas, as well, into the American *Billboard* charts at number 162.

"We were all a bit freaked out after the *Snow Goose* album," Latimer said. "When you get success of that sort, I don't know, we were voted 'Brightest Hope of the Year' by *Melody Maker* magazine in England. We did the album with the London Symphony Orchestra. After all of that success, you know, you say, 'What should we do now? What should we do?' We talked about it endlessly."

Eventually the band arrived at another concept—sort of—a kind of command performance that hinted at the greatness of the last record without repeating it. "We decided what we would do [was] . . . something based on the individual members of the band," Latimer said. "Instead of doing . . . *Son of Snow Goose*, which most intelligent people would probably do, we decided to do something completely different, and we did *Moonmadness*."

Latimer was at his jazzy, Santana-meets-David-Gilmour best. "Lunar Sea" and "Chord Change," both from *Moonmadness*, are prime examples of

Latimer's guitar greatness; surely he is one of the most underrated guitarists in all of prog rock, squeezing out solos, seemingly on the fly.

"*Moonmadness* has a much more open feel, and maybe [that is] because we didn't have time to mess it up," Latimer said. "We just went in and did it."

Given the time frame for recording—just a few weeks —it's shocking how sophisticated the music is. *Moonmadness* also benefits from at least one memorable gimmick—an endless groove is cut into side two, thus not allowing a turntable's arm to disengage.

Moonmadness can be placed squarely within the tradition of elite prog records of its day. Yes's *Fragile* was compiled and composed by five individual band members in a piecemeal fashion, yet became one of the band's most popular—and enduring—efforts. Similarly, *Moonmadness* was not a wholly planned effort comprised of individual artistic expressions. And, as Yes's work did for that band, *Moonmadness* sheds light on Camel's collective creative process. It was evident that the quartet had logged some serious miles on the road and were comfortable trusting one another's musical instincts. *Moonmadness* reached *Billboard*'s Pop Albums chart, coming in at number 118 in the U.S. and number fifteen in Britain.

By the end of March '76, as the band hit the road in support of *Moonmadness* (with saxophonist/flutist Mel Collins in tow) Camel had begun to come apart at the seams. Though the band was winning fans, the good reviews couldn't alleviate the tension between drummer Andy Ward and bassist/vocalist Doug Ferguson, which had finally come to a head. Ward simply told Latimer, "It's either him or me." Knowing Ward was the more musically competent of the two, Camel backed Ward.

It was difficult for Latimer, a close friend of Ferguson since his teenage years, but he dropped the boom on him, and the bass player was sent packing.

To stop the Camel ship from going adrift, the remaining three members of the band (Latimer, Ward, and keyboardist/songwriter Peter Bardens) agreed to bring in Richard Sinclair of Caravan, Hatfield and the North (which had recently dissolved), and the granddaddy of all Canterbury scene bands, the Wilde Flowers. Since the Hats' split, Sinclair had pursued a number of different ventures, from a musical equipment business to the short-lived band Sinclair and the South—a kind of twisted reference to the Hats.

Sinclair began asserting himself immediately after joining Camel in 1977: Caravan and the Hats were always interested in exploring the jazzier side of things as well as the more ridiculous and unadulterated aspects of rock songwriting, and Sinclair had a mind to bring these elements to Camel.

"It was probably a reaction against *Moonmadness*," Latimer said, "but we wanted to do more concise material, and we also wanted to get into jazzier areas. Richard could play all the jazz things we wanted—and some of them were quite complex."

The band spent months at Island Studios, tinkering with already written material and developing new music for what would become *Rain Dances*, their fifth studio record.

Rain Dances entered the U.S. *Billboard* charts on November 12, 1977, stayed there for five weeks, and peaked at 136 on the LP chart. (Over in Britain, the band scored a Top 20

hit with the album.) Further vindication came in the form of sold-out British dates, which were followed by a continental tour.

But with increasing regularity, it seemed, Camel were becoming a studio band. This was the era of new wave and punk, and with 1978's *Breathless*, Camel were slipping further down the path to becoming a streamlined, cybernetic band manufacturing the kind of sterilized prog-pop perfected by the Alan Parsons Project. (Appropriately, APP's 1977 record *I Robot* played on a well-trod sci-fi/progressive motif: that of man usurped by his own machines.) But if Camel did briefly stare directly into the abyss, the band never *completely* lost its soul. There was still plenty of emotion in the tracks.

Still, shellacking the LP with production gloss ("Summer Lightning" is rescued from sinking to disco-rock sap only by Latimer's burning outro guitar solo) couldn't mask the interpersonal pettiness undulating just under the surface.

It was during the recording of *Breathless* that Bardens officially announced he was leaving the band, due to creative differences with Latimer. He'd agreed to stay only to complete the LP, but touring and future recordings were out of the question.

After his time with Camel, Bardens was buoyed, perhaps exclusively, by his skill as a keyboardist. He hooked up with Them buddy Van Morrison for the recording of the latter's 1979 record *Wavelength*, then released a solo record, *Heart to Heart*. It wasn't long before Alan Parsons

Project stalwart Eric Woolfson invited Bardens to join Keats, a band formed by APP members when *not* working with the Project, a side project featuring members of APP.

In the mid-'80s, Bardens finally achieved that elusive hit record he'd been chasing. His "On the Air Tonight," recorded by blue-eyed soul man Willy Finlayson, the Scottish guitarist/singer formerly of Meal Ticket, became a Top 20 hit in 1984. Subsequently, Bardens released three solo records; his 1994 album *Big Sky* featured Mick Fleetwood.

Fans long held out hope that Latimer and Bardens would put aside their differences and renew their musical partnership. Peter Bardens died in January 2002 from complications of a brain tumor.

CAMEL: RESURGENCE

With Bardens gone, Camel recruited a cast of new musicians—opening what would become a revolving door of talented but constantly changing personnel.

Recorded at Trevor Morais's Farmyard Studios just north of London, in the green, leafy suburb of Little Chalfont, *I Can See Your House from Here* (the title taken from a very bad joke about crucifixion, which was oddly represented by a crucified astronaut on the LP cover art) was produced by Rupert Hine (who had recently finished recording with ex-Genesis guitarist Anthony Phillips and with Scottish prog-pop band Café Jacques, and who had just completed his own influential solo studio production single "Snakes Don't

Camel
(1973)

Mirage
(1974)

FMusic Inspired
by The Snow
Goose (1975)

Breathless
(1978)

I Can See Your
House From Here
(1979)

Curriculum Vitae
(DVD, 2003)

Dance Fast," which was reportedly constructed solely of vocal noises).

I Can See also featured Phil Collins on percussion; two new keyboardists (Caravan's Jan Schelhaas and Kit Watkins, formerly of American prog rockers Happy the Man); bassist Colin Bass; orchestral sections (recorded at George Martin's AIR Studios in London); a beautiful, slow-moving and bluesy ten-minute instrumental called "Ice"; and funky electronically sequenced rhythms, proving Camel were willing to collaborate with outside artists and keep up with music technology to effect different sonic flavors in their progressive rock.

By the end of October 1979, *I Can See Your House From Here* had reached number forty-five in the British charts. Into early 1980, Camel released singles, though the mainstream public largely ignored them. Unhindered, Camel were already onto the next project, *Nude*, a concept album based on the true story of a Japanese soldier who was stranded on an island in the Pacific, years after WWII had ended.

"I think this period was the beginning of some disintegration of the original energy of the band," says Bass. "It seemed everything was going off in different directions."

Nude marked the end of an era and the first true sign that Camel would never be the same again. After recording was finished, drummer Ward had called it quits. "I didn't so much leave Camel [as] fall off," said Ward in the DVD *Camel: Curriculum Vitae.*

Ward would soon briefly join Marillion, leaving Latimer as the only original member of the band, making Camel more the "Andy Latimer Project" than ever. As such, whatever Latimer said pretty much went. That prospect, in and of itself, didn't seem such a bad proposition.

"You must change," Latimer said. "I think most of us do. You have to change. I think that goes for people like King Crimson, too. You have to go and

The back cover of Camel's 1976 record, *Moonmadness*. *Left to right*: bassist/vocalist Doug Ferguson, keyboardist/vocalist Pete Bardens, drummer/vocalist Andy Ward, and guitarist/vocalist/flutist Andy Latimer.

experiment or else you'll go crazy. For me, personally, I have to keep on doing as many diverse things [as] I can."

Camel were dormant for most of the second half of the 1980s, largely due to near-crippling legal wrangling with former manager Jukes over songwriting royalties. Latimer moved to America in 1988, established a new label (Camel Productions), and kickstarted the band for the 1990s with strong efforts such as 1991's *Grapes of Wrath*–inspired concept record, *Dust and Dreams*, and 1996's tale of Irish immigration, *Harbour of Tears*.

Camel were experiencing a resurgence of interest in the 2000s when things came to a screeching halt. Latimer has been a strong character, in and out of music, and, God willing, he'll be back recording, touring, and delighting longtime and new fans

Stationary Traveler (1984)

alike, doing what Camel does best: surviving against all odds. As of this writing, Andy Latimer was living in England and recovering from stem cell transplant surgery.

(Michael Putland/Getty Images)

GENTLE GIANT

On Reflection

FORMED BY THREE BROTHERS, DEREK, RAY, AND PHIL
Shulman (who were all born in Scotland but raised in Portsmouth, England), Gentle Giant created intricate and multidimensional compositions that stand as some of the most complex music in progressive rock.

Though never as popular as their British prog compatriots Yes, ELP, and Genesis, Gentle Giant gained a loyal following through intense touring and memorable performances, just as they've served as inspiration for younger rockers, who'd one day stand on their tall shoulders to grab their own piece of prog history.

Prior to forming Gentle Giant, the brothers played in bands such as the Howlin' Wolves and the Road Runners and the blue-eyed soul/R&B group Simon Dupree and the Big Sound, which scored hits with the Eastern- and Mellotron-tinged 1967 psychedelic pop tune "Kites," the Top 40 British LP *Without Reservations*, and 1968's "For Whom the Bell Tolls."

There wasn't really a Simon Dupree, but Derek Shulman assumed his identity, just as the band began recording under yet another pseudonym, the Moles, a marketing ploy hatched by the brothers to make people think they were actually the

Beatles incognito. (This charade came to an end when Syd Barrett revealed that the Moles, not the Beatles, were indeed Simon Dupree.)

Simon Dupree soon discovered that writing and recording a hit record, especially one that was not indicative of the band's music, was the wrong type of success. "By default, we turned into a hit-single band," says Derek Shulman. "Therefore we started to play to audiences that weren't much bigger, and we weren't making that much more money, but the audiences were expecting hits as opposed to involvement."

The Shulman brothers became increasingly uncomfortable with being a pop band and wanted to write more serious music. The boys even turned down the possibility of stardom by refusing to work with material written by Simon Dupree keyboardist Reg Dwight—the future Elton John—and his friend Bernie Taupin.

"[Elton] actually wanted to join . . . Gentle Giant," says Shulman. "He'd played us things like 'Your Song' and 'Skyline Pigeon,' and myself and Ray said, 'Nah. Next. That's not going to work for us.' We wanted nothing to do with anything resembling a hit-making machine."

ACQUIRING THE TASTE
Simon Dupree folded, and Gentle Giant, whose name was inspired by François Rabelais's sixteenth-century work *Gargantua and Pantagruel* (a book Phil had read), formed in 1970. Along with the brothers Shulman (lead vocalist/saxophonist Derek, bassist/violinist Ray, and saxophonist/trumpeter Phil), Giant featured keyboardist/percussionist Kerry Minnear (a composition major who had attended the Royal Academy of Music with a concentration in piano and percussion), guitarist Gary Green (a blues rocker who'd been in a North London–based band called Fishhook), and former Simon Dupree drummer Martin Smith.

Encouraged by then-manager Gerry Bron to experiment, Giant

exploited the fact that they featured multi-instrumentalist members. "We had a group of characters who were generally good musicians and well trained and from different worlds," says Derek Shulman. "Ray was a classically trained violin player but also loved jazz. I was a singer, a pop singer, and had learned to play saxophones. Phil played trumpet and sax as well. Gary was an incredible blues player with incredible technique."

In 1970, the band recorded their self-titled debut album (appearing on the Vertigo label) with producer Tony Visconti (who Shulman says "introduced us to the recorder," an instrument the band later used onstage for "recorder quartets").

While Shulman admits that the band, during the writing and recording stages, behaved more as six individuals than as a single creative unit, the album is rarely ponderous, despite the fairly long compositions and many different elements the band stirs up.

Songs such as "Giant," "Isn't It Quiet and Cold?" "Alucard," "Why Not?" and "Nothing At All" display the band's multicolored stripes proudly, with church organ textures, bluesy guitar riffs, layered harmonies (four of the six members sing on the record), synthesizer-driven jazz-rock, touches of "early music" (at this time, composer/bassoonist/pianist/recorder player and professor at the Royal Academy of Music David Munrow was instrumental in a rebirth of interest in European Renaissance and medieval music), a flair for rhythmic bombast, and chamberlike retro-pop.

"We were babies on the first record," says Shulman. "Where it was going to go, we had no clue."

By the band's sophomore record, 1971's *Acquiring the Taste*, Giant had expanded upon and improved its sound to include Renaissance hymns (à la Palestrina and Holst, both Minnear influences), counterpoint vocal structures, backward audio snippets, orchestral drumming and percussion, angular musical sections (à la Bartók), rapid changes of complex tempos, a hint of

medieval balladry, intricately interweaving baroque musical lines, and Green's ever-present blues guitar grit in songs such as "Pentagruel's Nativity" (another reference to Rabelais), "Edge of Twilight," the title track, "The House, the Street, the Room," "The Moon Is Down," and "Plain Truth."

"Ray was the younger brother," says Kerry Minnear, "and he was the one who was musically most creative, in my opinion. Phil had great ideas, but most of the musical lines came from Ray. I remember he always wrote awfully difficult keyboard parts, too: The [finger] spacings would be different for every chord. In the earlier days, especially, Ray would write a line and then write another over the top of it. Yet, it wouldn't be parallel in any way. It could be totally independent. 'Pentagruel's Nativity' is an example of working together: I'd written the middle part, with the guitar riff and the strange vocal harmonies. Ray wrote the first section of the song, and I continued it."

Though Visconti is credited as producer of the record, the band believed they had enough experience under their belts to claim ownership of important musical decisions, a trend that would continue throughout the 1970s.

"[Visconti] was around on the second album but really was not involved at all," says Derek Shulman. "We said, 'We can do it ourselves.' We were quick learners. Ultimately, I think, we learned fairly well."

THREE FRIENDS & OCTOPUS
However, this teamwork approach was soon shattered when the band asked drummer Martin Smith to leave in favor of Malcolm Mortimore, a more technical player, influenced by jazz-rock fusion of the day (from the Mahavishnu Orchestra to drumming legend Tony Williams), who appears on the band's third release, the 1972 concept record *Three Friends* (the band's first record issued in America, via Columbia).

"I believe the actual concept was

Gentle Giant's big talent. *Left to right*: Derek Shulman, Ray Shulman, John Weathers, Gary Green, and Kerry Minnear. (Courtesy of Chrysalis)

Phil Shulman's," says Mortimore. "The story follows three friends from their early days at school to adulthood and shows how their lives are both different and strangely parallel. [Of] the three friends, [one was] an artisan, working all day; the second was a go-getter, a very ambitious materialist; and the third an artist."

Within the strict confines of thematic structure, Giant produced what may be its greatest work to date, with startling compositions such as "Prologue," "Peel the Paint" (check Green's guitar solo here), "School Days," and "Working All Day," among others.

"*Three Friends* was like our adolescent years," says Derek Shulman. "We weren't mature, but we weren't children anymore. But the music was quite good. I can say that without any compunction."

"Prior to forming Saga, the drummer in the band I was in bought an import LP from across the pond," says longtime Saga vocalist Michael Sadler. "He put the album on and after side one was done I said, 'I want to make music like this.' It was *Three Friends*. I had never heard anything like it in my life."

The band was all set to tour the record in America, marking Giant's first appearance in the U.S., when Mortimore was involved in an unfortunate motorcycle accident.

"Instead of allowing Malcolm to take some time off and get another drummer for the tour, my brother Phil said, 'If you want to be in the band, you have to be on this tour,'" remembers Shulman. "Phil made him strap a stick to his cast. When I think back on it, that was totally hilarious and spiteful. But such was life in the 1970s."

Mortimore simply couldn't continue, and the band hired touring drummer replacement John Weathers, largely a British R&B drummer, who'd spent some time as a teen playing in Liverpool-based Merseybeat bands and had played with Eyes of Blue, Pete Brown and Piblokto, Wild Turkey, and Graham Bond's Magick Band in the early 1970s. (An interesting side note: Just before Weathers joined, Crimson's Michael Giles jammed with Giant but declined the gig.)

"Then I got a call from Phil [Shulman]," says Mortimore. "He said that John [Weathers] was getting on really well with the band and was going to stay. I knew that page had turned, if you like. Once I got better, funnily enough, I wound up working with [Weathers's] old band— the Grease Band with Henry McCullough."

"Malcolm was a technician bar none," says Shulman. "But since the orchestration of the music was pretty complex, we needed someone to keep the middle ground."

That's exactly what Weathers had done for Giant: he banged out appropriate accents while pinning down the arrangements so listeners could have a deeper understanding of and appreciation for the music.

"John's playing style changed the way I wrote from [1973's] *Octopus* onward," says Kerry Minnear. "I gave more credence to the fact that he could hold things down, which allowed me to take the music into more complex directions."

Giant was an embarrassment of riches on all levels: *Octopus* brought not one but two cover designs. The British Vertigo release featured an iconic Roger Dean image, while the U.S. Columbia Records edition was cut in the shape of a jar. "The idea for the U.S. version, illustrated by Charles White III, was actually mine," says Shulman. "I bought an octopus in a glass canister in San Francisco and thought that would make a great cover image, and gave the concept to the record label, and they went with it. It cost a fortune."

Octopus was a triumph, further developing the band's approach (some would say even streamlining it) and sharpening the music's production quality (in part due to the stellar work of engineer Martin Rushent) with songs such as "The Advent of Panurge," "Raconteur Troubadour," "A Cry for Everyone," "Knots" (a "latter-day madrigal," says the band, that was influenced by British psychologist R. D. Laing, author of *The Divided Self*, investigating notions of normality and madness), the instrumental "The Boys in the Band," the drumming extravaganza "River," and others.

"'Knots' is so highly contrasted, and that is what I've always loved about prog," says Transatlantic and former Spock's Beard vocalist/keyboardist Neal Morse. "Even more than classical music, in my opinion, because you've got the heaviness of the electric guitar."

On an Italian tour to support *Octopus*, Phil Shulman, ten years Derek's senior (Ray is the youngest of the three Giant brothers), decided to leave, placing his personal life ahead of the music, opening a rift between his brothers that would not mend for years.

"The three Shulman brothers were serious about what they were doing," remembers Jethro Tull's Ian Anderson, who toured with Giant in Europe in early 1972. "The only one who had a bit of a sense of humor, back then, about what he did was the elder brother, Phil, I think. They would have furious arguments about [the music] when they came offstage in the dressing room, screaming and shouting because someone played a wrong note."

THE POWER AND THE GLORY

Oddly, without the presence of a major conceptualist like Phil, Giant appeared to grow stronger, having signed with Capitol Records, just as Minnear and Ray Shulman were turning in some of their finest work to date on such albums as 1973's *In a Glass House* (not released at the time in America) which opens with "The Runaway," a track that features the sound of shattering glass—a cacophony that coalesces into a pleasing rhythmic pattern ("That was a carefully looped sound effects tape," says Minnear); the 1974 concept record based on the idea of corrupted ideals, *The Power and the Glory* ("Each song was developed as an individual piece," adds Minnear, "and only the final song, 'Valedictory,' taking the theme from the opener 'Proclamation,' indicated a complete musical circle"); and 1975's *Free Hand*.

"When I heard *Free Hand* for the first time, I just totally got into the song 'Just the Same,' just the band's sense of rhythm, and the counterpoint vocal melodies of 'On Reflection,'" explains Dream Theater keyboardist Jordan Rudess. "I was studying to be a classical pianist and was seduced by Gentle Giant. While others were rebelling to

Black Sabbath, Gentle Giant played my songs of freedom."

Giant may not have been in the same sales category as Yes and ELP, but they were generating a serious buzz in America and Europe with their live show, which featured a multiple-member percussion assault, called the Drum Bash, among other spectacular stage antics. "I saw Gentle Giant a lot of times," says 21st Century Schizoid Band's Jakko Jakszyk. "I was taken by the fact that as multi-instrumentalists they were able to swap instruments in the middle of the show."

"We didn't trade off instruments to show off," says Minnear, "though it was a bit of a nightmare on the stage, to be honest. [laughs]. My cello playing is rather suspect."[12]

Though Giant were winning over fans on both sides of the Atlantic, they didn't make the commercial leaps that Yes, Tull, and Floyd had. While 1976's *In'terview* (which presented an album in the format of a journalist's Q&A with the band) and 1977's *Playing the Fool: The Official Live* (recorded in 1976) boasted classic Giant musical intricacies, soon the music would devolve into something much more simplistic, as evidenced on records such as 1977's *The Missing Piece* and 1978's *Giant for a Day!*

"Gentle Giant's record *The Missing Piece*, which I'd engineered, had some good moments on it, but the band were kind of chasing success, because they knew that the era of indulgence for indulgence's sake was going by the wayside, and artists, and even the fans, had to evolve," says producer Paul Northfield (ELP, Rush, Gryphon).

"On those records, there were songs that simply didn't transcend," says Derek Shulman, who reportedly wrote "I'm Turning Around," from *The Missing Piece*, at the last minute due to record label pressure for a hit. "There

was a desperation and the fact that the songs were a little more . . . contrived. We saw bands like Genesis and Yes and even Kansas, having hit singles on AOR [album-oriented rock] radio. We were playing shows with them supporting us as special guests and we watched them leapfrog over us, scoring hits. I wanted my share, but changing our approach just didn't work for us."

By 1980's *Civilian*, the band was winding down, as both Minnear and Derek Shulman said they were no longer interested in touring. "Life on the road was difficult, but even more so [was] the separation from my family," says Minnear. "Sally, my first daughter, was one year old during the *Civilian* album, so I just wanted more control over the time I spent at home."

However, for the ten years from 1970 through 1980, Gentle Giant (for the most part) were the epitome of what a progressive rock band should be, having written some of the most engrossing and dense music of the era. Time has revealed the sophistication of the band's material.

"Gentle Giant took a while to develop," says Shulman, "and our records eventually sold hundreds of thousands of copies. But it was gradual and eventual."

THE MISSING PIECE

Since Giant's dissolution, Minnear, who had become a Christian in the early years of the band, spent time working with the church (and continues to oversee the band's publishing company, Alucard Music); Weathers went on to work with the Welsh band Man. Ray Shulman has, of this writing, maintained a successful career in music and video production (as well as sound track work); guitarist Gary Green did session work (having appeared on Eddie Jobson's 1983 Capitol Records release, *Zinc*), and eventually settled outside Chicago, where he now plays live local shows; and Derek became a record industry bigwig, signing acts such as Bon Jovi, Cinderella, Pantera,

---

[12] The cover of *In a Glass House* features cellophane overlays of band members playing more than one instrument; for example, Ray appears to harness a bass guitar on one layer and bow a violin on another.

One of two covers issued for the 1972 *Octopus* album.

and Dream Theater to labels such as PolyGram, Atco Records, Mercury, Roadrunner Records (of which he was president), and has since established his own DRT label, which has rereleased the band's most vital efforts, causing many to reconsider the gravity of the Gentle Giant catalog.

In recent years, Green, Minnear, and Mortimore formed Three Friends, a tribute band–plus, which performs Giant's music. "I never thought I'd see Kerry or Gary again," says Mortimore. "We met at a Gentle Giant convention, run by the On-Reflection fan club/Internet mailing list, and debuted in 2008. It rekindled my interest in the music. Even the name of the band is perfect because it harks back to the original theme of the LP *Three Friends*. Kerry is not playing with us at the moment, but you could actually make another concept record, *Three Friends: Mach II*, based on the lives of the guys from Giant. Of course, not everyone in the original band is interested in playing the Gentle Giant material, but that's up to them. We're having fun. Life's too short. You've got to get on with it."

Three Friends (1972)

In a Glass House (1973)

The Power and the Glory (1974)

Free Hand (1975)

In'terview (1976)

The Missing Piece (1977)

(Fin Costello/Getty Images)

PROG FOLK

Out of the Mist

SINCE THE MID-1960S, BRITAIN HAD CHURNED OUT a number of virtuoso "folk baroque" guitarists, from Davy Graham and John Renbourn to Martin Carthy, John Martyn, and Bert Jansch, whose musical innovations in the use of odd time signatures and alternate string tunings (such as Graham's DADGAD) as well as their imaginative fusion of world music and traditional European styles carved a path for psychedelic/pop, "freak," electric, and progressive folk artists to follow.

Another big innovation came from the U.S., when artists such as Bob Dylan and the Byrds demonstrated that folk music could be electrified and still retain a sense of integrity.

Suddenly, folk music wasn't just a traditional art form. The floodgates were open for all kinds of experimentations. British bands, in particular, such as the Pentangle (of which Renbourn and Jansch were members), Donovan, the Incredible String Band, Fairport Convention, and the Strawbs, as well as faux-medieval, medievalesque, Renaissance, and Elizabethan progres-

Mandalaband's David Rohl, *right*, at Indigo Studios with rock idol Marc Bolan in 1974. (Courtesy of David Rohl)

sive folk-rock bands Gryphon and the Amazing Blondel seized upon the opportunity to push musical boundaries and the public's perception of what a rock (and folk rock) band could be.

Nat Joseph's Transatlantic, Chris Blackwell's Island, Polydor, even Elektra Records supported and encouraged this traditional folk and ethnic folk music in the U.K. "John Renbourn was bitten by this medieval Renaissance bug and made an album called *Sir John Alot of Merrie Englandes Musyk Thyng & ye Grene Knyghte*," remembers Graeme Taylor, guitarist for the British, medieval-tinged prog folk-rock group

Gryphon, which used such traditional instrumentation as harpsichord, crumhorn, recorder, and bassoon. "Then there was this sort of boom around the early '70s with groups like the Pentangle, which became quite popular by playing acoustic guitars. People say that there was a kind of wave of interest or renewed interest in medieval or Renaissance music in the early '70s. We didn't want to subscribe to one school or another. We wanted to create something new and different, but with the use of totally irregular instruments. Within the first six months we'd played enough around the country to make an impact and draw the attention of a talent scout, Laurence Aston, from a label called Transatlantic, who signed us and had also signed the Pentangle."

Influenced by jazz, jazz-rock fusion, Indian modalities, and the odd tempos typified by European art music, the five members of the Pentangle extended traditional songs to create folk-rock suites for records such as *Cruel Sister* and *Basket of Light*.

"Changing time signatures, [and] altering melodies were an extension of the experimentation we were doing at the time," says Pentangle vocalist Jacqui McShee. "We had a jazz-influenced rhythm section [double bassist Danny Thompson and drummer Terry Cox], and there was a lot of listening to Indian music, especially sitar music. Because of our folk background there were very few bands with the type of rhythm section we had. So, if you like, we were flying in the face of convention and [of] the traditionalists, who had a very blinkered attitude. But at the same time, we were making conscious decisions, for instance, to take a song like 'Jack Orion' [from 1970's *Cruel Sister*] and fill an entire side of an LP with it. Some traditional songs are very long, and in that case, we were speaking to a certain heritage. We were also expanding the long trad songs and breaking them up into sections form-ing mini suites, making each section, hopefully, reflect the mood of the telling of that part of the story. If it sounded good then it was okay."

Other bands let their freak flags fly, taking influences from just about anywhere and anything. For instance, the highly influential Incredible String Band began experimenting with song form to expand the musical boundaries of folk. Mike Heron, lead vocalist, songwriter, and multi-instrumentalist of the Scottish band, penned the thirteen-minute psychedelic epic "A Very Cellular Song" (from their popular 1968 record *The Hangman's Beautiful Daughter*, influenced by European baroque, Southern Indian, Bahamian spiritual, and even Bulgarian choir music, which was intended to, as Heron says, "take you on an outline of an LSD trip through different moods.

"It's also meant to have you connect, on an atomic, molecular level, with everything," says Heron. "It starts off with the radio playing and gradually gets wilder and wilder until it ends up sending you a message wishing you well. Using substances and creating this kind of music, and the connection between the two, is a very good question. I think in the early days, the first couple of albums, we were just smoking a lot of dope, and it was a very underdeveloped thing. In Edinburgh [Scotland] there must have been fifty people who were into smoking dope. We knew them all and all the dealers and everything. It was a small-scale thing, a hippie scene where everyone was reading Jack Kerouac. I think probably we had to smoke an awful lot of joints to write 'Cellular Song.' We may have needed that step [laughs], if you will. But then again, we never really saw it as that, because by the time Robin [Williamson, vocalist/multi-instrumentalist] came back from Morocco [and] we reformed the band, that was what we were doing. We would [smoke] and drop a bit of acid on the side, but it was not really radical. We found this music, the two of us, and the two girls [Dolly Collins and Licorice], that seemed to make sense to us and the generation around us."

"Some major artists, like the Incredible String Band, were using instruments like harpsichords," says Gryphon's Graeme Taylor. "That was harkening back to an older era. Even still, the Incredible String Band went into wonderfully ethnic music while using these instrumental tools and used them for their own means, as opposed to trying to re-create something I would consider 'authentic' or traditional."

Fairport Convention employed American West Coast influences in their music in the early years only to dive headlong into British folk, making them one of the most popular progressive folk acts of the early 1970s.

Taking their name from guitarist Simon Nicol's parents' home (one they owned in Muzzle Hill, North London), Fairport did their first gig in May 1967, eventually making a name for themselves by performing Bob Dylan and Joni Mitchell tunes.

Featuring three guitarists—Nicol, Richard Thompson, and Ian Matthews—bassist Ashley Hutchings (who was a member of the Ethnic Shuffle Orchestra with Nicol), Martin Lamble on drums, and singer Judy Dyble, Fairport were getting exposed not only to the scene in London but to a wider range of authentic British traditional music.

"Certainly folk music was something that Richard, Ashley, and myself had all heard as fresh listeners going out to clubs in London," says Nicol. "So we had absorbed the ethos, even if we were not scholarly about the music's background."

After Dyble split for Giles, Giles and Fripp, Fairport hooked up with singer Sandy Denny, a chilling and emotional singer, an expert interpreter of ancient song, who had been working with bluegrass band the Strawbs.

Although Fairport had yet to fully incorporate the sound that would make them famous, bringing Denny into the fold was a historic and fateful step in the band's evolution.

"Sandy, when she came along, had come directly from the folk clubs as a singer/songwriter, who had drawn on the tradition of the ballad form, as it was properly done—proper ballads without known writers; things that had been handed down from generation to generation," says Nicol.

Eventually Fairport progressed to more traditional music, recording songs such as "Nottamun Town" and "She Moves Through the Fair" (from the band's second record, *What We Did on Our Holidays*) and continuing to push musical boundaries.

"There was a big step made when we did 'A Sailor's Life,' which was a significant song on the third album [*Unhalfbricking*]," says Nicol, "where we took a straightforward story-song from a tradition and played with it in a way that wouldn't have been possible without the freethinking influence of West Coast American bands from around about that same era. And hearing Dave Swarbrick's fiddle work on the song, something just clicked. We knew there was something different happening here. This wasn't Jefferson Airplane."

After a tragic motor accident claimed the life of drummer Lamble, Fairport took stock of their situation and eventually rebuilt the band, then released what may be their crowning achievement—1969's *Liege & Lief*, which blurred the division between modern and traditional music, resulting a uniquely British folk music.

Songs such as "Matty Groves" (about infidelity and murder), the haunting "Tam Lin" (based on the Scottish ballad involving a pregnant maiden and fairies), and other traditionals demonstrated Fairport's ability to interpret distinctively British music with electric instruments. Like their progressive rock counterparts, Fairport would often work in odd

time signatures, an outgrowth of the structure of the song.

"If we were playing in strange time signatures, we were doing so because the song dictated it," says drummer Dave Mattacks, who'd replaced Lamble. "Many of the traditional songs have unconventional tempos, and we were attempting to be true to these."

By 1970, Denny had left the band to pursue a solo career (she appeared on Led Zeppelin's self-titled 1971 album on the track "The Battle of Evermore" but died tragically in 1978 from a brain hemorrhage as a result of a fall), and Hutchings went on to form traditional folk band Steeleye Span.

In the meantime, Fairport tapped bassist Dave Pegg (later of Jethro Tull) and continued to experiment on *Full House* (featuring the nine-plus-minute song "Sloth") and 1971's much underappreciated concept album, *Babbacombe Lee* (in the wake of Richard Thompson's leaving). In the grand British folk tradition (which speaks to all aspects of the human condition), the band based the record's concept on the real-life story of a Babbacombe, West England, man who was scheduled to be executed by the state but whose death was prevented three times owing to technical malfunctions.

"Dave Swarbrick is a big antique hunter, and he was in a shop, and there was a huge pile of papers all about the story of John Lee," says Mattacks. "He bought this package, and in it were a bunch of newspaper articles about him. It had its basis in reality."

"I thought it was an urban myth or whatever," says Nicol. "Apparently it had actually happened, and in 1908, Lee published a series of articles in the first person about his story, and this inspired Dave and the rest of us to write and produce an album telling a story through this young man's eyes. In those days it was okay to do a concept album, and this was like a mini opera, if you will, without being too pretentious."

For years after the mid-1970s,

Fairport became known primarily as a live act and, as of this writing, they continue to perform and host an annual music festival in Cropredy, England, in the heart of what Nicol jokingly refers to as the "folk belt."

"It is a self-mocking thing, I suppose," says Nicol. "We all tend to live around here, but it's not as if it's a great wellspring of folk-based musicians. We've just made it our own."

BARCLAY JAMES HARVEST

Formed in 1967 in Lancashire, Barclay James Harvest (BJH) sat on the edge of the progressive genre with their blend of acoustic folk, Mellotron-drenched doom rock, and orchestral accompaniment on records, while dabbling in symphonic rock on *Barclay James Harvest and Other Short Stories*.

"My interest lies in turn-of-the-century Vienna, turn of the nineteenth century," says keyboardist Stuart "Woolly" Wolstenholme, who was a member of a band called the Sorcerers prior to joining Barclay James Harvest. "I'd like to go back to a time when music started to question itself, rather than being a landscape on the wall. I think that is what Barclay James Harvest was about, in a way. It was not a straightforward rock band. It could be abstract. We were English. Even when we attempted to do rockers it was in a kind of twisted English way."

BJH released their self-titled debut in 1970, produced by Norman Smith (who was so instrumental in helping to shape early Pink Floyd's sound), which was a mixture of riff-based and orchestral folk rock (e.g., "Dark Now My Sky").

"After the first album . . . I think we had found a [musical] home with the fusion of the band sound with an orchestra," Wolstenholme says.

As one of the first few acts to be signed to EMI's Harvest label (Wolstenholme claims it was Barclay James Harvest that not only inspired but came up with the name of the label),

"With 1976's *Octoberon* we began experimenting with things like strings and a choir, although Barclay *had* used string orchestras in the early days when they worked with their arranger Robert Godfrey, from the Enid," says David Rohl, recording engineer and assistant producer. "Among the things we did was, we had Les [Holroyd, bassist] … sing into mirrors and recorded the sound bouncing off the glass to give his vocals a real crystallized feel."

BJH went from an underground to a full-blown mainstream pop band with prog sensibilities, their evolution to a large extent mirroring that of Genesis.

"When we were signed to EMI, there were no specific label for pop bands," says Wolstenholme. "When it became obvious that there was an underground music that was not about singles, EMI wanted to dedicate a label to these sounds. Because the artists on the label were becoming more and more diffuse, in the sense that Harvest was collecting artists who were more pop-oriented, we went to Polydor. It was a more mainstream label, and this was one step in our development, if you want to call it that, toward being a mainstream band."

Through the mid-1970s, records such as *Everyone Is Everybody Else*, *Time Honoured Ghosts*, and *Live* were built in large part around the songwriting craft of guitarist/vocalist John Lees, Wolstenholme, and bassist/vocalist Les Holroyd, and the power of the Mellotron.

"There was evidence, through the work of the Moody Blues and King Crimson, that the Mellotron was becoming a standard piece of rock equipment alongside the Hammond and even the piano," says Wolstenholme.

Songs such as "Beyond the Grave," "Hymn for the Children," "In My Life," "Titles," "Child of the Universe," and "The Great 1974 Mining Disaster" ranged in purpose and topic from paying homage to the

Beatles to raising social consciousness.

BJH took a bit of a left turn with 1976's self-produced *Octoberon*. It's a sometimes brilliant but slightly unfocused album, stretching and pulling the band's creative energies into areas of the experimental, mystical, countrified, and symphonic with tunes such as "Ra," the black-humor-laced "Suicide?" "May Day," and "Rock and Roll Star." *Octoberon* represents the peak of the band's progressive period.

"We tried many things in the studio," says David Rohl, who engineered the record. "Even if ideas wound up not working, we at least experimented whenever and wherever we could. For the song 'Suicide?' for example, when you hear the sound of someone walking, at the end of the song, that's Woolly in clogs moving up and down the stairs at Strawberry Studios. We also used a plastic dummy head with two microphones attached to it—one in each ear—for a great sound effect. The stereo head had an XLR cable, forty feet long, connected to it. We climbed to the top of a hotel in Manchester and threw the head off the roof and had it crash onto the pavement below to get the sound of what it was like to jump from a building. While that's pretty brutal, and not exactly high tech, that was an example of the kinds of experiments we were carrying out."

"We filled every possible space, especially on the *Octoberon* record," says Wolstenholme. "Plenty of rolling climaxes."

The musical pendulum would swing in either direction throughout the band's career from the mid- to late 1970s, as if elements within the band were fighting for supremacy. After 1977's *Gone to Earth*, BJH further aligned themselves with mainstream rock, having established themselves as hitmakers not only in Britain (where they scored numerous Top 40 albums) but also in Germany.

"The arrangements on *Gone to Earth* were a lot more layered and complicated than [they had been] in the past," says Rohl, who called upon his experience as the chief engineer at 10cc's Strawberry Studios in Stockport and his time at Manchester's Indigo recording studios for the sessions.

BJH made the same fatal error the Strawbs had a few years earlier, which was to ditch the Mellotron in the late 1970s. "By the time I left the band in '79, the latest thing was the Yamaha CS-80 polysynth," says Wolstenholme. "When I left the band, they dropped the Mellotron completely, because it had become a symbolic instrument of a certain sound, and also one symbolic of me."

Though BJH would continue to make records into the 1980s, their music and audience had shifted. The

band eventually broke up but returned in two competing forms (one led by Lees and Wolstenholme in the early 1990s, another by Holroyd post-2000).

Wolstenholme continues to work with his own Maestoso and David Rohl's reformed symphonic rock studio project Mandalaband. "In the Maestoso world, I can be anything I want," says Wolstenholme. "I can be sardonic, critical, romantic, bitter, and twisted. You wouldn't find that on a Barclay James Harvest record. Once you're beyond the cliché of the band setup, the freedom is incredible."

THE STRAWBS

Intrinsically tied to the British traditional music scene, and one of the best examples of a band moving from folk or bluegrass (as the Strawberry Hill Boys) to full-on prog rock, are the Strawbs.

The Strawbs' roots in American blues and folk and English minstrelsy, along with the band's use of the keyboards such as Moog, harpsichord, Hammond organ, and the Mellotron, created a progressive rock that was distinct from many of their contemporaries.

"We get bracketed with bands like the Moody Blues and King Crimson because of the Mellotron," says Dave Cousins, acoustic guitarist/leader/chief songwriter of the Strawbs. "Getting into English folk music and using those churchy, medieval harmonies, gave [the Strawbs their] individual characteristics."

Rarely had a progressive band had the ability to allow a composition to breathe while infusing it with such energy. Possessed of this strength, they created incredibly powerful and well-paced folk-based epics such as "Ghosts," "Autumn," "The Life Auction," "Out in the Cold/Round and Round," "The Antiques Suite," and "The Vision of the Lady of the Lake."

The band experienced an incredible evolution from the late 1960s into

the early 1970s. But the Strawbs' musical roots stretch back farther than modern rock. From his school days, Cousins was seduced by the music of skiffle master Lonnie Donegan, Leadbelly, flat-picking guitarist Ramblin' Jack Elliott, Pete Seeger, Woody Guthrie, and banjoist Earl Scruggs.

Cousins picked up the guitar (and later the banjo) and went on to form the Gin Bottle Four with his West London mate, guitarist Tony Hooper, who shared Cousins's love of skiffle, roots, jazz, and folk music.

The two school friends recruited mandolin player Arthur Phillips and formed the Strawberry Hill Boys. A series of personnel exits and entrances occurred until the band finally settled on the name "the Strawbs," then featuring double bass player Ron Chesterman and future Fairport Convention singer Sandy Denny.

Though not together for very long, this lineup cut the Strawbs' first album, *All Our Own Work* (which did not see the light of day until 1973, but included a version of Denny's famous "Who Knows Where the Time Goes?")

By mid-1968, Denny had split for Fairport, and, strangely enough, the Strawbs became the first British act signed to the American independent label A&M. The band went on to record their self-titled debut for the indie—a conceptual, orchestral affair with overtures to Middle Eastern music produced by Gus Dudgeon (later of Elton John fame) and featuring the haunting symphonic closing piece "The Battle."

Despite arrangements by Tony Visconti and appearances by session musicians, including John Paul Jones and Nicky Hopkins, A&M hated the end result (they'd thought they were getting a folk band but instead received a faux-symphonic folk rock band) and forced the Strawbs to record new material.

"Initially A&M were only really interested in Sandy," says Cousins. "But they figured they owed us good-

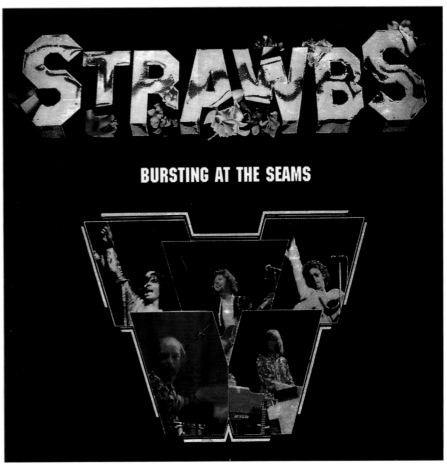

The Strawbs:
*Bursting At The
Seams* (1973)

will, so they sent us money to record."

Undeterred by the label's reaction, the Strawbs continued their spiral toward progressive folk rock, releasing such records as *Dragonfly*, produced by Visconti and featuring cellist Claire Deniz, with keyboardist Rick Wakeman serving as a session player on piano.

The album's centerpiece, the sprawling "The Vision of the Lady of the Lake," expands upon the Arthurian legend and reconfigures it with Greek mythological/Christian symbolism, featuring Leslie-effected Hammond organ.

"'The Vision of the Lady of the Lake' was written about the seven deadly sins," says Cousins. "But I twisted it by turning it on its head. In order for [the hero] to get the woman of his desires, he had to kill her, but he just couldn't do it. In the end, he is overwhelmed by the sins coming back at him. It's ultimately about sacrifice, and I think I have made sacrifices in my life that helped me write about it."

Personnel changes threatened to derail the band (notably, Deniz and Chesterman both left), but the Strawbs pushed on. Added were key members Tony Hudson, a percussionist and sitar player, and electric bassist John Ford, taking the band farther from its bluegrass/rootsy beginnings.

The Strawbs recruited Wakeman as a full-time member and recorded the live album *Just a Collection of Antiques and Curios*, for which

Cousins employed a multitude of banjo tunings. ("I would put the banjo in different tunings to get the modal drones," he says. "These tunings were not discordant in and of themselves. But if you try to play those notes on the piano, it may become discordant. Rick had to ripple around the chords, and that was what gave the Strawbs its sound.")

Wakeman and Cousins quickly became friends, and Cousins was ecstatic when the Royal Academy of Music trained pianist, whose haunting Mellotron work on David Bowie's 1969 hit "Space Oddity" caused a major stir in many musical circles, agreed to be a member of the Strawbs.

"I was never more surprised than when he said yes," says Cousins. "Then I thought, 'Crikey: We are now a band. We have this guy who plays organ like a loony.'"

The public and press paid special

attention to Wakeman (*Melody Maker* called him "tomorrow's superstar"), who was sending the Strawbs farther down the path of electric folk and progressive rock.

Wakeman seemed to enjoy the spotlight: When the Strawbs appeared on the television show *Top of the Pops* in 1971, the young keyboardist pressed a paint roller onto the keys to produce sound in the song "The Hangman and the Papist."

"If it hadn't been for that or the fact that he was in the Strawbs, I don't think [Wakeman] would have become as quickly famous as he did," Cousins says.

On the strength of the U.K. Top 30 *Antiques and Curios* (the Strawbs' first foray into British chart success), the band recorded *From the Witchwood*, a British Top 40 success.

Everything was going well until Wakeman decided it was time to leave his mate Cousins and take advantage of a more lucrative opportunity. While on tour in the States with the Strawbs, Wakeman had agreed to claim the keyboard chair with Yes, who had been making big noises with a new guitarist, Steve Howe, and record, *The Yes Album*.

"Rick needed to expand musically, and [Yes] offered him a lot more money than we could have," says Cousins, laughing. "I learned an awful lot from watching Rick play the piano. I've learned to play octaves [with my] left hand, and that's how a lot of the Strawbs' songs have developed since then."

More changes followed. Hooper, thinking the band had gone too far afield of its original sound, left after the recording of 1972's semi-concept record *Grave New World*, a reflective and spiritual album that follows a character's life from birth to death and features an all-important keyboardist/Mellotron player Blue Weaver (Wakeman's replacement) and the *electric guitarist* Dave Cousins.

By the time the band came to record 1973's *Bursting at the Seams*, the Strawbs had further cemented their path toward full-on (prog) rock by adding a full-time electric guitarist, Dave Lambert, a friend of Cousins, which helped to develop an audience in the States. Unsurprisingly, it was the band's highest charting record in the U.S. (it reached number 121) at that time.

Fans immediately responded to the diversity of tones and colors on *Bursting*, be it the short, haunting track "The River," the midtempo power-chord rocker "Lay Down," the music hall–esque Ford/Hudson composition "Part of the Union" (a Top 2 song in Britain), or the Mellotron-laced epics "Down by the Sea" and "Tears and Pavan."

The Strawbs would continue to explore their progressive side on their U.S. breakthrough records, 1974's *Hero and Heroine* and '75's *Ghosts* (arguably the band's creative pinna-

cle), for which the band saw further personnel changes: Ford and Hudson left to pursue opportunities together as songwriters (under the moniker Hudson Ford), and Weaver bailed (later to resurface on the Bee Gees' sessions for *Saturday Night Fever*).

Cousins and Lambert recruited drummer Rod Coombes (Stealers Wheel), bassist Chas Cronk (who appeared on Wakeman's *Six Wives*), and classically trained pianist/keyboardist John Hawken, late of the original Renaissance.

By the time the Strawbs came to record *Hero and Heroine*, everything was falling into place: high studio production value (producer Tom Allom layered Mellotron to achieve a thick wall of sound), lyrical themes brought to life by often restrained playing, and epic and superior material; chief songwriter Cousins was at the top of his game.

"Dave is the most incredible writer," says Hawken. "I don't know where he's tapped into but it's the same sort of line that people like Paul McCartney and Elton John are tapped into. He certainly hasn't received the notice he should have . . . To me he should be way, way up there and receive more acclaim than he ever did. He has been consistently writing for years, and you'd think that he would eventually run out of ideas. He doesn't."

From the opening, croaking Moog synth tones and the heavily chorused E-minor string sound of "Autumn," audiences knew immediately that this was a changed Strawbs. The song and the entire record breathe and throb as nothing else in the band's history.

"*Hero and Heroine* had an advantage inasmuch as we went down to Devon, where [Cousins] was living at the time, during a very lovely summer, and we rehearsed in this little peaceful country hall with nothing around for miles," says Hawken. "Dave did a lot of writing in that neck of the woods—tremendous appeal and stunning

countryside. It's very inspirational."

Songs such as the drenched-in-vocal-harmonies "Shine On Silver Sun," the Mellotron-monolith title track (which was "written about cocaine, I suppose, if you want to simplify it," says Cousins. "But it can also represent lovers, of course"), and the suicidal "Out in the Cold"/"Round and Round" account for some of the Strawbs' best-loved material.

Because *Hero and Heroine* scored in the Top 100 in America (Top 40 in the U.K.), and the band went on an international tour to promote the record, all of a sudden fans of Yes (which Wakeman had left by this time) and Jethro Tull were mentioning the Strawbs in the same breath.

"There is only one other band that I think has any resemblance to us, and that is Jethro Tull," says Cousins. "We can headline . . . a folk festival in Canada and at the same time headline a prog rock festival in America, within three months of one another. There are very few bands that can do that."

"We used to call it gothic rock," says Hawken, "which I think filled it beautifully."

The Strawbs followed up *Hero and Heroine* with the strong but somewhat dark record *Ghosts*. "I was hospitalized for a suspected brain tumor [due to dizziness] during that time," says Cousins. "I had a lumbar puncture [a spinal tap], which is the most god-awful thing to have. I had to sing the album lying on my back."

Like Jimmie Rodgers on his final recording sessions, Cousins toughed it out—but he has also lived to tell about it. "I would sing, 'Go to sleep my babies, don't you wake up . . .' [from "Ghosts"] and have to lie down. Then they spooled the tape and I'd get up and sing the second line and lie down. A very harrowing experience, I can assure you."

"There was a darkness about those songs, and [about] Dave [Cousins]'s in particular," says Hawken. "Hearing them was like viewing an Edward Hopper painting. There's always a black area about it."

Despite the dire portent, the record is full of life, featuring "Lemon Pie" (a great straightforward 1970s rock song with a touch of harpsichord), "Where Do You Go (When You Need a Hole to Crawl In)?," the Cronk-penned "Starshine/Angel Wine," "The Life Auction" (a vertigo-inducing song about the greed involved in selling belongings of the dead), "Remembering/You and I (When You Were Young)," and the church-organ finale "Grace Darling," recorded in the chapel in Charterhouse with a children's choir (and based on a real-life nineteenth-century heroine of the same name, the daughter of a lighthouse keeper who had helped to save lives of those in a sinking ship off the coast of northeast England).

"I remember when we recorded that: The chapel had a glorious natural echo," says Hawken. "You could hear the sounds dying away. That wasn't any effect: That was the sound whistling down the length of the chapel to these beautiful stained-glass windows. It was a magic experience."

The music is enhanced by sonic textures—the result of experimentation in the studio, such as the matrix of heavily echoed variable speed harpsichords opening "Ghosts." "It was like an explosion in a harpsichord factory," says Hawken. "The engineers gradually reduced the amount of echo on the track. It was a nice technique to introduce the song.

"The classic one is, in fact, the beginning of 'The Life Auction,'" continues Hawken. "I wanted an elongated echo for the piano, and I wanted it to be uneven. The engineers got one of the tapes off of the console and attached its spindle to a broom handle [and] tied it up with adhesive as we were recording. I was playing the chord and [an engineer] would shove [the reel] out the window and bring it back [into the studio] and shorten the length of the tape. There's your uneven echo."

Ghosts was the band's highest-charting record in the U.S. (scoring in the Top 50). But big changes were afoot. After a few lukewarm reviews of the album, and feeling that the musical winds had shifted as to work against the band's momentum, Cousins thought the best direction for the band was to distance itself from its past and, in a stunning move, rid themselves of the Mellotron (and therefore Hawken). The result was the accessible, fairly successful album *Nomadness*.

"[When] we dropped the idea of the Mellotron, which is the most stupid [thing] we ever did, that was the end of an era, I'm afraid," says Cousins.

Nomadness was the Strawbs' last album for A&M (much to the label's chagrin), as the band eventually found a home at Polydor. But what followed—*Deep Cuts, Burning for You*, and *Deadlines*, some of which contain choice material (e.g., "Hanging in the Gallery," "The Golden Salamander," "Burning for Me," "Alexander the Great")—simply didn't stack up to the band's reputation or its work of the past. Simply put, the Strawbs' best and most progressive days were behind them.

"There's an album called *Heartbreak Hill* that's not well known, because it didn't come out at the time it should have," says Cousins, who adds that the record was officially remastered in 2006. "That record has very progressive playing; it has strong arrangements and vocals that go way above anything we've ever done before. But sadly our management decided . . . they were not supporting the group anymore, and the album got left aside. We never should have left A&M. That was a serious mistake. But that wasn't my decision. A&M were desperate that we should stay with the label, but our managers decided otherwise. That was the end of the band, essentially, at that time."

Cousins went on to have a career in radio, while the Strawbs lay dormant for most of the 1980s, returning later in the decade to the studio to record *Don't Say Goodbye*, which featured Tony Hooper.

The band wouldn't become an entity again—writing, recording, touring, and establishing their own label, Witchwood—until the twenty-first century. As of this writing, the band continues, and in 2009, the Strawbs released a studio album with new material, titled *Dancing to the Devil's Beat*, featuring, along with Cousins, Cronk, Lambert, Coombes, and Rick Wakeman's son Oliver on keyboards, replacing Hawken (who left the reformed Strawbs due to health issues and lack of interest in touring).

Wakeman does double duty as the keyboardist for Yes and the Strawbs (something even his musical wizard father didn't pull off). "After [Yes] had finished a Canadian tour [in 2008], Dave [Cousins] asked if I was available for the next album, and it was something I really wanted to do, as I have always been a fan of the Strawbs and their songs," says Wakeman. "It's great to perform live with Yes and Strawbs, but there is also something great being involved in adding to the recording legacy that a band has."

In actual fact, the Strawbs' legacy is an underappreciated one that hopefully will continue to grow through the years. "I think a lot of people who have remained fans really do equally enjoy the music and the lyrics," says Cousins. "Many people have gotten married to our songs, especially the end part of 'Autumn.' Many people got married to 'Grace Darling.' We have had that profound influence on people. I remember I had met a friend [Bill Levenson] who put together the double record *Halcyon Days*, the best-of compilation, and my description of [the Strawbs] was that among all the bands that came to America to perform, we were the top of the second division [of the progressive rock bands]. We just both kind of laughed and he said, 'Nah. You were the bottom of the first division.'"

RENAISSANCE
TURN OF THE CARDS

Recording engineer Dick Plant, who worked on 1974's *Turn of the Cards* remembers Renaissance singer Annie Haslam had "a perfect voice for the contemporary orchestral folk material Renaissance wrote." Haslam has called the early and mid 1970s "magic."

THE ORIGINAL RENAISSANCE

Before John Hawken was a member of the Strawbs, he helped establish Renaissance with former Yardbirds drummer Jim McCarty and vocalist/harmonica player/guitarist Keith Relf, after leaving his pop/rock 'n' roll band the Nashville Teens in 1968.

"I got a call from either Jim or Keith, can't remember now, who had rang me and asked if I'd come down for an audition for a band they were putting together," says Hawken. "I had bumped into them on the road. The Teens and the Yardbirds had played together a few times. They'd said they were thinking of putting something together with more of a classical influence. Was I interested?"

An initial jam with Hawken, Relf, McCarty, and bassist Louis Cennamo (who'd play with Colosseum and later with Relf in Armageddon) and pedal steel player B. J. Cole (who later dropped out) confirmed the direction the band was to go in: a four-piece with less blues and more folk and classical influences.

"I remember we were playing the song 'Island,' which was like one of Keith's and my songs, and right in the middle of the song, suddenly John Hawken runs into this Beethoven," says McCarty. "We said, 'God, this is great. Let's keep that.'"

"We did some weird wacky stuff [in Renaissance]," says Hawken. "You look back and say, 'Oh, God, why did you play that chunk of Beethoven's Sonata no. 13 Pathétique in the middle of a song? Why?' Well, it's because we could."

This was not the Yardbirds or the Nashville Teens. The band that would be dubbed Renaissance seemed to be onto something different from what any of the individual members had done in the past. "Toward the end of the Yardbirds we wanted to do something a bit more poetic, if you like, not so heavy," says McCarty, who'd learned to play guitar for his post-Yardbirds duo with Relf called Together. "A bit more folky. We were listening to Simon & Garfunkel and Dylan. We had had enough of heavy rock."

Relf was looking to handle all of the vocals himself, but as it so happened, the often-delicate turns in the

Gryphon: *Red Queen to Gryphon Three* (1974)

Barclay James Harvest: *Time Honoured Ghosts* (1975)

Barclay James Harvest: *Gone to Earth* (1977)

The Strawbs: *Dragonfly* (1970)

The Strawbs: *Grave New World* (1972)

The Strawbs: *Ghosts* (1975)

The Strawbs: *Just a Collection of Antiques and Curios* (1970)

Renaissance: *Scheherazade and Other Stories* (1975)

Illusion: *The Island Recordings* (2003)

music called for a sweeter, gentler voice. "Jane [Relf] used to turn up there to hang out with her brother Keith and make tea," says Hawken. "Then one day [Keith] handed her the mic and said, 'Will you sing this?' It was the song 'Island.'"

Before long the band had recorded its self-titled debut, produced by Yardbirds bassist Paul Samwell-Smith, a five-song platter that rivals much of the classical rock of the day. While not completely devoid of psychedelic blues (or of blues in general) Renaissance was a new beast.

Hawken lets loose on more than one occasion with aggressive piano work that elevates tunes such as "Kings & Queens," "Innocence," "Bullet," "Island," and "Wanderer" from folk rock to classical folk rock of the highest order. Embellishment and elaborate runs on the acoustic piano and harpsichord perfectly fit the mystique of the band and even hark back to a sound the Yardbirds were experimenting with on their hit song "For Your Love."

"[Hawken] really has a gift," says McCarty. "You could play him an idea with a few chords and he really does something beautiful with it."

Once the first record was released, Renaissance hit the road in America for a tour that ended up being a self-confidence-sucking one (especially for singer Jane Relf). "Jim and Keith had come off a very stressful year with the Yardbirds and it was all starting to fragment, break down," says Hawken. "The bottom line was they didn't want to go on the road."

"There was no big record company keeping [the Yardbirds] going," says McCarty, "and the only way to make money was to get on the road. At that point I was just tired and fed up. I found it difficult to get back into touring again and to do all of that all over again."

The decision was made that McCarty and Relf would remain part of the band, but only in the capacity

of producers/songwriters/session men, while Hawken and Jane Relf remained to augment a touring lineup by adding vocalist Terry Crowe (formerly of the Nashville Teens), drummer Terry Slade, bassist Neil Korner, and another Nashville Teen alumnus and future Renaissance mainstay, guitarist Michael Dunford.

The band's second studio record, *Illusion*, which Hawken calls a "mishmash," tapped this new crew as well as others, including keyboardist John Tout, drummer Terence Sullivan, bassist Jon Camp, and lyricist Betty Thatcher—all important musical figures in the next phase of Renaissance's development. (McCarty and Relf also appear.)

"Then Louis left and Jane, once she realized that Keith was not going to tour, didn't want to go back on the road either," says Hawken. "So it was down to me."

"We were a very insecure band, I think, at that point," says McCarty. "That was one of our problems. I think John was okay, but if you put that many people who are insecure into a situation, it's not the best basis for a touring band."

As a result, Hawken had taken a job with Spooky Tooth, who had generated a buzz with a cover of the Beatles' "I Am the Walrus" from *The Last Puff* album. Before he exited, Hawken hired vocalist, Binky Cullom, for an upcoming tour. Hawken turned it over to keyboardist Tout, whom he had gotten up to speed on the arrangements, and that was the end of it. He was free of Renaissance.

In the mid-1970s (after his stint with the Strawbs), Hawken and original Renaissance members McCarty, Jane Relf, and Cennamo as well as guitarist John Knightsbridge and drummer/percussionist Eddie McNeill formed the band Illusion, a name taken from Renaissance's second studio album. (They no longer had rights to the name.)

Illusion recorded two studio records, *Out of the Mist* and *Illusion*, in

the wake of a freak electrocution accident in 1976 that claimed the life of original Renaissance member Keith Relf.

After Hawken's exit, Renaissance became a cult favorite behind singer Annie Haslam, the once-cross-eyed, Northern English–accented girl who was sent to elocution lessons at the age of nine—and thrown out of her school choir for singing too loudly.

Not exactly an auspicious start to a life that would become totally immersed in music—and one that made Haslam one of the few undeniably great female singers in progressive rock.

"You couldn't understand anything I said," says Haslam, "and when I was thirteen the family lived in Cornwall and I picked up an accent there. It really wasn't until I moved to London and began working for a dress designer, with people who spoke the Queen's English, that I began to lose my strong accent."

After her stint in the clothing business (she'd go on to design some of her famous, gypsyish stage clothing herself), Haslam began taking her talents for singing seriously and signed up for vocal lessons with opera singer Sybil Knight. Before long, she answered an ad placed by Renaissance, who were looking for a vocalist, and became perhaps the most important ingredient in the band's appeal.

Unlike many of the artists to which they were compared, Renaissance allowed the piano and female voice to came to the forefront, as they do for *Prologue*, the first record with the lineup of Camp, Tout, Sullivan, Haslam, and guitarist Ron Hendry. Songs such as "Kiev" (reflecting the band's puzzling obsession with Russia and its great composers), "Sounds of the Sea," and the title track (which has no lyrics) feature Haslam's incredible range.

After the release of *Prologue*, Dunford, Tout, Camp, Sullivan, and Haslam produced, arguably, the band's first great record, 1973's *Ashes Are Burning*, featuring electric guitarist Andy Powell.

Once again, piano takes command in many of these diverse songs (we hear symphonic patches, Afro-Cuban percussion, and impressionistic rhythmic pacing), particularly in future fan favorites such as "Can You Understand?" and "Carpet of the Sun," as well as "On the Frontier" (cowritten by McCarty) and the title track, which was inspired by a near-death experience as told in Betty Thatcher's lyrics.

Nineteen seventy-four's *Turn of the Cards*, boasting tracks such as "Running Hard," "Black Flame," and "Things I Don't Understand" (cowritten by McCarty in his last appearance on a Renaissance record), solidified the band's sound. Most importantly, sweeping orchestral passages; tuned percussion; interlocking, counterpoint, and simultaneous acoustic piano and guitar lines; layered harmonies; and Haslam's soaring, angelic lead voice mark the tension-filled nine-minute closing track, "Mother Russia" (featuring Russian scales and inspired by the book *One Day in the Life of Ivan Denisovich*, by Aleksandr Solzhenitsyn, based on the story of a 1950s prisoner of the Soviet gulag, the track was the record's eerie crowning achievement).

"I think that the real thrust of the music came from John Tout's piano," says coproducer and recording engineer Dick Plant. "I don't think Renaissance ever wanted to do anything that they couldn't reproduce onstage."

Having said this, Renaissance went all out for its 1975 studio album, *Scheherazade and Other Stories*, which featured the twenty-five-minute "Song of Scheherazade," recorded with the London Symphony Orchestra.

A point of confusion: Renaissance based its song on the story of *One Thousand and One Nights*; the track bears no musical connection to the well-known classical work "Scheherazade" By Nikolai Rimsky-Korsakov

"There are three versions: Ravel,

Rimsky-Korsakov, and Renaissance," says Haslam.

For the record, Thatcher wrote beautiful imagery for Haslam to sing, and the vocalist delivers fantastical lines with equal whimsy, vulnerability, conviction, and dread. "Betty wrote several songs about me: 'Ocean Gypsy' was based on me and my relationship with Miles Copeland, while 'Trip to the Fair' was about the first date I'd had with Roy Wood [ELO, the Move], who I lived with for four years and was engaged to," says Haslam. "What happened was, one night Roy and I had been out drinking [laughs] and we left to go to the fair on Hampstead Heath; I think it was at Easter time. It was like twelve o'clock at night when we decided to leave. We got there and [the fair] was closed. Next day I called Betty to tell her about the date and my evening was turned into lyrics for a song."

"Song of Scheherazade" (along with a rousing rendition of "Ashes Are Burning") was a flash point of the band's well-received double LP *Live at Carnegie Hall* (which went to number 55 on the U.S. charts), documenting Renaissance's historic run at the famed New York City venue. Renaissance sold out three consecutive nights at Carnegie, becoming the first British band to do so.

Nineteen seventy-seven's *Novella* album followed, bringing such memorable tunes as "Midas Man," "Can You Hear Me?" (another brilliant orchestral number), and "Touching Once (Is So Hard to Keep)," just missing the U.S. Top 40.

Renaissance was at an all-time popularity high, finding themselves playing to sold-out audiences and receiving radio airplay on FM radio stations in the U.S., particularly in the northeastern part of the country, in Pennsylvania and New York.

"When we first came over I don't think we went to the West Coast for a couple of tours, actually," says Haslam, who, as of this writing, lives

in Pennsylvania. "We were concentrated on the East Coast of America, because that was where they were going crazy over us. I think our music was accepted on the East Coast and maybe not anywhere else."

Featuring arrangements by Louis Clark (who'd worked with ELO), 1978's *A Song for All Seasons*, bolstered by the British Top 10 hit "Northern Lights" (an ode to Haslam's homesickness on her many trips to America), was the first Renaissance record to make the U.K. charts since the band's debut. But, like so many other progressive rock bands, faced with a change in attitude, musical industry directions, and cultural upheavals, Renaissance hit a rough patch in the late 1970s.

Whether it was a sign of the times or the band no longer having the courage of their musical convictions, fans were spooked by Renaissance's newer material on such uncharacteristic records as 1979's *Azure D'Or* and 1983's *Camera Camera*.

"We had a hit with 'Northern Lights,' and that's when we were encouraged to write more commercial music," says Haslam. "We did a turnaround musically instead of trying to take our music into the 1980s . . . It was too radical. I think we should have stayed our course."

By the early 1980s, only three longtime Renaissance members were left (Haslam, Dunford, and Camp) and before anyone knew it, the band had silently disappeared. Haslam, Dunford, and Tout would return in 2000 with *Tuscany* (produced by Roy Wood), and in the fall of 2009, Haslam and Dunford celebrated the band's fortieth anniversary with a nine-city U.S. tour (unsurprisingly, favoring the East Coast), performing many of their classics.

"Everybody was integral in all of this," says Haslam. "It really was magic. It was a great combination of people that made that band special. It was a great time, an interesting band, and I don't think it'll ever be like that again."

(Courtesy of Afraká and Blu and Blu Music)

PROGRESSIVO ITALIANO

Musica Rock
Romantica

FORGIVE THE CRUDE GENERALIZATIONS: AMERICANS WERE and are known for their rhythm, the Brits for their studied, mathematical approach to music, and the Italians for their romance.

Bands such as Osanna, Il Balletto di Bronzo, Banco del Mutuo Soccorso, Premiata Forneria Marconi (PFM), Le Orme, New Trolls, Locanda delle Fate, Museo Rosenbach, Arti + Mestieri, and many others had set the standard, first drawing on American and British influences, then looking inward and pulling from their country's rich cultural history.

"Rock, blues, jazz—they weren't born here in Italy," says Il Balletto di Bronzo's Gianni Leone, a onetime member of Città Frontale. "That doesn't mean I stopped myself from playing it. We here in Europe have another musical tradition. That's not to say that we all must sing 'O Sole Mio,' which I hate. But our tradition is an important one, and it's contributed to why progressivo Italiano has been recognized around the world."

"You have to remember that in the 1950s we had American rock 'n' roll," says Vittorio De Scalzi, guitarist/flautist for New Trolls, who grew up in Genoa, a major port city in Italy that imported many records from America and Britain. "In Italy it was very popular. Then something was changed with Jimi Hendrix and Vanilla Fudge. . . . Rock 'n' roll became progressive rock, and we played our own style of it."

In Italy there were countless bands, with names as lyrical as their music, some only managing to release one record in their career. But they flooded the field with their spin on a passionate, sometimes academic, approach to experimental and classical rock.

One of the first major Italian progressive rock releases to fuse classical and hot-rodded blues-rock guitar riffs (à la Cream) was 1971's *Concerto Grosso No. 1 per i New Trolls*, rife with Ian Anderson–esque jazzy flute playing and sweeping symphonic arrangements by Argentinean composer Luis Bacalov—the final section ("Shadows") of which is dedicated to Jimi Hendrix.

Prior to *Concerto Grosso*, New Trolls were largely a straight-ahead, if unfocused, light psychedelic rock band influenced by Vanilla Fudge (with strings attached), experiencing success in Italy with the hit "Una Miniera." "It was really the idea of producer Sergio Bardotti to have the interaction between our rock band and *musica baroque*," says New Trolls' De Scalzi.

In the wake of *Concerto Grosso*, bands created classics of the genre by the dozen: Premiata Forneria Marconi's *Storia di Un Minuto* and *Per Un Amico*; Il Rovescio della Medaglia's *Contaminazione*; Il Balletto di Bronzo's *Ys* (a concept album inspired by but not based on the ancient mythological city of the same name consumed by the sea); Semiramis's *Dedicato a Frazz* (with a

pastiche of symphonic passages and beautiful/sci-fi-esque vibraphone-enhanced melodic runs); Museo Rosenbach's *Zarathustra* (based on Nietzsche's nineteenth-century treatise on religion and morality, *Also Sprach Zarathustra*); Reale Accademia di Musica's self-titled debut; Campo di Marte's self-titled concept record debut concerning European colonialism and the mistreatment of Native Americans; Latte e Miele (aka Latte Miele)'s *Passio Secundum Mattheum*; Biglietto per L'Inferno's self-titled release; Area's disorienting concoction of rock and jazz (and other genres) titled *Arbeit Macht Frei*; and Banco del Mutuo Soccorso's politically charged *Io Sono Nato Libero*.

"A lot of new groups formed in a few years," says Aldo Tagliapietra of Le Orme. "What we wanted to do was change the world, change the music, and change society."

Much as in the United States (or as in any country for that matter), each region and each city in Italy possesses its own artistic personality, a fact that was exacerbated by the country's political tensions throughout the 1970s. Progressive rock in Italy was shaped as much by the musicians as by their times and location.

Italy's motor city, Turin, for instance, produced Arti + Mestieri—a jazz-rock/art rock band that thrived on unrest and improvisation. Like the title of one of their songs, "Positivo/Negativo" (from the band's 1974 debut album, *Tilt*), Arti + Mestieri mix light and dark, seemingly representing the cultural tension of their surroundings.

"Turin is the city of the car Fiat," says keyboardist Beppe Crovella. "Having Fiat in Turin was both positive and negative. It created a lot of jobs, but by the same token, the more people who flooded in, the more restless the population became. It meant more people didn't get along and there was less harmony."

Even the band's signature image,

the iconic funnel (featured on the cover of *Tilt*), speaks to this, as if Arti + Mestieri are sending a message regarding their ability to channel cultural diversity. "That cover was exhibited at the Museum of Modern Art in New York because it has become so famous," says Crovella.

In Venice, Le Orme formed after the dissolution of the Corals (a garage band Aldo Tagliapietra fronted) and released what some regard as one of the best Italian progressive rock records, 1973's *Felona e Sorona* (a concept record based on a cosmic romance), which makes overtures to European art music. Yet the music flows very freely, as it does on releases such as *Verità Nascoste*, *Contrappunti*, and *Uomo di Pezza*: You'll find moments of piano sonata and fugue, counterpoint melodies, as if lush, classical romanticism were in the band's DNA.

"Venice is a strange town, but during the age of Serenissima [the historic republic of Venice], it was one of the most important towns in music," says Tagliapietra, who handles vocal, bass, and guitar duties for Le Orme. "In Saint Mark's Church they used to perform concerts in stereo: a choir on one side of the church and a second on the other, with listeners and churchgoers in the middle."

Milan, of course, is a progressive arts center of Italy that thrives on new blood and ideas (there's always something to learn in the city), and it just so happened to have spawned one of the more enduring Italian progressive rock bands, Premiata Forneria Marconi.

This vitality can be detected in PFM's rich blend of rock, European orchestral music, chamber music, baroque stylings, church hymns, and opera on records such as *Storia di Un Minuto* and *Per Un Amico* before the band began diving into jazz-rock fusion for 1975's *Chocolate Kings* and 1977's *Jet Lag*.

"We have always made a promise to ourselves that no one album will be the same as the one before it," says

PFM drummer Franz Di Cioccio. "It has always been about growing with each record."

It's no surprise that Rome's Banco del Mutuo Soccorso should be singing of politics given the topsy-turvy climate of violence in the capital city in the 1970s. Just as *neorealismo*, an artistic movement in Italian cinema, was exploding in Italy, the progressives, on some level, reflect this openness to reality. The mere appearance of this record and the nearly sixteen-minute opening track "Canto Nomade per un Prigioniero Politico"—a song for a political prisoner—dispel myths about prog rock being purely an escapist genre.

Similarly, Naples-based band Osanna (formed by the unification of two separate bands, I Volti di Pietra and Città Frontale) released what they themselves dubbed the "first Italian rock opera," 1973's *Palepoli*.

Viewed through the lens of Italy's civic unrest throughout the 1970s, *Palepoli* could be interpreted as a statement on empire, the lack of human harmony, and the modern world's greed. Even the artwork seems to confirm this: We catch a glimpse of Dutch Renaissance painter Pieter Bruegel the Elder's sixteenth-century painting *The Tower of Babel*, and the LP's gatefold presents a panoramic view of humanity (give or take a dash of Hieronymus Bosch). In the background is another Bruegel painting, *The Fight Between Carnival and Lent*, bringing into sharp focus the idea that man's existence is inherently schizophrenic and irreparably caught between the sacred and the profane.

Naples also spawned Il Balletto di Bronzo, which recorded the apocalyptic *Ys*, mentioned earlier. "The story tells about a man who remains alone in the world after a catastrophe," explains Bronzo keyboardist Gianni Leone. "He meets three other men: The first one, represented by the second section, 'Primo Incontro,' is deaf, and immediately also the survivor becomes deaf;

the second man, in 'Secondo Incontro,' is blind, and he becomes blind too; the third man—'Terzo Incontro'—is dumb, and our protagonist becomes dumb. Then, *e buio fu*—darkness, the end of everything."

Other bands would continue to push rock Italiano's musical boundaries. Classically trained violinist Don V. Lax came to Italy when he was seventeen, to attend one of the oldest music conservatories in the world, Rome's National Academy of St. Cecilia. Lax, who claims to be half Romanian and brought up on classical and gypsy music, hadn't been exposed to popular music until he immersed himself in it in the late 1960s and early 1970s music of Joni Mitchell, James Taylor, and the Beatles.

After attending a Quella Vecchia Locanda (QVL) concert in Rome, Lax was impressed with the band and asked if they were looking for a violinist. As it happened, they were, and they set a date to rehearse in a little farmhouse (from which the band derived its name) outside of Rome, where the members of QVL (French drummer Patrick Traina, lead singer/flute player Giorgio Giorgi, bass player Romualdo Coletta, lead guitarist Raimondo Maria Cocco, and keyboardist Massimo Roselli were living.)

QVL's debut is arguably the band's most adventurous record, containing Eastern European–tinged music (their 1974 sophomore effort, *Il Tempo della Gioia*, does not feature Lax). The opener, "Prologo," showcases multitracked vocals, a high level of musical interplay, and simultaneous runs of piano, flute, guitar, and violin, which shape the jagged, multisectional song structure.

"I think the Italian feeling for storytelling really came into the music," says Lax. "The music was so free that it expressed all the different aspects and archetypes of the story we were telling. For example, take the concept of the first record. You're not sure if the main character is from

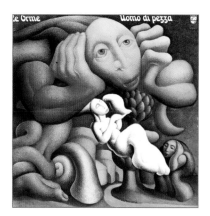

Le Orme: *Uomo di Pezza* (1972)

Le Orme: *Felona e Sorona* (1973)

Le Orme: *Verità Nascoste* (1977)

another planet or got lost and has amnesia. He doesn't know what he's even doing on this planet. He goes through this journey of life on planet Earth and sees things that shock him and bring him to grief. He falls in love and then has experiences of pain and suffering and moments of complete emotional and spiritual awareness that bring him great joy. The record ties together very well. It's really like a continuum. Even the drum solo on the first side of the vinyl ends and then begins on the next side."

One of the most operatic and distinctive bands from Rome, Banco del Mutuo Soccorso, which first appeared on a compilation tape, *Sound '70*, would soon be introduced to the world through their 1972 debut record.

While the Italian melodic and operatic elements are obvious (singer Francesco Di Giacomo's obvious range and passion were a Banco sonic signature), the influence of British proggers was also present, a condition that Banco wouldn't totally overcome until the 1980s, when the band nearly completely changed musical direction.

Gianni Nocenzi's use of acoustic piano, the band's musical interplay (particularly the call-and-response between the organ work of Vittorio Nocenzi, who studied piano and organ at the university level, and the electric guitar riffage of Marcello Todaro in the hypnotic "Metamorfosi"), studio effects employed by veteran songwriter/producer Alessandro "Sandro" Colombini (e.g., the rapid panning from left to right in "R.I.P. [Requiescant in Pace]"), and the operatic/impressionistic moments of the multidimensional eighteen-and-a-half-minute tune "Il Giardino del Mago," demonstrate Eastern and Central European baroque influences.

The follow-up, a concept album examining the evolutionary theory of life on the planet (i.e., a look at man's ability to rise above his primal instincts), was called simply *Darwin!*,

and builds upon the band's multigenre pastiche compositional style. We hear elements of synthesizer-driven British progressive rock ("Cento Mani e Cento Occhi"), orchestral touches, passionate vocal pleas ("750,000 Anni Fa . . . L'Amore"), and Mediterranean flavors (synths that mimic folk instrumentation widely used in the area, such as accordion as in "Danza dei Grandi Rettili").

Darwin! also possesses what the debut only hints at in places: a strong sense of sonic experimentation. We hear moments of compositional complexity, rich textural chord voicings, and traditional European instrumentation mixed with sound design, custom-made synth noises, and even musique concrète ("Ed Ora Io Domando Tempo al Tempo ed Egli Mi Risponde . . . None Ne Ho!").

Banco, as do many of the Italian progressive rock bands, presents a lyrical approach: The music is less pulse-conscious than melodic. For example, Banco drummer Pier Luigi Calderoni or Arti + Mestieri skinsbeater Furio Chirico often dispense with groove in favor of following a guitar or keyboard line.

Banco's 1973 *Io Sono Nato Libero* is the band's most fully formed recording, featuring the abovementioned "Canto Nomade per Un Prigioniero Politico" and the multi-tracked voice and acoustic guitar magic that is "Non Mi Rompete"—a celebration of personal freedom (the title translates roughly as "let me be"). Despite the music's sonic layering (particularly apparent in "No Mi Rompete"), the intricate moments rarely become cumbersome.

Io Sono Nato Libero was such a definitive artistic statement that it helped to convince Emerson Lake and Palmer that they should sign Banco to ELP's new label, Manticore. By 1975, Manticore had released *Banco*, which contained English-language versions of songs from previous albums and unreleased material, which was followed by *As in a Last Supper*, an English version

of *Come In Un'Ultima Cena*, a richly textured record evoking images of the country's ancient past while moving smoothly through odd times.

Banco's biggest musical rivals, PFM, were also signed to Manticore. Di Cioccio remembers how it came to be: "Our manager, Franco Mamone, the father of progressive music in Italy, made all of this possible. [He] took a tape of our music and gave it to Greg Lake and said, 'This is my band in Italy.' You know, you give a tape to a rock star and they say, 'Yeah, I'll listen to it when I get home.' They probably will never hear it. We were very lucky, because he heard the tape and said the band was great. . . . So he said he wanted to see and hear the band for himself. He wanted us to come to the Manticore [Studios in Fulham, London]. . . . Turns out they loved us, and Pete Sinfield said we had the same power as King Crimson but were Mediterranean. That is what started us on [our] international career."

The opportunity that ELP presented bands such as Banco and PFM was a double-edged sword: Recording music in English meant, inevitably, the ability to reach a wider audience—a new world—in Britain and the States, the very home of the musical vein in which the Italian bands were working.

However, the problem with mucking about with the band's music and image spoke to the public's sense of nationalistic pride: Italians didn't always look kindly upon musicians who catered to English speaking countries.

"I loved working with PFM," says Pete Sinfield, who wrote lyrics for PFM's *Photos of Ghosts* and *The World Became the World* (which were English versions of material found on PFM's 1972 record *Storia di Un Minuto* and 1973's *L'Isola di Niente*—loosely translated as "Isle of Nothing"). "PFM represented a kind of bright Mediterranean free spirit side, and they were warm and funky. A bit fast, as was the drummer Franz [Di Cioccio], like Carl Palmer. But it was

Premiata Forneria Marconi: *Storia di un Minuto* (1972)

Premiata Forneria Marconi: *Per Un Amico* (1972)

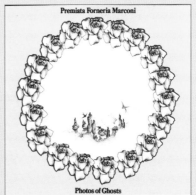

Premiata Forneria Marconi: *Photos of Ghosts* (1973)

Premiata Forneria Marconi: *The World Became the World* (1974)

Premiata Forneria Marconi: *Chocolate Kings* (1975)

Il Rovescio della Medaglia: *Contaminazione* (1973)

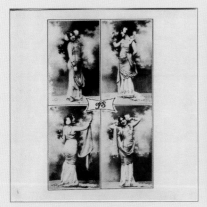

Il Balleto di Bronzo: *Ys* (1972)

Museo Rosenbach: *Zarathustra* (1973)

Locanda delle Fate: *Forse le Lucciole non si amino pui* (1977)

New Trolls: *Concerto Grosso per 1* (1971)

New Trolls: *Concerto Grosso number 2* (1976)

Banco del Mutuo Soccorso: *Darwin!* (1972)

Banco del Mutuo Soccorso: s/t (1972)

Banco del Mutuo Soccorso: *Io Sono Nato Libero* (1973)

Banco del Mutuo Soccorso: *Come in un'ultima Cena* (1976)

Semiramis: *Dedicato a Frazz* (1973)

Arti + Mestieri: *Tilt* (1974)

Arti + Mestieri: *First Live in Japan* (2006)

Osanna: *Palepoli*
(1973)

terribly frustrating, because some of my best lyrics are on the two albums I did with them, and I found it was difficult for them to pronounce all of the words in English in a way that some of us are accustomed to."

"Peter Sinfield said the music would be more universal if new lyrics were written, and I agree with him,'" says Di Cioccio. "If you write lyrics that reflect only a small part of your life or your country, then people aren't going to be interested in your music. *Per Un Amico*, which means, 'for a friend,' for instance, addressed political situations in Italy at the time. Basically, we were saying, 'Hey, friend, instead of talking and talking, don't waste time. Make something. Do something.' At that point it was very hard to live here in Italy. The early '70s had a lot of fighting, and it started one of the worst periods of Italian life with the Red Brigade [aka Brigate Rosse, a rogue communist guerilla group]. So the story of the record was not so important for the rest of the world."

"We shouldn't forget about the fact that PFM did an album called *Chocolate Kings*, which is an anti-American album about excess," says Sinfield. "I said, 'You're touring America. You can't do something so blatant.'"

"Pete Sinfield offered a lot of advice," says Di Cioccio. "He also said [we'd] be better off using PFM as the band name. But the problem was, people didn't know what PFM stood

for. When people asked what it meant, we would joke about it and say that it stood for 'Pass the Fettuccine and Macaroni.' Or 'Please Fuck Me.' But that is not true. We took our name from the Marconi bakery."

In some ways, performing in English hurt Banco as it did all of the Italian bands. As backward as it sounds, part of what gives the music its mystique is the fact that English-speaking people don't always understand the words. (Ironically, it was the Italians, in many cases, who supported the English progressive bands such as Genesis, Van der Graaf Generator, and Gentle Giant before they were fully accepted in Britain. "Our style must have appealed to them," says Van der Graaf Generator keyboardist Hugh Banton. "We figured it had to do with the perceived operatic qualities of our rock music.")

PFM's ability to communicate with an audience was fundamentally changed upon translation (e.g., the English version of Le Orme's *Felona e Sorona*, translated by Van der Graaf Generator guitarist/vocalist Peter Hammill, is now a collector's item.) Yet PFM's *Photos of Ghosts* ranked on the *Billboard* Top 200 Albums chart. PFM and Banco were breaking through: The *New Musical Express*, when PFM toured Britain in 1974, even compared flautist/violinist/guitarist Mauro Pagani to Niccolò Paganini, calling him a master.

As if averting the language barrier altogether, Banco entered a heavily instrumental period in the mid-1970s, composing the score for a 1976 Luigi Faccini film about love and political unrest in Sicily, *Garofano Rosso* (based on the Sicilian author/political dissident Elio Vittorini's first novel, *Il Garofano Rosso*), and, in 1978, . . . *di Terra*, an instrumental symphonic rock record featuring the Orchestra della Unione Musicisti di Roma—what Banco call their most complex music.

Banco would return (more or less) to form with *Canto di Primavera* (though the record contains some

instrumental tracks), with Di Giacomo's vocals taking the musical lead once again. *Canto di Primavera* also marked a change in musical direction for Banco—a condensation of their creativity—that roamed far from the band's progressive early days. Banco, arguably for the first time, were clearly attempting to write a hit single.

Banco stands as an example for the entire rock progressivo movement in Italy: They might have been misguided in the late 1970s and in the 1980s, and even began imitating some of their British and American counterparts. But they've clawed their way back to their roots, continuing to perform music from the glory days of the early and mid-1970s.

Italy might not have beaten Britain or the U.S. to the experimental rock boom, but their enduring music is one of the most beloved strains of progressive music.

"Progressivo Italiano has been recognized around the world," says Il Balletto di Bronzo's Gianni Leone. "What we were doing in those years, not really even being aware of what we were doing, really can't be topped and can't be repeated."

"There really was a magic about the time, at least for a little while," says Beppe Crovella. "You could feel it in the art, the schools, the workers, everyday life. And I think that spilled over into the music."

Osanna: *Suddance*
(1978)

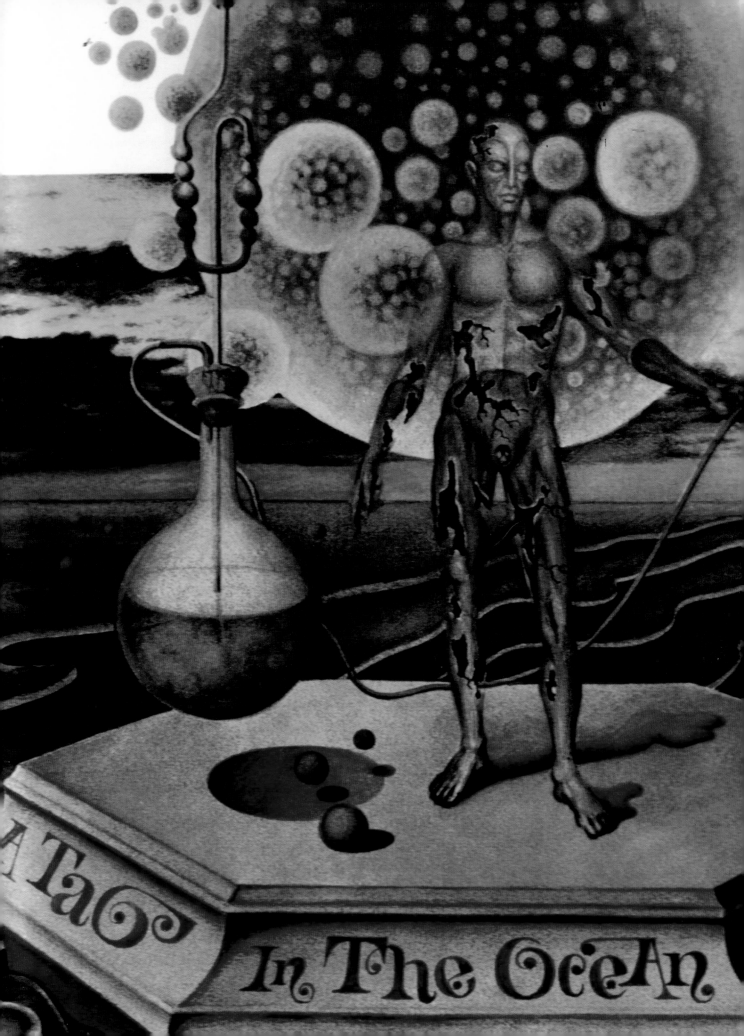

GERMAN PROG AND THE KRAUTROCKER

IN THE LATE 1960S AND EARLY 1970S, GERMAN ROCK BANDS
came in all shapes and sizes, ranging from the avant-garde and experimental to
the electronic, minimalist, avant-garde, Wagnerian, conceptual, and (paradoxically) quintessential British progressive.

While many similarities exist between these German bands, there were far
more points of divergence. Several factors contributed to this, including the rise
to prominence of record labels such as Pilz, Sky, Ohr, and the Hamburg-based
Brain; the geographic locale of a particular band; the political and socioeco-
nomic conditions of the city in which a band was based; and even the nature
of the German psyche.

"I think all the German rock bands were very idealistic people," says Milla
Kapolke, bassist for Grobschnitt, a band formed in Hagen in the mid-1960s.
"At this time, German bands were not in it purely for the money. They didn't
give a shit about selling lots of records."

"I guess it came down to a common guilt in Germany—you were not supposed
to admit that you were German," says Amon Düül guitarist/vocalist John Weinzierl.

"We grew up not knowing why. We didn't see the war, but we had all of these disasters, disasters that our parents made, shoved in our face. We didn't want to be new nationalistic Germans. We just wanted to be ourselves."

"It was frowned upon if you listened to American or English music," says bassist Dave Anderson, the only Englishman during his time with Amon Düül. "It was a clear, definite decision to develop a different style and sound."

"Even our band names were different," adds Weinzierl. "In those days, everybody was called the Beatles or 'the' something. We didn't want to have an English name. Amon is related to the Egyptian sun god. One of the bands we used to listen to was Canadian, called Hapshash and the Coloured Coat, and they released a record [in 1967] called *Featuring the Human Host and the Heavy Metal Kids*, which featured a mythology that included the word Duul, or Dyyl. We took our name from that. Later we placed in the umlaut dots to point out that we are German."

GERMAN SCENES

Musicians were allowed to grow independently of and isolated from other artistic scenes in Germany, and the fractural nature of the musical landscape created a diverse brand of art and progressive rock, which has inspired generations of artists from Porcupine Tree and the Jesus and Mary Chain to Sonic Youth, Stereolab, Radiohead, Air, and Primal Scream.

"[In] every little village in every city there was live music," says Charly Maucher, bassist of Hannover's Jane, a band that reached its psychedelic/prog peak with the three-track 1976 release *Fire, Water, Earth & Air*, the double LP *Live at Home* (also 1976), and 1977's *Between Heaven and Hell*.

"In England it seems like most of the movers and shakers were in London at some point, but not every important band in Germany was in Munich or Berlin," says Kapolke.

Proximity didn't always equate with musical homogeneity, either. For instance, Düsseldorf produced the minimalism and orderliness of Kraftwerk as well as the messy musical interactions of Neu!

Hamburg (initially) fostered the acid-induced workouts of the English natives Nektar as well as the avant-garde art rock of Slapp Happy, a group led by English keyboardist Anthony Moore, American guitarist Peter Blegvad, and German singer Dagmar Krause, who collaborated with Britain's politically charged Henry Cow—kindred spirits who appeared on Virgin Records along with Slapp Happy—on 1974's *Desperate Straights* and 1975's *In Praise of Learning*.

"Slapp Happy reminded us how great short song form could be, and how flexible," says Henry Cow drum-

---

KLAUS TO THE EDGE

Klaus Schulze, an original member of Tangerine Dream, spawned his own career in electronica after abandoning the drums for the synthesizer in the early 1970s.

Schulze, much like Manuel Göttsching (see Space Rock sidebar), not only embraced emerging keyboard/sequencing technology (EMS, Moog, ARP, and later Fairlight), he successfully circumvented the limitations of contemporary recording equipment to produce layered compositions independent from his American and British rock influences.

"An analogue synthesizer could not store sounds," says Schulze. "But I made records like *Irrlicht* [1972], *Cyborg* [1973], [and] *Picture Music* [1975] with them. Up until *Moondawn* [1976], *Body Love* [1977], and *X* [1978], which I recorded in a small studio in Frankfurt [Panne-Paulsen studios], I only had a two-track Revox [reel-to-reel analog tape recorder], so I had to play everything in one go, like in a live concert."

Schulze began incorporating percussion (courtesy of drummer Harald Grosskopf) and swing feel, which lightened the repetitive nature of a milestone record such as *Moondawn*, for instance, and helped to enhance Schulze's adventures in sound design ever since.

"[Schulze] was a master of synthesis," former Santana drummer Michael Shrieve told the author in 2006. Shrieve first worked with Schulze on Japanese percussionist Stomu Yamash'ta's 1976 extraterrestrial kung fu musical extravaganza, *Go*. "I loved all of the sequencers pumping this rhythm stuff that he was doing, but one of the things that drove me crazy was the drum patterns. He had these powerful rhythms . . . and yet I didn't like the groove."

KLAUS SCHULZE
Trancefer

Trancefer (1981)

"When I played with *Go*, I listened to [Shrieve], because he helped me to adjust my sequencers," says Schulze. "He talked to me about body movement and told me, 'Klaus, walk with the rhythm you've made.' It was a strange request, but I did, and I ended up adjusting my grooves to the point that I could walk with them. From that point on, I learned that you could groove with machines and not to be so mathematical."

mer Chris Cutler, who formed Art Bears with Cow guitarist Fred Frith and Slapp Happy's Krause in 1978.

Cologne-based Triumvirat, formed in 1972 by classically trained keyboardist Jürgen Fritz, recorded impressive symphonic material such as 1974's *Illusions on a Double Dimple* and 1975's *Spartacus* – something akin to what their British progressive rock brethren had been doing some years earlier.

Interestingly, the city also was home to the talents of the musically adventurous Can, formed in 1968, which took rock experimentation to its very limits (nearly to the point that the musical fiber disintegrated) with 1969's *Monster Movie* (credited to the Can), 1971's double album *Tago Mago*, and 1972's *Ege Bamyasi*.

Their 1973 offering, *Future Days*, perhaps Can's most accessible effort of the 1970s (and the last to feature vocalist Kenji "Damo" Suzuki, who replaced Malcolm Mooney after the latter's nervous breakdown) is a satisfying, if disturbing, listen at times.

Can's avant-garde approach, which helped to spawn the genre known as "krautrock," was an amalgam of backward vocals; Michael Karoli's guitar effects processing; tape loops of rhythmic patterns; Holger Czukay's wheezing and wobbling bass lines; plucked and sawed stringed instruments; Irmin Schmidt's bleeping and spiraling keyboards; funky/bluesy syncopated grooves (courtesy of the magic hands—and feet—of drummer Jaki Liebezeit); Suzuki's profound/nonsensical panting, chanting, and ranting; organic simple chord jams; hissing sheets of electronic white noise; and cavernous echoes (applied during the mixing stage).

"This was one of the rare periods when the record industry was running behind the music, not manufacturing it," says Cutler. "We all benefited from the album culture. For a short span, *novelty* was popular and record companies were falling over one another to sign the strangest bands

and unearth new ones."

TANGERINE DREAM

Tangerine Dream, an innovative synthesizer-based band formed in 1967, produced textural and undulating programmed soundscapes via Moog, Mellotron, organ, and VCS-3 synthi, an approach best captured on *Phaedra* (1974), a Top 20 British hit; *Rubycon* and *Ricochet* (both 1975); and *Stratosfear* (1976), featuring the much-heralded lineup of Russian-born keyboardist/guitarist Edgar Froese, keyboardist Chris Franke, and keyboardist/flutist Peter Baumann.

The Dream's percolating, wordless music evoked otherworldly visual images while expressing basic human emotions, inducing altered states of consciousness. Despite some of the genuinely terrifying sonic turns of *Phaedra* and *Rubycon* (something like a bad trip), the meditative aspects of Tangerine Dream's spontaneously composed songs fulfilled the band's musical destiny as transcendental impressionists (an approach only hinted at on their debut, 1970's *Electronic Meditation*).

"All the rhythmic aspects of what they did came from synthesizers and sequencing, as opposed to playing," says producer Mick Glossop, who engineered *Rubycon* and *Ricochet*. "Ninety percent of what they did was improvised. One of them would sit down at the synthesizer and start making a sound and the others would respond.

"If they felt there was something they had done that was worth listening to, they'd come into the control room and have a listen," continued Glossop. "They would perform overdubs or take a theme from one part that was improvised and copy it and place it somewhere else. It was like a cut-and-paste function in a word processing program."

Mainstay Froese proclaimed, in a statement that's largely true of most German prog artists/krautrockers, that Tangerine Dream was not striving to be a pop band at all, but aimed to be

"far away from all the silly things."

Though conventional rock instruments became more prominent in Tangerine Dream's live performances and studio recordings by the late 1970s, Froese and the band have stayed true, more or less, to their electronica musical roots, churning out stellar efforts such as 1980's *Tangram* and 1983's *Hyperborea*, and even finding commercial success via Hollywood film scores, including those for William Friedkin's 1977 gripping thriller *Sorcerer*; 1983's *Risky Business*, starring Tom Cruise; the film adaptation of Stephen King's best-selling *Firestarter* (1984); 1985's horror-comedy *Fright Night*; and 1987's *Three O'Clock High*.

"They were a unique band, not just because they played three banks of synthesizers," says Glossop. "They shaped music until they achieved the sound they wanted. The whole approach to music was quite different."

GROBSCHNITT

Grobschnitt is one of two major German bands that resembled their British progressive rock counterparts closely by translating musical drama and campy theatricality into "gold" with 1974's *Ballermann*, 1975's slightly absurd *Jumbo*, and—considered by many to be the band's crowning achievement—1977's fantasy-based concept record, *Rockpommel's Land*.

The brainchild of keyboardist Volker "Mist" Kahrs and founding member/drummer/lyricist Joachim Ehrig (aka "Eroc"), *Rockpommel's Land* told the musical adventure of a troubled boy named Ernie, who escapes life's doldrums by hitching a ride with Maraboo, a paper airplane that transforms itself into a giant bird.

It's little wonder that *Rockpommel's Land* struck a chord in fans on the Continent, the U.K., and America: The music blends chirping acoustic riffing, stratospheric synthesizer flights of fancy, and odd electronic noises (manipulated by Eroc) that perfectly capture all the confusion, joy, oppression, and wonder inherent in the plot.

Yet because the record, delivered with straight-faced conviction, was a slight departure from the band's earlier psychedelic efforts, audiences took a while to warm to its overtures toward classical and British folk. (Even the fantasy-based cover was purposefully Roger Dean–esque.)

"When [Grobschnitt] played *Rockpommel's Land* live in 1978, there was no applause," says bassist Milla Kapolke. "The people didn't want to hear it. I could compare it to Yes, maybe, when they did *Tales from Topographic Oceans*, which some people didn't like at first. For some it's their greatest album. *Rockpommel's Land* is the same way: It's the most popular and [commercially successful] record Grobschnitt has, and it's what people want to hear most when we perform live."

By the time audiences began appreciating *Rockpommel's Land*, Grobschnitt had changed its musical style yet again. "The band followed [*Rockpommel's Land*] with *Merry-Go-Round*, a much more song-oriented album," Kapolke says. "After *Merry-Go-Round* the band wanted to go in yet another new musical direction. With every LP we finished, we said, 'This is not our music anymore.' That makes *Rockpommel's Land* something rather special."

ELOY

Like their German rock compatriots Novalis and French, Mahler-influenced symphonic rockers Pulsar, Hannover-based Eloy were, at times, derivative of Pink Floyd, but built a cult following that continues into the twenty-first century, thanks to the band's layered, Wagnerian sound.

Inspired by H. G. Wells's riveting sci-fi classic, *The Time Machine*, Eloy's band name was, itself, a kind of backhanded homage to the German scene.1

"The name spoke to the situation of the music business in Germany in the late '60s," says Eloy guitarist/vocalist producer Frank Bornemann, who founded the band in 1969. "Most German bands performed the well-known hits of artists from the U.K. and USA. We were a nation of cover bands, really. I thought that by naming the band Eloy, in a strange way, maybe I could change things and build a more promising future."

After releasing their independently produced first single, "Walk Alone/Day Break," in 1970, Eloy offered its full-length, self-titled debut in 1971—a heady mixture of psychedelic blues-rock grunge à la Black Sabbath and Deep Purple (the song "Today" is a close cousin to "Hush"), followed by 1973's *Inside*, a creative touchstone in the band's early career.

While urban American blues and psychedelia still accounted for much of the band's output, Eloy ventured into long-form composition and traditional European influences to achieve a similar musical amalgam brewed by Procol Harum.

"The time was right to start playing a brand of progressive rock that was German," says Bornemann.

A NEW DAWN

Inside attracted the attention of EMI Germany, and Eloy eventually signed to its progressive music sub, Harvest, home of their musical forefathers, Floyd.

"We changed a lot at that time: our rhythm guitar player, Manfred Wieczorke, started playing keyboards; Fritz Randow replaced Helmut Draht on drums; and I became lead vocalist," says Bornemann.

These personnel shifts set in motion a series of events that would forever shape Eloy's musical direction. Though a 1973 single, the (largely) instrumental "Daybreak" (different from the song appearing on the band's debut) failed to find an audience, and 1974's *Floating* was a lateral artistic move, each successive record steeled the band's commitment to progressive rock.

By 1975, having acquired bass player Luitjen Jansen, Eloy gathered enough creative courage to compose the Moog-laden concept album *Power and the Passion* (originally slated to be a double record), which told the tale of time travel and social intolerance in the Middle Ages—a cinematic story befitting the majestic, "big sky" LP cover photograph.

Through live performances and German radio airplay, Eloy generated a buzz, but growing tensions threatened to destroy the band. Not long after the release of *Power and the Passion*, Bornemann was Eloy's only remaining member.

Instead of folding up the band, the guitarist guided the ship through a turbulent period by recruiting fretted/fretless bass player Klaus-Peter Matziol, drummer/lyricist Jürgen Rosenthal, and keyboardist Detlev Schmidtchen—generally recognized as Eloy's most creative lineup.

The quartet banged out 1976's symphonic *Dawn*, centered on the concept of a spiritual entity's attempt to contact the living. With roaring sound effects, soaring orchestral strings, and Schmidtchen's sonically saturating Moog and Mellotron work, the album recalls many of the British prog milestones from the early '70s. The band even cheekily references Yes's "Ritual: Nous Sommes du Soleil" in the lyrics of the life-affirming "The Sun Song."

"We were four totally different characters, but still able to create music and to play together," says Bornemann

OCEANIC ELOY

Eloy were on the verge of commercial breakthrough—one radio-friendly single away from changing their world—but didn't give into the temptation of scoring a hit record. Instead, the band devised, of all things, yet another concept record, the four-track *Ocean*, hatched from the fertile mind of Rosenthal.

"The Eloi, like the Carlovingian kings, had decayed to a mere beautiful futility." —Wells, H. G. (Herbert George). *The Time Machine*. Electronic Text Center, University of Virginia Library.

Nektar: *A Tab in the Ocean*
(1972)

Nektar: *Remember the Future*
(1973)

Can: *Tago Mago*
(1971)

Amon Düül II: *Yeti*
(1971)

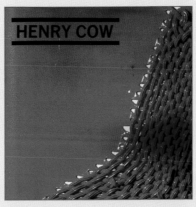

Henry Cow and Slapp Happy: *In Praise of Learning* (1975)

Eloy: *Colours*
(1980)

Ash Ra Tempel: *Schwingungen*
(1972)

Tangerine Dream: *Rubycon*
(1975)

Grobschnitt: *Rockpommel's Land*
(1977)

Based on the myths and legends of Atlantis, *Ocean* possesses many of Eloy's musical hallmarks: bombastic drumming (a tradition begun by dynamic player Fritz Randow), Gilmour-esque bluesy guitar solos, and sweeping, ethereal synth passages.

"*Ocean* was the record that really solidified our reputation as a serious recording band," Bornemann says.

It also flew in the face of convention. While the Sex Pistols and British punk bands were conquering the world, 1977's *Ocean* became the band's best-selling record to date (and remains so, as of this writing), moving hundreds of thousands of vinyl platters with its escapist morality tale.

"*Ocean* struck a chord, I think, because it taps that feeling in us that there's still much to explore and discover about the world," says Bornemann. "But it also sought to make predictions about the future."

SILENT CRIES

Eloy followed up *Ocean* with 1979's *Silent Cries* and *Might Echoes*, which continued in the band's epic-opus compositional approach, but creative difference split the band (Rosenthal and Schmidtchen quit).

Eloy pressed on with the addition of guitarist Hannes Arkona (who joined the band for dates on the *Silent Cries* European tour) and keyboardist Hannes Folberth, a lineup that helped the band greet the 1980s with a new outlook, a slightly different sound, and a new record—the muscular *Colours*.

Though Eloy consciously curbed some of their progressive tendencies throughout the 1980s, they retained a sense of their conceptual glory days throughout the decade and into 1990s with releases such as 1981's *Planets*, '82's *Time to Turn*, '83's *Performance*, '84's *Metromania*, and 1998's *Ocean 2: The Answer*, which Bornemann asserts is the positive flip side to 1977's *Ocean*.

"Everything that I wrote was, in a way, a reflection of my soul and my senses," says Bornemann. "I've been completely honest with everything I've ever done."

MIGHTY ECHOES

While it is true that Eloy's recorded output has been spotty over the last two decades, the band have been resuscitated back to life by their first release in twelve years—2010's *Visionary*, a seven-track, symphonic effort featuring bassist Klaus-Peter Matziol and keyboardist Hannes Folberth.

"If music is played well and has the ability to touch people's hearts," says Bornemann, "then it doesn't matter what you call it: progressive or not. The label is meaningless at that point. It's just music."

ASH RA TEMPEL

Formed in 1970 by legendary synthesizer player (then-drummer) Klaus Schulze, guitarist/bassist Hartmut Enke, and guitarist/synth player Manuel Göttsching (who later recorded Terry Riley–influenced, synth- and guitar-based electronica heard on 1976's *New Age of Earth* and 1984's *E2-E4*), Ash Ra Tempel may be Germany's greatest jam band.

"I almost compare Ash Ra Tempel to Cream and even Jimi Hendrix," says Göttsching. "We weren't Cream or Hendrix, but we played freely, touching upon a theme, as those artists often did when they performed live."

AMON DÜÜL

With releases such as 1969's *Phallus Dei*, 1970's *Yeti*, and 1971's *Tanz der Lemminge*, Amon Düül nurtured their music as it sprang from assorted vamps, chordal drones, and guitar/bass riffs. Rife with feedback and studio and guitar effects, the band's music was so visual and trippy, it was once believed to have been conceived on LSD. (This is untrue.)

Much of what we hear on the

GERMAN SPACE ROCK: WHAT IF?

As Pink Floyd, Hawkwind, and, to a degree, the Moody Blues were creating theatrical fantasy trips in the U.K., dubbed "space rock," Germans such as Amon Düül (later renamed Amon Düül II) on their artists' commune twenty kilometers outside Munich, Berlin's Ash Ra Tempel, and the Darmstadt-based Englishmen Nektar explored both the inner and outer cosmos, in some cases, asking profound questions.

One of the more trance-inducing German bands of the subgenre, Popol Vuh, formed in Munich in 1969, and initially experimented with electronics and synthesizers. By the early 1970s, the band had begun incorporating acoustic instruments such as the harpsichord/cembalo, sitar, and oboe on 1971's *In den Gärten Pharaos*, 1973's *Seligpreisung*, and 1974's *Einsjäger & Siebenjäger*, creating something akin to classical/world/electronica rock.

Throughout the 1970s and 1980s, keyboardist Florian Fricke worked closely with celebrated German film director Werner Herzog on sound tracks for movies such as 1973's *Aguirre*, the *Wrath of God*, 1979's *Nosferatu*, and 1982's *Fitzcarraldo*.

Amon Düül II: *Tanz der Lemmingei* (1971)

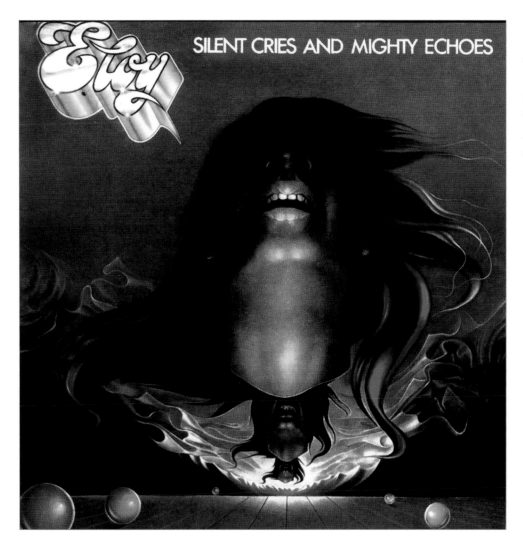

SILENT CRIES AND MIGHTY ECHOES

Eloy's 1979 record, *Silent Cries and Mighty Echoes* (left) followed in the creative footprints of 1977's breakthrough concept album, *Ocean*.

band's early efforts came directly from jams. The double record *Yeti*, for instance, is a shining example of the band's boundless musicality, as if a single album format couldn't contain their creativity.

"When we were doing *Yeti*, we were interested in using a real multitrack machine," says Amon Düül's guitarist/bassist John Weinzierl. "But for some reason, our engineer recorded it on two-track. We freaked out because we went into the studio wanting to use the technology. That's why *Yeti* became a double album. We did one album on two-track again and the other with sixteen with some improvisations, including 'Yeti Talks to Yogi.'"

While some of the band's music is arguably more accessible on later records (e.g., 1973's *Vive La Trance* contains nods to Eastern European, cabaret, glam, world, and classical music in "Fly United," "Ladies Mimicry," "Im Krater Blühn Wieder Die Baüme," and the seven-plus-minute anti-Western rant "Mozambique"), one would be hardpressed to call the band conformists. That is, at least until the late 1970s and early 1980s, which yielded 1978's new-wavish *Only Human*—for all intents and purposes a guitarist/violinist/saxophonist Chris Karrer solo record—and 1981's *Vortex*.

NEKTAR

Signed to the Bellaphon label in 1970 and bolstered by moving melodies and funky, fast-paced extended psychedelic blues-centric jams, Nektar created clas-

sics of the prog and space rock genre: 1972's *Journey to the Center of the Eye*; 1973's *Remember the Future* (a thirty-six-minute suite spanning both sides of the original LP); and perhaps their best-known effort, 1972's *A Tab in the Ocean*, the title track of which asked the musical question, What would happen to global politics and everyday life if the entire planet were spiked with LSD?

"We were all on the same wavelength," says Nektar guitarist/lead vocalist Roye Albrighton. "All we wanted to do back then was create music. People say we were prophesizing, but that wasn't it at all. It had nothing to do with that. We weren't prophets. We simply asked, *What if?* through our music."

(Waring Abbott/Getty Images)

SONG FOR AMERICA

Can the U.S. Export Prog?

A FUNNY AND PARADOXICAL THING about America: It was ahead of the curve on so many musical forms, from blues to jazz to hip-hop, yet when it came to "progressive" rock, it wasn't until the mid-1970s that U.S. bands began making any noticeable commercial impact. And when ELP were fading, when Yes were floundering with *Tormato*, when King Crimson hadn't released a studio record in four years and Genesis had moved, with each studio record, away from their more expressive and arty past and more toward a straightforward, hard-driving rock and pop style, bands like Kansas and Styx were carrying the flag in the mainstream in a high-profile way.

By 1980, Kansas's *Leftoverture*, *Point of Know Return*, *Masque*, *Song for America*, *Monolith*, *Audio-Visions*, and *Two for the Show* (a live double LP) had achieved precious-metal status in the U.S. alone, while containing some of the band's most epic rock recordings.

Similarly, Styx performed a hybrid form of pop and progressive rock that was, in part, inspired by the first wave of British bands. "When I wrote 'Lady,' I was listening to 'The Court of the Crimson King,'" admits Dennis DeYoung, the classic voice of Styx.

KANSAS

Kansas have caused so much controversy simply for being who they are. Rarely has a band inspired such division among fans and critics alike.

Some have said that Kansas, almost impossible to categorize, wound up in the progressive bin by default: Straddling the line between progressive and radio-friendly rock, they possess qualities of the great British progressive rock bands, from Yes to Gentle Giant, while incorporating homegrown influences such as American folk, Native American, and country and western motifs and imagery—a virtual grab bag of musical goods.

One can point out the blues influence of the band's early bar days in songs such as "Stay Out of Trouble" and "Two Cents Worth." But what would we call "Angels Have Fallen," which gleans elements of folk, Americana, and classical? "Roots rock"? This definition and description conjures a whole other scene.

Then we come to songs such as the orchestral and often quaint "Lamplight Symphony" and the multi-tempos and European-church counterpoint melodies of "Hopelessly Human." The latter makes a very peculiar mess: Drummer Phil Ehart's rhythmic punctuations and patterns—specific "notes" struck on toms and roto-toms—mesh well with the counter-melodies spun by the band. Yet throughout the song, straightforward blues-informed rock guitar and basic syncopated patterns are continually reprised (mostly during vocalist Steve Walsh's philosophical monologues).

Ehart literally plays nothing more than "one" and "three" on the hi-hat and "two" and "four" on a tom, yet the song doesn't seem to follow a simple pop or straightforward rock structure. For instance, the chorus is very nearly tucked into the violinist/vocalist Robby Steinhardt–sung "verses," rendering Walsh's "verses" de facto choruses (though there's no repetition of lyrics in Walsh's "choruses," as is generally the case with rock songs). It's all a bit confusing, contradictory, and odd. And none of it makes the picture any clearer or brings us closer to the answer to the question: *What the hell kind of music does Kansas make?* Some experts weigh in:

"I think Kansas is more of a progressive rock band than [Styx]," says DeYoung. "I always thought that. I always thought that we were a song-based pop-rock band with progressive rock overtones. That's what I always thought we were. I always thought song first, not arrangement. I think a lot of prog bands, they were more about the musicality and musicianship and the technical aspects of playing and the virtuosity, more like what I would call faux-classical musicians in rock."

"Kansas was even weirder because they had a violin," says Utopia bassist Kasim Sulton. "It was like, 'Who puts a violinist in a rock band?'"

"Here's a question for you," says Saga vocalist Mike Sadler. "I would ask people who had been listening to Kansas prior to their commercial success if they would continue call them prog? To me, it's the other way around: They got introduced to the prog community through success on the radio."

"We just made no sense to anyone, and we made no sense to ourselves," says Ehart. "There was just something about when the six of us started playing. The problem was, there really were . . . not many committed, full-time musicians in Topeka, so you had to pull from wherever to make a band. That's what made Kansas so freaking odd. We weren't a group of guys that shared musical tastes and we all came up in bands together. We really didn't. We had kind of gotten to a point in our lives when we were all that was left. Everybody else had gotten real jobs or gotten married. That was where the original six came from. It was kind of an attrition, survival of the fittest. We had formed White Clover, the five of us, with me and Dave [Hope, bassist] and Rich [Williams, guitarist] and Robby and Steve. We hadn't even added Kerry [Livgren] to the band yet."

"Kansas were signed with Rich as the only guitar player," says producer Jeff Glixman, who was a member of Ehart's pre-Kansas band White Clover with Williams, Walsh, and Hope. "Phil thought they needed strength in songwriting, so they brought in Kerry."

"I had a vision for this band as far as who I wanted to be in it," says Ehart. "I want to make this clear: Kansas came from all of us. But as far as who I wanted in the band, I remember starting with Dave and Rich because I had played with them in White Clover. I remember telling Rich, 'I want to go full time with this,' and Rich says, 'I'm in.' Steve was washing windows in St. Joe, Missouri, and I had called him and he said, 'Yeah. Let's do it.' I had seen Robby, and I had never played with Robby in a band before, but I had seen him in a band in Lawrence, Kansas, and I had seen him play violin and thought, 'He has got to be in this band.' The five of us started playing as White Clover and we recorded, down in Liberal, Kansas, and sent our reel-to-reel tapes to Don Kirshner."

"I remember wanting Steve to sing Kerry's songs," Ehart continues. "I had already played in a band with Kerry, an earlier formation of Kansas. I always told Kerry, 'Steve needs to sing your stuff.' He said, 'Really?' I said, 'This is the perfect combination.' It was just something I always heard in my head."

"The first time I met Steve, he drove up in . . . a car, and he had just been in a motorcycle wreck," says Glixman. "His arm and leg were sanded down to the bone and he was cut up. When he sat down and started playing Hammond organ and singing, I said, 'God, this is the most amazing guy I've ever heard.' He was nineteen, twenty years old."

"We had a band in Topeka [White Clover], and we were looking for a keyboard player, and he came over as an organist," says Ehart. "The big Hammond C-3 with the foot pedals. We heard him and we said, 'That's great, but we're kind of looking for

The mid 1970s Kansas. *Left to right*: bassist Dave Hope, guitarist Richard Williams, drummer Phil Ehart, guitarist/keyboardist Kerry Livgren, vocalist/keyboardist Steve Walsh, and violinist/vocalist Robby Steinhardt. (Neal Preston/CORBIS. Courtesy of Legacy Recordings)

Kansas: *Two for the Show* (1978)

someone who can sing.' He said, 'Well, I can sing, too.' And he sang 'Walk Me Out in the Morning Dew' just on the organ. We all stood there with our mouths open. It was like, 'Who is this guy?' It was like, 'Man. Me and this guy have got to work together.'"

"Phil is a kind of visionary," says Glixman. "Some people assign that description to others in the group, but I would have to give it to Phil. He saw it and he heard it before anyone else did."

"Putting the people together is about as much as I can take credit for," Ehart says. "But I had to believe in these guys, they in me, and us in each other that we could do this. Once we added Kerry to the band and became Kansas, it just took off as something none of us had really been prepared for."

Despite their considerable talents and admirable Midwestern determination, Kansas aren't considered by some purists to be a progressive rock band, largely because of their two massive radio hits and R&B- and country-tinged tracks such as "Can I Tell You," J. J. Cale's "Bringing It Back," and "Two Cents Worth." But then, where would we place "Magnum Opus"? "Cheyenne Anthem"? "Icarus (Borne on Wings of

Steel)"? "Song for America"? "Death of Mother Nature Suite"? "The Pinnacle"? While these songs are not esoteric musical excursions of the avant-garde variety, they often proved challenging for mainstream musical tastes.

"All the guys in Kansas were self-taught," says Ehart. "You know, sticky-carpet gigs, frat parties, rodeos, biker bars. When we read about other people, you know, 'He graduated from the Royal College of Music,' what the hell? We're just so much more Americanized. Our background, I can say for all six of us, was in the Midwest. Robby, playing the violin, did have quite a bit of classical training to learn how to play that instrument, because, realistically, that's the only way you're going to learn that instrument, unless you're going to be a fiddle player. But Robby was never a fiddle player. His dad was the head of musicology at the University of Kansas, and Robby grew up with that. By the time we were all nineteen or twenty, we had all dropped out of college and concentrated on what we were doing."

Like any other band of its generation, Kansas aspired to success (they wouldn't have allowed themselves to be signed to a record deal if not), but what's

amazing is that they didn't come up with a hit record until 1976's *Leftoverture*.

They were an unlikely fit for rock stardom—initially, the band hadn't realized just how lucky they were to be signed and given a chance. "Don Kirshner discovered us—out in the middle of freakin' nowhere in Enola, Kansas, where we staged a concert giving away free beer," says Ehart. "We knew that when Kirshner and his people came to see us we had better have some people there. We said, 'How are we going to do this?' So we bought a bunch of kegs and gave away free beer, and that was how we had a bunch of people show up. So when Wally Gold, Kirshner's right-hand man, shows up, there are people wrapped around the theater. He's thinking, 'They are like the Beatles.' But in actuality they showed up to drink beer.

"To be discovered by a guy who

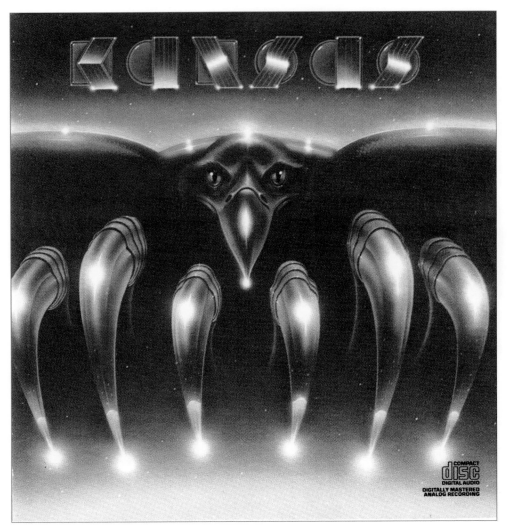

Kansas' 1975 record, *Song For America*, straddles many musical lines. "They were doing some things that we wish we could have done," says keyboardist Mike Ponczek of the American progressive rock band, Ethos (Ardour), signed to Capitol Records in the mid 1970s.

had his own rock TV show?" Ehart continues. "He started this label, Kirshner Records. He saw something in us that nobody else did, which was the violin and Steve's singing. We were naïve in those days. We worked real hard and our parents always told us that if you work really hard, you will get to do what you want to do. [laughs] Wrong. Little did we know that nine-

ty-nine out of one hundred bands never get that opportunity. Ever."

The band went to New York City to cut their debut. The recording was, as Ehart put it, "a freakin' joke." For one thing, Kansas were told not to bring their gear because the studio, the Record Plant, was well stocked.

"We went in to record and all the gear was crap," says Ehart. "It was junk,

beat up, studio gear that . . . [was] not quite as good as we had imagined. Those were songs that we had been playing for years. No click track, no overdubbing—well, maybe some overdubbing because of the vocals and leads and stuff, but on a lot of those songs like 'Death of Mother Nature Suite,' 'Journey from Mariabronn,' which is a complicated song with all those starts

Kansas (1974)

Kansas: *Masque* (1975)

Kansas: *Leftoverture* (1976)

Kansas: *Point of Know Return* (1977)

Kansas: *Monolith* (1979)

Proto-Kaw: *Before Became After* (2004)

and stops, and 'Apercu,' it was 'One, two, three go. Okay, next song.'"

"Lonely Wind" escapes the realm of the secular musically, spiritually, and lyrically. "Lonely Wind" is a white man's symphonic gospel song, complete with mournful violin playing filtered through European influences.

Kansas, the state, does have a history of evangelicalism, as the cover of the debut record indicates, featuring a painting by John Steuart Curry, *Tragic Prelude*, with Kansas radical abolitionist John Brown as the center image with a Bible in one hand and a Sharps rifle (also known in Kansas as a "Beecher's Bible") in the other.

"That album cover was a painting I had seen as a young teenager in the state capitol building," says Ehart. "I remember standing there thinking, 'If I ever have a band, this is going to be my album cover.' What did I know? I specifically remember telling some of the guys and they said, 'Are you kidding?' But it was like a no-brainer. Anyway, we get this onto an album cover—our first record. I couldn't find a picture of that mural anywhere, but my neighbor across the street, Don Richards, was the state photographer and had a picture of that in slide form. What are the chances of that? I got the slide from him and sent it to CBS Records and they put a crappy logo on the front.

"The photograph on the back was taken by this doofus named Don Hunstein, and I say that in all respect," continues Ehart. "It turns out he was one of the most famous rock photographers of all time. He was putting us out in front of Mack trucks and McDonald's, eating hamburgers. Then we looked up into the sky coming out of the west, the western sky of Kansas, and this big storm was coming in. It was one of those storms that spawns tornadoes, and there was one point in the plains of Kansas called Burnett's Mound, they didn't even call it Burnett's Hill, 'cause it wasn't even a hill. It truly was a

mound [and the highest place in Topeka]. We went up there and that storm came behind us and the sun came through the storm—the storm was behind us—and the sun is out in front and it was [an atmospheric condition] that lasted about thirty seconds. Then the sun went behind the clouds, the winds started blowing, and it turned into a crappy day. Don went back and touched up all the houses in the background, so they're all gone. It looked like we were standing out in the middle of the plains."

Whether they intended it to be or not, the 1975 epic tune "Song for America," from the band's sophomore record of the same title, is an anthem for all progressive rock bands in the U.S.

No British, Italian, Finnish, German, French, or any other European band wrote or could have written "Song for America"—one of the most enduring of Kansas's tunes, and certainly one of the greatest non-instrumental American progressive rock songs to be written prior to 1975. And no American band—prog or not—wrote this kind of material. "'Song for America' is one of the songs among many that sets us apart from a lot of the corporate rock bands at that time," says Ehart.

Rivals Styx, roughly a year later, would make their own statement about American society—a society Dennis DeYoung had feared was in danger of decline—with "Suite Madame Blue," which fuses sobering criticism, tough love, and pleas for a new start in the U.S. (The Italians PFM did it with *Chocolate Kings*, also the same year, but their take seemed more inciting than insightful.) "I've got three themes in my music, but I didn't know it at the time—my relationship with my wife and what that meant to me, the state of our country, and the belief that winners are losers who got up to give it one more try," says DeYoung.

Song for America also boasts the Livgren-penned grand haunter "Lamplight Symphony," which opens

with rumbling timpani; the wheezing organ, evocative jazz piano, and suspended chords underscore the song's gripping plotline (about a grieving husband visited by the ghost of his wife, who soothes his pain by explaining that they'll be together someday). Even more fascinating is the band's blues in 11/8 ("Lonely Street"), the first song on side two of the original LP. Is this not the epitome of what it means to be an American band, influenced by blues and roots music while adding complexity?

Closing the record, "Incomudro—Hymn to the Atman" could very well be the most spiritual song of the entire Kansas catalog. The term *Åtman* (or *atman*) is a Hindu (as well as Buddhist) term referring to the soul. In this case, Livgren, the songwriter, is speaking of the soul's attainment of nirvana through reincarnation, the circular nature of our spirits, the Zen attitude of meeting life with a smile, and the simple act of meditating to achieve a higher state of consciousness.

Kansas followed *Song for America* with *Masque*, a fan favorite, featuring "Icarus (Borne on Wings of Steel)," "All the World," and the gnarly "Mysteries and Mayhem" (about being cursed by God to forever wander the earth, as in the biblical story of Cain and Abel in Genesis), which complements the following song, the aforementioned "The Pinnacle"—impressive, occasionally sprawling compositions all. Sandwiched between them are more straightforward songs, such as "Two Cents Worth," "It Takes a Woman's Love (to Make a Man)," and "It's You"—the Kansas schizophrenia at work.

"It amazes us how [*Masque*] is a favorite for so many Kansas fans," says Ehart. "It sounds odd. It has a dark cover. It was a record we came off the road [to record], did in a hurry, went back on the road in a hurry. It has real light and poppy songs like 'Two Cents Worth' and 'It Takes a Woman's Love' and yet also 'The Pinnacle' and 'Mysteries and Mayhem.' To me,

Masque is kind of a metamorphosis. We were in a cocoon—a [caterpillar] changing into a butterfly, if you will.

"By *Masque*, [Kirshner] needed a hit," Ehart continues. "The first record did fifty thousand [sales], the second album 150, and *Masque* got up to 250. So he was making money. It wasn't like he was losing money. But Kirshner was all about publishing hit songs, and, by accident, 'Carry On Wayward Son' came along and *kaboom-o*. It was a success, because in those days there was such a thing as artist development and such a thing as FM radio where a band could go out for three or four albums and actually build a following. On tour we went from the Kinks to Queen to Bad Company to Jefferson Airplane to the Beach Boys to Billy Joel and Hawkwind. Mott the Hoople. We just went from band to band to band as an opener. Radio at the same time was playing 'Song for America' [an edit] and 'Icarus,' and we were starting to get a following. So when you hear 'Mysteries and Mayhem,' heck, yeah. It's very obvious it was pre-*Leftoverture*. We had things like 'Icarus,' where Kerry was starting to write this really impressive material. If you pay attention to what we are writing and how we are writing, you can tell that something's coming."

That "something" would be the band's critical, artistic, and commercial success, *Leftoverture*, an album recorded in just seven weeks. Songs "*The Wall*," "Questions of My Childhood," "Miracles Out of Nowhere," "What's On My Mind," "Magnum Opus" and "Carry On Wayward Son," the last song to make the record, have become classics and set a standard in musicianship and audio fidelity. Sections that could have been imbalanced and muddy are sharp and possess a kind of glow. Where older Kansas material seemed to absorb darkness, *Leftoverture* is bright and detailed; each individual instrument in the mix can be heard, and the integrity of the song isn't compromised. We hear with crystal clarity every crack of the bullwhip ("Magnum Opus") and every crisp beat banged out on a throaty tom-tom (which is partly the result of the studio's pecan-wood walls and tile floor), a perfect fusion of songwriting and production.

"Things just sounded great," says Ehart. "Everyone was singing and playing well . . . and we were focused and well rehearsed. We were all starting to see money for the first time, so people could actually eat, which was a new concept for a starving musicians."

The rehearsals for the record would prove to be the most productive of the band's career; Livgren, who had contributed so much to the previous albums, was at his creative peak, and the band could do no wrong. "Every day at rehearsals it was like, 'What did Kerry bring today?'" says Ehart. "That's how 'Carry On Wayward Son' got on the record. After we heard it, it was a no-brainer, you know? And it almost didn't make the record.

"We had already finished rehearsing for *Leftoverture*, and we had worked up the songs, and as we were breaking down our gear on the last day," Ehart continues, "Kerry had one more song that he said he would like to play for us down at the studio. Once we got down there and heard the song, we were all going, 'Yeah. That is a really serious song there.' So that song made it by the skin of our teeth. If someone would have said, 'Nah, we have enough stuff,' 'Carry On Wayward Son' [might] never have surfaced.

"The freakin' idiotic drum part that was at the beginning?" says Ehart. "You know, 'Don't you cry no more ...' *boom-boom, boom-boom, dat*. When we were recording the song, we were actually starting to overdub, and we learned that song in the studio. That drum part you hear was only supposed to be a marker. I'd go back in and put down some mind-numbing part that, you know, went *skeetly-deeddely doodley doop*. Something like that. Something a bit more impressive, because at the time I was into impressing people, as we all were at an early age. So we went on to record that song and that *boom-boom, boom-boom, plat* was just there. We'd do the guitar parts and we'd have to hear that. We recorded the vocals and we'd have to listen to that. So it started to grow on us. I remember Jeff Glixman turning to me and saying, 'I think you ought to leave that drum part in there.'"

Upon its release, *Leftoverture* soared to number five on the *Billboard* charts, and "Carry On Wayward Son" would forever be a staple of FM radio and an audio standard. Major rock bands from Heart to Foreigner would request their records sound like *Leftoverture*.

That's why it was a surprise to find that *Point of Know Return* was a bit of a sonic mess. Not that the band suffered commercially. *Point of Know Return* went to number four on the U.S. charts and sold more than four million records in the U.S. at last count. And the songs were there—the title track (which saw heavy radio rotation) and the clincher, "Dust in the Wind." The ubiquity of that song—which reached the country charts—was and is frightening.

The odd times, strange arrangements, and same weird amalgam of symphonic prog were all present. But something was missing. "You listen to *Point of Know Return* and it was like, 'Whoa. What happened there?'" says Ehart. "We ran into some recording problems—the studio we were in shut down and we had to move to another studio, and then another one in L.A. That record was moved all over the place."

Due to the success of *Leftoverture*, the rock 'n' roll lifestyle and excess perhaps did a number on Kansas. Personal problems invaded the band's production process, causing havoc. The songwriters weren't on the same page and weren't working together—or at all, in some cases. Far from presenting the cohesive vision of *Leftoverture* (which by comparison feels like a concept record), *Point of*

Somewhere to Elsewhere
(2000)

Paradise Theater
(1981)

Pieces of Eight
(1978)

time for us."

The band went on a massive stadium tour of North America to support 1979's *Monolith*, which helped the record go gold, but the members of Kansas were going in different directions. Walsh released a solo record, *Schemer-Dreamer*, and returned to the band for 1980's *Audio-Visions*. "Steve and Kerry started doing solo albums, and once you do that, you don't give the band your best material," says Glixman. "It is too bad. Neither one of them did alone what they did as a unit. They never wrote together as a unit, per se, but their collaborations were exceptional."

If *Monolith* was the closing chapter to the band's 1970s escapades, then Kansas's second consecutive self-produced record, *Audio-Visions*, was the beginning of new creative directions, opening different vistas. Even Peter Lloyd's cybererotic album cover artwork seemed an attempt by Kansas to distance themselves from their past and appear futuristic. *Audio-Visions* presents a much slicker (more so than *Monolith* a year prior), more refined Kansas, who were further polishing their prog tendencies to create muscular, deceptively complex songs.

The band was getting very good at smoothing out the jagged edges—the self-aware weirdness that made the band Kansas—and turning their work into formulaic commercial rock. That isn't to say that *Audio-Visions* contains bad music. But the band had reached its pinnacle in balancing a commercial sound with its proggy side to the point that the adventurous qualities of the music were sometimes buried in production gloss.

Walsh quit the band, seemingly for good. Singer John Elefante stepped in, and Kansas enjoyed two hits in as many years: a Top 20 song, "Play the Game Tonight" (from 1982's *Vinyl Confessions*), and "Fight Fire with Fire" (on *Drastic Measures*), the video for which was in heavy rotation on MTV.

Know Return limped to the finish line.

To make matters worse, the band was booked for a national tour and needed music sent to radio stations across the nation before they set foot on a tour bus. Walsh was nursing throat issues (he even threatened to quit—and did only temporarily before rejoining), while the rest of the production team and band were floating in and out of studios just to complete the project. It was nothing short of a nightmare.

Whether anyone could really see it, the band's greatest commercial *and* progressive period was drawing to a close.

"It really was the end of a cycle," says Ehart. "It wound down at that

"After that, the band went on hiatus," says Ehart. "Actually, we disbanded. Kerry, Dave Hope, Robby, Steve had all left the band, and Richard [Williams] had gone fishing. It was just basically one of those things that I thought, 'Well, if we are going to keep it going, we are going have to take a shot *now*.'"

Kansas re-formed (minus Livgren), with Steve Walsh and Steve Morse of the Dixie Dregs, and went on to deliver the explosive 1986 comeback commercial rock record Power and the Bob Ezrin–produced concept record, 1988's *In the Spirit of Things*.

Though the band's sound was virtually unrecognizable to fans of the classic lineup (Steinhardt was gone, and so was the violin element), Morse's rifle-fast pick-every-note riffing, Walsh's inhuman range, and Ehart's sophisticated pounding made for a potent (if only mainstream) heavy rock combination.

"That was an incredible time for Steve Morse and Kansas," says Ehart. "I think it was Steve Morse's foray into a real band—a real democracy. He was running his own show with the Dregs. He was great. He had his growing pains like anybody else, of course. Billy Greer [bassist] had just joined the band, and these were the MCA years. We did two records with MCA, the *Power* album and the Bob Ezrin record, *In the Spirit of Things*, which we consider one of our best records ever. Putting Steve [Morse] and Steve Walsh together was a lot of sparks. I met Steve Morse at a Robert Plant concert and he said he wanted to come over and audition, which was funny that he thought he *needed* to audition. We jammed a little bit, and he and Steve started working on material. Steve told me he wanted to step in as a guitar player and take the Kerry role. He said, 'I'm not good enough to write the way Kerry did.'"

Ultimately, Morse's growing pains meant he constantly had to fight for his musical ideas, which led to the guitarist quitting the band. Soon after, MCA dropped Kansas.

"You'll hear people talk about Journey, Chicago, Styx, Foreigner, and Boston, and we are never mentioned with those bands," says Ehart. "Then people mention Yes and Genesis and ELP and we are never mentioned with those bands either, which is fine. We are not like any of those bands. We're very much an anomaly. That's why reviewers hated us—we didn't fit into a bowl.

"Many years ago our agent tried to get us on Farm Aid," Ehart continues. "We are the band Kansas, right? But they told us that we were not the kind of band they wanted on the bill. We're used to being the ugly stepchild. We are what we are, and that's exactly why our fans love us."

STYX

Nineteen seventy-seven's *The Grand Illusion* and 1978's *Pieces of Eight* may be the best examples of Styx balancing commercialism with prog, but the band had recorded a string of quasi-prog records in the early and mid-1970s, including *Styx, Styx II, The Serpent Is Rising, Man of Miracles*, and *Equinox*. Throughout their career Styx straddled the line between prog and pop, with such songs as the classically inflected "Clair De Lune" (a piece composed by Claude Debussy), "Come Sail Away," "Castle Walls," "Pieces of Eight," "Father O.S.A.," "Crystal Ball," "A Day" (which falls somewhere between blues, folk, jazz, and liturgical rock), "Little Fugue in G," "I'm O.K.," the thirteen-minute "Movement for the Common Man" (featuring Aaron Copland's "Fanfare for the Common Man"), "The Grove of Eglantine," "Man of Miracles" (its use of timpani and basic opening theme eerily echo Kansas's "Magnum Opus," which appeared nearly two years *after* Styx's *Man of Miracles* record), and "Best Thing" (with its "Knife Edge"–like organ honks).

"*Equinox*—that, to me, is our com-

ing-out album," says Dennis DeYoung, Styx's lead vocalist and keyboardist for thirty years. "It had 'Light Up,' 'Lorelei,' 'Suite Madame Blue,' 'Midnight Ride.' We had made four records before this that, in my opinion, were not very good. But *Equinox* was it."

The proof, as they say, is in the pudding. Fittingly, "Lorelei" (the second track on *Equinox*), a song aglow with the romantic euphoria, scored a number twenty-seven spot on the *Billboard* Top 40 chart in March 1976. *Equinox* hit number 58 on the Top 200 Albums chart.

DeYoung had emerged as a solid songwriter, one who was arguably the most accomplished player and singer/arranger in the band at that point, having written, or cowritten with guitarist/singer John Curulewski and guitarist/vocalist James Young, Styx classics such as "Light Up," "Suite Madame Blue," "Born for Adventure," "Lorelei," "Lonely Child," and "Mother Dear."

As the band's fortunes swelled, so did the instances of stage theatrics on tour. "We used to do a sword fight onstage [during 'Born for Adventure']," says DeYoung. "In the middle of the song, this guy would come out with a big pirate hat and cape, and he would throw me a foil in the middle of the guitar solo, and we would sword fight. You talk about pretentiousness, you're talking to the number-one guy."

Despite the band's newfound success, Curulewski, while a great foil for DeYoung (and also a great songwriter in his own right), decided to leave the band to focus on his personal life and his own music. (Tragically, Curulewski died in the late '80s from a brain aneurysm.) Seemingly undeterred, Styx brought in Alabama-born guitarist/vocalist/songwriter Tommy Shaw (who made his Styx debut with 1976's *Crystal Ball*) just as audiences were packing venues like never before. Shaw's presence was felt immediately in the music: "Mademoiselle," cowritten by DeYoung and Shaw, reached number thirty-six on *Billboard*'s Top 40 chart just as *Crystal Ball* soared to number sixty-six of the Top 200.

"We needed someone to sing the high part in 'Lady,'" says DeYoung. "Tommy Shaw sat at the piano, and he could do it. He never picked up a guitar. He played some tapes of his songwriting. I said, 'This guy is the *guy*.' I didn't even care if he could play guitar. The fact that he *could* was a bonus. I wanted a songwriter in the band. You know, I told you the most important thing—songwriting—and that is why he got hired. Unbeknownst to me, he was a very good live performer."

By 1977, Styx appeared to be nothing more than a knockoff of more successful progressive and quasi-progressive rock bands on either side of the pond.

"We started making records in 1972 with a very distinct style, right?" says DeYoung. "'Lady' was written before I ever knew who Queen were. The problem was, we weren't really discovered in the United States until 1975, because our first four albums were completely buried and nobody knew who we were. So, we were doing that high-harmony, pop–progressive rock thing in 1972. I remember when Kansas backed us up for the first time, back in, I think, it was 1974. Kerry Livgren came backstage and said to us, 'Man, we were really influenced by the *Serpent Is Rising* album.' I thought to myself, 'Geez. I *hate* that record.' We were before Kansas. Boston. Queen. But we were not yet as successful as all those guys. So we appeared to many people as second-generation to those bands.

"Here's my problem with progressive rock: After the first fifteen minutes, it [is] like, 'Man, that guy can play like that,'" says DeYoung. "But then these prog rock bands went into what I call 'musical masturbation,' and you can do it, but it had better have a song in there. You take

me on a journey, but I want the song first. Then I can go with you."

"Do you want to go so progressive that you leave a market behind?" says Rik Emmett of Triumph fame. "American bands . . . are going to figure it out a lot quicker than someone who comes from the hinterlands. You won't figure it out as quickly as a bunch of guys from Chicago who have a band called Styx. Those guys are going to figure it out and get it right, and they are going to get it right over and over again. To the point that people say, 'They're not a progressive band. They are just a rock band.' In a sense, they are. But in another sense, they're doing things that borrow from the progressive community. They took from Yes, and in truth Dennis DeYoung is a kind of music theater guy, really. Now we are coming back to it. What is progressive rock? It has to have drama. It is almost like music theater in a way, isn't it? It doesn't make it much different from when Mozart was putting on *The Magic Flute*."

This musical drama is something Styx had done very well on *The Grand Illusion*, which plays like a concept album expounding on the paradoxes of fame.

It's easy to be deceived by the pomp and circumstance of the record. The opening title track trumpets out of our speakers with something resembling a classical rock march—a fitting oeuvre for such a record.

"The lyrics were warning, 'Don't buy this. Don't believe in this. Don't be fooled by the radio, the TV, or the magazines. They'll show you photographs of how your life should be, but they're just someone else's fantasy,'" DeYoung continues. "We said, 'We see you in the audience. You're looking at us up here. I know what you're thinking and it ain't true. This is a grand illusion for your entertainment.' This was 1977. That was all bullshit. That is what I said. But 'please buy our tickets anyway.'"

The Grand Illusion went to number six on the *Billboard* Album chart

and spawned two hit singles: "Come Sail Away" (number eight) and "Fooling Yourself (The Angry Young Man)" (number 29).

"I discovered Styx when I was looking through my dad's record collection," says Oliver Wakeman, current keyboardist for the Strawbs and Yes, two gigs his father Rick also won decades ago. "I had a demo copy of *The Grand Illusion*. It obviously had been given to Dad because he was on A&M Records as well. I remember putting this record on . . . and hearing 'Miss America,' which blew me away. Then I started to listen to the other tracks, 'Fooling Yourself,' 'Castle Walls,' 'Come Sail Away.' This whole album from start to finish I thought was superb. . . . It kind of made me realize that as a keyboard player you can rock out a little bit. You don't always have to just write the ballads because you play a keyboard."

"The Oberheim was my signature sound," says DeYoung. "Hammond organ and Oberheim and whatever else was handy, basically. I had a Moog 10, which I used on 'Lady.' I also used an ARP 2600 on some records. ARP Pro Soloist sometimes. But mostly Oberheim. If it had keys, I played it."

The band's next studio record, *Pieces of Eight*, was a conceptual record ruminating on the fame and fortune the band had recently experienced.

"I told the guys after *The Grand Illusion* that we had made more money in one year than we could ever have imagined," says DeYoung. "It was ridiculous. What did it mean to have this fame and this money? What did it mean if you were Lords of the Ring, suddenly? When you make a lot of money, you find out who your friends are. You find out who your family is. That's what *Pieces of Eight* is about. 'The search for the money tree/ Don't cash your freedoms in for gold.' That's me telling myself what I needed to hear."

Despite their diversity, the band

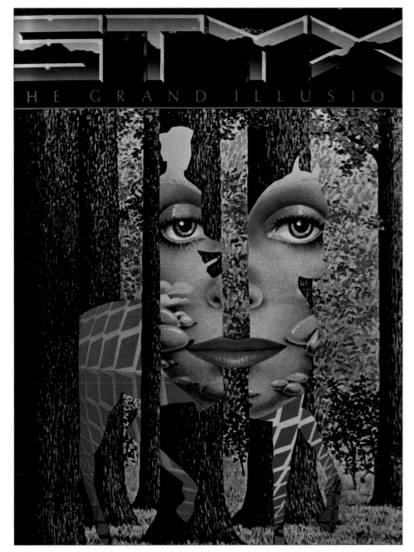

The cover of Styx's *The Grand Illusion* is a cunning knockoff of surrealist René Magritte's 1965 painting, *Carte Blanche* (aka *Le blanc-seing*).

Kilroy Was Here, the latter two (ironically) being concept albums and inspiring extravagant rock shows.

"After we started writing songs, I started to get ideas about how to stage [*Paradise Theater*]," says DeYoung, who portrayed Pontius Pilate for a theatrical production of *Jesus Christ Superstar* in 1993, and in 1997 presented the musical *The Hunchback of Notre Dame*. "I said, 'I have some ideas to stage this theatrically as the old theater house coming back to life.' It worked. It was our most successful tour. It set the record at that time for the most people in an indoor arena tour."

When the band hit the road to support *Kilroy Was Here*, Styx presented more musical theater: DeYoung, for one, wore a costume complete with heavy robot boots, and during the performance, band members read lines from a script.

Prior to the live-action show, a ten-minute film was shown, outlining *Kilroy*'s convoluted plot involving a former rock star wrongly accused of murder and silenced by the head of the Majority for Musical Morality, Dr. Everett Righteous.

"There will be those who think that we should have never changed," says DeYoung. "I know when the Beatles first made *Revolver*, I thought they had lost their minds. Now I think differently. *Paradise Theater* is more like *Cornerstone* than *Pieces of Eight*. Show me the prog rock on that one, because I don't know where it is. It's not there. Yet that was even a bigger seller. It was a pop rock record and I'm not ashamed of that. Now that I still wander around this country of ours, I see that people still like 'em. Mission accomplished."

feared they were being pigeonholed. "After 1978, the *Pieces of Eight* record, I felt I was being tagged as 'Mr. Prog Rock,'" DeYoung says. "I had done it for almost eight albums. I looked around and I said, 'I think prog rock is going to die.' At that moment, we went to [England for the first time]. I was in love with the Beatles and the English music scene, and we arrived on the shores of England just as we were being called a dinosaur, being vilified by the English press. We were in the rapturous throes of the Sex Pistols and the beginning of the punk movement. I saw that and I said, 'Jesus. What is this thing?' I thought, 'If [the press] were looking to the antithesis of what we do, they've found it.' For me, 99 percent of it was antimusic. I thought it was a social movement, and I'm interested in writing songs and music."

The story goes that punk and its minions may have tried to kill prog, but they were unsuccessful. As proof, *Pieces of Eight* was selling millions of units, and a 1979 Gallup poll revealed that Styx were the U.S.'s most popular band among teenagers.

Of course, the band would continue to have less and less to do with prog rock as they recorded *Cornerstone* (which spawned the Fender Rhodes–driven number-one hit "Babe," which DeYoung confesses was his first time using that particular electric piano), *Paradise Theater*, and

TUBULAR BELLS

Mike Oldfield

TUBULAR BELLS

Exorcising Mike Oldfield

MIKE OLDFIELD WAS JUST FIFTEEN WHEN HE RECORDED THE
album *Children of the Sun* (issued through Nat Joseph's Transatlantic Records
in Britain) with his sister Sally Oldfield as the folk outfit Sallyangie. The duo
didn't stir up much attention (though it has become something of a cult hit)
and broke up after the release of debut, at which time Mike decided to join
forces with another sibling, his brother Terry, with whom he formed Barefoot.
But Barefoot didn't make much of an impression either, and it too broke up.

Oldfield was a shy and insecure youth who holed up in his bedroom to
escape the perils of his dysfunctional family (his mother was a heavily medicat-
ed manic-depressive). He created his own world by listening to Bartók, John
Renbourn, Bert Jansch, flamenco guitarist Paco Peña, and others, and learning
the ins and outs of a variety of instruments and fingerpicking guitar technique.
He gained a reputation on the British music scene as something of a guitar
prodigy. At age sixteen he was asked to play bass as a member of Kevin Ayers's
the Whole World backing band.

Consisting of keyboardist and arranger David Bedford, who'd later forge a
musical relationship with Oldfield; Soft Machiner Robert Wyatt on drums; saxophonist Lol Coxhill; and Ayers himself (who had recently signed with EMI's
progressive sublabel Harvest), the Whole World (along with Richard Sinclair on
bass and others) cut two records: *Shoot at the Moon* and
Whatevershebringswesing, the former being the follow-up to Ayers's oddly enter-
taining solo debut, *Joy of a Toy*—a slightly loony hybrid of psychedelia, studio

experimentation, and pop, rooted as much in British literary tradition (evocative of childlike wonder à la Lewis Carroll) as musical tradition.

While a member of Ayers's band, Oldfield began tinkering with his own ideas, even experimenting in the studio environment until Ayers lent him a tape recorder to construct his compositions. Oldfield customized the device to allow for multitracking.

Oldfield went from label to label in England, playing them portions of his unfinished work, but no one bit. The question was raised: "How could we sell an eighteen-minute instrumental?" Oldfield didn't have an answer, except to continue working on his recording project—even when it was at times inappropriate.

One promising lead was Virgin Records' retail store, which had recently opened in London. (Prior to this, Virgin was a mail-order retail music business.) Oldfield's demo caught the attention of both Tom Newman and Simon Heyworth (the in-house producers/engineers of the soon-to-be Virgin label), who knew Oldfield from sessions he'd done as a bass player with singer Arthur Louis at Virgin honcho Richard Branson's Manor Studio.

Without the proper mechanism in place to support a young artist, Virgin turned the eighteen-year-old away. Disappointed but determined, Oldfield pushed on and again made a run at releasing his massive instrumental via an established label. Still no luck.

Some months passed and it occurred to Oldfield that perhaps he should try Virgin again: They'd seemed receptive, and maybe their business

operations had evolved or fundamentally changed. Oldfield returned to Branson, and this time the barely formed label did not let the quiet but persistent composer slip away: Oldfield became Virgin Records' first signing.

Oldfield was committed to his original material. He was all but done with the Whole World, living at Branson's newly built Manor Studio in Oxfordshire, working for the better part of six months (from the autumn of 1972 through the spring of '73) on his composition, which was based on the structuralism of classical composing but also used rock instrumentation and amplification. The composer layered tracks and played most of the instruments himself, using an enormous number of tracks to achieve his goal.

"Mike is a multi-instrumentalist," says Heyworth, one of three recording engineers for the record that would become *Tubular Bells*. "He wanted to play everything. If he heard it in his head, he wanted to be able to play it."

Tracked in the days before digitization, *Tubular Bells* stands as a legendary feat of musical production. "It was difficult, because there were only sixteen tracks," says Heyworth. "We didn't have computers then. I had a track sheet, which was a roll of paper that we would roll out on the floor and was divided into blocks of a minute, or something like that, in colored crayons to mark which track certain bits of music were on. Mike would point to the chart and say, 'At this point a bit of music starts . . .' and then he'd say, pointing someplace else, 'At this point, something else starts. . . .' So, you'd have to plan it all out ahead before you got to the mixing

stage. Where does everything fit? Where is everything going to go?"

Nerves were frayed, tempers flared, and tapes were many. "I became a very adept tape operator," Heyworth says. "It all became really complicated. There were points where we would have to mix all of the tracks down and make more space for more overdubs. We were forever overrunning and going into the next section and erasing what we had spent hours recording."

The Manor's production crew was stretched to its very limits, using whatever effects and creative innovations they could to help realize Oldfield's dream. Effects such as "taped motor drive amplified organ chord" or double-speed guitar were created in the studio.

The production of the record became more and more nerve-racking and detailed as the weeks wore on. For one thing, Oldfield continued to insist on playing all of the instruments, from electric, bass, and acoustic guitar to glockenspiel, Farfisa organ, and grand piano. But it soon became apparent that Oldfield couldn't play *everything* himself. Others needed to be contacted for contribution, such as Jade Warrior's flautist Jon Field, Edgar Broughton Band drummer Steve Broughton, vocalists sister Sally Oldfield and Mundy Ellis, string bassist Lindsay Cooper (not to be confused with the bassoonist Lindsay Cooper, who performed with Henry Cow and Hatfield and the North—both Virgin artists), and "master of ceremonies" Viv Stanshall, of Bonzo Dog Band fame. (It's Stanshall who introduces instruments by name as they state the lead melody, including the clanging

Tubular Bells (1973)

Hergest Ridge (1974)

Ommadawn (1975)

Incantations (1978)

Five Miles Out (1982)

Crises (1983)

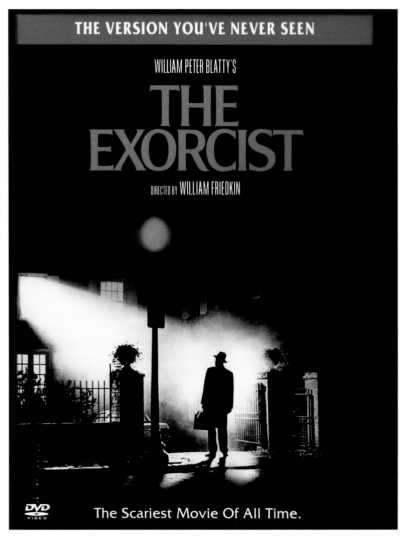

THE VERSION YOU'VE NEVER SEEN

WILLIAM PETER BLATTY'S

THE EXORCIST

DIRECTED BY WILLIAM FRIEDKIN

DVD VIDEO

The Scariest Movie Of All Time.

Mike Oldfield's chilling *Tubular Bells* perfectly captured the mood of William Friedkin's horror blockbuster, *The Exorcist*.

When Bedford tackled the *Orchestral Tubular Bells* project (a record that he admits was Richard Branson's attempt to "milk the '*Tubular Bells*' phenomenon"), he learned just how complex the piece is. "I had to listen to all the tracks to replicate them in the orchestra, and I'd discover little themes that changed throughout the piece," says Bedford. "The piece was never written out before. Oldfield may have written a few chords down, but it was nothing like this. I probably know the actual notation of the piece better than he does."

Despite its complexities and subtleties, critics scoffed that *Tubular Bells* was little more than a pale, boring pastiche of greater, more serious works by such composers as American minimalist Terry Riley. Admittedly, Riley's *A Rainbow in Curved Air*, with its repetitive and cyclical aspects, and even Steve Reich's *Piano Phase* (for two pianos) from 1967 seem to be forerunners to *Tubular Bells* and other long compositions such as *Ommadawn* and *Incantations*.

Audiences couldn't have cared less one way or another. "*Tubular Bells*," a three-minute edited version of the composition (under the title "Now the Original Theme from *The Exorcist*"), reached number seven on the *Billboard* Hot 100 chart (and took up residence there for ten weeks), and the album of the same title hit number three on the Top 200 Albums chart. (The record went gold in the U.S. in March 1974 and to date has sold more than thirteen million copies across the globe.)

Tubular Bells catapulted Oldfield to stardom and was the foundation stone in Virgin's industrial complex, one that willingly supported experimental music through the mid-1970s by signing bands such as Hatfield and the North, Gong, and Henry Cow.

bells of the song's title, in the "Finale.") "All Mike wanted was his music played correctly," says Jon Field.

After an excruciating process, *Tubular Bells* (one song in two parts, each spanning a single side of the original LP) was finally completed and released in May 1973, and by July it had soared to number one on the British charts.

Meanwhile, across the pond, *Tubular Bells* was being imprinted on the minds of music listeners in a slightly different way, due to its inclusion in the horror blockbuster *The Exorcist*, released in December '73. An edit of the massive composition and even a rerecorded section of *Tubular Bells* were released as singles on both sides of the Atlantic.

Despite how perfectly the icy open bars of *Tubular Bells* capture the mood of director William Friedkin's wintry and insidious film, the composition stands on its own merits—Oldfield himself didn't see *The Exorcist* until years later.

"You can say that *Tubular Bells* is a collection of three-minute pieces, if you want to be unkind," says David Bedford, who later arranged *Tubular Bells* and conducted the Royal Philharmonic Orchestra for Virgin's 1975 release Orchestral *Tubular Bells* (featuring Oldfield on guitar). "That is, just three-minute instrumental pieces, without any singing, vaguely linked together. But I did a proper musical analysis once, and the themes did progress and lead into other themes quite logically."

(Richard E. Aaron/Getty Images)

Marshall
100-watt head

2 H.H. power
heads

2 8-12"
custom
cabinets

PA

ers 25w Celestions)

DY LEE

nberger

Nady
transmitter/

APLS50A EQ

BGW 750C

Custom 2-15"

PA

PA

PA

RUSH

Modern-Day
Warriors

ondary Kit
ns: T... ...mons
ass dr...
ingerland snare
mons tom-tom modules
ons snare module
ons Clap Trap

als: Zildjian
-hat
de
ash
ash
hina

YOU RARELY SEE THEIR NAMES
in the tabloids. They don't aspire to
live the Hollywood life. Or crash parties or cars, or trash hotel rooms. They
retain a measure of anonymity while
successfully inspiring excellence in
themselves and their devotees.

They're not American. Or
English. They're Canadian. In other
words some of the most *un- rock 'n'
roll* rock 'n' rollers in rock 'n' roll.

But as much as any British progressive band featured in this book,
Rush are the personification of the
idea that the music is all that matters—moving with the times (not

A mid-'80s Rush. *Left to right*: bassist/vocalist Geddy Lee, guitarist Alex Lifeson, and drummer/lyricist Neil Peart. (Courtesy of Mercury/PolyGram Records)

Moving Pictures (1981)

bowing to the trends), loved by fans, and utterly confusing critics.

Bassist Geddy Lee is as normal as they come—he talks about baseball, makes an offhand joke. His is the kind of down-to-earth talk that drives music writers and critics mad.

Rush guitarist Alex Lifeson is another story, but one with a similar ending. Thinking of Lifeson, you might recall the numerous schizophrenic and sizzling guitar solos he's ripped out during the course of his career—in the "Overture" in "2112," "Emotion Detector" (from *Power Windows*), "Xanadu" (*A Farewell to Kings*), "La Villa Strangiato"

(*Hemispheres*), "The Spirit of Radio" and "Freewill" (*Permanent Waves*), "The Necromancer" (*Caress of Steel*), and "Mission" (*Hold Your Fire*), among others—yet little of his persona seems to hint at the feral qualities of his guitar solos. When you meet Lifeson, you're struck by a welcoming glow. He's understated. Intelligent. Patient. When you ask him a question, he ponders it for a moment and then returns to your inquiry, issuing you a conscientious and earnest answer.

"Alex is a lovely chap and terribly diplomatic," explains Rupert Hine, who coproduced Rush's late-1980s and early-1990s records *Presto* and *Roll the Bones*. "He would always try to absorb everyone's opinion and try to make his parts work as well as anybody's. So he was used to pleasing the producer and, hopefully, himself."

"We are low-key people," Lee told the author in 2000, "and not very image-conscious. We think like musicians and we act like musicians. I

value my privacy tremendously but [I] refuse to stop my life. Some people are more fiercely private. Neil [Peart, drummer], for example, is a very private person . . . and that's the way he chooses to live his life."

Peart has said that he would like to be "completely anonymous when I'm not onstage." But because of the popularity of Rush, which has spawned the teeming number of aspiring and aging rockers to whom Mr. Peart has been an inspiration, and owing to the massive amount of firepower the drummer brings with him onstage (two drum kits, an acoustic and an electronic), it's a certainty he'll always be anything but.

Peart's work is so detailed and seemingly so precise that sometimes critics have squawked that he consciously "subdivides" his beats, or that he has no genuine "feel." These criticisms are patently absurd, even though Peart has said that his preparedness is a character "flaw."

"It's only in the recent five or ten years that [Peart] has started to try to be spontaneous," says producer Paul Northfield, a native Brit who moved to Canada in the late 1970s, who has engineered such Rush albums as *Permanent Waves*, *Moving Pictures*, *Exit . . . Stage Left*, and *Signals*. "In the early days, every last little accent was worked out to the extent that even when they did videos—which [Peart] used to hate—he was the only one who could get everything note-for-note perfect. [He] could shoot a video a year after they'd recorded the album and every shot of him playing would be right on the money."

"Neil was always very, very prepared," longtime Rush producer and native Brit Terry Brown told the author in 2000, about his many years working with the drummer. "But he would continue to prepare himself in the studio for hours on a fill that was giving him a particularly hard time. He would work on that fill and play a verse and a chorus going into a fill and keep going over the sections of material constantly until he was totally comfortable with it. Then he would put his sticks down, light up a smoke, and he'd always play it perfectly after that."

"Once he'd settled on what he wanted to play, he never deviated from that," adds Northfield. "To give you a quote, Neil is so obsessive about the details that Geddy has said that Neil Peart is the only person he knows who rehearses to rehearse."

"I don't think I've worked with a combination of players with such musical ability and talent before or since, particularly Neil, who is an absolute phenomenon," says Hine. "He's the only drummer, and I've recorded some jolly good drummers, some very big names, but never have I ever sat behind the console and listened to someone playing and actually had to stand up to watch him because I could not understand what was he was doing. When we recorded the song 'Bravado' [from 1991's *Roll the Bones*], I was amazed at how all the sixteens [beats] are complete, and yet he's moving both hands to achieve this 'gaduun' sound on the floor toms. I'm just at the point of being intrigued by how he is doing this when he introduces ride cymbal beats. At that point, my head exploded. I thought, 'You can't do that without at least three arms.'

"It was a relatively simple-sounding piece," Hine continues. "It was not one of their manic seven- or eight-minute pieces with tricky time signatures. But listening to all of his playing at once . . . was astounding. Even when I [was] soloing his drum tracks and muting everyone else's [from the mixing desk], I was still confused. I'm turning to the engineer [Stephen Tayler], saying, 'Can you understand that? Can you, in your mind, ascertain which limbs are doing what?' I'm listening to this and the engineer is counting up the limbs and suddenly his face gets white and he looks at me. In the middle of a take, I walk into the studio and stand in front of him and I still can't work it out. All my years of making records suddenly mean nothing."

FLY BY NIGHT

We can trace Rush's progressive-rock roots back to 1974, when Peart joined. Drummer John Rutsey, who appeared on Rush's self-titled debut, departed before the recording of the band's sophomore album, *Fly by Night*, and Peart (who'd been playing in a St. Catharines, Canada–based band named, interestingly enough, Hush) emerged after an audition that impressed Lee and Lifeson ("He had really short hair with shorts on," Lifeson remembered. "So this weird-looking guy comes down with this small kit of Rogers drums, and he played like a maniac.")

"I think in the early days we had the difficult task of existing at a time when the people who influenced us still existed," said Lee. "We were obviously influenced by a lot of English prog rock bands and [bands like] Cream and Led Zeppelin. . . . [S]o we paled in comparisons to our prototypes. I can understand that criticism."

Without a doubt, the band changed its musical direction when Peart joined. "There was a lot of enthusiasm for Peart," Terry Brown said, "and Lee and Lifeson had already sussed out the fact that Peart was a writer and a thinker and was going to be a very stabilizing influence on the band. You could tell that they were very excited about the new addition. I think right from the beginning there were high hopes that it would be a fantastic success." A division of labor was immediately decided upon: Lee and Lifeson would handle the songwriting; Peart, because of his obvious skill and enthusiasm, would write the lyrics.

It wouldn't be until 1975's *Fly by Night* that the band showed signs of carving out their own progressive style. The opener, "Anthem," based on the Ayn Rand novel of the same name about individual freedom, bubbles over with adrenaline. It also hints at the kind of complexity that would become a Rush trademark: The band deftly moves from 7/8 to 4/4 (and back again), demonstrating that they've begun to move on from their straightforward blues-based rock material.

The band's newfound momentum was maintained throughout the first side of *Fly by Night* on tracks "Best I Can"; "Beneath, Between, and Behind"; and the band's first attempt at recording a long-form piece, an eight-and-a-half-minute sci-fi sonic battle titled "By-Tor and the Snow Dog." (ELP had their "Tarkus" suite, Rush "By-Tor and the Snow Dog.") It and "Rivendell" (referencing a safe elfin haven in *The Lord of the Rings*) represent the members' shared obsession with Tolkienesque fantasy.

CARESS OF STEEL

There was plenty more where that

1975's *Caress of Steel*: once the property of the hardcore Rush fan.

came from. The band's follow-up record, *Caress of Steel* (dedicated to Rod Serling), is liberally sprinkled with sword-and-sorcery imagery. For one thing, the layered menacing electric guitar tracks evoke images of dark forests, expansive otherworldly landscapes, evil wizards, and wispy specters.

What *Caress of Steel* is best known for is the band's long-form compositions. The closing track of the original LP's first side (track four on the CD) is a three-part composition, "The Necromancer," which runs nearly twelve and a half minutes and tells the tale of three travelers—men from Willowdale—who journey into "dark and forbidden" lands of the title's namesake.

Caress of Steel remains a signpost

along the highway of the ever-evolving progressive hard rock movement that valued wizards and warriors as much as wah-wah pedals and whammy bars.

Rush stood at the gates, perhaps even opened the gates to a new breed of musician. Funnily enough, their most progressive (i.e., most ambitious) material was written just prior to or during the punk era, making them a harbinger as well as a throwback to the British progressives of the decade's early years.

Unlike some other progressive rock bands, Rush survived and even thrived in the punk era, thumbing their noses at the critics and the haters. (Perhaps the band's hard rock cred helped to insulate them a bit?) Rush would change musical direction, but by

then punk would be long over and the band would have brought along a fan base that had grown up on epic scores from *2112*, *A Farewell to Kings*, and *Hemispheres*. By then, they had nothing to prove to anyone but themselves.

DOWN THE TUBES

Caress of Steel may have been a proclamation of progressive hard rock and a success on one level, but it missed the mark on others. Actually, it flopped.

"In terms of creative and psychological survival, [*Caress of Steel*] changed us," Geddy Lee told the author. "I mean, *Caress of Steel* wasn't difficult to make. It was just . . . a weird-ass record. . . . There was just a lot of negativity around how the record was received."

Peart claimed that the band was

"playing all of these divey bars" just on the outskirts of major cities for the tour, and it began to set in that they were on their way down, not up. (Rush also opened for Kiss, Nazareth, and Mott the Hoople during their lengthy North American tour for *Caress of Steel*. Not every gig the band played was at a hole-in-the-wall—some were arena venues.)

Supposedly, morale got so bad among the band and the road crew that they adopted a black humor, dubbing their jaunt through the U.S. the "Down the Tubes" tour. Rush had one more record to make for Mercury, and (they thought) one last shot to make it.

The "Down the Tubes" tour was good for one thing: Rush began to piece together and perform bits of the title track for their next record, *2112*, onstage.

2112 AND *A FAREWELL TO KINGS*

Nineteen seventy-six's *2112* was a watershed moment in the band's history. "*2112* was a much more commercial record than *Caress of Steel*," explained Brown. "In fact, we'd gotten a bunch of ideas together while were doing *Caress of Steel* that were carried through into *2112*."

Once again, Rush took inspiration from Ayn Rand's concept of individual freedom versus the will of society/ruling government (specifically, the novel *The Fountainhead* and its main character, architect Howard Roark) to fashion the basis for the record's title song.

The side-long epic "2112" was composed of several movements and involved an idealistic young dreamer and a futuristic, authoritative government and its prohibition of art of all kinds. In simplest terms, the priests of the Solar Federation, from their temples, run a nanny state via monstrous computers and plan and supervise all human activities, stunting personal ambition and free thought in the process. The hero sees—or dreams

of—how man's creativity once touched the sky in a world time forgot. It's a paradise for him and it soon becomes clear to the dreamer: He either lives free or dies in the hopes of entering that dreamland.

2112 is an example of the band's fusion of the ancient and modern, as well as its ability to juxtapose these two motifs for effect: Priests and temples; atmospheric domes and "Templevision"; supercomputers and ancient seers; electric guitars and "ancient miracles"; a Tchaikovsky reference *and* soaring sci-fi sound effects all appear in the *2112* "Overture." It all seems so natural. Everything fits together.

"We fought back with *2112*," Lee said, "which was probably the most important record we ever made. Without a doubt. Other records may have been more popular and sold more, but that record saved us."

Because of the buzz generated by *2112* (the record hit number sixty-one on *Billboard*'s Top 200 Albums chart, and songs "The Temples of Syrinx" and "A Passage to Bangkok" became live favorites) and a follow-up live album, *All the World's a Stage* (which hit the *Billboard* Top 40), and owing to the newfound enthusiasm in and around the band, Rush and Brown couldn't wait to get back into the studio to make the next record.

A Farewell to Kings, recorded at Rockfield Studios in June 1977 in Wales (the destination for many progressive/pomp/space rock bands in the 1970s, including Van der Graaf Generator, Queen, and Hawkwind), presents another strange duality of the Rush catalog. Despite the record's title, Rush—as many prog rock bands had done before them (and as countless others would do after)—looked backward for inspiration.

The album's centerpiece, "Xanadu" (arguably one of the high points of the band's most progressive period), an eleven-plus-minute descent into madness, is based on the Romantic poet Samuel Taylor

Coleridge's meditation on immortality and paradise, "Kubla Khan."

Musically, the terrain of "Xanadu" mirrors the layered topography of Coleridge's poem. The song opens with bird chirps, wind chimes, volume-controlled guitar, and buzzing, droning synth tones recalling nature and capturing the expanse of the stately pleasure dome of Xanadu. Lifeson's snaky 7/8-time guitar riff slinks in softly and grows in venom and potency (and volume) as the bass and drums erupt underneath it. Wind sounds, most probably made by synth, whip around the speakers and perfectly capture the blizzard conditions surrounding the "frozen mountaintops" of Xanadu/Shangri-la.

Other tracks include the title song, "Closer to the Heart," "Madrigal," "Cinderella Man," and the album closer "Cygnus X-1, Book One—The Voyage," based on the binary star system (the first black hole scientists ever recorded).

In "Cygnus X-1," the menacing wash of synthesizer and the sustained ringing of gamelan-like bells echo in the chasm of deep space. The roaring, whooshing noises call to mind a rocket ship shifting into hyperdrive. The atmospherics come to a calm, as though we're floating through the weightlessness of space, when a focal point—a bass line—slowly grows in loudness and clarity in the stereo mix, as if we're viewing the rocket ship Rocinante's lurch toward the massive Cygnus X-1 system.

Throughout, Rush play choppy, quirky, heavy rhythms, even an aggressive 11/8 rhythm toward the end of the track, suggesting the unpredictability and chaos within a black hole, perhaps mirroring the extreme physical distress and mental anguish the rocket ship operator/speaker experiences upon discovering, and then passing into, the black hole of Cygnus X-1.

A Farewell to Kings is a prog rock success on many levels—it showcases the band's ability to synthesize a number of distinctive elements and regale its audience with epic tone poems. The band capitalized on their growing appeal when "Closer to the Heart" reached number thirty-six on the U.K. charts in February 1978, just as *A Farewell to Kings* soared to number thirty-three in the U.S. (and number twenty-two in Britain).

What's more, the music circumvented the critics, making the press irrelevant. While some critics tried to understand the band's appeal (John Rockwell, writing for the *New York Times* in January 1979, recognized that Rush answered a "need"), ultimately, fans found their way to the music without the help of the press.

"In a lot of ways, [critics] have the last word," Lee said. "But I think a good record will cut through that."

HEMISPHERES

How do you follow up a successful prog rock album? By going even bigger the next time around. Rush's 1978 effort, *Hemispheres*, is, in some ways, far more ambitious in scope than its predecessor, *A Farewell to Kings*.

The opening track, "Cygnus X-1, Book II: Hemispheres," which encompasses the entirety of side one on the original LP, continues the saga of our traveler from "Cygnus X-1, Book One."

Using the metaphoric schism between passion and intellect (partially inspired by a reference in the 1975 book *Powers of Mind*, by financial markets writer Adam Smith), "Cygnus X-1, Book II: Hemispheres" is a good measuring stick for the band's growing songwriting confidence.

Arguably, outside of "Xanadu," "Hemispheres" is the band's most heady, complex and smooth material. Its eighteen minutes whiz by you in a flash. Although he's not introduced until later in the piece (part three, "Armageddon"), the Rocinante pilot mysteriously returns from the void, having been flung from the black hole/interdimensional time warp to a place of the gods, where Apollo and

Dionysus are in battle for the very souls of human beings. As they did in "Book One," Rush successfully combine ancient mythology and sci-fi imagery into one narrative.

Despite the sleek veneer, "Hemispheres" was a bit of a bitch to get together. Lifeson spent a lot of time achieving his guitar tones, perhaps more than for any Rush record had in the past. "It was harder to record the guitars with *Hemispheres*," said Brown. "It was harder to nail performances. It certainly wasn't coming as easy as *A Farewell to Kings*."

The band was in England, first in Advision and then Trident, for three months in 1978 for the production of *Hemispheres*. By the time final vocals needed to be tracked, Rush were behind schedule—the vocal melodies hadn't been written. (They would be in Rockfield Studios.) Because the compositions were in keys that made it difficult for Ged to sing, the process was further slowed.

"Ged was fit to be tied," Brown said. "It was hard work for Ged. Hard work for everybody. You didn't have the kinds of tools available then to lower a track that you have now. The only way you did it back then was to slow the tape machine down. You were stuck. You either cut the track again or you persevered. [Rush] are all perseverers. They all want to go farther than they can actually handle. [*Hemispheres*] was the start of all that happening."

PERMANENT WAVES

Just as our space-traveling hero achieved balance in "Hemispheres," so did Rush by the end of the 1970s. Arguably, the band's three studio records following *Hemispheres*—1980's *Permanent Waves*, 1981's *Moving Pictures*, and 1982's *Signals*—to varying degrees married their progressive tendencies with the order of the day: new wave.

Inspired by the likes of Peter Gabriel, Ultravox, Japan, Talking Heads, and a host of British New

Romantic bands, Rush set upon a new course with *Permanent Waves*, the title of which was itself an expression of the band's need to create more song-based material (i.e., music that was built to last). Toward this end, Rush had bandied about recording another epic, this time based on the Arthurian tale of Sir Gawain and the Green Knight. But an extended work was not in keeping with the band's new aesthetic.

Instead, the boys spliced and diced "Sir Gawain" to arrive at the nine-minute multisectional song titled "Natural Science," concerning the delicate balance between nature and science.

Other songs speak to individual choice ("Freewill") or the commercialism of music and the ever-encroaching hand of marketing in art ("The Spirit of Radio"), a theme that's echoed in the closer "Natural Science." "Jacob's Ladder" is an almost spiritual concoction of odd times on the subject of inspiration. Then there are the deceptively difficult little tunes about relationships, "Entre Nous" and "Different Strings" (those are Lee's lyrics and that's illustrator Hugh Syme on piano).

The use of studio technology helped *Permanent Waves* become one of the band's cutting-edge productions. "There were no big surprises in making *Moving Pictures* and *Permanent Waves*," says engineer Paul Northfield. "*Permanent Waves* was a twenty-four-track session, and *Moving Pictures* was one of the first forty-eight-track sessions I did, so you could use more tracks. You could have maybe ten tracks for your drums, where in the past we would have used seven tracks."

Permanent Waves went to number three on the British charts, soared to number four on the *Billboard* U.S. Top 200, and reached platinum status in Canada (striking gold in America) within three months of its release. It set the stage for the band's most popular work: *Moving Pictures*.

Hemispheres
(1978)

MOVING PICTURES

"You could feel it in the control room," Brown said. "There was magic going on. Those two records—*Permanent Waves* and *Moving Pictures*: The energy coming out of the studio and onto the tape was just magic."

"The atmosphere of Le Studio [in Morin Heights, Quebec] was pretty special because it was an idyllic spot," says Northfield. "It was overlooking a lake and was one of the first successful residential studios in the world. That contributed to it being a great experience. *Moving Pictures* was on another level because [Rush] came in very organized, with everything worked out and demos done. They knew exactly what they were going to do."

"We took a couple of months to record *Moving Pictures*," remembered Brown. "We did *Fly by Night* in three weeks—start to finish. Time to make records progressed as they moved forward through their careers."

Some of the band's most revered compositions appear on *Moving*

Pictures. It might be difficult for people to relate today to how shocking it was to hear the distinctive synth sweep opening "Tom Sawyer" for the first time. This mixture of heavy rock (approaching metallic) with an aggressive keyboard riff was truly groundbreaking when it was appeared.

"Geddy had the Oberheim [polyphonic] that could play a high string line through a Minimoog," Northfield remembers. "The OB-X is what Geddy used for that big sweeping sound in 'Tom Sawyer.' That was made with an OB-X cross-modulation sound."

Aside from being the band's most fruitful collaborative effort (between Max Webster lyricist Pye Dubois and Peart), the rhythmic meter of the lyrics and stark imagery are as powerful as the musical elements in the song.

Just as important to the enjoyment and longevity of the tune are its thundering and now-legendary drum parts and drum breaks, fluttering between time-signature changes (4/4 to 7/8).

Moving Pictures sharpened and perfected the music of *Hemispheres* and *Permanent Waves* by presenting challenging, literary-based, muso-friendly songs such as "Limelight" (on dealing with fame); "Red Barchetta" (based on the futuristic geo-socio-politico-industrial short story by Richard S. Foster), "A Nice Sunday Drive," which uses a vintage car (a red Ferrari Barchetta) as a symbol for personal freedom *and* the fight against government-imposed regulation); and "The Camera Eye" (inspired by John Dos Passos's trilogy of novels *The 42nd Parallel*, *Nineteen Nineteen*, and *The Big Money*—a cacophony of American voices captured at the turn of the twentieth century). Despite "The Camera Eye's" length (eleven minutes), its economy of words and music lightens the song. It feels breezy, unburdened—qualities that may have been elusive in the band's music prior to 1980.

Suddenly, Rush were everywhere: On MTV. On radio. In magazines. (*Moving Pictures* has gone platinum four times over in the U.S. alone, and reached number three on the *Billboard* and British charts after its release in 1981.) Rush were hailed as musical heroes for extolling the virtues of technique and songwriting, much in the same way Yes, ELP, Jethro Tull, and Genesis had been before them.

"*Moving Pictures* just blew them up," Val Azzoli, former cochairman and co-CEO of the Atlantic Music Group, said in a 2002 interview I conducted. (Azzoli worked with Rush manager Ray Danniels booking Rush, among other operational duties, from the late 1970s through the late 1980s.) "They had all these critically acclaimed records—*2112* was one of them. They became a very successful touring band but never sold a lot of records. They were playing small clubs like Cobo Hall in Detroit opening for every band in the world. When *Moving Pictures* came out, they started playing bigger arenas—Madison Square Garden for three nights."

The band solidified its global domination with the live double album *Exit . . . Stage Left* (a platinum-certified release in the U.S. and a Top 10 entry in the U.K.), featuring the second-most-copped drum solo in rock history (the first being John Bonham's in "Moby Dick").

But success is a funny thing: Some progressive rock fans are wary of formulaic music but, at the same time, want their favorite bands to continue to create a familiar brand of music. This became abundantly clear when Rush recorded and released *Signals*, the follow-up studio album to *Moving Pictures*.

Signals was a clear shift in musical direction, and the band's move toward a more keyboardcentric sound confused longtime listeners. "Subdivisions" (that's a Minimoog Lee's using in the extended instrumental sections), "New World Man" (a Top 30 U.S. hit and a nod to the minimalistic, reggae-rock stylings of the Police), "Countdown" (describing the excitement of a space shuttle launch—"space rock" for the '80s generation), "The Analog Kid," and the four-on-the-floor quasi-dance track "The Weapon" all demonstrated the band's desire to write tight compositions. Perhaps none of these were fully understood or appreciated at the time, even by those close to the band.

"There was a lot of changes going on in [musical] direction then," Brown said, "which I really wasn't enthused about. The band was moving toward electronics, keyboards, which I really

didn't hear as part of the band. . . . I didn't understand enough about [electronics and keyboards] or feel it was something I could participate in."

"[W]e need to move onward," Lee told writer Geoff Barton of *Sounds* in May 1983. "Come the first inkling of stagnancy and we're off and away again."

Indeed. Despite the fact that the band had used keyboards in the past, it's hard to imagine "Between the Wheels" (from 1984's *Grace Under Pressure*), the rolling undercurrent of syncopated rhythms in "Middletown Dreams" (from 1985's *Power Windows*), the evocative piano tones and wispy sonic orchestration of "Second Nature" or the Vivaldi-esque atmospheric feel of "Mission," both from 1987's *Hold Your Fire*, without the appearance of *Signals*.

With ever-increasing frequency, keyboards (and synthesizer programming) shaped the structure, form, and production of the band's music. Coupled with the material's stark qualities and the austere characteristics of the many synths used by Lee (and guests), the shift left many fans in the cold.

Some were in disbelief: Where did their Rush go? Gone were some of the band's hallmark traits: the grinding ("Limelight"), chordal/arpeggiated ("Fly by Night"), and wah/flanging effect–inflected ("The Spirit of Radio") guitar riffs of yore.

Rush were simply going in other directions, curtaining their progressive rock tendencies and getting with the keyboard technology of the 1980s. The playing followed: Peart's style became uncluttered, not quite as busy (though he tapped into an electronic percussion craze led by, for one, King Crimson's Bill Bruford), Lifeson's axe pickin' evolved texturally and emotionally, and the bass came to the fore, filling the role of a lead instrument with an economy of notes.

Fans who didn't come along for Rush's 1980s synthesized ride perhaps

didn't comprehend the mission of the music from the get-go: to progress.

PROGRESSIVE

After parting ways with Brown, the band hit a streak of bad luck in finding an appropriate producer. Brown had worked with Rush very nearly since the beginning of their recording career. How could they replace him? But that was just it: Brown was the past, and Rush weren't looking for a replacement as much as someone who could help guide them through their new direction.

After months of searching and preproduction (writing, arranging, demoing scratch recordings), producer Peter Henderson appeared. That's when the fun began. "It was a long, involved project that just wouldn't end," Lee said in 2000. "The recording process applied a lot of pressure on our families and personal lives, and it was a pretty tense affair all around. It was thirty-five degrees below zero and it was snowing and I hadn't seen my family in ages. And we never took days off. We were working insanely. I could never make a record like that again. Never.

"It was one thing to have a million opinions when you know that you have one guy sitting there, who you trust, who is a father figure, who ultimately you trust to say 'yea' or 'nay,'" Lee continued. "But when he's not there, and you're in the floating world for the first time, you have to step up and make those decisions [yourself]."

"They bit off a big chunk with *Grace Under Pressure*," said Brown. "It was the first record without me for a long, long time. I think it caused some stress and was aptly named."

The intense production cycle was evident in the music: "Distant Early Warning," "Red Lenses," and "Between the Wheels," late Cold War–era songs, speak of international and interpersonal concerns, as well as the necessity to stem environmental erosion, political polarization, and global disaster.

Grace Under Pressure hit the *Billboard* Top 10, but its icy synth tones convinced some that it was merely a continuation of the direction the band had carved out with *Signals*. Unfortunately for a portion of the Rush fan base, more of the same followed—*Power Windows* and *Hold Your Fire* are either terrific examples of the band doing what it wants or cluelessly heading down the wrong path.

Adjectives used to describe records in the wake of *Signals*—*Grace Under Pressure, Power Windows* and *Hold Your Fire*—range from *slick* and *sleepy* to *limp* and *timid*. It is unpopular to say or even suggest so, but this type of opinion is unfortunate and perhaps uninformed: Music on these '80s Rush records can be quite powerful and inventive.

By the close of the 1980s, *Presto* appeared to redefine the band's sound yet again. Producer Rupert Hine, whose name had been bandied about by the band earlier in the '80s (Hine said he was asked to produce Rush prior to working with them in 1989 but declined), was on a mission to bring Lee's voice down from the upper stratosphere and get him singing in the lower registers in an attempt to smooth out the band's overall sound.

"I talked to Geddy very much about [his voice] during the final meetings for *Presto*," Hine intimates. "I just really don't like those voices up on the ceiling. That was always the reason why I passed [previously]. You know, how could [you] produce an album if you don't like the singing? . . . But I did talk to Geddy and I said, 'In order to do this, I need to get this off my chest'—and I did. Geddy said to me, 'So, what would you do about [my high singing]?' I immediately, without missing a beat, said, 'Well, for starters I would lower your voice an entire octave. I wouldn't even bother to change the key. I would drop it an entire octave, because then we would hear Geddy Lee the human

being. We'd actually *hear* you. And we can get a sense of what you are like as a person. There is a good chance that your character and personality will come through in a conversational range rather than . . .'" [Hine squeals and shrieks some nonsense vocals.]

"'None of us have a clue who this person is,'" Hine continues. "'He just sounds like a bit of a freak. When you want to go up high, you can't because you're up there already.' He chuckled and laughed when I told him this, so graciously, and soon I was to get to know Geddy very well and understand him a bit as a person."

Still, hanging onto anything that would identify the band with the vintage '70s might have been just as perilous as trying something completely new. "Rush had already done the heavy stuff in the '70s and [made] the more Police-like sonic change in the early 1980s, and they were in a dangerous place," Hine says. "Atlantic wanted them to do a big record, and that change in production was me. One of my goals was, 'We need you to get back to being a power trio: guitar, bass, and drums, but not in a retro way. Not revisiting old Rush. Not going back to the Police era or the more medley '70s.' Just doing whatever happens between the three of them. Although there were some little splashes of keyboards, a lot of the slightly more atmospheric sounds were in fact things I did with Alex. So they served a similar purpose of wash or sustain but were born from guitar origination, creating more air and less density than you tend to get with keyboards.

"Rush are a glorious example of a three-piece," Hine says. "That's in common with the most progressive of rock bands, going back to Hendrix and Cream. There is so much room with a three-piece."

Presto was a breath of fresh air and a reminder of the band's guitar-based legacy—something fans were waiting for. The partnership between Rush and Hine (and Tayler) contin-

ued through 1991's *Roll the Bones*, a ten-song CD centered on the theme of chance, which produced the live favorite "Bravado"; the title track (featuring, of all things, a rap interlude); "Dreamline," which shot to number one on the *Billboard* Mainstream Rock chart; and the production piece "The Big Wheel" (ruminating on the fickle hand of fate).

"During that record, we were thinking in a sort of cinematic way toward the soundstage," Tayler says. "I tend to mix as if the band were laid out in front of me and there's a depth to the music. I think with *Presto* and *Roll the Bones* I was trying to create this panorama in front of you. I'll often record things on different combinations of microphones, with close and ambient [room] mics, and those get switched in and out a lot during the mix. Sometimes by doing that you can make certain aspects of the mix bigger and louder."

SOLIDIFYING THE LEGACY

In the early 1990s, when the so-called alternative and Seattle grunge sound changed the way record labels did business (as they searched high and low for the "next Nirvana"), an explosion of indie bands using distortion, tortured lyrical imagery, sloppy playing technique, and sonic dissonance conjured the punk revolution of the 1970s.

Rush weren't killed off during the first go-around of the underground music assault in the '70s, and they were too well established to disappear. More to the point, in many ways, they could relate to the emerging indie phenomenon. After all, Rush *were an indie band*, having recorded on their own independent label, Moon Records, before Mercury released their debut album. (Rush have maintained a kind of independent status ever since: In 1977, SRO Management, Rush's longtime representation, founded the label Anthem for Rush and a few other acts, most

Neil Peart's titanic technique, colossal kit, and ability to compose intelligent drum parts have inspired countless drummers. (Fin Costello/Getty Images)

notably, Max Webster. The label is still around and in good shape as of this writing.)

All that youthful energy certainly motivated Rush. In the wake of the grunge revolution, Rush released their most hard-driving, groove-based record in years, *Counterparts*, which recalled pre-punk, shit-kicking Brit rock bands such as Cream and the Who. The result was a kind of metallic, progressive R&B album—yet another new creative avenue for Rush.

Rock radio responded in kind, spinning songs like "Cold Fire" and "Stick It Out," placing them in heavy rotation alongside popular music of younger "alternative" and metal artists—the Lollapalooza generation—such as Tool, Soundgarden, Marilyn Manson, Smashing Pumpkins, Primus, Alice in Chains, White Zombie, Danzig, Helmet, Nirvana, and Pearl Jam, some of which were influenced by Rush.

The band had been validated, their approach revered and recognized as being relevant in the decade of feedback and distortion. "The era that begat Rush appreciated players," says bassist and band friend Jeff Berlin. "If the band [came] on the scene now, they would disappear after six weeks. Emerson Lake and Palmer or a U.K. or Asia or these progressive rock bands of that era would die a horrible death today."

LIMBO

Rush were MIA for five long years, in part due to the crippling double tragedies Peart experienced at the end of the 1990s. After a tour to support of their 1996 record *Test for Echo*, Peart's daughter, Selena Taylor, was killed in a single-automobile crash (her Jeep overturned) on an Ontario road near Toronto in August 1997.

"That was a very difficult period," Lifeson told the author in 2002. "Peart and his wife left Canada for a while. Geddy went over a few times to spend some time with them. I went over and spent some time with them. . . ."

Then the unthinkable grew worse: Less than a year later, Peart's wife Jacqueline Taylor succumbed to cancer. "It came upon her very quickly and she was gone in five months," said manager Ray Danniels in 2002.

It was a crushing blow, a devastating experience for anyone and everyone who'd touched Peart on a personal level. "I would say for a long period of time no one was capable of functioning properly," said Lee. "It was a heartbreaking time for everybody. It's a very sad part of my life. My heart still breaks for what Neil had to go through. His losses are incalculable. . . . He essentially lost everything that was important to him."

"His life revolved around his daughter and wife and touring," adds Paul Northfield.

As soon as the initial shock wore off, some began questioning the band's next move. Rush had been out of the record-making game for years—an eternity by pop music standards. "I'd say [to these people] that it was hard for me to explain . . . but I can't think about that now. I think of it as a guy I've known for most of my life who's gone through this awful thing," Lee said. "We were worried about him."

Peart took some time to find himself again, get away from Canada and see the U.S. He didn't let his grief destroy him. "With what [Peart] went through, I am surprised the man got out of bed for two years," Danniels said.

"It was a tough road for him: I don't know how he survived it," Lee said.

CLOSER TO THE HEART

I caught up with Lee when he had finished his solo debut, 2000's *My Favorite Headache*, a record Lee called a "recuperative" project, and after we spoke, an announcement was made that Peart had rejoined Rush. The band was formulating plans to write material for a new studio album, soon to be titled *Vapor Trails*.

"Neil is feeling more positive these days," Lee said at that time. "I think he's ready for work. . . . I would say that it's a very positive time at the moment."

But it was slow going at first. Lee said the first few months of writing for the then-upcoming studio record was difficult. Lee and Lifeson had been apart for years, and the first experiments in collaborating "we were not thrilled about," Lee said. "We worked very hard for about four months, and then we took a break."

When Lee and Lifeson reconvened, they immediately went to work on some of the problem areas of their writing approach. In blister-breaking moments of discovery, the pair jammed in July 2001. A good portion of the record was based on those jams. "Then everybody was more confident and everyone was more focused and more determined [to write and record], and we had a clear picture of what the job was," Lee said.

"You have to go through certain motions to get to the point where you are confident in your hands and in your head an in your heart, and [that] takes a while," said Lifeson.

Lifeson and Lee had been jamming for the better part of a week without discussing song structure or arrangements—just playing—when they called old trusted friend Paul Northfield to seek his opinion as an "objective sounding board" and ask him to report on the progress of the boys' work.

Northfield also assisted Lee and Lifeson with arrangements, slugged it out with Lifeson to achieve appropriate (read: extra-aggressive) guitar tones, and created an environment in which Peart could rehearse his drum parts. "[Northfield] was a busy boy," Lee said.

"It was an emotional record for them to do," says coproducer Northfield. "Neil's trauma and drama of losing his daughter and wife within the space of a year . . . [H]e may never have recorded or played again. . . . When he started that record, he hadn't played drums for about two years. He certainly didn't pick up a pair of drumsticks for eighteen months after his daughter died."

"It was important to create an atmosphere around him that was gentle [and] private, and one that allowed him to be nurtured," Lee said. "A lot of the early stages of the project were about that: Alex and I trying to find each other as playing partners and [the] three of us trying to develop a comfortable environment where we [could] get beyond our emotions and get beyond the past and get into what we love doing, which is making music."

Vapor Trails exposed the band's raw musical nerve. Lee called the record "rich and quite a meal. It's the longest Rush record by far we have ever done, and a certain level of intensity seems to exist from song to song

Rush (1974)

Fly By Night (1975)

2112 (1976)

Permanent Waves (1980)

Signals (1982)

Grace Under Pressure (1984)

that, I think, we set out to do."

"There's still a tension there," Lifeson chimed in.

"On past records we had a tendency to focus on intense sound and not intense performance, and that was something Alex was tuned in on very early," Lee said. "I think he was the first one who mentioned there should be more life playing."

Given the circumstances, it's amazing the band recorded such a coherent record. Songs include "Ghost Rider" (a commentary on the road winding out in front of Peart—and away from his old life), "Ceiling Unlimited" (about madness masked by grief, hope as an eternal spring), "Sweet Miracle" (on finding love), "Nocturne" (a poignant song about working through the day's problems on a subconscious level, in your sleep: "In a way, [Peart's] nightmares were helping him sort out his situation," Lee said. "At the end of this incredible night of dreams, he woke up and realized what he had to do next"), and opener "One Little Victory" (about not taking life for granted).

"['One Little Victory'] makes a statement about being back, at the same time dealing with every little success you have and how you measure it," Lifeson offered.

Arguably, without *Vapor Trails*, the band couldn't have written 2007's studio effort, *Snakes & Arrows* (produced by Nick Raskulinecz)—a tighter, more cohesive record. By 2007, Peart (seemingly) had time to decipher what the hell his life meant as well as focus on the events unfolding on the global stage—everything

from war to religious radicalism.

Songs such as "Far Cry," "The Larger Bowl," "The Way the Wind Blows," and "Faithless" recall themes from earlier Rush lyrics but benefit from a new perspective. Peart isn't repudiating his former beliefs: He's simply presenting a clearer, stronger case for them (e.g., "Faithless," a biting critique of organized faith, stresses individualism and the power of love).

Despite the deep subject matter, the lyrics are generally life-affirming, not bleak or desolate. "[They're] sometimes just telling it like it is," Lee said in 2007.

"Some people say we never left progressive rock, and some people lament the fact that we don't write any more twenty-minute songs," Lee said. "It's hard to look backward, but if we find ourselves at a point where we think it is appropriate to do a twenty-minute song again, I certainly wouldn't discount it."

***

As of this writing Rush are on a new high. After spending time on the road, motorcycling through America to clear his mind, Peart remarried and appears to have turned a page in his life. The band has been touring regularly since 2002, releasing live albums and concert DVDs filmed in places from Germany to the U.S. to Brazil. It seems fans and critics alike have taken notice.

As the years have gone by (and particularly in the 2000s), with the global reach of the Internet, Rush's stature has grown in the music community. Incredibly, *Rolling Stone* mag-

azine, not always the friendliest to prog bands, featured Rush in a multi-page article in 2008; hip political spoofster Stephen Colbert of Comedy Central's *The Colbert Report* interviewed the band and surrendered the television studio floor to them (twice); Jason Segel and Paul Rudd develop bromantic feelings when they discover a common love of Rush in the comedy flick *I Love You, Man* (Rush even make a cameo appearance in the film); a children's choir sings "The Spirit of Radio" for a climactic scene in the supernatural thriller *White Noise 2*; bands from Dream Theater, Savatage, and Queensryche, to Fates Warning, King's X, Metallica, Megadeth, and Foo Fighters are unabashed in claims of being influenced by Rush. Rush are even featured in the popular video game *Guitar Hero 5*.

Either the band has recruited new fans over the last decade, or decision makers at major publications, gaming manufacturers, and Hollywood production studios were raised on "Tom Sawyer."

"As we age, the ratio of bad press to good has gone up in our favor substantially," Lee said. "There is a definite school that says rock should be pure and be approached in a particular way, and because we mixed everything up, we are fusion artists [we were criticized]. We mix up all kinds of stuff: Sometimes we get very technical—maybe that's not in the same spirit that some critics believe in, which is fine for them. [But] there's a place for bombast in the world, and it's fun to do."

Power Windows
(1985)

Hold Your Fire
(1987)

A Show of Hands
(1989)

Presto
(1989)

Time to Roll
(1992, bootleg)

Snakes & Arrows
(2007)

(Courtesy of Naoju Nakamura)

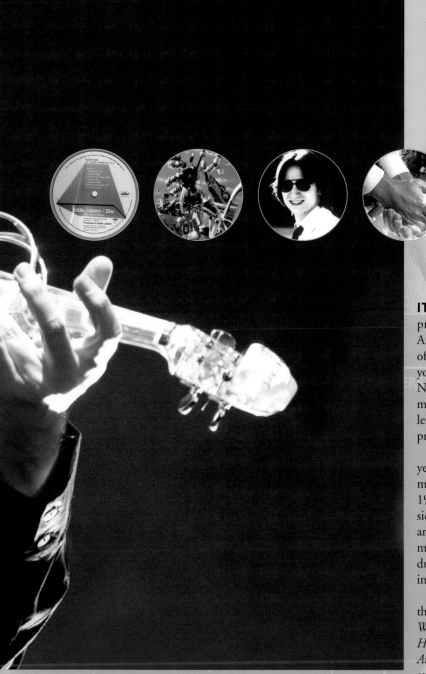

U.K.

Sunset on the Empire?

IT WAS A STRANGE TIME FOR THE
progressive rocker: The music press in
America—and Europe—launched an all-out
offensive to eradicate prog from the planet. If
you played a Moog, you were Public Enemy
Number One; diddled your guitar strings for
more than a few seconds, you were a wanker;
left time in your set for a drum solo, you were
predictable, boring, and self-indulgent.

Yet despite the open hostility, the "twilight
years" of the genre (or so the history books
might describe them), comprising roughly
1977 through 1980—an era in which the classic progressive bands were changing their M.O.
and the ascendancy of a new form of popular
music was unavoidable and inevitable—produced some of the genre's most potent, enduring, and stellar outings.

Peruse some of the titles that appeared when
the genre was said to be in decline: *Songs from the
Wood* (by Jethro Tull); *A Farewell to Kings* and
Hemispheres (Rush); *Going for the One* (Yes);
Animals (Pink Floyd); *Wind & Wuthering* (released
at the end of '76) and the double live *Seconds Out*
(Genesis); the Homeric *The Odyssey*, a Peter Jenner–produced effort featuring Mike
Oldfield and future Police guitarist Andy Summers (David Bedford); *World Record*

(Van der Graaf Generator); *Forse le Lucciole Non Si Amano Più*, one of the finest late-'70s Italian progressive rock records, largely the work of keyboardist Michele Conta and guitarist Alberto Gaviglio (Locanda delle Fate); the ELP-esque *Symphonic Pictures*, *Sunburst*, and *Ticket to Everywhere* (Schicke, Führs & Fröhling); *Live, Listen Now!*, and *K-Scope* (Phil Manzanera and Phil Manzanera's 801); National Health's self-titled debut; *Somewhere I've Never Traveled* (Ambrosia); Atlantis-inspired concept record *Ocean* (Eloy); fantasy-based *Rockpommel's Land* (Grobschnitt); and Hungarian band Omega's *Időrabló* (English version: *Time Robber*) and *Csillagok útján* (English version: *Skyrover*).

"Punk was just starting to happen, but it was still a great time for progressive rock," says Eloy guitarist, vocalist, and founder Frank Bornemann. Britain did prog rock bigger and arguably better than anyone. So it's no surprise that in the genre's supposed darkest hours, the northern island held its ground and produced a leading light of visionary music: the briefly burning but brilliant band U.K.

If ELP were the first prog rock supergroup, then U.K. were the last great one, culling the talents of drummer Bill Bruford, bassist/vocalist John Wetton, keyboardist/violinist Eddie Jobson (Roxy Music, Zappa, Curved Air), and soon-to-be jazz-rock guitar god Allan Holdsworth (Soft Machine, Tempest, Tony Williams Lifetime). Quite rightly and shrewdly, these stalwarts ignored the punk revolution and partied like it was 1969.

The band was separated into two camps: Bruford and Holdsworth on one side and Wetton and Jobson on the other—four musicians embracing rock, hard rock, pop, jazz-fusion, ambient, European art music, classical, and something else entirely.

"You had these two jazz guys [Bruford and Holdsworth], and then you had these glamour pop and rock guys [Eddie Jobson and John Wetton]," says Stephen W. Tayler, a former Trident Studios engineer who got the call to engineer the U.K. debut. (Tayler had worked with producer/Brand X keyboardist Robin Lumley on the 1978 Bruford record, *Feels Good to Me*, featuring Holdsworth). "The band was split down the middle."

Looking at the writing credits, this would appear to be the case. Wetton and Jobson wrote or cowrote nearly all of the material. "It was always really Eddie's project and mine, and we were the two protagonists," Wetton told the author in 1995.

While this was the case, allowing the "pop" side of the quartet to lead the way was sure to cause controversy. "There wasn't a lot of compromise on that first record," says Jobson. "We all did what we did and somehow it came together. Everybody had a strong identity and had been doing what they did for so long that difficulties arose when there was a call for compromise. I think in those early days, just getting together and fighting for what you wanted in the rehearsal and just going in for a fairly short time and recording it yielded a pretty good result."

"U.K. didn't really want a producer for the project," adds Tayler.

"To be honest, it was a lot of responsibility for me. . . . Often I felt I was in the middle of all of this stuff and I was just having to get on with the work. A lot of the record was done individually, unlike [with] Brand X. This was very much bass and drum going down with a bit of a token keyboard or guitar. Allan . . . was a very solitary character. He was very sensitive to people around him during that time. He liked to work on his own, just with me a lot of the time. Even on Bill's records he did [this]. . . .I loved working with him, but it felt like he . . . didn't like being tied down to the structure of the music and wanted to just play. I think he felt he was required to play riffs on parts . . . which he certainly didn't like.

"Then [Holdsworth] would argue with Bill, even though they were kind of coming from the same side," Tayler continues. "They were very much looking out for themselves. This is what produced a brilliant album, but I wouldn't say they were really pulling together. It is an unusual record because it does seem to walk that line between the real progressive rock side and jazz. I can tell you that the record was cut in winter, 1977 into 1978," says Tayler. "It was dark outside, it was dark in the studio, and the mood surrounding the project was quite dark."

This darkness is reflected in the music. From the thirteen-minute opening suite ("In the Dead of Night/By the Light of Day/Presto Vivace and Reprise") through to "Thirty Years," "Alaska" (the side-two opener), "Time to Kill," "Nevermore," and "Mental

U.K.: *Danger Money* (1979)

U.K.: s/t (1978)

U.K.: *Live: Night After Night* (1980)

Roxy Music: *Stranded* (1973)

Roxy Music: *Siren* (1975)

Eddie Jobson: *Zinc (The Green Album)* (1983)

U.K., '79. *Left to right*: Eddie Jobson, John Wetton, and Terry Bozzio. The emotional arc of guitarist Allan Holdsworth's solos was missed. (Courtesy of EG and Polydor)

Medication," the band complements themes of despair, lucidity (or lack thereof), denial, illusion, and the ravages of time with musical moments of luminescence and shadow.

"My writing is often inspired by a great sound, and in the case of U.K., most of the writing was done on the Yamaha CS-80," says Jobson, who also dazzles with his Plexiglas electric violin throughout the U.K. debut. "I was lucky enough to buy the first one in England—right before the beginning of the U.K. project. I usually find a sound and then it makes me want to write something around it. That could be a synthesizer sound like [on] 'Alaska,' an instrumental song that came about because I found the sound I liked on the CS-80 synthesizer."

When the record was completed, U.K. had achieved a true fusion of musical styles and had produced, arguably, one of the last groundbreak-ing progressive rock albums of the 1970s. Yet even this confirmed musical success couldn't motivate the quartet to remain a unit. Wetton asked Bruford to leave at the close of the band's first world tour, Holdsworth bolted to rejoin the drummer's jazz-rock band, and the Wetton-Jobson writing team was free to pursue poppier pastures. The band would continue through the end of the decade as a three-piece with Jobson, Wetton, and Zappa alumnus and percussion phenom Terry Bozzio handling drum duties.

"When you get people together of such varying backgrounds, and there is such a great divide between those back-grounds, everybody feels, 'Well, I don't need to make that much effort to accommodate a person on the other end of the spectrum,'" Jobson reasons. "Just doing that one record, or at least the touring afterward, I think every-body, particularly the people on the out-side edges, which was probably John on the one side and Allan on the other, the differences start to really become exaggerated. Those tensions tend to manifest themselves in a more pronounced way, I think. That's why the original band did not last very long."

U.K. never recaptured the original lineup's odd chemistry and creativity, although the band's sophomore effort, *Danger Money*, and the live recording from Japan, *Night After Night*, have their moments.

"I've found that every record that I've ever done has impacted somebody somewhere," says Jobson. "For whatever reason, listeners have that one record for which it all comes together. That's one of the more fulfilling aspects [of] recording. You usually don't find out about it for twenty years. Someone comes up to you and says, 'You know, that one record you made changed my life.'"

(Ebet Roberts/Getty Images)

THE RETURN OF THE KING (CRIMSON)

ROBERT FRIPP'S WITHDRAWAL FROM HIS MUSICAL LIFE IN general, his life apart from England in New York City, his spiritual self-discipline to effect change, and his application of the philosophical concept of "small independent mobile intelligent unit" were filtered and translated into the schizophrenic 1980s Crimson edition—lineups composed of tiny units, or two halves, completing the whole.

"King Crimson lives in different bodies at different times, and the particular form [that] the group takes changes," Fripp once said. "When music appears which only King Crimson can play, then, sooner or later, King Crimson appears to play the music."

Fripp admitted that the new Crimson lineup was the one he had been waiting to establish for four years: longtime Peter Gabriel bassist Tony Levin (the New Yorker also played Chapman Stick; Bill Bruford; and Kentucky native Adrian Belew, who had seemed destined to play the hotel circuit as a member

"To sing or not to sing?": a question that's haunted Crimson guitarist/vocalist Adrian Belew for decades.

of the cover band Sweetheart until Frank Zappa rescued him from a life of buffet lines and room service. Belew had also recorded and toured with David Bowie, having cut the live *Stage* and 1979's *Lodger* and appeared on two Talking Heads records (as well as being part of their large stage band), most notably, 1980's *Remain in Light*.

Having Bruford return was a no-brainer—he was a link to Crimson's past glory, a recognizable face to long-time fans, and his artistic approach could meet the unique challenges facing a drummer intending to become a member of Crimson.

"Bill was pivotal in that Robert needed him but at the same time resented him, in my opinion," says Patrick "Paddy" Spinks, Crimson manager from 1980 to 1985. "Bill was an astonishing and creative drummer who also put on a show onstage. The friction between them was part of the success of that King Crimson. Subsequent versions of KC never had that same dynamic, in my opinion."

The intensity level would grow between band members as creative ideas clashed. Specifically, the differences mounting between Belew and Fripp boiled down to a disagreement over what should and should not be deemed Crimson material.

Belew's strong sense of melody and willingness to write lyrics (a task that was previously left to some outside the band) helped to transform Crimson from intricate instrumental band to progressive band with pop music sensibilities. Belew also brought a keen sense of sonic experimentation via guitar effects, which matched the strides in music technology being employed by Levin and electronic drummer Bruford, all of which enriched Crimson's guitar-driven blend of pop/neo-industrial/post-punk/Euro art/new wave/ethno prog rock.

DISCIPLINE

In one sense, every musician in Crimson was a small, independent mobile intelligent unit and each smoothly interfaced with the others, making the band work. Because of the freedom each member was allowed, a kind of Fripp-esque self-discipline was required for the music *not* to turn to chaos.

Fripp was excited by the prospect of getting back together with a band, and the quartet began working up new material in 1980. Dubbing themselves "Discipline," the band debuted in a tiny basement nightclub, Moles, in Bath, England. Despite the audience being on top of the band, the show was a success—or at least it was enough of a positive sign that Discipline should continue.

"I started working with Robert with the League of Gentlemen in 1980 and continued as he formed Discipline as the 'rehearsal' King Crimson," says Spinks. "Robert wanted to find out if the lineup of Discipline was worthy of being called King Crimson."

Sensing that Discipline contained an adventurous soul similar to that of the original Crimson, Fripp made a command decision to allow this new band to carry on the Crimson legacy. The time was right for Crimson to officially return—or perhaps Crimson were right for the times.

"It was quickly obvious that this was King Crimson," says Spinks. "I encouraged Robert to call the band King Crimson, as it would always be easier to market. But I can't say that it helped. Robert makes up his own mind."

Whatever the band was called, or going to be called, not everyone took to Crimson's cross-genre music right away. Some older fans didn't understand how this new Crimson fit in with the '70s band they loved so much.

On the surface Crimson were radically different from that behemoth: Instead of delivering bombastic emotional crests and grand overtures, they exposed audiences to hypnotic, cyclical, knotty patterns; interlocking dual guitar parts that were only hinted at when David Cross was in Crimson; gradual shifts in pitch, inflection, accent, and synchronization; as well as world/African/Balinese musical influences.

Some fans didn't understand, couldn't process, or didn't very much like what they were hearing at first: Where was the violinist? Why no Mellotron? No saxophone?

"I remember the first Discipline tour—it was probably Germany—and someone threw meat on the stage," says Spinks. "The crowd was expecting '21st Century Schizoid Man' and got angry when they did not get it."

"Robert said that when the band started again in 1980 and did the album *Discipline*, they were booed off the stage, playing that record," relates Stick player/Warr guitarist Trey Gunn, who'd become a member of Crimson in the 1990s. "While I was never booed, I've definitely experienced that thing of 'The audience cannot go with us.' That's what it means to be on the edge."

Crimson continued to push in all directions, meeting the growing field of electronics head-on. Instead of using hanging gongs and racks of metallic percussion, Bruford combined electronic and acoustic drums, including tube drums, a gong bass drum, Simmons pads, and a very effective wooden rhythm box called a tongue or log drum (its dark pitch is heard in "The Sheltering Sky" and "Discipline"), which Bruford said "is a Californian toy that I picked up in a tourist shop for twenty-five dollars."

Likewise, throughout his time with Crimson in the 1980s, Belew used a Roland guitar synthesizer, the GR-300, while running other effects to garner textures and tones that manufacturers never intended or had ever dreamed of. In this sense, Belew was doing with the guitar what the great keyboard pioneers had accomplished in the late 1960s and early 1970s, before mass-market synthesizers were available: conducting research and development with disregard for standard factory-issue sounds.

"Crimson has to keep reinventing

itself," Adrian Belew told the author in 2001. "In the 1980s, that quartet with Tony Levin, Bill Bruford, Robert, and myself—we were the first guys to try all those tools. Bill was one of the first electronic drummers I ever heard of. Tony Levin was the first Stick play-er I'd heard of, and Robert and I were using the guitar synthesizer."

All three albums Crimson released in the 1980s (1981's *Discipline*, 1982's *Beat*, 1984's *Three of a Perfect Pair*) seem connected by slender musical threads. They chart a course from a monologue (*Discipline*)—the need for someone tes-tify (as was the case for the reformed Crimson; it had a reason to exist, to say something to an audience)—to a pas-sion and dialogue between two people (*Beat*), to broadcast, industry, and mass appeal (*Three of a Perfect Pair*). Fripp

BRIAN ENO: OBLIQUE STRATEGIES

During the mid- and late 1970s, in collaborations with David Bowie and the German ambient/rock outfit Cluster, Brian Eno moved further into ambient territory, having released such groundbreaking work as *Music for Films* and *Music for Airports*, on an artistic kick that was, arguably, established with 1975's *Discreet Music* and his second, more settling collaboration with Fripp, *Evening Star*.

The music Eno performed and recorded with Roxy Music provided a great launching point for his latter, impressionistic work. (By contrast, the post-Eno Roxy Music, of the early and mid-1970s—the Eddie Jobson years—achieved a glam/art-rock mixture on records *Stranded*, *Country Life*, and, to a degree, 1975's *Siren*, featur-ing number-one British hit "Love is the Drug.")

After Eno's own quasi-proggy period, exemplified by *June 1, 1974* (featuring the all-star cast of Nico, Mike Oldfield, Kevin Ayers, John Cale, and Robert Wyatt), Wyatt's *Ruth Is Stranger than Richard*; his own *Here Come the Warm Jets*, *Another Green World*, and *Before and After Science*; Phil Manzanera's 801's *Live*; and 1974's symphon-ic parody, *Plays the Popular Classics*, with the Portsmouth Sinfonia, Eno turned his ambitions toward ambient explorations.

In some of the recording sessions for the abovementioned records, Eno employed a custom deck of cards, dubbed *Oblique Strategies: Over One Hundred Worthwhile Dilemmas*, reportedly inspired by the ancient *Chinese Book of Changes* or *I Ching*.

Developed by Eno and painter friend Peter Schmidt, OS cards present possible resolutions to creative dilem-mas through instructions such as "Don't be afraid of things because they are easy to do," "Be extravagant," "Ask your body," "Emphasize differences," "Is there something missing?"

"He would break out these *Oblique Strategies* cards, hi-tech tarot cards, to figure out his next move," says bassist Percy Jones (Brand X). "It was totally different from what you were used to in terms of a session. It must have been the element of chance involved that interested him. It was almost like he was letting the music grow on its own to some degree.

"A similar anecdote with [Eno]," Jones continues, "was when he gave everybody in the studio a piece of paper and we had to write down a number from one to ninety-nine or something. Then he said, 'Number three: Percy, you play an F sharp. Number four: Phil, you hit the crash. Number five: Fred Frith, you play a C minor.' He went through this list, like ninety-something of these things. It got to the point where Phil [Collins] was throwing beer cans across the room, trying to hit a bicycle wheel in time. Nothing came out of that, though, but it just shows the length Eno was willing to go in the studio."

Fripp & Eno: *(No Pussyfooting)* (1973).

"The first time I met Brian, he said he was not a great musician," explains drummer Dave Mattacks (ex–Fairport Convention), who appears on *Before and After Science*. "I wouldn't say working with him was the antithesis of capturing a good performance off the floor, but it was certain-ly the other side of that understanding. You're deconstructing sound to an excessive degree, and, without sounding like some woolly-headed liberal, the ends justified the means. He really zeroes in on the textural aspect, cre-ating a mood. That later work with U2 and Daniel Lanois is a perfect example."

"More than most," says guitarist Fred Frith (Henry Cow, Art Bears), who appears on Eno's *Before and After Science*, "[Eno] was able to set aside the things he could already do in favor of learning something new about himself."

once explained that the symbols on the front and back covers of *Three of a Perfect Pair* could be interpreted as an evolution from a relationship between a man and woman to the family unit.

Fripp himself has said, rather honestly, that the band's contract with Warner Brothers was for three records—the label perhaps wanted more from the band, but Fripp/Crimson would only agree to the minimum requirement of three albums stipulated in the agreement.

The first record to appear, *Discipline*, leans more toward the cyclical and orderly (with guitar processing capturing the sounds of nature, acting as the fly in the ointment) than does *Beat*, which is looser, more deranged, and adds more overt ethnic musical influences. By comparison, the strongest material on 1984's *Three of a Perfect Pair* includes the art of industrial noise via electronic drum and fretless synth guitar, among other instruments and devices (e.g., "Man with an Open Heart," "Dig Me," "Industry," "Nuages (That Which Passes, Passes Like Clouds)," "No Warning").

Discipline remains the most potent and coherent of the three, however, and is arguably the record the band tried to top for the next three years. It is also the only record of the three, for the most part, from which material was performed live prior to recording.

The lead track, "Elephant Talk"—likely the first song most fans heard from this new Crimson—stomps on Crimson Old with animalistic ferocity. (The song itself recalls the natural habitat of the African plain, conjured, for example in the elephantine trumpeting and insect buzzing created via an Electro-Harmonix Polychorus effects unit.)

"Frame by Frame" (which is a phrase Belew used to express his frustration with what he perceived to be as Fripp's intellectualizing of every little detail of life and music) ratchets up the intensity level. The antagonistic Belew-Fripp partnership is represented musically by a tapestry of interlocking and divergent guitar lines.

"The original riff was written by Robert," Belew said. "It's a seven-note riff. The idea was that both guitarists play the riff, and then one guitarist takes one note away each cycle. What you get is something like a strange delay that's gone awry."

Belew sings a melody line over this complex musical matrix, as if he were writing for the Top 40, which, in and of itself, is not a bad thing (as it creates great tension). "It has always been my decision to sing or not to sing, so to speak," Belew said. "I mean, you have to make a judgment call as to whether the music is so strong that singing would be an interference or interruption, or if the music is a spot to start from. It is never really perfect. We don't write songs the way most people do, sitting down and drumming out three or four chords and writing a melody over that. 'Frame by Frame' doesn't seem like something you'd sing over, but I figured out a way to do it and thought, 'Yes, I should sing over it.'"

Ultimately, Belew and Fripp complemented each other well, conversing to create a dialogue, flipping roles as per the requirements of the musical setting: While Brit Fripp plays with the utmost precision, spinning hypnotic guitar lines, American Belew spews whimsical and cyber-processed noise chaos.

Other songs on *Discipline* underscore the band's global music approach. "The Sheltering Sky" (a title taken from the Paul Bowles novel of the same name, involving an American couple's journey through the Sahara with a friend) slips from African to Asian avant–rock pop. "Matte Kudasai," based on a Japanese phrase meaning "please wait for me," falls somewhere between Asian and American blues music. (Check Belew's slide playing/seagull effects.) "Thela Hun Ginjeet," an anagram of "Heat in the Jungle," features Belew's account of being accosted by armed Rasta toughs.

The title track behaves much in the same way "Frame by Frame" does, operating on the basis of interlocking guitar parts. It seems to be guided by one of the basic tenets of Balinese music, which is the idea of cyclical patterns, a feeling of a piece of music having no true beginning or end (much like the Celtic knot emblazoned on the cover of *Discipline*, which also speaks to the teachings of Gurdjieff and Bennett; the cover, not surprisingly, was created by John Kyrk, a disciple of J. G. Bennett.)

Interlocking and interweaving guitar lines and Bruford's 17/8 and 17/4 rhythmic patterns (spread across tongue drum/log drum, kick, and roto-tom) create a tension but not much release, highlighting the influence of cyclical music on Fripp and Crimson.

"Indiscipline" is philosophically and musically the other side of the coin to the title track: The dynamics of the piece, the searing and screaming effects-processed guitar lines, and the general sonic mess it makes, as well as its irreverence (i.e., humor), are the antithesis of the orderly, serious manner in which the title track progresses, reinforcing this concept of duality and schizophrenia at the very heart of what made the band tick.

BEAT

Crimson were looking for constant inspiration and stimuli, having accepted that they were working outside the normal parameters of accepted rock music. Because of this, the limits of their musical vocabularies and comfort zones were constantly being tested.

"Mostly the music . . . [is] like a mathematical puzzle, so you have to learn it correctly," Belew said. "The real rough part for everyone comes in the designing and finding out what to play in the music. We paint ourselves into a corner and try to figure out how to get out. I always use this analogy: It's like someone gave you a box of twenty-four crayons and poured out three or four of them and says, 'Now here's what you get to use.' All the other things that you might normally bring to someone else's music or to your own music just won't work."

This approach may have been why the band's second album, *Beat*, was inspired by the wayward, rambling, and bohemian lifestyle of the Beat poets. *Beat* engages the listener in a way *Discipline* doesn't. It feels interactive, yet it's difficult to tell if this sensation arises due to the romanticism of the lyrics (in some cases) or the narrative framing of the songs.

The song "Sartori in Tangier" references the Moroccan port that played host to Beat writers such as Allen Ginsberg and William Burroughs, the latter of whom wrote his nonlinear novel *Naked Lunch* in Tangier in a drug haze. ("Satori" is a Zen Buddha phrase for the process by which one begins to understand the nature of the mind and self, experiencing sudden enlightenment. *Satori in Paris* was a Kerouac novel. Interestingly, Crimson use the word *sartori* and not *satori*.)

The record seems to be informed by the confused and "cut-up" fashion in which *Naked Lunch* was constructed: References in the lyrics appear later in the album's song sequence. Each of the songs seems to be describing separate scenarios ("Sartori in Tangier" and "Requiem" are instrumentals) and yet all seem connected, as if each were part of a larger unified story.

"Neurotica" is a rambling, fantastically confused account of a wild city, initially inspired by Manhattan (we hear sirens, the scream of a subway train as it whizzes by, a police whistle, among other noises), as if we were viewing these seemingly random images through the eyes of a narrator drugged out of his mind.

The opener, "Neal and Jack and Me," is not just an ode to the band's life on the road; it's a reference to Neal

---

Fripp: inventing a new genre?

BEYOND KING CRIMSON: ROBERT FRIPP, EXPOSED

By the late 1970s, guitarist Robert Fripp had been recalled to the music business by Eno and Bowie, having fully emerged from the ruins of King Crimson and his self-imposed sabbatical, to undertake a new beginning.

The time away from Crimson must have done Fripp some good: His playing on 1975's *Evening Star*—a collaborative effort with Eno, similar to the duo's 1973 record, (*No Pussyfooting*)—Bowie's 1977's *Heroes*, and 1980's *Scary Monsters*, represents some of the guitarist's most monstrous and inspired performances this side of the Crimson juggernaut.

"I've witnessed it once, the only session I ever did with Eno for the *Nerve Net* record [1992]," says onetime King Crimson Warr guitarist Trey Gunn. "Eno lured Robert into a kind of playing that I have never, ever heard him play before, and that no one had ever done before. That was something that Robert claims used to happen a lot, and it came out of Eno making suggestions. For instance, Eno wanted Robert to do one more guitar solo, and I was there with [producer] David Singleton when Eno said, 'Robert, go in there and I will conduct you.' Eno was making all of these weird gestures with his body. Up to that point, I'd never heard Robert play anything remotely like that. It was like a Debussy flute part that was utterly chromatic and melodic. Somehow, his encouragement to Robert has . . . probably given blossom to a couple of genres."

Furthermore, Fripp's famous "sky saw" tone was an Eno creation that's a hybrid texture of mechanical grinding noises and a violin-like screech achieved via an electric guitar signal sent through the VSC-3 Synthi synthesizer (where it is further manipulated digitally).

Fripp creates a repeating looped signal (a few seconds long) and then allows the tape signal to decay with slight sonic degradation. Waves of sound are layered but don't disappear, and Fripp sends textural pieces soaring with his signature sustain, creating a kind of dronescape continuum.

The guitarist can thank Eno, in part, for helping to inspire and devise his tape-looping system, famously dubbed Frippertronics. "The (*No Pussyfooting*) record, that title, came about because Robert wrote on a card, 'No pussyfootin', and put it on the mixer board," says Gunn. "This meant: 'If we are going to go somewhere musically, let's really go there. Let's not hedge and go back. This isn't rock music, this isn't pop music, let's go for it.'"

With signal-delay tape loops, Fripp created a bed structure and then layered changing musical ideas/phrases on "top" of it, until a tremendous fabric of sound was woven. The technique was one Fripp would use for his first solo album, 1979's *Exposure* (originally conceived as the last installment of a proposed trilogy, which was to include

Cassady and Jack Kerouac and *their* experiences, which were the basis for Kerouac's *On the Road*. (The emotional "Heartbeat" was the title of the autobiography of Carolyn Cassady, Neal's wife.)

"Sartori in Tangier" begins with Levin's sensitive touch on the Stick, then segues into a thrusting groove: Much as a pianist would, Levin uses his left hand to hold down two repetitive notes and his right hand plays the melody. When the band picks up steam, we hear Fripp playing a violin-like sinuous lead (à la David Cross's performance in "The Talking Drum") that hints at the hypnotic whining of a

snake charmer's flute, or pungi (Belew once likened the sound to that of Turkish trumpet)—a fine example of musical technology converging for an intelligent ethno-rock performance.

Similarly, "Waiting Man" practically sums up the new ethos of the band, with interlocking guitar lines, the use of technology (from the Chapman Stick and electronic drums to guitar processing via dual GR-300 guitar synths), the punchy bass line harmonizing with Bruford's Afro-Latin percussion (courtesy of the Simmons pads), a passionate vocal performance, and Belew's ghostly guitar roar.

"Two Hands" (with lyrics written

by Belew's wife Margaret), "The Howler" (which evolves from tinny funk to prog disco to soul rock) and closer "Requiem" make you realize just how far-out this "commercial" music was and wonder why (and how) Crimson ended up on Warner Bros. Records in the first place.

The music is all over the place: "Requiem," in particular, dissolves into near chaos. (Fripp's wild playing fries up some free-form rock-jazz as Bruford's subtle and sizzling ride, snare, and kick patterns propel the sonic mess along). It's perhaps the closest thing to the 1970s Crimson this version of the band would ever get.

Daryl Hall's *Sacred Songs* and Peter Gabriel's sophomore "rip" record, both of which Fripp produced).

Prior to making *Exposure*, Fripp transplanted himself to New York City's Hell's Kitchen and gradually eased into the flow of making music again.

He jammed and/or recorded with underground and New York new wave/punk artists Talking Heads, the B-52s, and the Ramones, and even played onstage with Blondie in May 1978, one of Fripp's first live performances in three years. Not long after, Fripp founded his dancey new wave outfit the League of Gentlemen, having resurrected the band in which he appeared with Gordon Haskell in the 1960s.

Featuring Phil Collins, Daryl Hall, Eno, Gabriel, future Crimson bass/Stick player Tony Levin, Jerry Marotta, and drummer/producer Narada Michael Walden, *Exposure* could have been, in the best of all possible worlds, a kind of autobiography—the likes of which Crimson fans had yet to see. Yet throughout, Fripp keeps his distance, testing the waters, searching for a way to express himself, and leaving the listener in a maze—an intriguing labyrinth, but a labyrinth nonetheless.

While Fripp used some subterfuge to subvert the presentation of this material, something of the guitarist's personality does come through. For one thing, the album opens with a taped snippet of Fripp talking, perhaps half jokingly, about the commercial potential of this batch of songs.

Featuring some fine melodies; overtures to musique concrète (taped voices, one of which belongs to Fripp's fearless guru J. G. Bennett); ambient passages of sustained guitar noise created via Frippertronics; punky, violent bursts of sonic energy; and even moments of intimacy (e.g., in "Here Comes the Flood," initially recorded by Gabriel for his 1977 solo debut, appearing here, quite rightly, in an understated manner), *Exposure* was as much a

Robert Fripp: *Exposure* (1979).

culmination of the guitarist's exile from Crimson as it was a summation of his time *with* Crimson, and his view of a future Crimson.

The knotty, odd-time workout of "Breathless," the Hall-sung "North Star," and the off-kilter "Disengage" (sung by Van der Graaf Generator's Peter Hammill, whose unhinged vocal performance lies somewhere between visionary satire and absolute lunacy) use Fripp's past as a launching pad to foreshadow early 1980s Crimso tunes such as "Matte Kudasai" and "Frame by Frame."

Fripp's goal of rejoining the musical world, which he dubbed, "The Drive to 1981," was, in retrospect, a way of reconciling himself with the fulfillment of the guitarist's spiritual enlightenment, the advent of punk, and his eventual return to the mainstream. *Exposure* was just one step in that process, a process that would carry him back to King Crimson.

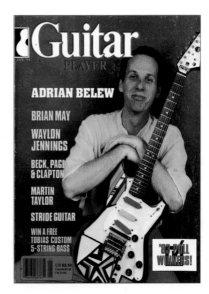

Belew graces the cover of *Guitar Player* magazine, January 1984.

Fripp's life and music philosophies: *Guitar Player* magazine, January 1986.

The 1990s double-drumming duo, Bruford and Pat Mastelotto (*Modern Drummer*, November 1995).

Bruford: pioneering electronic drummer (*Music Technology*, June 1987).

Some music writers either disregarded this fact or made a sharp (even veiled racist) point: This wasn't rootsy rock based on African music, but some Eurocentric concoction that pandered to a white, middle-class audience.

When some European (and American) artists reached out to include more "world" musical influences, they (incredibly) baffled critics, who either didn't grasp the appeal of the music in the first place or failed to see that music in general shouldn't be boxed in or limited by geography or societal boundaries.

Music is a continuum, and, as such, prog rock not only helped to erase so-called lines between genres but went a long way to expose the fact that attempting to erect barriers between musical styles is backward, perhaps even wrong-minded, thinking.

Progressive rock, then, was and is a logical, if not necessary and organic, creative branch in popular musical evolution, connected on some cellular level to many more "legitimate" forms of music and genres than it's given credit for, and something the *Beat*-era Crimson embodied.

THREE OF A PERFECT PAIR

Prior to the release of *Three of a Perfect Pair*, Adrian Belew said his lyrics would reflect the Western world's passage from the Industrial Age to the Information Age. Not only was this prophetic, but, once again, Crimson created an interesting dichotomy in the music.

Belew molds his guitar sounds into something akin to drills, power saws, and electrical tools of all sorts for songs on the second side (of the original LP)—the sounds of industry, the old age. More to the point, the guitar effects heard throughout the record capture the stuttering, beeping, and staticky tones of a dial-up Internet modem connection and fax signal transmissions—years before the Internet was given its name and commercialized.

The song "Industry" is a good example of a contemporary composi-

When the band toured *Beat*, fans in attendance booed punk and ethnic music that played through the loudspeakers before the band took the stage. However, they cheered for Crimson when they applied African, Indonesian, and other wide-ranging musical motifs to rock. The irony wasn't lost on some, who accused Crimson of a form of "cultural impe-rialism," a charge also leveled against Peter Gabriel, particularly after the release of his *Security* record.

Funnily enough, the European progressives were slammed in the late 1960s and early 1970s for using their own heritage and bringing it to rock, when that same heritage helped to shape, at the least on some level, the basis for rock 'n' roll.

Discipline
(1981)

tion bordering on a kind of linear Steve Reich–ish art music. For the piece, Bruford combines acoustic with electronic drumming to almost unnerving effect. The plodding, rhythmic, machinelike pace of the song and the strange guitar blasts and textures underscore the music's fusion of emotion and reserved complexity—the human and robotic together.

The album concludes with the sonically charged "Larks' Tongues in Aspic Part III," bringing echoes of the past and yet encompassing all that was new about this 1980s Crimson—a duality to the end.

When the *Three of a Perfect Pair*

tour wrapped in Montreal in July 1984 (for years, the show existed as a bootleg until being released on CD as *Absent Lovers* on Fripp's Discipline Global Mobile label), Crimson disappeared again into the ether.

Fripp expressed that Crimson had ceased to be something that possessed that "X" factor and had become a highly skilled group of individuals who merely played together, playing less for the band and more for themselves.

"No discussion followed the end of the tour to address either working together or not working together," Fripp wrote in his online diary in January 2001.

"In retrospect it was inevitable," says Spinks. "Robert can only do the same thing for so long; then he has to move on. It's a kind of self-destruct mechanism, but it's him being completely honest with himself."

The members scattered to the corners of the earth: Bruford went off to work with Patrick Moraz; Levin resumed his studio and tour work (which he never truly left) with Gabriel, Stevie Nicks, James Taylor, Pink Floyd, Cher, Robbie Robertson, and others, Belew fronted his own band the Bears (and did sessions with Cyndi Lauper, Paul Simon and Jean Michel Jarre, among others), and Fripp began working on a new standard tuning for the guitar, recorded with the likes of Toyah Wilcox, David Sylvian, and Peter Hammill, and taught guitar craft seminars and classes in music for the nonmusician at the J. G. Bennett–affiliated Claymont Society for Continuous Education in West Virginia.

Despite certain pop choices the band made during the writing and recording stages of *Three of a Perfect Pair* (songs such as "Man with an Open Heart" and "Model Man" stressed Belew's and Crim's mainstream music sensibilities), the series speaks more of musical evolution than cold calculation.

Beat
(1982)

Three of a Perfect Pair (1984)

The Compact King Crimson (1986)

Absent Lovers: Live in Montreal 1984 (1997)

(Michael Putland/Getty Images)

THROWING IT ALL AWAY

Genesis, Yes, and ELP

GENESIS ARE EITHER THE BEST OR WORST example of what it means to be a "progressive" rock band: Their music changed so drastically (albeit gradually) over a ten-year period as to render them a straight-up mainstream pop-rock group, one that defined the times in which they lived. Had Genesis been plotting to become a pop band all along?

It was in the late 1970s that Collins expressed aspirations of becoming a solo artist. In 1981 he dropped *Face Value*, which contained the massive hit "In the Air Tonight"; the single reached number two in Britain and number nineteen in the U.S.

One career had fed the other. As Genesis gained in popularity throughout the late 1970s, the road was paved for Collins's solo career to take off. On his own, Collins could vent his frustrations about life as a drummer and lead singer and, more importantly, administer himself a form of therapy for the pain and heartache of his first marriage falling apart—options that were not always available to him as a member of Genesis. In some cases, listening to Collins's solo material became embarrassing: Collins lifted the veil to reveal, in some cases, work that seemed almost too personal and emotional, making us feel as if we were eavesdropping on the man's private conversations and personal thoughts.

When Collins's solo albums (*Face Value*; *Hello, I Must Be Going!*; *No Jacket Required*; . . . *But Seriously*) went global, Genesis benefited from the lead singer/drummer's newly acquired high profile, and the band soared to the heights of superstardom, playing stadiums around the globe.

Collins's gradual move away from his earlier career became complete when it seemed more people in the world identified him as a singer first, a drummer second. Collins was even using (gasp!) Roland TR-808 and TR-909 drum machines, LinnDrums, and Simmons electronic drums, creating a mathematical and even mechanical feel to some of his own and Genesis's material in the 1980s.

"It was funny," Robert Berry (GTR, 3) relates. "Carl [Palmer] walked up to Phil Collins when 3 played at Madison Square Garden for the Atlantic Records anniversary concert [1988], and he said, 'What are you up to?' Carl wanted to talk about drums, and Phil wanted nothing to do with drums. He just wasn't a drummer at that point."

Bolstered by Collins's debut solo album success, Genesis's 1981 record, *Abacab*, reached the Top 10. Songs such as "Abacab," "No Reply at All," and "Man on the Corner" all charted in the U.S. Top 40 (with "Abacab" reaching number nine in Britain). Although this direction had been hinted at on records as early as *Selling England by the Pound*, . . . *And Then There Were Three*, *Wind & Wuthering*, and *Duke*, and despite the strong material on *Abacab*, the band had reached the point of no return.

Though classic Genesis trademarks

Like the Eagles' Don Henley, Genesis' Phil Collins emerged as a triple threat in the 1980s: a songwriter, vocalist, and drummer who successfully juggled these three musical attributes. (Larry Hulst/Getty Images)

run rampant in "No Reply At All" (keyboardist Tony Banks employs the same hand-over-hand piano technique used in *The Lamb Lies Down on Broadway*"), the song was a way for Collins to get back to the music he loved. By using the same horn section featured on Collins's solo record, *Face Value*, Genesis crossed into soul and R&B pop.

"Abacab," while being one of the most driving songs the band would ever record, confuses as much as it pleases.

Perhaps "Abacab" is a metaphor for the band's music in the 1980s—slightly vapid, vague, and ingenious in its ability to get people talking, listening, and debating, while not really (seemingly) being about anything of any real substance. (Collins turned this approach into pop gold with "Sussudio," from 1985's *No Jacket Required*.) In that sense, Genesis acclimated well to the corporate 1980s.

"I guess Genesis became less progressive as they continued and songs became shorter," Steve Hackett told the author in 2002. "The single held sway over the *War and Peace*–type epics. . . . I'd like to say something controversial here: You could say that Genesis started out . . . the reverse of the Beatles, I think. the Beatles started out sounding arguably the most stupid band and then ended up sounding the most intelligent. I think vice versa for Genesis. I'm not knocking the individuals, who I consider great musicians and writers. I'm just saying in terms of the tunes, I'm not sure [that] making the hit single your raison d'être is the best way, long term, to come up with the most interesting music."

"After a certain point, I'm not sure you could call Genesis progressive," says drummer Jerry Marotta. "You wouldn't call [Phil Collins's solo song] 'Sussudio' progressive either. The progressive aspect of that band took a backseat when Peter Gabriel left. Every time we went into the studio with Peter there was never any talk about what kind of record we would make. Nobody ever used the

word *progressive*. We all went into the studio with our different approaches, influences, and backgrounds. Peter encouraged that. That's what made those records so great, and that is why no two of them sound alike."

Admittedly, flares of progressiveness do crop up in Genesis's music throughout the 1980s and early 1990s, but these were fading.

After the massive success of 1986's *Invisible Touch* (the title track reached number one on the U.S. *Billboard* Top 100 charts—the only Genesis single to do so—the band hit the road again to support a new batch of hit songs and then took some time off. The band would return in the early 1990s with the release of 1991's *We Can't Dance*—"a mixture of songs that came together quickly and other longer, more constructed tunes such as 'Fading Lights' and 'Driving the Last Spike,' explains Nick Davis, who coproduced the album with the band.

The song selection on *We Can't Dance* gave longtime prog fans new hope. But in reality, the trio's days were numbered. By 1996, Collins had announced that he was leaving the band, reducing Genesis to a duo—Mike Rutherford and Tony Banks, who recruited Scottish singer Ray Wilson and drummers Nir Z and Spock's Beard's Nick D'Virgilio for the recording of 1997's studio album, *Calling All Stations*.

As one would imagine, the record didn't break into the Top 50 in the U.S. (it fared better in the U.K., where it soared to number two, perhaps purely on name recognition). But the sales and support for the record just weren't there, rendering touring impossible.

Calling All Stations was one of the most genuinely progressive records Genesis had made in years (it sounds a bit like Marillion did at roughly the same time period). But apparently it wasn't prog enough for older fans to be convinced that the band had shed its pop tendencies.

"I thought the material was okay," says D'Virgilio. "I didn't think it was their best work, but I thought it was all right. I think it was safe. That's a good word to use. With all of this stuff and the incredible jams they'd done earlier on, they weren't doing much of that at all [on the record]. Especially with Phil having left the band, they could have taken a little bit more of a left turn. They could have gone a little more muso with it, and it may have been a bigger record. But it was a tough thing: Phil Collins was such a big part of that [band]. Tough shoes to fill."

"Genesis are held up to be the virtual paragon of what progressive rock tries to attain," says the Tangent's Andy Tillison. "I think they did some tremendous music in between *Trespass* and *Wind & Wuthering*. So basically we're looking at 1977 as the turning point, which is what I consider to be the last of the great Genesis albums. After which they became an indisputably highly successful, sophisticated pop group. . . . From my perspective, they have not made a good record for thirty years, and that's a long time not to have made a good record. Yes completely reinvented themselves, then went back to what they were before. But they still pack them in at stadiums. You can't really knock them for that."

YES: CHANGES

After a tour to support *Drama* and the release of a live double album, *Yesshows*, Yes broke up—for good, it seemed—in 1980. Hopes of a reconciliation between the members were dashed as the gang were scattered to the four corners of the musical globe: Steve Howe had found new life as a member of Asia; Rick Wakeman continued his session work and recording his critically acclaimed concept record *1984* (based on George Orwell's novel); Jon Anderson collaborated with Greek progger Vangelis on a few projects and released his own solo recording *Songs of Seven* (and

. . . And then there were three: Genesis, 1978. *Left to right:* Mike Rutherford, Phil Collins, and Tony Banks.

appeared on Wakeman's *1984*); Trevor Horn resurrected the Buggles, with some assistance and contribution from keyboardist Geoff Downes, who'd joined Howe in forming Asia.

Meanwhile, drummer Alan White and bassist Chris Squire hadn't given up hope of forming a stadium-rock band. Prog rock veteran and composer Dave Lawson met with Chris Squire.

"After hearing me play on a Synclavier in the studio, Chris asked me to come out and to meet Alan White," Lawson says. "I've got some recorded tracks of us playing. After I did a film called *Deathwish II* with Jimmy Page, I mentioned playing with Chris and Alan to Jimmy. Jimmy knew of Chris. In fact, Jimmy put some guitar tracks on the recordings we did. It appeared as though we were becoming a band, to be called XYZ [as in ex–Yes and Zeppelin.]

"Unfortunately, the band never happened because of political reasons, and that was the end of that," Lawson says. "But a while later, when Yes start-

ed to put the band together again, it was assumed that I would join the band. Alan White even said, 'I'm begging you . . .' when I said I couldn't do it because I was so busy with sessions."

Enter South African guitarist/studio hound/multi-instrumentalist Trevor Rabin, who'd recorded with his band Rabbitt in the 1970s and Manfred Mann's Earth Band in the early '80s. Since Howe had his hands full with the wildly popular Asia, Rabin was a shoo-in for a new project, dubbed Cinema, which was to be produced by former Yes singer Trevor Horn.

"Trevor Rabin came in with a different set of fresh ideas, so, it made it all feel very new and exciting," says Chris Squire.

While Rabin was helping the band write new material, Trevor Horn was directing the band's overall focus and sound. "Trevor [had] kind of had enough of the singing and realized he could use his talents to a much better degree in producing the band," says Gary Langan, an engineer for Yes who

worked with the band on 1980's *Drama* and went on to find his own success with the Trevor Horn–produced studio project, the Art of Noise.

The band needed to be reimagined, if they were to have a fighting chance in the 1980s. Moog solos were out. Twenty-minute pieces, out. Indecipherable cosmic messagings kept to a minimum. "Horn had quite firmly decided that Rick Wakeman was not going to come back into the fold," adds Langan.

But redefining a monster band like Yes, even if they were being labeled a dinosaur, is not an easy (or possibly even wise) decision. Who could perform with the band and yet retain some of its core values of musicianship and songwriting? If not Wakeman, then who?

Patrick Moraz was busy with his solo album *Future Memories II* and, more importantly, being a keyboardist and vital part of the Moody Blues' resurgence in the pop world with the success of the well-crafted 1981 record

Produced
by DAVID
HENTSCHEL
and
GENESIS

Gelring/Hit
&Run Music
Publishing
Ltd.

(P) 1978

Charisma
Records Ltd.

Charisma
Label →

45

CB 309

B

Made in
England

BALLAD OF BIG
(Collins/Banks/Rutherford)
GENESIS
Taken from the forthcoming album
"AND THEN THERE WERE THREE"

"Ballad of Big," the flipside of
Genesis' breakthrough single,
"Follow You, Follow Me."

Long Distance Voyager. ("Although they had done the *Octave* album, and it was well received, it was not the kind of big comeback record the band was looking for," says Moraz, who replaced original keyboardist Mike Pinder and made great use of keyboard technology and orchestration skills to enrich the Moodys' sound. "When they were thinking about recording a new album, which became *Long Distance Voyager*, I was able to emphasis the full scope of [my] creative imagination by bringing them sounds that they were not even thinking about then," says Moraz.)

There seemed only one logical choice—one so wild it just might work; a look back to move forward. Tony Kaye appeared, and everything took off.

"After Tony Kaye, everything was beginning to get settled. With some shrewd talking, Jon Anderson was approached to sing for the band, which he was more than willing to do," says Langan.

With Anderson onboard (originally it was believed Rabin would be the singer), the name Cinema was dumped as it became apparent that the personalities that were assembled could only be called Yes. Anderson's voice was and is too distinctive to pretend otherwise. Some still harbored doubts about the project.

"I so hated the *Drama* record—it was torture for me—that when Trevor said that we're going to do another Yes album, I said, 'I'm not sure I can do that, mate,'" says Langan. "Then Trevor said, 'No, no, it is going to be different.' I told him, 'Trevor, if it starts to turn out like *Drama*, I'm going to really think about taking a backseat, because I can't do that again.'"

Langan, at least initially, seemed to have cause to worry. *90125* was the result of an arduous nine-month process. Kaye exited the sessions at one point due to disagreements with Horn, leaving keyboard, synth mapping, programming, and other production duties to the likes of Lawson, Langan, and Jonathan "J. J." Jeczalik (who

helped to form the Art of Noise).

"When you have someone like Tony Kaye," Langan says, "who is struggling to keep up with technology, you can see it in Trevor's eyes that he's thinking, 'We could do this another way, and we can do it a lot quicker if I were to use so and so . . .' He'll gently just push Tony out the way and we'll get to work the way that Trevor wants to do it. Before you know it, you are on the sidelines and you don't even see it coming. He can be that ruthless, but that is the way he is. The guy generates hits.

"I also want to say that there's nothing wrong with Tony as a keyboard player," Langan continues. "He's just not a programmer."

Said Tony Kaye in 1984: "The seven months I spent in England working on *90125* was the longest time I spent in eons."

"Owner of a Lonely Heart" is a microcosm showing Horn's progressive studio approach. "All of these tracks were cut as a band to begin with," says Langan. "It really was 'Owner of a Lonely Heart' that started out as a bit of programming, with a set of LinnDrums in the beginning."

"The acoustic guitar sound for 'Owner of a Lonely Heart' was originally mapped out by me on the Synclavier and later played by Trevor Rabin," adds Lawson.

"The track was built from there," says Langan. "[Squire] would put a bass track down. Then Alan would have done a drum track and then the guitars and keyboards and other samples and things. That's how Trevor used to make his pop records—built up a layer at a time, because he did not like dealing with a live band. I think that is something Trevor has in common with Eddy Offord—they both crafted records."

Through Rabin's impressive pile of material, Horn's ever-growing production skills, quite a bit of synth programming, and a ton of multitracked instruments, the album titled *90125* (its catalog number) revitalized Yes and

put Horn and Langan on the map as a production team par excellence.

Heard over the radio at the time of its release, not only did "Owner of a Lonely Heart" not sound like classic Yes, it had a frightening sonic freshness. Between Rabin's reverb- and harmonizer-soaked guitar solo and the interesting use of panning techniques throughout, nothing compared to the song.

"Ahmet Ertegun at Atlantic was just over the moon," says Langan. "We had helped to revive this dinosaur band. I think the success of the record was down to the chemistry and combination of people involved. Primarily, if I'm being honest, I'll put that down to Trevor and myself, because there is an art form that Trevor and I had in making records. We were able to impart that on this Yes album."

"That was my favorite Yes," says Peter Banks. "I thought the *90125* album was fantastic. That was when I started liking the band [again] because they at least sounded different. Obviously Steve [Howe] wasn't happy with it. But I thought that band was great. I saw them play quite a few gigs in the States. . . . My only complaint was the hidden keyboard player and the hidden guitar player, Billy Sherwood. I thought that was kind of stupid. Having another keyboard player underneath the stage, I thought that was . . . like circus time. Having a stunt keyboard player. What is that all about?"

"Around the 1980s/*90125* period, when samplers and sounds were needing to be loaded under the stage and stuff, there were guys doing that," says former Yes member Billy Sherwood. "When I toured with them in the 1990s on the *Talk* tour, I was onstage with them and there were still guys changing disks and putting up the next synth sounds. It was more technical things they were doing down there than musical. A lot of people have the illusion that there were guys down there playing the parts for everybody, but the reality was that it was more technical. You couldn't have Tony Kaye onstage . . . changing discs and that kind of nonsense."

Yes were as strong—and controversial—as ever, touring both sides of the Atlantic. On the road, the band had the opportunity to play for audiences who had missed them in the 1970s, performing '80s renditions of songs such as "Starship Trooper" and "I've Seen All Good People." Anderson even dusted off "Soon," the cathartic climax of the epic "The Gates of Delirium," for the shows.

The follow-up to *90125* wouldn't materialize until 1987 and the release of *Big Generator*. Yes placed themselves in the unenviable position of having to follow a hit record, and the band appeared to be putting it off.

It's little wonder. *Big Generator* got off to a rough start. For one thing, it took nearly two years after the band's '84 world tour in support of *90125* to get down to recording. The process began, as it had for *90125*, in a slew of recording studios.

At every turn, *Big Generator* stresses the need to leave behind the old ways and enter a new world. Fittingly, the song "Big Generator" refers to the power of creation in the universe (what some call "God"), and the entire song cycle of the album (in particular side two of the original LP) feels like a meditation on and a communication with this energy; a spiritual journey to enlightenment, capped off by the ecological prayer and plea for global awareness called "Holy Lamb (Song for Harmonic Convergence)."

Big Generator is quite an extraordinary accomplishment indeed, having garnered two U.S. Top 40 hits— "Rhythm of Love" and "Love Will Find a Way," cementing Yes's return. The Yes saga might have ended on a peaceful note, except trouble was brewing once again. It wouldn't be long before Anderson flew the coop and the band was split in half, opening the door to yet another supergroup.

"It's ironic that I wrote the song 'Perpetual Change' in 1970, because it really almost should be an anthem to describe Yes," Squire says.

MEANWHILE, GTR

Disenchanted with Asia's musical direction and internal strife (e.g., Wetton's battle with personal demons), Steve Howe in the mid-1980s found himself recording with the likes of Frankie Goes to Hollywood and the techno-pop band Propaganda, both produced by Trevor Horn for his ZTT label.

Back in 1982, Howe had recorded an acoustic bit for the song "Up in the Air" for the Dregs' *Industry Standard* (Howe exchanged analog tapes with Dregs guitarist Steve Morse) and discovered how much he enjoyed working with another axe man.

At the same time, former Genesis guitarist Steve Hackett began to formulate ideas to put together a new band. After discussions with manager Brian Lane, contact was made with Howe, and the two met in 1984 and traded licks, and something just clicked. It was in these early days that Howe and Hackett had decided that they would front this band with two lead guitarists, who could splash the musical canvas full of sonic color using nothing but guitars and guitar synthesizers.

Though both Howe and Hackett had the reputation of widening the bandwidth of possibilities of the guitar in the realms of electric and acoustic, crossing over into synthesizer territory seemed just as good a reason as any to form a band in the mid-1980s.

At this point, anything the keyboards could do, guitarists felt they should be able to do as well. Using a variety of MIDI-controlled synth modules such as Roland GR-700 and GR-300 units, OSCars, Synclaviers, Fairlights, Emulators, and so on for sonic options and layering, Hackett and Howe were able to play sound samples of pipe organs, cellos, bells, harps, calliopes, drums, or anything they wanted. They'd discover odd and unexpected ways in which stored keyboard sound samples (and other sonic textures) interface with the nuance of guitar technique.

For prog rock fans it was a dream come true. The combined star power was undeniable even for cynics, and people would come out in droves to see these two guitar titans on the same stage for an evening. For the two iconic guitarists, it may have also been a shot at redemption; Howe could position himself as the "classic" Yes guitarist in a modern recording setting post-*90125*, and Hackett could grab the much-deserved spotlight. The truth was, Howe had experienced massive success with Asia, and Hackett had been charting solo records in Britain since—and during—his Genesis days. In fact, the first eight Hackett studio solo albums charted. In short, GTR was full of musical possibilities and held the promise of a true collaboration between two skilled musicians. It sounded nice on paper; living it was to be another story. . . .

The first step after Hackett and Howe began exchanging tapes was to establish a band around them. Ex-Marillion drummer Jonathan Mover got the gig, along with bassist Phil Spalding.

The band was christened GTR (an abbreviation commonly used by sound engineers on their mixing boards to denote guitar inputs) and tapped Asia's Geoff Downes as producer, in the hopes that his knowledge of keyboards and synthesizers would be beneficial for the record. The rehearsals and recording sessions were going swimmingly.

"When the Heart Rules the Mind," which became a Top 20 hit in the U.S., was one of the more dynamic and successful pieces on the record (sketched out early in the writing process) and features beautiful nylon-stringed acoustic guitar passages juxtaposed with layered, arena-rock guitar bigness.

"[The main melody] was a line written on nylon guitar and a line that transplanted to the voice," Hackett told the author in 2002. "It was changed to accommodate voices and harmonies. There [are] some harmony parts on that track that would have done credit to the Beach Boys, I think."

Other songs include "You Can Still Get Through," "Jekyll and Hyde" (the bell sounds you hear at the opening of the song were created by the attack of two guitar synths), the deceptive "Imagining" (Hackett begins the track with finger-style classical guitar as Howe floats above it with orchestral strings via guitar synth; the tune ends with Howe and Hackett trading licks in something resembling flamenco style), and two solo pieces: "Hackett to Bits" (which is a "whammy-bar extravaganza" reinterpretation of the title song from Hackett's 1978 record *Please Don't Touch!*) and Howe's twelve-string electric showpiece "Sketches in the Sun" (highlighting Howe's ability to play a delicate melody and rhythmic ostinato simultaneously).

Despite the success of the tracks, some within the band felt the record held more potential than it ultimately delivered. "GTR took a long time to get going and lasted a short time after it came out," says Mover. "It was a wonderful experience for me, because it gave me international notoriety and playing with Steve and Steve was amazing. But it was also a big disappointment, too, on some levels. The kiss of death to that was Geoffrey Downes. No offense, but Geoffrey wanted to do Asia Part II. Before GTR chose Geoffrey as a producer, we were progressive rock. You had a lot of songs in odd times and songs that were nine, ten, eleven minutes long, with different sections and breakdowns.

"Geoffrey destroyed a lot of the record," Mover continues. "He chopped up a lot of the odd times and made them even. He had taken out a lot of the countermelodies and rhythms that Hackett and I were kind of doing and was turning it into a pop record. Me, Mr. Mouth, like I was with Fish, I came into the studio . . . and I started listening . . . and the polyrhythms and double [kick] and ambidextrous stuff I was playing are all gone. I looked at Geoff Downes and said, 'Who the fuck do you think you are, chopping my drums up? I didn't play that. That's not what I would have thought of.' Steve Howe got a little bit snippy with me, and said, 'You have no idea. You have no experience. You're the youngest one here. We know what we're doing.' I looked at Steve Howe and said, 'You can take your fucking record and shove it up your ass.' I quit the band. I was twenty or nineteen years old.

"I stormed out of the studio. Hackett came running out after me, and I really have to extend my thanks to the guy, because he said, 'I know what you're going through. I've been there. Don't quit. Hang in there. We will make this thing really great live. You're going to fuck up your career and you're going to blow a great opportunity. You have just got to trust me to stay with it.' I cooled off and I didn't quit. Geoff is a sweet guy but he is not a producer."

"I personally think the record was mixed too brightly and not compressed enough, but I shouldn't be widging about things that are old issues," Hackett told the author. "I always felt 'When the Heart Rules the Mind' sounded better on FM radio because it came across with a certain amount of compression that aided the mix . . . and so it brought the power of the band alive, to my mind."

"The GTR record, well . . . I was slightly less happy with the overall sound [compared] to the first Asia album," Howe told the author in

2005.

"The record was a failure on three levels: Musically it didn't make the mark it should have; production-wise the sound of the record is horrible and it does not translate because it is bathed in so much reverb that you can't even hear half the shit that is going on; and thirdly and most importantly, I think Geoff Downes was overwhelmed by Steve Howe," Mover adds. "When you're producer of a band, with individuals on five individual levels, you've got to be the king. You have to have everybody looking at you. Not you siding with Steve Howe because you had this little thing. That wasn't fair to Steve Hackett."

The record was released, and by July 1986, *GTR* had gone gold in the U.S. After "When the Heart Rules the Mind" charted it was followed by "The Hunter" (written by Downes), also a Hot 100 single. Despite the success, nothing could save the doomed supergroup; the subsequent tour broke the band's back.

"Hackett and Howe traveled separately on the road," Mover says. "They stayed on separate floors in the hotels we stayed in. They each had their own tour managers. It cost us a fucking fortune and me, Phil, and Max [Bacon, vocalist] had to pay part of it. And they never spoke to one another. The only time they got within thirty feet of one another was onstage. It was a drag, because in the beginning it was fun. The two of them are great guys. I was angry with each one of them for not letting a good thing happen."

Eventually Hackett, who had convinced Mover not to quit, did just that, leaving Howe at the helm. "After the tour of '86, which ended in September, we got together at Steve Howe's farm house in Devon, England, to start working on the new record," Mover says. "Hackett didn't show. But we started material. The material was great. We did three songs the first week we were out there. The music was in the progressive vein. . . . I was really happy with the direction."

Mover eventually left the band, having accepted an invite to join soon-to-be guitar god Joe Satriani. GTR attempted to record a second studio album sans Mover and Hackett, but the record failed to gain label support and the project collapsed.

"There was a lot of politics going down between management and the record company, and the next thing we knew, GTR had folded," says Mover's replacement, drummer Nigel Glockler (Saxon, Asia).

"The combination of progressive and pop was an area that couldn't be sustained for very long," Hackett said. "Those are very different sensibilities."

ELP AND 3

"Of all the people I've worked with," says Robert Berry, "the only guy I was afraid of was Keith Emerson, because I saw him as this rocket scientist, [a] crazy keyboardist [who] wasn't going to be easy to talk to. Like a nutty professor that I wouldn't be able to get an honest conversation [from]. It turned out to be totally different than that. A couple glasses of wine, he likes to tell jokes, he's funny, down-to-earth. Not the nutty professor at all. I lucked out with Carl Palmer and Keith both because they treated me with a lot of respect. Immediately, they let me be on their level—we were a three-piece band with three voting members. . . . They are just fantastic musicians and top of the heap when it comes to musicians in the rock world."

The appearance of 3 capitalized

on Emerson's return to the spotlight with Emerson Lake and Powell in 1986, whose debut record was a Top 40 hit on both sides of the Atlantic. (The song "Touch and Go" reached number two on the *Billboard* Mainstream Rock chart.)

Drummer Cozy Powell's hard-hitting percussive attack in recordings by Rainbow, Robert Plant, Jeff Beck and others made him a shoo-in to replace Carl Palmer, who was busy with Asia. Powell suggested the band tackle "Mars, the Bringer of War" from Gustav Holst's *The Planets*—something Emerson, for some reason, had fought to avoid—and the new-fangled lineup had recorded "ELP"'s greatest material since the mid-1970s.

"Upon hearing that, I called them up and wished them best of luck, and let them use the ELP logo," Palmer told the author in 2005. "They had to play the material I had cowritten for ELP, and the record company was promoting the back catalog. From a financial point of view, I could gain half the ball of wax, if not the complete ball. I was never quite sure why they didn't wait for me; I think it was a big mistake. . . . I look at the positive aspect of it."

Apparently, and intriguingly, Simon Phillips (yet another drummer with a last name that begins with the letter *P*) was contacted. "They knew of my playing and the records I'd done," says Phillips. "I was doing sessions from 1974 onward. I don't remember when I first met Keith. I was contacted by management for what would have been Emerson Lake and Phillips. We talked more about

the business end of everything, and I was not knocked out about how that was going. I was very busy at that time because I was working with Mike Oldfield."

If there were any hard feelings on anyone's part, they obviously had melted away: Phillips eventually hooked up with Emerson in a short-lived touring band called the Best ("Terrible name," says Phillips), featuring Joe Walsh, the Who's John Entwistle, and Jeff "Skunk" Baxter, and Palmer rejoined the keyboard wizard when they formed the band 3 with Robert Berry.

Much of 3's debut record, . . . *To the Power of Three*, was catchy, commercial rock with some progressive flair, what allmusic.com calls "alternative pop" (e.g., "Chains," "Lover to Lover," "Runaway," "Talkin' Bout," "On My Way Home," written in dedication to Tony Stratton-Smith). "The real die-hard progressive fans were down on 3—the types that would rather sit down next to a coffee table with headphones and listen to the music," Berry says. "3 was trying to be accessible the way Rush was—write accessible music, get people educated, get some radio play, keep people liking it . . . There's an art to that."

The standout track, the seven-minute "Desde La Vida," is a gutsy move by the trio, featuring a fusion of electronic and acoustic drumming. "Palmer had a digital drum sampler made by a German company, Dynacord, at that time," Berry says. "I was already trying to bridge the gap between what I thought was going to happen in music, and I believe Mr.

Abacab
(1981)

Genesis
(1983)

Invisible Touch
(1986)

We Can't Dance
(1991)

The Way We Walk: Volume Two, the longs (1993)

Calling All Stations
(1997)

Seconds Out
(1977)

Mister and some other bands were out there too. I said to Carl, "If we can not only meld your electronic and acoustic set but meld the drum machine with your playing, it would have a really tight groove. I think we would fit into the modern sound.'"

When 3 took their show on the road, they decided to tour small clubs throughout America and play ELP and Nice favorites such as "Hoedown," "Fanfare for the Common Man," "America," and "Rondo" along with material from the band's debut. They even made a stop at Atlantic Records' fortieth anniversary party at Madison Square Garden, an appearance that went well, despite the Aaron Copland debacle mentioned earlier.

"Carl and Keith wanted something new," Berry says. "They wanted to play clubs and be real close to the fans. Keith told me on the bus that this is one of the most fun times touring. With ELP, he told me, 'We would be fighting.' As 3, the three of us just got along great."

It was a party until the unthinkable happened—the record label pulled support in order to get 3 off the road and back into the studio. "Geffen said, 'Okay, we're shutting the tour down now, so you can start recording the next album,'" Berry says. "'Talkin' Bout' was number nine, and we were a new band, with a new fan base. I said, 'Wait, if we have another hit song, which was going to be 'Lover to Lover,' if it was only to hit the Top 100, are you saying that's a

bad thing? And, anyway, we haven't toured Japan, where we are huge. . . .' They said, 'Next album!' Keith said, 'You know what? I cannot forge a new path for myself away from ELP without support from the record company.' . . . It was our first album, and if it wasn't for the record company—what they did—we would have made a second album. That second album would have been a more middle ground like Asia— a combination of mainstream and progressive material. Emerson didn't want to go through that assembly-line production kind of thing. So he was basically done with it. Someone like Keith Emerson only comes around once in a lifetime. But you can't record epic albums, make little money doing it, and remain a band."

(Pete Cronin/Getty Images)

MARILLION

Doin' It in "Style"

IN THE 1980S, A NEW BREED OF ROCK, DUBBED NEO-PROG, helped to resuscitate a fading and once greatly revered sound. Though bands of the neo-prog subgenre initially relied heavily on formulaic musical devices and compositional approaches pioneered by classic bands of the late 1960s and early 1970s (e.g., synth solos, expansive multisectioned compositions), they represented a vibrant, virulent strain of experimental music that codified progressive rock into a style that successfully incorporated such unlikely musical elements as funk, hard rock, and even punk.

While 1970s behemoths were tarred as "pretentious and boring" for their self-important indulgence of classical (or faux-classical) musical flourishes and ornamentation, the '80s bands, while less visionary and groundbreaking than their predecessors, rightly picked up on the more immediate hard rock and techno dance vibes of their contemporaries to carve out their own niche in the prog rock universe.

Case in point: Marillion. Originally dubbed Silmarillion (a reference to the J.R.R. Tolkien novel of the same title) by founding member and drummer Mike "Mick" Pointer, Marillion emerged from the post-punk music scene in Britain at a time when progressive bands such as Yes, Emerson Lake and Palmer, Genesis, and Gentle Giant had either died an unceremonious death or drastically changed their M.O. to become virtually unrecognizable to longtime fans.

Marillion existed as a bridge between punk and classic progressive rock, even to the point of the band being dubbed "the New Genesis." The band's lead

Fish: no "sausage-machine" songwriting. (Courtesy of Ami Barwell)

vocalist, a certain Derek William Dick (aka Fish), was instrumental in leading the charge: His towering, raging stage presence (he spit bars like a lunatic poet) complemented the band's driving tempos and its sometimes rough-around-the-edges sonic assault, which boasted a sensibility that bordered on the new wave. (The singer even pulls a Johnny Rotten by referring to himself as the Antichrist in the autobiographical song and the band's first single, "Market Square Heroes.") A lot of music fans hadn't seen a band perform in the progressive rock musical vein with quite the same intensity. It was an unusual combination, but it seemed to thrill a small but growing number of fans (later called "Freaks," after a B side to a single released in 1985).

"We had come up just as the punk and new wave movement was starting to run out of steam," says Marillion guitarist Steve Rothery. "What we were doing was kind of, in some respects, a throwback, but it was also influenced by the energy of punk and new wave. . . . It was a nice hybrid, you know? It was the kind of music I believed in and I wanted to play. From the early days we recorded at a studio [in Hertford] of [a] band [called] the Enid, and they were symphonic rock, if I could use that term, and exactly [at] the other end of the spectrum from where we were coming."

"When I met up with the Marillion guys, everybody came from a certain background, musically," says Fish (a nickname he picked up because he, much like Yes's Chris Squire, spent a lot of time in the bath). "I mean, Pointer was into Rush and . . . Neil Peart, Steve was into the Genesis/Hackett/Camel thing, and . . . the one name that was prevalent was Genesis. Well, Genesis and Floyd. I think having a guitarist like Steve Rothery, we were always on the kind of Genesis line. Steve and I, more than anybody else, kind of guided it in the early days. When Mark Kelly came on, he brought the kind of Yes synth stuff. But the energy from punk was there. And we weren't the only ones: You had bands like Simple Minds. Jim Kerr and Charlie Burchill were huge Genesis fans, but they embraced more of the punk ethic in the early days."

"I grew up in a little fishing town near Whitby in North Yorkshire, England, and one of the big things there was an annual folk festival," adds Rothery, who joined Silmarillion in 1979. "So I kind of absorbed some of that, I suppose, in my musical identity. A lot of what I do comes more from a traditional English folk background than blues or jazz or classical, for example. At the same time, I kind of loved Pink Floyd, Camel, King Crimson, Yes, Genesis, many of those early '70s bands,

because I found them incredibly fresh and exciting. When I discovered [them] in the mid-1970s, all of my friends went into punk rock, basically. They were rebelling by doing punk rock and I was rebelling by not getting into prog rock [laughs]. I think that is kind of where my development started, really."

Adding to the strange nature of the band, Fish used theatrical props and elaborate costumes to dramatize his stage performances of such songs as "Grendel" and "Forgotten Sons" (for which he'd wear ancient armor and army fatigues and/or a helmet, respectively) and applied multicolored greasepaint to his face. (Fish explained that when he was young he was a shy, chubby boy, and rather than be ridiculed as such, he turned into the class clown. Fittingly, when this harlequin grew up, he wore a greasepaint mask and, quite literally, on occasion a jester's cape, to steel his stage resolve so he could brave the crowds. Fish's use of war paint was as much a defense mechanism as homage to Peter Gabriel/Alice Cooper theatrics.

"I think the thing that appealed to me about progressive rock was that it wasn't in bed with fashion," says Fish. "Even though I wore a kind of mask, I knew that you didn't have to dress up in outrageous things to be prog rock."

Marillion began in earnest in the early 1980s, after the band dumped the "Sil" from its name and took onboard its flamboyant lead singer. Fish remembers the long and winding road leading up to his joining Marillion: "I was eighteen; I did what I wanted to do," recalls Fish, a self-proclaimed college dropout who's "never been good with authority.

"When most of my friends were getting into [fixing] cars and knew the differences between various carburetors . . . and fog lights, I was getting into music," Fish continues. "I was reading music magazines and buying albums. . . . But I needed a line of work. I was an axe man, and I don't mean guitar. A friend of my father suggested forestry, so I got into it. . . . But it didn't feel right. I was wearing the wrong shoes. I did other various jobs, and by 1980 I was singing in a band called Blewitt, that played in the Scottish Borders. We were doing covers of Average White Band, Steely Dan, Ry Cooder, Little Feat, and stuff like that. It was a whole different type of music [from Marillion]. It was good experience for me because I had never sung before. I really wanted to write progressive rock, yet the band didn't have a keyboard player. Plus the guys were doing it more as a hobby. . . . I wanted something more than just playing pubs."

Fish bounced around from job to job, band to band, and auditioned for a band in the south of England, but "that didn't work," Fish says. "They were British heavy metal, and they didn't think my voice was loud enough. I got pissed off by that and I came back and joined a band in Retford in mid-England, which featured my friend bassist Diz Minnitt. But that came to nothing. We wound up attempting to start another band, this time up in Cambridge. Couldn't do it up there either. So, I went back to the Scottish Borders."

Fish and Diz were planning to buy a cottage and open a recording/rehearsal studio, but neither of these dreams materialized. "Then we found an advert in a music magazine, I believe *Musicians Only*, from a band looking for bassist/vocalist," says Fish. "When we called Marillion, we basically bullshitted each other on the phone. They said they played all of these gigs and had T-shirts and merchandise or some bullshit and we said we knew Robert Plant. No one was being honest. They had only done four or five gigs or so. But we got the audition and I remember singing lines around the music I was given—[the] music was instrumental and very Camel-oriented. My first impression was that the guitar player was incredible."

Both camps suspended disbelief long enough for Fish and Diz to win the gig. From the outset, the band set high standards for themselves.

Founding member Brian Jelliman was out in favor of keyboardist Mark Kelly, who was up on the new technology. Much in the same way Keith Emerson, Patrick Moraz, and Rick Wakeman used Moog, Kelly utilized portable organs and grand pianos, a PPG Wave 2.2 (a polyphonic analog/digital synth that could produce thousands of waveforms and featured sequencing capabilities and sound samples), and a Yamaha DX-7, generally referred to as the first affordable and portable digital synth (it did for keyboards what Digidesign's ProTools did for home recording).

"The band evolved over the next two years," Fish says. "Members came in, members were fired, and whatever."

A buzz was building around the band with the clown-faced front man. Marillion's strong local followings in St. Albans, Bedford, Milton Keynes, their home base of Aylesbury, and even London (most notably at the Marquee) caught the attention of EMI, which had rejected an early demo made by the band.

EMI tapped David Hitchcock, who had worked with Genesis, Camel, Caravan, and Renaissance, to produce the band's early recordings. Songs such as "Market Square Heroes," inspired by Aylesbury Market Square; "Three Boats Down from the Candy" (keyboardist Mark Kelly's debut as a songwriter for Marillion); and the seventeen-plus-minute controversial epic "Grendel," based on the John Gardner book of the same title (complete with "Apocalypse in 9/8"–like odd meter), were eventually released as the band's first 12" EP/single.

The songs were a mixed bag of pop and Genesis-style prog, with Fish's thick Scottish accent neatly tucked away amid hints of Peter Gabriel, Dave Cousins, and Peter Hammill vocal inflections.

Laugh as some critics did, Marillion continued to gain fans, playing numerous shows around England and outside the country throughout 1982 and 1983. Strangely, the band even attracted attention from the heavy metal press and hard rock fans, who

identified with the band's frontal assault. "You've got to look at the Marillion's rise in popularity in terms of the whole 'New Wave of British Heavy Metal' happening in the early '80s," says Fish. "Suddenly, there was a throwback to the Led Zeppelin/Deep Purple stuff, which was all around when progressive rock was about in the '70s. . . . It wasn't as if there was a schism between the progressive rock thing and the punk thing. The way I see it, out of the punk thing came the New Wave of British Heavy Metal. Those guys wanted something that was a little more complicated, which was the same thing I wanted when I was thirteen or fourteen years old."

By being associated with the NWOBHM bands and being featured regularly in a British metal magazine like *Kerrang!*, suddenly, the band had a roughness, an edge (even if it was only a perceived musical edge), something that a lot of the earlier prog rock bands lacked.

STICKING TO THE "SCRIPT"

Marillion's first full-length record for EMI, *Script for a Jester's Tear*, is a bit like an adolescent dressing in adult clothing. The Genesis-style musical arrangements and flowery vagueness of the lyrical content only add to the artificiality. Even the album's title speaks to Marillion's modus operandi: witty but also calculated, lacking in any spontaneity. This perception, justified or not, would dog the band for most of the 1980s.

Just as the first wave of progressive rock bands had, Marillion needed a visual translator, someone who could successfully complement and package their music with art. The cover illustration of *Script*, airbrushed by Mark Wilkinson, reinforced the perception of Marillion as pretenders to the prog rock throne.

Overall, there's a naïve ambition, an arrogant cluelessness about *Script for a Jester's Tear*. The music is a bit like Fish himself: The songs are of an adult nature, but their truer, deeper meanings are masked by dramatic prog rock trappings and escapist language.

Not everyone viewed Marillion as being purely derivative. The band impressed with its chops, stage show, and willingness to discard trends even at the risk of being ridiculed for doing so.

"Fish was very aggressive onstage," says Nick Barrett of 1980s prog rock band Pendragon. "[He] was spitting out the words with the passion and venom of a punk [singer]. This is not strictly a limp-wristed prog. It gave Marillion a lot of credibility, in my opinion."

FUGAZI

Fugazi, Marillion's most diverse record to date, was the result of the band's growing pains and the dizzying effect of being behind schedule and in and out of recording and rehearsal studios, having EMI breathing down their necks for new material, and a producer (Nick Tauber) so overwhelmed from the pressure he was backpedaling (forcing the band the work long hours in order to hand the record in under the deadline). The band was on the road before the record was finished, for a tour that was meant to promote *Fugazi*.

Fugazi was torturous to put together, beginning with the search for a new drummer to replace Pointer, who'd been asked to leave. (After Marillion, Pointer would go on to form the neo-prog outfit Arena in the mid-1990s with Clive Nolan of Pendragon.) Jonathan Mover, world-class drummer, auditioned for the drum chair and won it.

Everything seemed to be going well, but, as Mover remembers, a fateful conversation involving Fish's idea for a concept record caused major eruptions within the band. "We were already writing individual songs that had nothing to do with each other, and [Fish] wanted to do a concept record like *The Wall*," Mover says. "Over dinner one night he said, 'We need to attach all of these songs and

make them a theme. What do you think?' The other three guys, who were very much afraid of Fish, said, 'Well, maybe, I don't know.' Then he looked at me, [and] as his buddy, and I said, 'That's a stupid idea. We are writing individual songs [and] there is no theme . . . unless you want to scrap these songs and start from scratch.' I didn't realize it then, but that was the wrong thing to do.

"So, not long after, I woke up and the other band members were sitting on the couch with their heads hung low, looking very sad and meek. I asked, 'What's up?' They told me, 'Fish said it is you or him.' They embarrassingly told me, 'We can't lose Fish. He's the leader of the band. This isn't going to work without him.' They just said, 'Sorry.' I went upstairs and it felt like someone stuck a vacuum up my ass, turned it on, and sucked all the life out of me. I came to the bottom of the stairs and [Fish] walked out and opened my hand and he gave me one of his fish earrings, and the next thing I know I had a plane ticket home. It was devastating to me. It was a really hard blow. I thought my dream had come true. I realized that it's all a tap dance and a game and you have to play the game right if you're not the leader."

Fish reflects on that time period, both personally and creatively, with a mixture of amazement and embarrassment. "I look at interviews I did at the time and now I say, 'Who the fuck is *that*? What was I thinking?'" Fish says.

Mover would go on to play with Steve Hackett, whose onetime drummer, Ian Mosley, had played on Hackett's *Till We Have Faces* and *Highly Strung*. In an ironic twist, Mosley replaced Mover in Marillion. "I found out that Ian Mosley had gotten the gig and I think he was one of the guys who had auditioned originally," says Mover. "I knew he had played with Hackett, so I later called Hackett's manager and asked him if Steve was looking for a drummer,

because I knew Ian was now playing with Marillion. Even though Steve's manager said that the position had already been filled, I made him a proposition: 'I'd like to audition for the position, anyway. If I get the gig [Hackett] can pay for the hour. If I don't, I'll pay for it.' The manager called me back about an hour later and said, 'Steve Hackett thinks you have big balls. Thursday. One o'clock . . .' and gave me a location. I showed up, met Steve, and we played for about maybe two or three minutes, and he said, 'The gig is yours.'"

MISPLACED CHILDHOOD

Marillion was touring extensively in the mid-1980s behind *Fugazi* and a then newly released live record, *Real to Reel*, in late 1984. But it wouldn't be until *Misplaced Childhood* that the band went international.

Misplaced Childhood is a highly personal album for Fish. But it's also a concept album, about an adult looking back at his life, his past loves, his excesses, his loss of innocence, and his search for a kind of spiritual rebirth.

For the recording, the band convened at Hansa Studios in Germany in February 1985. Marillion was more prepared for the production process than they had been for perhaps any record up to that point. "That in and of itself was unique inasmuch as we had rehearsed it for about a month in England," says producer Chris Kimsey (ELP, Rolling Stones, Peter Frampton). "The record company were keen to know what the singles were, what the songs were, but I kept them away. We actually went to Berlin to record the album, because [it cost less] to go to there."

Living in Berlin for four weeks (writing, recording, and mixing) had a tremendous impact on the band. As David Hentschel had achieved with Genesis for the *Wind & Wuthering* album by bringing the band to Relight Studios in Holland, Kimsey fostered an atmosphere of freedom away from England, and this fed into an uncommon musical continuity.

"Most of this stuff had been written before we went out," says Fish, "but as an environment for writing, it was fantastic. This was pre–[Berlin] wall falling. So what you had was a very tense city, a bohemian city, and for someone like myself, it was incredible. You are living life to the absolute fuckin' max."

"Apart from the verse structure of 'Kayleigh,' [which] I had written before we'd gotten together, everything else came together in about a week or so," says guitarist Rothery. "I wrote probably about seventy-five-percent of the music on *Misplaced Childhood*. I used a Roland [GR-300] guitar synth on a few of the tracks, including the 'spider' section of 'Brief Encounter' from 'Bitter Suite.' It was a way of exploring different textures and approaches from the viewpoint of having something that is a guitar but sounds slightly like a keyboard. I [had used the same synth] on the previous album, *Fugazi*, most notably for the intro of the song 'Assassing.'"

As the recording wore on for a few weeks, EMI, having been blown off by Kimsey earlier in the process, was getting antsy to hear *something*, preferably a lead (hit) single, and hounded the band and Kimsey for the goods. "I said, 'Well, the single won't be [ready] just yet, because we're making a concept album,'" Kimsey says. "They completely freaked out and they said, 'You can't make a concept album.' The idea of a concept record—they didn't know what it meant. It just confused them. So we just sent them the second song we recorded, which was 'Kayleigh.'"

"From a musical point of view, EMI didn't understand us," Fish says. "We hadn't had any real hit singles. . . . Initially, we were going to do side one and side two, no singles. Chris Kimsey fell into our game plan, and we kind of kept it hidden from EMI for quite a long time. . . ."

"The record company was demanding something pretty much after the first week," Rothery says. "Even when we recorded 'Kayleigh,' we had a huge fight with the record company, because they wanted the B side of 'Kayleigh,' which was 'Lady Nina,' to be the A side. It was really a deal breaker. It was nearly a mutiny. Fortunately, we got our way. It is funny, but you have to stick to what you believe. We weren't thinking about singles; we were just making the album."

It's been proven time and time again ——another tenet of progressive rock—but record companies refuse to listen, sometimes for their own good: Let the band (and their producer) present their own musical vision, because you never know what will connect with people. If bands are left to their own devices and are allowed to evolve, both the artist and the label most likely will be rewarded.

Misplaced Childhood is living proof. The video for "Kayleigh" was on heavy rotation in America on MTV, a channel still in its infancy, and was an anthem for many a young person's love found and lost. "Kayleigh" placed in the U.S. Top 40, and *Misplaced Childhood* reached number 47 on the *Billboard* U.S. Top 200 Albums chart. It was even bigger in Europe, where the album went to number one, "Kayleigh" went to number two, and "Lavender" reached the Top 5.

CLUTCHING AT STRAWS

Marillion were on top of the world with the success of *Misplaced Childhood*. In 1986, they opened for Queen in Germany, in front of 130,000 people, and become a genuine commercial and artistic force. However, this only meant that the band was expected to perform in more places with increased frequency. It's a little bit like the law of diminishing returns: The more time you spend on the road to support your current record, the more fans you gain, but the less time you

actually have to write and record the follow-up to your next record.

Fish, in particular, was having a hard time juggling a personal life with the burdens of being in a successful band. And his partying was spiraling out of control.

"Money wasn't the driving force," Fish says. "We were just happy to be in a band, making records. We really just wanted to make music. But by the time you get to *Clutching at Straws*, you start to realize, 'Wait a minute: there're an awful lot of people making an awful lot of money off this band, and the people who are at the core, the energy of the entire unit, the creative end of the unit, we [are] getting paid less than everybody else.' On the top of that, we were away from our families. . . . I just got sick of it. I just wanted to stop."

"The band was touring a lot in Europe, and they were under great stress because of the success of *Misplaced Childhood* and were exhausted," confirms Kimsey. "This industry never recognizes the kind of pressure they put on artists. [A band] becomes a cash cow and the label and management . . . don't realize that there are egos and human beings involved."

All of that frustration found its way into 1987's *Clutching at Straws*. You can hear it in a song such as "That Time of the Night (the Short Straw)," in which Fish uses drink imagery and a dog-on-a-leash analogy to describe his state of mind and the dynamic between artist, manager, and music industry machine.

"In the middle of it, the band found out that someone had severely ripped them off," Kimsey says. "So it wasn't a very fun album to make, really. Being back in England, instead of everyone being together in Germany, they'd go home and bring their day-to-day problems into the studio. That was a bit of a labor of love, that one."

Fish admits that *Clutching at Straws* is his favorite Marillion record, but "it was a torturous process putting it all together," he says. "There were casualties along the way, and I was one of them. By the time we got off the tour we were sick and tired of each other. We had been together for too long. We didn't have a break from each other."

Clutching at Straws reached number two on the British charts, one slot shy of its predecessor. Marillion were stuck in a merciless vicious cycle of rehearse, tour, write, record, tour. Not slowing down was a mistake that would cause irreparable damage to the band.

"We should have taken a break from each other after *Clutching at Straws*," says Fish. "We didn't, because the machine was too big and . . . the machine needed so much money to keep it going forward. We had no time between *Misplaced* and *Clutching*. We had to go to work. We came off the *Clutching* tour, we had a month off, and then we went right backing back into fucking writing another album," Fish says. "The record label said 'We want another 'Kayleigh.' I said, 'Wait a minute. This isn't what I signed up for.'"

Ultimately, Fish, Marillion's charismatic front man, left the band to save his sanity and work at his own pace. Plenty of rumors spread at the time as to why Fish had exited a successful band, namely that his exit was due to problems with alcohol and drugs, as some stories had indicated. "That's bullshit," Fish says. "It was something that was very useful for the management and . . . others concerned to try to deride the fact that I left the band. It was very easy to use the drug-and-alcohol brush on me. It was bollocks."

Fish calls any allegation of drug or alcohol abuse misguided and unin-formed. "I have never been an alcoholic. I have never been dependent on alcohol," Fish says. "I have never been dependent on drugs, and I have never been a drug addict. I've used every-thing, but . . . it was never anything that has caused a problem to me pro-fessionally. . . . What was bothering me at the time was a psychological thing; I just felt like we were being used. That's why I left. It suited people to make out as if I was . . . some kind of rogue fac-tor, and they went out there and tried to keep the band together when singer Steve Hogarth joined."

Kimsey confirms Fish's assertion: "I remember [Fish] being into Jack Kerouac at that time. And what I mean by 'being into' Kerouac is read-ing Kerouac; not *doing* all the drugs."

Fish suspects that certain ele-ments, after realizing what a loss it would be for the Scot to leave the band, forced the situation, perhaps for financial gain. "You've got to remem-ber that it was in EMI's interest to have two units," Fish says. "They wanted the Peter Gabriel/Genesis vibe. They wanted the lead singer doing an album *and* they wanted the old band doing albums with a new singer. Best of both worlds."

TRANSFORMATION

With Fish out of the picture, the hunt was on for a new singer/lyricist. It took several months to find the right man.

"Steve Hogarth is a musician as well as a singer, whereas Fish never was," says Rothery. "So he can graft an idea quicker and he . . . is a very talented writer who can come up with vocal melodies. We started working

with lyricist John Helmer before Steve joined, so, we already had some lyrics written for *Seasons End*. Steve came in and he sang some things in the audi-tion that pretty much stayed in that form until we made the record."

The press welcomed Hogarth like a conquering hero, as did the fans: The first post-Fish Marillion record, *Seasons End*, went Top 10 in Britain (with three singles, "Hooks in You," "Easter," and "The Uninvited Guest" charting). The transition appeared to be a smooth one.

Similarly, Fish's first solo record, 1989's *Vigil in a Wilderness of Mirrors*, contains material that the band had been working on prior to his exit. "If *Vigil* and *Seasons End* had been com-bined in one album, it would have been an incredible," says Fish. "But you have to look at the time—it was 1988. We . . . started writing in May 1988. I left the band in September and didn't finish writing the *Vigil* album until June the following year [1989]. We never would have been able to take that much time to write another album with Marillion. Both parties were forced to work the way they did."

Some will debate what ranks as Marillion's post-Fish pinnacle. They'll point to the concept album *Brave*; *Anoraknophobia* for its eleven-minute centerpiece "This Is the 21st Century" (an ode to the mysteries of life); *Marillion.com* because of its use of recording technology to create such var-ied music as the dub/reggae track "House"; *Holidays in Eden* for its flirta-tion with pop music ("Splintering Heart," "The Party," "No One Can," "Cover My Eyes"); *This Strange Engine*

Script for a Jester's Tear (1983) *Fugazi* (1984) *Misplaced Childhood* (1985) *Clutching at Straws* (1987) *B'Sides Themselves* (1988) *Less is More* (2009)

Afraid of Sunlight
(1995)

(album cut "Estonia" hints at the Mediterranean romanticism of the Italian progressive rock, while "Memory of Water" bridges epic rock and electronica); *Seasons End*, which features crowd-pleasers "The Uninvited Guest" (about global warming) and "Easter"; 2004's double album *Marbles* for its Eastern-flavored grandness ("You're Gone," Marillion's first Top 10 single in Britain since "Incommunicado" in 1987; "Fantastic Place"; "The Invisible Man"; the symphonic-soul arena rock of "Neverland"; and "Ocean Cloud," dedicated to sea voyager Don Allum, the first man to row the Atlantic in both directions); 2007's *Somewhere Else* (on which the song "Faith" recalls the melody and acoustic guitar work of the Beatles' "Blackbird" and the Mellotron

flutes of "Strawberry Fields"); or 2008's *Happiness Is the Road*, a 110-minute double-disc set that sees the band experimenting, once again, with atmosphere and odd instrumentation, such as glockenspiel, harmonium, zither, and dulcimer. Virtually none of these records sound like the 1980s version of Marillion.

Afraid of Sunlight is one of the more coherent albums in Marillion's post-'80s catalog, which struck upon what prog rock had always strived for: a blend of soulful melodies, sonic expansiveness, rock's energy, and European symphonic influences.

Fans clutch tightly to nostalgia, hoping for a time when Fish will return to Marillion. But this seems unlikely. Fish warns that, for various reasons, a

reunion tour "just has never happened."

"I am totally independent now, and it's great," says Fish, who says he has faced some serious financial burdens since going solo. (Circa 2000, the *Fellini Days* album period, Fish says he was more than "nine hundred thousand pounds in debt.") "I don't sign on for the fame and stardom stuff. It is just not me. So I am very grateful to have maintained a fan base. That was one of the reasons why I don't get involved in sausage-machine album writing. There are some people out there who think they have to make an album every twelve months and people will buy it no matter what because they're fans. I don't take that approach. If I'm going to do something, it has to be at least as good as what I did before."

(Mick Hutson/Getty Images)

DREAM THEATER

The Soul of Prog?

HERE'S A BAND THAT SURELY SITS BETWEEN MODERN AND postmodern while presenting a strange and intriguing dilemma. They synthesize the various aspects that made Yes, Genesis, ELP, Iron Maiden, Deep Purple, Queensrÿche, Pink Floyd, Dixie Dregs, Metallica, and Rush such successes (individual technical prowess, a command of odd times, the willingness to expand song form in the pop arena) while injecting venom, adrenaline, and a certain musical athleticism into their craft.

It should be noted that Dream Theater suffers from bias on some level as being perceived as a "music school" band. There is some truth in this, however. "I went to Berklee after high school," guitarist John Petrucci told the author in 2001. "[Bassist] John Myung, who I grew up with, went to Berklee too, and that's where we met [drummer] Mike [Portnoy]. He was from Long Beach, [Long Island], and that was the core of the band when it started in 1985."

Keyboardist Kevin Moore, who'd known Myung and Petrucci from is childhood days in Kings Park, New York, had attended SUNY Fredonia in western New York in the 1980s, where he studied music. When he left Fredonia to come back to Long Island, he hooked up with Portnoy, Myung, and Petrucci to form the band Majesty: The name was reportedly inspired by Portnoy's description of the climax to the Rush song "Bastille Day" as "majestic."

"We have known each other for a long time," says Fates Warning guitarist Jim

The modern prog supergroup, Liquid Tension Experiment. *Left to right*: Jordan Rudess, Mike Portnoy, Tony Levin, and John Petrucci. (Courtesy of Magna Carta Records)

Matheos. "I first met Mike when Fates Warning was playing on Long Island back in 1986 or 1987 on the *Awaken the Guardian* tour and Mike was out in the audience. I guess he was a big fan and after the show he gave me a Majesty tape with his phone number on it. I went home and listened to it and I was just blown away by it. We became friends and have stayed friends."

Majesty then recruited singer Chris Collins, but when he proved inadequate for the vocalist job, he parted ways with the band. After a year of auditions, Majesty found Brooklyn singer Charlie Dominici, who joined the band just before it changed its name to Dream Theater after answering an ad that ran in (as Dominici recalls) *The Island Ear*, a

Chroma Key: *You Go Now* (2000)

Long Island music paper. Before long, the band hit the club scene as Majesty—blowing the crowd away with its prowess and volume.

"As Majesty, the crowd always loved us," says Dominici. "The gigs were fun, but I always had to contend with the volume onstage. I had a hard time hearing myself above the band."

Pumping up the volume appeared to work, in any case. Majesty had gained a small following and even impressed competing and friendly bands alike on the Long Island–New York City live music circuit. So much so that there was a complaint: The name Majesty was already being used by a Nevada-based band.

"It was Mike's dad who gave us the name Dream Theater," Dominici remembers. "It was the name of a movie house [in California]. We all liked the name because it was very suggestive and also just sounded pretty cool."

Dream Theater continued to perform the New York area clubs until they got a break. "Chuck Lenihan, a guitarist formerly of the Long Island hardcore band Crumbsuckers, also of the Genitorturers, knew of us, and that led us to getting signed to Mechanic/MCA," says Dominici. "He told the label about us and they came to one of our rehearsals. They signed us pretty much immediately."

Before long, Dream Theater's debut, *When Day and Dream Unite*, was released, and there was little doubt that the band had patterned themselves after the Dixie Dregs, Iron Maiden, Rush, and Yes.

On one hand you could say that Dream Theater are an outgrowth of white-boy music run amok: pure head-banging adrenaline featuring shredding but little soul. There's a feeling floating out there (and quite insulting it is) that middle-class white kids—especially middle-class white kids from Long Island—have no life experience to draw from, so one of the ways they can excel in music is to become technical wizards, nothing more.

On the other and, they, as progressives had before them, soared where angels fear to tread. Hearing current vocalist James LaBrie sing is a bit like experiencing Otis Rush's guitar playing—it's so brash, dramatic, even passionate, and yet so strident at the same time, it slices your brain. These are great (and very different) talents—you have to be prepared to fully appreciate them.

SCENES FROM A MEMORY

Sensing his voice and songwriting approach weren't appropriate for Dream Theater's ever-increasing musical aggressiveness, Dominici exited the band. Dream Theater then recruited a new lead singer, James LaBrie, who'd worked with prog metal band Fates Warning as a guest vocalist on the song "Life in Still Water" for the band's 1991 breakthrough record, *Parallels*. On the strength of LaBrie's booming, almost operatic vibrato, and the band's new material, Dream Theater were signed to the Atco label (a division of Atlantic Records), releasing their sophomore record, *Images and Words*, in 1992. (Gentle Giant's Derek Shulman, then an executive at Atco, signed the band.)

The song "Pull Me Under" reached the Top 10 of the *Billboard* Mainstream Rock Tracks chart and saw rotation on MTV; other songs from *Images and Words* such as "Another Day" and "Take the Time" fell within the Top 30 on the same chart the following year. The album itself reached the *Billboard* Top 200 albums chart, climbing to number sixty-one, and the Heatseekers chart in 1992, landing at number two.

Though the band's two subsequent studio records, *Awake* and *Falling into Infinity*, reached higher chart positions on the *Billboard* Top 200 (thirty-two and fifty-two, respectively), *Images and Words*, which plays like a loosely held-together concept record (revolving around the idea of eternity and the passage of this world to the next), is seen, rightly so, as the band's commercial breakthrough, even peak. *Images and Words* stands as the only record that has gone gold in the U.S. Like Yes's "Roundabout" or Rush's "Tom Sawyer," Dream Theater's "Pull Me Under" is perhaps best remembered as a defining moment for a progressive band that more often than not only flirted with pop music success.

Rush references abound in the Dream Theater universe. Even as late as 2009's *Black Clouds & Silver Linings*, the band dabbled in Rush tribute in "The Count of Tuscany."

"Mike Portnoy is so in love with the idea of constructing drum parts," says Paul Northfield, who engineered 2007's *Systematic Chaos* and 2009's *Black Clouds & Silver Linings*. "At a certain point, drummers who love Neil, what they like about Neil is that his performances gave them something to aim for. It is much harder to play like [session drummer] Steve Gadd, in my opinion, because . . . to

play like Steve Gadd you almost have to *be* Steve Gadd. Sometimes it's about the push and pull and the feel. Unless you can go back to Steve Gadd's influences and learn to love the music he loves, you won't capture that feel. Neil offered complicated drum parts that they could learn."

***

Flash forward to 2004. Dream Theater opened for Yes at an outdoor arena in New York and I noticed something startling: A group of middle-aged men—they took up half a row of seats—were knocked out by Dream Theater's performance. They were so amazed that when Yes came out they exited promptly. These guys were old enough to remember Yes the first time around and yet appeared more excited about Dream Theater. There was certainly something more than meets the eye about Dream Theater.

Not long after the band's tour with Yes, I asked Yes guitarist Steve Howe to comment on Dream Theater's appeal. "I've probably heard them more than the other guys, because when I get to a gig, I usually stay there," Howe said in 2005. "I don't leave, go to the hotel room and come back again in a fleet of limos. I've heard them . . . and sure, they have made some very heavy records at times, but what they did on our tour was try to accommodate a Yes audience—tried to please them as much as they pleased themselves. They did a nice set, I feel. In there was the drama and individual prowess of each individual member, and I think that is what the progressives were good at, like ELP were . . . and Yes were . . . trying to show off that side."

And there was no drum solo that reminded the writer of Neil Peart—that was long gone. While Dream Theater are still impacted by Rush, the band has worked hard to develop their own vision. Portnoy, in particular, has worked to develop his own style.

"Neil [Peart] is in many respects

more meticulous," says Northfield, who worked with Rush on classic albums such as *Permanent Waves* and *Moving Pictures*. "Mike is a true obsessive-compulsive, as he would freely admit, and he is first of all a music fan. He likes to do things quickly and off the cuff, and he has phenomenal technique and just sort of blasts through things effortlessly, which is his strength."

Nineteen ninety-nine's *Scenes from a Memory* and the subsequent *Six Degrees of Inner Turbulence* (2002) are dense and dark. It isn't hard to respect a band that has (with the exception of the crossover attempt *Falling into Infinity*) taken a stance to steer clear of commercial music.

Dream Theater have brought the audience to them, not the other way around. I asked Portnoy prior to the release of *Six Degrees of Inner Turbulence* (a double record with one disc dedicated to a single song) about criticisms of the band going commercial.

"My God!" raved Portnoy from Frankfurt, Germany, where he was on tour with supergroup Transatlantic, in mid-November 2001. "If an album [composed] of a forty-minute song is an attempt to be more accessible, then we are the luckiest band in the world. I mean, we have done things on our own terms this time around. In the past we probably have been accused of trying to go 'accessible' or scale down, maybe at the request of the record company or pressures from the outside industry. I think this album is a very brave step in the opposite direction."

Against the odds, there's little this band can't accomplish, thanks to a sense of determination, which has helped propel them throughout the years. Dream Theater, as its name suggests, had once envisioned (as aspiring unknowns) themselves as a band that would tour the world, play uncompromising music similar to the progressive rock and metal of the band's youth, and stay true to their ideals.

Mike Portnoy is a goal-driven

Transatlantic: *SMPT:E* (2000)

individual intent on achieving certain benchmarks that seem to appear (to some) as the prerequisites for rock "awesomeness." Through tribute bands to the Who, the Beatles (Yellow Matter Custard), and Rush (during the tour to support 2002's *Six Degrees of Inner Turbulence*, Dream Theater even dedicated part of their live show to cover Iron Maiden's *The Number of the Beast* and Metallica's *Master of Puppets*); his side projects such OSI (with Kevin Moore and Fates Warning's Jim Matheos), Liquid Tension Experiment (Tony Levin, John Petrucci, Jordan Rudess, Portnoy) and Liquid Tension Trio (no Petrucci); as well as his willingness to perform with a number of other artists (the supergroup Transatlantic being one of them), Portnoy seems to be the soul, one of the driving creative forces of Dream Theater, possessing a lot of energy—like an excitable kid, who's hit upon the most amazing luck by landing in a rock band. He's also a kind of managing editor of Dream Theater.

"He is," confirms keyboardist Jordan Rudess, who joined Dream Theater in 1999. "He lives for rock 'n' roll and this business, and has a tremendous perspective on so many things that are involved in being a rock band. . . . He's into making set lists and goals and recording albums and concept albums. It is his life. By playing in the tribute bands, all his fantasies come true. He just loves the

Who, Led Zeppelin, the Beatles. That is one of his talents—to bring things into reality, as he did with this band."

"How do I deal with Portnoy?" asks Portnoy's bandmate in Transatlantic and former Spock's Beard singer/keyboardist/main songwriter Neal Morse. "Do you mean, 'Where does the three-hundred-pound gorilla sleep?' Mike is very New York, energetic, and has a lot of force to his opinions. It's a different experience working with everyone. I think it's interesting that everybody in Transatlantic reflects the stereotype of his native land. Mike is loud. [laughs] You really see what a product you are of where you're born."

"He always has a million things going on and a million ideas in his head," explains Fates Warning's Jim Matheos, who was initially tapped as the guitarist for Transatlantic but had to back out due to scheduling conflicts. "A lot of ideas. He gets really passionate about stuff, especially in the studio. He really gets into a part and into what he's recording. I love that about him."

Portnoy certainly makes things happen. In 1998, he called Morse about the possibility of forming a new band project. After Matheos bowed out, Morse suggested the Flower Kings guitarist/vocalist/head honcho Roine Stolt, and Portnoy invited Marillion bassist Pete Trewavas, and this supergroup was born.

Transatlantic's 2000 debut, *SMPT:E*, contains some of the most ambitious (and melodic) material any of the members' respective bands had ever recorded. And it was Portnoy who'd helped to stretch the elongated first song on the debut—a six-part thirty-minute dynamic opus with a big glorious major musical theme, titled "All of the Above"—to its very limits.

"I remember that very moment when we were recording that, and it was the very first song we recorded," says Stolt. "We were in a studio in upstate New York [Millbrook

Studios] and we [had] just met. We were putting together this song within the first two days, listening to pieces, and rehearsing pieces and then recording another section and then stopping the recorder and rehearsing some more and doing another piece. Basically, we were recording and writing at the same time. We were building it bit by bit.

"By the time we were reaching the end of the song," Stolt continues, "there's a big guitar solo and a crescendo—a final ending—and after that I just kept doing some guitar soundscapes with lots of echoes and delays. This was going on for maybe a minute or two and the rest of the band had already stopped. Mike was getting up from the drum kit and looking at his watch saying, 'Keep going. Keep going. We're trying to pass the-thirty minute mark, because I've never recorded a song like this before.' He really tried to push it. The longer the better, he thought. We even have it on tape. I did a mix of the album, too, and I think on my mix I kept all of [his talking]. I tried to push up the overhead microphones for the drums because I could hear Mike saying, 'Keep going. This is awesome.'"

***

Dream Theater were still fairly young in 1993, and their influences—from Steve Vai to Steve Morse—were clearly on display. And as such, perhaps we shouldn't be too hard on them. Everyone has to start somewhere.

Though some hero worship still slips through, Dream Theater have forged their own sound. There's music and emotion there.

Dream Theater understand that when bands work in odd times, they have a responsibility to make the song groove and to make it accessible to the man on the street. Geddy Lee commented in *Bass Player* magazine in 1988 on Rush's ability to play smoothly through odd time signatures: "After a certain point, [odd time signatures] become more musical and less mathematical. But that's only after learning to feel comfortable with a particular time signature. Like with us, playing in 7 is now so comfortable we almost never have to count it."

By the time Dream Theater reached their third studio record, 1994's *Awake*, something had come alive inside them, namely ferocity and the ability to move through odd times with alacrity. Add to this the fact that singer LaBrie seemed to find his "voice" on *Awake*, as dynamic tunes such as "The Silent Man," the acoustic section of the three-part opus "A Mind Beside Itself," and "Lifting Shadows off a Dream" stress. In some cases, the venomous Dave Mustaine growl LaBrie injects into the goth-metal gospel tune (of sorts) "The Mirror" (written about Portnoy's struggle with alcoholism) is just as effective, maybe more so, than his signature supreme vibrato.

The band was expanding in other areas as well. "Space-Dye Vest," for instance, seems to wallow in self-pity, a sentiment underscored by Moore's choice of self-effacing, self-aware, utterly sad, and somewhat satirical audio clips, somehow poking fun at the fact that the speaker is experiencing a clichéd human emotion (though the pain is no more unreal for it). Likewise, "Ytse Jam" might have been the band's answer to Rush's "YYZ," but "Erotomania," the instrumental section of "A Mind Beside Itself," is Dream Theater coming into their own. Though strains of influences reveal themselves (for example, it's hard not to think of Steve Morse's speed-demon picking in Petrucci's gnarly guitar runs), 1994's *Awake* is unlike most records of the time.

By the time Dream Theater were ready to record *A Change of Seasons* with new keyboardist Derek Sherinian, the band relied on a tried-and-true method: recording tried-and-true material belonging to other artists such as Deep Purple, Led Zeppelin, Genesis, the Dixie Dregs, Kansas, Queen, or Elton John.

The danger in covering well-known songs is that they will inevitably be compared to the originals. Dream Theater took that risk with *A Change of Seasons*, on which cover songs serve as a lifeline for a band confused by the recent exit of its founding member keyboardist, Moore.

The twenty-three-minute title track—the only original song on the record—became the band's first magnum opus, veering in a direction Dream Theater had only hinted at in the past with tracks such as "Learning to Live," "Metropolis—Part 1," "Scarred," and "Voices," but there had never been anything this extravagant on record. (Even here, however, the song was written back in 1989 and was meant to be included on 1992's *Images and Words*. Fans knew the song existed and that it had never been released; evidently, Dream Theater decided there was no better time to give the people what they want).

Aside from the occasional busy drumming, the obvious use of odd times, and the winding undercurrent of guitars and keyboards, the song seems like an attempt by Dream Theater to marry complexity and accessibility. The floodgates had opened: Dream Theater would continue to rope in listeners with their technical prowess and challenge them with such long compositions as "Trail of Tears" (*Falling into Infinity*) and the 1999 concept album, *Metropolis Part 2: Scenes from a Memory*.

After a period of recording dormancy (the band's label experienced personnel changes, none of them too kind to the band), the band finally released 1997's *Falling into Infinity* after the dust settled. Dream Theater were secure in a contract, but there was a catch: Hearing something commercial in the band's music (or simply trying to squeeze whatever money they could out of the band), the label suggested DT carry on in the direction they'd hinted at with *A Change of Seasons*. Attempting to do so spelled near disaster for Dream Theater, who nearly tore themselves apart trying to please the label and essentially be something they were not.

At a sensitive time in the band's life, Magna Carta Records threw some in the band a lifeline and proposed that Petrucci and Portnoy put together a supergroup, which was dubbed Liquid Tension Experiment and featured bassist Tony Levin. They recruited Dregs keyboardist Jordan Rudess, who had slipped through the band's fingers a few years earlier.

Rudess tells a long, crazy tale as to how he joined Dream Theater: "One day I got a call from the Dream Theater management about the possibility of coming for an audition to their group," Rudess says. "They had gotten my name from Kevin Moore, who had mentioned me in passing at some point as someone whose keyboard playing he respected. So it was a recommendation plus the fact that [the band] had been looking in a magazines for a keyboard player, and they had seen in *Keyboard* magazine [that I] had won a readers award . . .[for] Best New Talent. I thought I should call them, but I didn't know who they were and didn't know anything about Dream Theater. A friend had been writing for some magazines at that point and had interviewed them and had a copy of *Images and Words*. I listened to it and it seemed really interesting to me. It really had that progressive rock sound that I love, but it also had metal virtuosity, which I hadn't really heard mixed with progressive rock. Granted, Yes and Genesis were paying some complicated stuff, but there was something about the intensity, speed, clarity, just the whole focused-playing thing that really turned me on.

"They ended up inviting me to this big convention, Foundations Forum—a big heavy metal convention they were headlining. I decided I

Dream Theater scored a rare hit early in their career with 1992's *Images and Words* (left).

In 1993, DT recorded at British prog's ground zero.

would do the Forum, but I needed some more time to think about the band thing. At the same time that that happened, I got a call from the Dixie Dregs management about joining *that* band. Jerry Goodman [electric violinist] had heard me play at NAMM show and he was talking about me to some of the guys in the group, and I think that Jan Hammer's manager, Elliot Sears, was telling the Dregs about me. So anyway, they got my

number and I ended up sending off a copy of *Listen* [Rudess's 1993 solo record] to Steve Morse to hear. In the same week, I learned all the Dream Theater material and all of the Dregs stuff. I had gone through an audition with the Dregs as well. At that time I had a choice: I could either do the Dregs or I could join Dream theater. I ended up doing the Foundations Forum thing and then got counseling from Steve Morse to do a couple gigs with the Dregs to figure out what I want to do. I decided at that point it was better for me *not* to join Dream Theater, because I felt like Dream Theater was going on the road for a very long time and they were a pretty new band; they didn't know which direction that were going to go in.

"After that, I got a call from [Magna Carta label chief] Peter Morticelli about joining this group that Mike Portnoy was putting together called the Liquid Tension Experiment, although it was not called that at that point," says Rudess.

"Mike was putting together what he called a supergroup. They had Tony Levin on bass, they had me on keyboards, and they didn't know who they wanted on guitar but that was to be determined. So I thought to myself, 'This is cool. I didn't join Dream Theater and now I am getting a call from the Dream Theater drummer for this. I will do that.' Then I found out that John Petrucci was going to do it as well. I ended up doing two albums, and both of those were among Magna Carta's most successful, and for us it was personally successful because I had a great time with the guys and enjoyed hanging out and writing music with them. At the end of making the second Liquid Tension album, the guys approached me about joining the band again. I was in a different headspace then, but it wasn't only that. Dream Theater was in a different space. Everybody was in a different place. Dream Theater had just completed their Awake tour, they had done the *A Change of Seasons* thing, *Falling into Infinity*. They were more solid, and it seemed like the band was going to stick around. I was older and I felt more comfortable, and I knew I could work with them."

Dream Theater had the difficult task of breaking the news to

Sherinian, but once the band shed the keyboard player, it was as though a mental load had been relieved—the entire *Falling into Infinity* time period was weighing heavy on the band, and Sherinian, as great as he was and is, could only serve to remind the band of less-than-stellar days.

"They were excited about me being a composer, and they had these windows of parameters and would police those parameters pretty carefully," says Rudess. "Initially, I thought [the writing process] was similar to [that of] Liquid Tension Experiment but I soon learned that this wasn't the case. There were a different set of parameters by which Dream Theater operates. They brought me into the band because John really wanted to have a writing partner. . . . I had to learn quickly what kinds of things worked and what things didn't. But to this day my job and what they expect me to do is push the boundaries a little bit and to challenge the listener and offer things that would not be within the normal spectrum of a metal band. So I convince them to go in directions that I normally wouldn't. Sometimes my role involves getting my ideas rejected. You know, 'This is too crazy an idea for Dream Theater.' I had a whole musical life before that band and it included some pretty bizarre styles. I feel like I want to bring in all of these styles."

Rudess, who studied at Julliard from ages nine through nineteen (until he heard Gentle Giant's *Free Hand*, got his hands on his first Minimoog synthesizer, and gave up the idea of being a concert pianist), had an immediate musical impact on the band's sound. In the wake of *Falling into Infinity*, and instead of folding, Dream Theater released what may be its *2112*, the concept record *Metropolis Part 2: Scenes from a Memory*, perhaps the densest single disc the band had ever recorded. They even refer to themselves as "the orchestra" in the record's liner notes,

as if we were watching and listening to a theatrical production.

The band was not catering to anyone, except perhaps themselves. For one thing, the concept of the album is almost indecipherable without CliffsNotes. The basic skeleton involves the fictional 1928 murder of a young woman, reincarnation, one man's mental regression into a past life, a journey of self-discovery, a belief in the afterlife, and a possible reference to the triumph and tragedy of the Kennedy family, tying together the "sleeper and the miracle" and "dance of eternity" motif of "Metropolis—Part I."

Although the music and the story line could have been more closely entwined, the album is on the whole extraordinary, if at times slightly derivative (e.g., the whirlwind of sound in the Zappa-esque, vibraphone texture–led jam of "Beyond This Life," the Pink Floyd–ish gospel voice of "Through Her Eyes," a Indian-inflected lead heavy metal guitar line à la Metallica's "Wherever I May Roam" in "Home"). Perhaps in an attempt to win back progressive rock fans—and fans in general—the band went for broke, throwing everything but the kitchen sink into their new record.

"One of the things that we did on [*Six Degrees of Inner Turbulence*] as well as *Scenes from a Memory* is we wrote the record in the recording studio and recorded as we wrote," explained Petrucci in 2001. "We skipped a demoing period, and so the core of the music and the core of the construction of the songs is very, very instinctual. A lot more of the crafting happens while we are actually recording the overdubs. Similarly, with *Falling into Infinity*, we were set up in such a way [that] if we had a live performance that was good, we'd keep a lot of it."

As much as they did on any record up to that point and perhaps since, the band moved very smoothly through odd times. Portnoy, in particular, navigates them very well, often

playing very tricky, off-kilter tempos.

"I've been playing in 7, 9, 11, 23, just as long as I've been playing in 4," Portnoy said. "I treat all numbers equally, you know? There's no reason playing in 7 should be any more difficult than 4. It is just a number."

Rudess added important elements to the band's music and conducted and arranged parts for a gospel choir for the production. "I definitely think I added some things to the band that they didn't have before," says Rudess. "One of the main things is, they didn't have someone who could orchestrate keyboard parts. Derek and Kevin, they were wonderful keyboard players, but they were coming from an approach that, 'Okay, I'll do this particular keyboard part and maybe add a string line here.' . . . My approach has been to [record] many tracks and then layer them. If I'm doing an actual orchestral sound, I will layer some strings and then I'll do a horn part, and then I'll do the winds. Then I'm layering synth textures. Also, I like to create my own synthesizer sounds. Usually I'll tailor the sounds to what I'm hearing in my head as opposed to relying on a factory patch. . . . I think there's a noticeable difference that comes out in the music when you are sound-designing for the exact music that you are creating."

"Fans adore the record," said Portnoy. "The tour was completely sold out, night after night around the world. The success from *Scenes*, the fact that we were able to make that on our own terms . . . opened the door and gave us the ultimate freedom to finally do whatever the hell we wanted without any outside interference or direction."

In an incredible twist of fate, the band's live album and boxed set from that tour, *Live Scenes from New York*, which contained the entirety of the *Metropolis Part 2: Scenes from a Memory*, was released on September 11, 2001, with cover art that depicted Manhattan and, in particular, the Twin Towers, up in flames. (The band and Elektra Records recalled the set, issued an apology, and repackaged the release.)

Their next studio album, 2002's *Six Degrees of Inner Turbulence*—a double record with one five-song disc featuring unrelated tunes and the second disc dedicated to a forty-plus-minute composition in eight parts, following the lives of six emotionally or mentally disturbed and deeply misunderstood individuals fending off their own ever-darkening troubled minds.

The band had arrived at Bear Tracks in March 2001 and delivered the finished record in October. "We locked the place and threw all our gear in there and wrote and recorded simultaneously," Portnoy said, "as we had done with *Scenes* and Liquid Tension."

Dream Theater took the show on the road through America, to Europe and Asia, expanding their global reach. Amid this, the band was receiving some of the best reviews of its career, from unlikely sources. *Entertainment Weekly*, which would have ordinarily turned their noses up at such progressive rock music, dedicated well over a page to a review of *Six Degrees of Inner Turbulence*, grading it a "B," saying this post-9/11 world could use a bit of fantasy.

"It makes you wonder which act is gutsier: Eminem slamming another teen-pop star or Dream Theater ignoring, and thereby dissing, every style of music that's existed since 1976," wrote David Browne in February 2002.

This is only partially true, of course. Dream Theater do ignore *some* trends, but they pick up on plenty of others (as the Radiohead-inspired tune "Disappear" indicates). At worst, *Six Degrees of Inner Turbulence* is an update of Yes, Genesis, and ELP with dashes

of Tool, Metallica, and post–Van Halen guitar histrionics thrown in for good measure. Other records followed, such as the heavy metal and grunge extravaganza *Train of Thought*, the triple-disc *Live at Budokan*, 2005's eight-track *Octavarium*, and 2007's *Systematic Chaos*.

Despite its dark moments, Dream Theater—with all of its fretboard, keyboard, vocal, and rhythmic acrobatics—offers a sense of hope that anything is possible. The production process for *Systematic Chaos* ("the title of which is an accurate description of our music," says Rudess) was infused with creative possibilities.

"It wasn't a conceptual thing," says Paul Northfield, who engineered and mixed the album, ". . . but the production process was a bit of a systematic chaos. At some point it was like they were sitting around and then all hell would break loose and things would happen very quickly. For one thing, Mike had two drum kits set up, as he often does, and wanted to be able to record with either one of them instantly. He wanted to turn around and work his John Bonham basic kit or his big progressive kit. Using two kits may have influenced him to play certain ways. I know he used the smaller kit for 'Constant Motion.' It was all quite tricky, because you have something like thirty or forty channels of drum miking. So it was all quite complicated to set it all up. But once it was set up, you would be in position to record. So that is the way we made that record. . . ."

Systematic Chaos also sees Dream Theater on a new label—Roadrunner.

Unlike other labels Dream Theater had been on, Roadrunner gave the band free rein to do what they wanted musically and artistically, and because they were working with a new record company—for the most part, a heavy metal label—Dream Theater felt they needed to make a suitable recording because of it. "I think the feeling came from within the band that we should deliver an album, as Mike would say, that is ballsy, has a lot of chunk—a heavier album," says Rudess. "It's not as though we changed our style per se because Roadrunner asked us to. It is more [that] we realized that it made sense to direct the music a little bit in a particular way."

Dream Theater followed up *Systematic Chaos* with their tenth studio album, *Black Clouds & Silver Linings*—a great summation of the band's career thus far. Throughout the dark moments of the band's career, its members have managed to see the positive side of a lifestyle that could have chewed them up and spit them out.

"We are fortunate to have the career we do, where we have a lot of exposure and tour the world and play our music," said Petrucci. "Bands in this style do exist. But because we came up when we came we did, [because of] the timing, we were able to forge our own path."

"Everything we do is swiped up by fans," Portnoy said. "They stand by us through thick and thin. It's their devotion that makes it possible for us to exist . . . because they are so supportive, whether it is a triple live CD or a double studio CD. I'm very grateful that we are able to do to what we do."

Awake
(1994)

A Change of Seasons (1995)

Metropolis Pt. 2: Scenes from a Memory (1999)

Live at Budokan (2004)

Octavarium (2005)

Systematic Chaos (2007)

Dream Theater, changing the face of progressive rock: *left to right*: bassist John Myung, guitarist John Petrucci, vocalist James LaBrie, keyboardist Jordan Rudess, drummer Mike Portnoy. (Courtesy of Roadrunner Records)

PROGRESSIVITY CONTINUES INTO THE TWENTY-FIRST CENTURY

THE RESURGENCE OF PROGRESSIVE ROCK IN THE 1990S AND
the 2000s was the result of the coalescing of forces such as the Internet, the
burgeoning festival circuit, the growth of independent labels and mail-order
companies, economics (i.e., an influx of money in the so-called prog field and
a spike in listeners' disposable income), and the musicians themselves, who had
grown tired of not seeing and hearing the music they loved being reflected in
the mainstream.

As they did in the late 1960s and early 1970s, it seems that popular bands
are increasingly calling the shots and taking musical leaps that at once echo the
past and catapult rock into a new dimensions.

Evidence of "progressivity" is everywhere, from bands (many of whom are
on major recording label that, ten years prior, would have shied away from such
acts) such as electronic experimenters Radiohead and Floyd- and Queen-inspired
Muse, to the Mars Volta (whose forty-five-minute jams have become legendary),

sci-fi conceptualists Coheed and Cambria, Icelandic impressionists Sigur Rós, Americana proggers the Decemberists, psychedelic pomp rockers Bigelf, and Tool, a kind of Crimson-on-steroids art-metal band.

"What a band like Radiohead did, for instance," says Jacob Holm-Lupo, guitarist and founder of Norway's neo-Gothic White Willow, "was take something vaguely progressive and then create something that had not gone before. When [1997's] *OK Computer* came, that was a huge turning point for a lot of people. It really combined elements of classic prog and something totally new."

"Before Chris [Pennie] started recording with us as our drummer, Taylor Hawkins—from the Foo Fighters—cut tracks [for 2007's *Good Apollo I'm Burning Star IV, Vol. 2: No World for Tomorrow*] and I can tell you he's a big progressive rock fan," says Coheed and Cambria guitarist Travis Stever. "His style reminded me of an early-Genesis Phil Collins. The roots of progressive rock run pretty deep in popular music, I'd say."

Others bands such as Opeth, Pain of Salvation, Enchant, Threshold, Shadow Gallery, Mastodon, Trans-Siberian Orchestra, and Symphony X continue to combine prog rock's exploratory sense of adventure (and sometimes excesses) with heavy metal thunder.

"There has always been a lot of guitar-keyboard interplay in our music, but as time went on, the classical influence of Bach and Beethoven gave way to modern-sounding stuff, like twentieth-century art music and film scores," says Symphony X founder and guitarist Michael Romeo. "But we never lost sight of metal. I think our common influence of classical music and progressive music, along with the heavier stuff, led us to where we are now and what we do."

"For me, I've collected all the styles of music I like and molded them into one," says Opeth gui-

tarist/vocalist Mikael Åkerfeldt. "It was never a big problem going from [one] extreme to the other, like a death metal part to a calm acoustic part. It just always made sense for me, given the kinds of bands I've listened to, whether it was a metal act or a classic progressive rock band."

"In order to create something that's true for you that sometimes requires sacrifice," says Coheed and Cambria drummer Pennie. "You have to say, 'I don't care if anyone likes it.' With progressive rock, they are either going to love it or hate it."

THE FLOWER KINGS

Prog's third wave, as it's often referred to, broke in the 1990s. The Swedes, in particular, were instrumental in leading the way, helping to shape progressive rock as we know it today. (Not surprising: Sweden has a history of producing trailblazing experimental rock artists, from Algren's Trädgård to Bo Hansson and avant-garde Samla Mammas Manna.)

Bands such as the Flower Kings, Landberk, Änglagård, and Anekdoten took an emotional (yet retro) stance against the tide of corporate control, offering nonconformists everywhere an alternative to popular music.

"When we started out in 1991, it felt like the underground progressive community was establishing itself," says Jan Erik Liljeström, vocalist/bassist of Anekdoten. "We didn't know much about how to reach out to distributors, but through personal connections and [later] the Internet, we were able to get ourselves a name in the prog rock community fairly easily."

As the 1990s rolled on, the interest in prog rock began to grow, thanks in no small part to the World Wide Web, which connects prog fans from all over the world. Record labels, catering to fans of progressive music, were open for business: Magna Carta, Laser's Edge, Cuneiform, InsideOut Music, Cyclops, Syn-Phonic, Galileo, Kinesis; France's Musea, established in the mid-

1980s, was coming into its own.

Others, such as Leonardo Pavkovic's Moonjune, Snapper Music's Kscope, and Shawn Gordon's ProgRock Records, were soon to follow and underwrite adventurous prog rock and jazz-rock recordings by legends and relative unknowns alike.

Annual festivals, such as ProgDay, NEARfest, Baha Prog in Mexico, RoSfest, and 3RP (the Three Rivers Progressive Rock festival in Pittsburgh), dedicated to prog music cropped up (and continue to crop up), causing family men and wayward sons and daughters across the globe to interact over a weekend of live music.

"I remember I played ProgFest with Kevin Gilbert [Sheryl Crow, Toy Matinee] in 1994, when we did *The Lamb Lies Down on Broadway*," says Spock's Beard's Nick D'Virgilio. "I had no idea that there were labels and festivals that promoted progressive rock."

It is from this burgeoning milieu that the Flower Kings sprang and thrived. "I wasn't aware that there was something happening with progressive music outside of Sweden," says guitarist Roine Stolt. "I began thinking: 'I have all of this recording equipment. Why not try to make an album today with what I see as . . . prog rock?' That's what led to my recording the solo record *The Flower King*."

Prior to the release of *The Flower King*, Stolt did whatever he needed to in order to survive. (He had previously been a member of the Swedish symphonic prog rock band Kaipa, which he joined in the mid-1970s, when he was seventeen.)

"I played in every possible style you can imagine after that," Stolt says. "Blues, folk, rock, Latin, heavy rock. Whatever. That was the best education I could have gotten."

This stew of influence sweetened the music of the Flower Kings for albums such as *Retropolis*, *Flower Power*, *Stardust We Are*, *Space Revolver*, and *Back in the World of Adventures*.

"I started the band because I want-

Sense of Adventure: The Flower Kings' Roine Stolt. (Courtesy of Ulei Frey)

Unfold the Future (2002)

bers of the Flower Kings, such as bassist Jonas Reingold and Hungarian drummer Zoltan Csörsz. "They develop riffs on marimba, and that had a similar effect on me as, say, when I heard and still hear 'Dawn of Light . . .' [from Yes's 'The Revealing Science of God']. These things let you know that you are on the verge of twenty minutes of escape. But it's not just escape: You're going places with these bands."

"I hope that when people hear the Flower Kings they know that this is a band not interested in seeing its music played on the radio," says Stolt. "There's a sense of adventure in the Flower Kings music that much of today's music simply lacks. People look back fondly at records like *Topographic Oceans* or *Relayer*. What they loved about those albums they can find in the Flower Kings."

SPOCK'S BEARD: THE HEALING COLORS OF SOUND

One of the major bands to emerge from prog's third wave were Americans Spock's Beard, who are often compared to Gentle Giant due to their use of syncopated patterns

ed to play and write music," says Stolt. "When I write songs, I want to write songs about something that matters to me, and something that connects with the other part of Roine Stolt, the family man, the private person."

Since the turn of the century, the Flower Kings have continued to fuse disparate genres for releases such as 2001's *Rainmaker*, 2002's *Unfold the*

Future, 2004's *Adam & Eve*, 2006's *Paradox Hotel*, and 2007's *The Sum of No Evil*, even making a conscious move to downplay Tomas Bodin's vintage keyboard sounds on latter records.

"You receive a certain feeling when you put on 'The Truth Will Set You Free' from *Unfold the Future*," says the Tangent's Andy Tillison, who has recorded with Stolt and other mem-

Opeth: *Blackwater Park*
(2001)

Coheed and Cambria: *In Keeping Secrets of Silent Earth: 3* (2003)

Muse: *The Resistance*
(2009)

Radiohead: *OK Computer*
(1997)

Riverside: *Rapid Eye Movement*
(2007)

Sigur Ros: *()*
(2002)

Spock's Beard: *Day For Night*
(1999)

The Mars Volta: *Frances the Mute*
(2005)

Tool: *Aenima*
(1996)

and counterpoint melodies.

A performance by Yes in 1972 in California changed forever Neal Morse and his brother, guitarist Alan, the founders of Spock's Beard.

"It was the *Fragile* tour," Neal says, "and I am not exaggerating when I say that it changed my life. Yes had this magic."

"I saw Steve Howe with a pedal steel and knew it wasn't exactly country music, but that rock music could have this whole other sonic palette," says Alan Morse. "That was an event that opened up a whole lot of things."

When Neal graduated from high school, he followed his aspirations of being a professional musician. "I had been trying to, all through the '80s, get a record deal as a singer-songwriter in Los Angeles," says Morse. "I used to write a lot of songs in the vein of early Elton John and Billy Joel and later on Marc Cohn. That was my vision for myself as an artist for years. But it never happened."

After Morse spent some time in Europe, he returned to America, but his career in music was still in traction. A self-help forum, sponsored by an educational service called Landmark, changed Morse's view of music and life path.

"In the '90s I was very depressed," says Morse. "I asked, 'What's the point? I've failed.' What Landmark made me realize is that I had commingled the realms of music and the music business. They helped me to remember what inspired me in the first place. I remembered Yes opening for Black Sabbath when I was twelve years old. A lightbulb went off: I never got into music for the business in the first place. It was like, '*That's* what it's all about.'"

"Neal and I came up with a slogan: 'Fuck it! Let's do what we love,'" says Alan Morse.

A week after taking the Landmark course, Neal began writing music for what would become Spock's critically acclaimed debut, 1995's *The Light*, recruiting bassist David Meros

and drummer Nick D'Virgilio (whom the Morse brothers met at a blues jam in L.A.).

"No one did prog in the mid-'90s," says D'Virgilio. "Spock's Beard played ProgFest in 1995, and that was when everything just took off. We met Thomas Waber, who owns the label InsideOut, and that eventually led to a deal with this record label, a mail-order company, GEP, Giant Electric Pea . . . and they released *The Light* in Europe."

"Spock's were something different," says keyboardist Martin Orford, formerly of Britain's IQ, who runs the GEP label. "These were long tracks but with catchy 'pop song' melodies. There was clearly a proper songwriting team at work here, and I was much impressed."

Beard's sophomore effort, *Beware of Darkness*, followed, featuring veteran Japanese organist/Mellotron player Ryo Okumoto, as did a live record in 1996, *The Official Bootleg*.

"It just snowballed," says D'Virgilio. "There were people who supported this music, particularly in Europe. We'd play in small clubs and it was a surprise to everybody that bands were playing this kind of material."

The Beard continued to release crowd-pleasers, such as 1998's *Kindness of Strangers*, 1999's *Day for Night*, and the live *Don't Try This at Home* (recorded in Holland). The following year's *V* featured the longest composition of the band's recording career (up to that point), "The Great Nothing."

"The Great Nothing" tells the tale of a veteran musician who's on the verge of conceding a worthless pursuit, when out of the blue he hears a single note of music, which inspires him to write songs again (thus reflecting Morse's own experience with the music business).

"In the song, when I talk about 'one note timeless came out of nowhere . . .' I'm talking about music saving me," says Morse. "I'm going through my life, feeling like I've

missed my calling and . . . becoming a miserable partier, a drunk. I was a major drinker. I remember the times I asked my girlfriend to bring me a beer in the shower. My motto was [that] a beer an hour would keep the hangover away."

By the time Morse was writing material for the next Spock's Beard record, the 2002 concept double album titled *Snow*, about an albino teen with the power to heal through touch, he was in the process of being spiritually transformed.

"I was becoming a Christian through the course of Spock's Beard," says Morse. "Even as early as a song like 'The Water,' from the first album, you can hear me reaching for God."

Snow was a success, selling tens of thousands of copies, but soon after its release, Morse announced he was leaving Spock's Beard, claiming he felt the pull of a religious calling.

"I felt . . . at that time that God was calling me out of [the band]," Morse says. "I prayed about it for nine months and all I ever felt was . . . 'You know what you need to do. It's time.' I feel like He let me be with the band and let us have our dream together for a while, and then it was time for me to move on."

For a time it appeared as though Spock's Beard might have been in trouble. They'd just parted company with their most prolific writer and cofounder, a unifying force for the most part.

"Neal never gave any indication that he would quit," says D'Virgilio. "He just came in one day out of the blue and dropped the bomb. We were a bit miffed. We were just finally getting to a point where we could have gone to the next level and were about the break a little bit. Then we got the rug pulled out from underneath us."

Nevertheless, Morse's solo material has helped to shape a new rock subgenre—CPR (Christian progressive rock)—with the release of albums such as 2003's concept record about

Morse's spiritual journey, called *Testimony* ("*Snow* took two years to write, and *Testimony* took about a month," Morse says), 2004's *One*, 2005's *?*, 2006's *Cover to Cover*, 2007's *Sola Scriptura*, and 2008's *Lifeline*.

Morse even reactivated Transatlantic—the supergroup he had formed with Dream Theater's Mike Portnoy, Marillion's Pete Trewavas, and the Flower Kings' Roine Stolt, recording and releasing 2009's *The Whirlwind*, the band's first record since 2001's busting-at-the-seams *Bridge Across Forever*.

Meanwhile, Spock's Beard continues to motor along. The same instinct to say, "Fuck it all" that birthed Spock's Beard has kept it alive. D'Virgilio stepped up to the microphone as lead vocalist, pulling a Phil Collins. (D'Virgilio continues to sing and play drums in the studio, but skinsbeater Jimmy Keegan handles the drumming duties when the band performs live.)

Post–Neal Morse, Spock's Beard have released 2003's *Feel Euphoria*, 2005's *Octane*, *Live in '05: Gluttons for Punishment*, 2006's eponymous album, and 2008's *Live*. At press time, Spock's had released their tenth studio record, appropriately titled *X*. It's been a long journey, full of ups and down, but the band has fought against the tide to become one of America's premiere progressive rock acts for the new millennium.

"After Neal left, we didn't waste any time," says D'Virgilio. "We knew what we needed to do and just went for it. Now, I'd say, we have a better idea of what we're doing and how to work together, and I think it shows in the music."

PORCUPINE TREE

For all intents and purposes, England's Porcupine Tree might be the best example of a modern band balancing elements of the experimental and melodic while watching their sales volume steadily rise with each studio release.

Alternately described as progressive rock, post-progressive, neo-psychedelic, progressive metal, experimental/ambient, and even trance/club, Porcupine Tree are in the enviable position of being a work in progress while maintaining a loyal fan base.

"I think what's really interesting is that I very often get spoken about in the terms of someone who is making progressive rock, and for many years I resisted that and felt that was only a part of the story," says Porcupine Tree mastermind and multitalent Steven Wilson. "What I do understand and have come to appreciate now about my style and approach over the years is that everything I do does have a certain progressive sensibility about it. I have definitely learned from listening almost exclusively as a teenager to progressive music—from Can to Mahavishnu to Henry Cow—which is not the type of music I listen to very often now. But it's certainly almost in my DNA."

From 1989 through 1990, Wilson (with the help of conceptualist/friend Malcolm Stocks) hatched his farcical Porcupine Tree. Some of the early material itself was a kind of satire, such as a track like "Hokey Cokey," on the ridiculousness of pop music, and music in general, almost to the point of creepiness.

Passing them off as long-lost relics of prog rock's golden era, Wilson distributed three private cassettes of his music on a limited basis: *Tarquin's Seaweed Farm: Words from a Hessian Sack* (featuring fan favorite "Radioactive Toy"), the rare (reportedly only ten copies were ever pressed) *The Love, Death & Mussolini EP*, and *The Nostalgia Factory . . . and Other Tips for Amateur Golfers*.

Wilson fed the mystique surrounding Porcupine Tree by creating an imaginary discography complete with band history and "band members," giving them names such as Mr. Jelly, Sir Tarquin Underspoon, and the Evaporating Flan.

In 1992, Wilson released Porcupine Tree's proper debut, *On the Sunday of Life*, through Delerium Records (a mail-order company) and it did surprisingly well, selling a thousand copies each in the CD and vinyl formats.

"Delerium put out the first Porcupine Tree album, and I realized that there were a lot of people out there craving that kind of music," says Wilson. "I said, 'Okay, if I'm going to do this, if I'm going to carry on, it can't just be a nostalgic thing. I want to do something genuinely progressive.'"

The eerie thirty-minute antidrug single called *Voyage 34*, released in 1993, followed, and combined elements of the ambient trance club culture of London and progressive rock. With 1993's *Up the Downstair* and 1995's *The Sky Moves Sideways*, Wilson

Stupid Dream (1999)

Lightbulb Sun (2000)

In Absentia (2002)

Deadwing (2005)

Fear of a Blank Planet (2007)

We Lost the Skyline (2008)

Steven Wilson in his home studio. (Courtesy of Steven Wilson)

The Incident (2009)

moved away from the trance field and into more of the ambient/prog arena.

By 1997's *Signify*, Porcupine Tree had begun working as a band unit and less as Wilson's studio project.

"We were all spending the same amount of time together onstage and in vans, and there was a sense of it being a collective and a cooperative," says former drummer Chris Maitland.

"With Porcupine Tree, it has been a slow evolution," says keyboardist Richard Barbieri, formerly of Japan, who'd worked with Wilson's pre–Porcupine Tree project No-Man. "The first couple of albums I was on I was just playing a bit on the album and then going home. *Signify* really marked the first time—and first album—to have a band sound."

Nineteen ninety-nine's *Stupid Dream* (released on Snapper) and the live *Coma Divine* both had a much more classic progressive rock, even Floydian, feel. "You don't hear many digital synthesizers in any of my projects, including Porcupine Tree," says Wilson. "Richard [Barbieri] is very much someone who loves old analog sounds, and that's somewhere where we really bond, in our love of Moog synthesizers and Prophet 5 and classic synthesizers. So a lot of that sound, what you might call sound design, comes from processing organic elements."

The band continued to explore and streamlined its approach with 2000's *Lightbulb Sun* (some fans have even described the album as a pop effort) and 2002's alternately dreamy and metallic *In Absentia*, the first PT record to appear on a major label (Lava/Atlantic), and the first to feature drummer Gavin Harrison, on the concept of "what makes serial killers [tick]," says Wilson.

"I think the entire record hangs together very well," says Barbieri. "*In Absentia* was a real turning point for us."

Two thousand five's *Deadwing* was based on a script for a psychological thriller (initially titled "Lullaby"), which Wilson wrote in collaboration with art designer Mike Bennion, who'd been working with the band since *On the Sunday of Life*.

"To Steve's credit, he's remarkably

prolific—his credits are about as long as your arm," says Bennion. "I think a lot of bands have a very short shelf life and they're not nurtured by the record company. It's a very unusual trajectory for a band these days, and I think he has allowed Porcupine Tree and Steven to get better at what they do."

Two thousand seven brought *Fear of a Blank Planet*, partly inspired by the Bret Easton Ellis novel *Lunar Park*, the summation of Wilson's view that our decrepit, reality-TV, and downloaded culture continues to be eroded by a technology that alienates us from society.

"*On Fear of a Blank Planet* we are talking very much about the whole digital technology era and the fact that although information technology brings the world into our front room, it also creates more a sense of universal paranoia," says Wilson.

The four-track *Nil Recurring* (recorded during the *Blank Planet* sessions) appeared on the band's own Transmission 5.1 label and is as powerful a socio-political statement as the record that spawned it. "There's a sense that this 'Nil Recurring' implies a constant nullification of life experience," says Wilson.

The record's themes of isolation and alienation are reinforced by the sometimes dark, penetrating, and eerie sonic textures created by both Wilson and Barbieri. "Richard is never going to give you a conventional sound," says Wilson. "He is very much a sonic architect, a secret weapon, who creates strange soundscapes."

When Porcupine Tree came

IQ

Marillion's breakthrough opened the door for other like-minded progressive rock bands to gain a little bit more credibility with critics and the public at large. Bands such as IQ, Pendragon, Pallas, Andy Glass's folky-symphonic band Solstice, It Bites, Twelfth Night, Spain's Galadriel, Poland's Exodus, Mexico's Cast (dating from the late 1970s), Italy's Nuova Era (formed with the express mission of playing '70s-style prog rock), Slovenian-Italian band Devil Doll, and others were slowly making prog rock a viable musical and commercial force once again.

"It seemed all of a sudden some people just got tired of the punk movement," says Pendragon guitarist/vocalist Nick Barrett. "When a band like Marillion were just starting to break, it seemed to make it okay for others, like us, who were closer to a band like Camel, to go out and perform."

Of the prog rock bands that emerged in the 1980s, IQ remains one of the most seminal. Formed from the ruins of the Giln and the Lens, inspired by the likes of Yes, Genesis, and classical masters, IQ initially performed many musical styles. Much like their contemporaries Marillion, IQ stood between two musical worlds: punk and prog rock.

"We were a prog band, amongst other things, that was unquestionably working-class and therefore didn't fit either social model of working-class punk or upper-middle-class prog rock artist," says keyboardist Martin Orford. "My father worked in a factory that made yacht masts, as did I for several years, whilst [guitarist] Mike Holmes's father worked in Southampton Docks, and neither of us attended any special music schools or classes. We were hardly brought up in poverty, but we were not living in the lap of luxury either. When the band moved to London, we survived for many years on only three and a half pounds a week each for food, which bought the ingredients for an ongoing vegetable stew, but not much else.

"The effect this had on the music was an interesting amalgam, and we certainly played prog rock faster and harder than anyone ever had before," Orford continues. "Punk had changed a lot of things in the U.K., and people expected hard-hitting, high-energy entertainment whatever the style of music. [I]f Genesis had sat on chairs while playing twelve-string guitars to some of the audiences we faced in our era, they would probably not have gotten out alive."

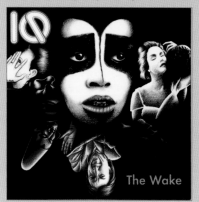

IQ: *The Wake* (1985)

"All the bands were pretty competitive with each other at the time, and that was a real incentive for us to keep pushing forward," says vocalist Peter Nicholls, who followed in Peter Gabriel's footsteps by donning greasepaint to help dramatize IQ's songs onstage. "The Marquee in London was probably the focal point of much of that energy and attention. In the early days, we used to stand outside when our 'rivals' were playing there and wish we could play there too. When Genesis played a surprise date there in 1982, we spent the whole evening up on the roof listening to the gig. It was a magical club, very atmospheric."

IQ went on to release such neo-prog staples as 1985's *The Wake* (a concept album that was inspired by and expanded upon Edgar Allan Poe's "The Premature Burial," centered on "what happens to the central character's through New York City on their 2009 tour to support their double studio album *The Incident*, one was immediately struck by the band's strange relevance. There were no great arena rock effects, no dazzling light displays, no flying pigs or gigantic cardboard bricks; instead, the crowd was captivated by the fifty-five-minute title song of *The Incident*, which occupies the entire first disc of the release.

It was hard to shake the notion that one was witnessing prog rock history in the making. (Perhaps a bit like seeing Genesis perform *The Lamb Lies Down on Broadway* for the first time?) Though "The Incident" references *Sgt. Pepper's*—a nod to prog rock's origins— it was obvious that the crowd was "listening to the future," to steal a phrase from author Bill Martin, proving that Porcupine Tree are at the forefront of progressive music in the twenty-first century.

"I shouldn't be making music for anybody else but myself," Wilson says. "Myself and [vocalist] Tim [Bowness] definitely reached that point when we made [1994's] *Flowermouth* record [as No-Man], because until that moment we had been making music to try to please the record company, try to please the management, to try to sell records. It hadn't worked anyway. We weren't selling any more records. Finally we said, 'Fuck it. If we're going to go down, let's go down in a blaze of glory and at least we can be proud of what we've done.' I've never looked back since with Porcupine Tree, No-Man, Bass Communion, Blackfield, or anything I've ever done."

IQ 2005. *Left to right*: guitarist Mike Holmes, bassist John Jowitt, vocalist Peter Nicholls, drummer Andy Edwards, and keyboardist Martin Orford.

spirit after he'd died," says Nicholls); 1993's *Ever*, 1998's concept double album *Subterranea* (on the subject matter of surveillance and an oppressive regime's social experiment), which spawned a multimedia stage production; 2000's *The Seventh House* (which sandwiches plaintive piano balladry in between Zeppelinesque heaviness); 2004's *Dark Matter* (featuring the twenty-four-and-a-half minute cautionary tale "Harvester of Souls"); and 2009's *Frequency*.

Because of its musical and thematic ties to progressive rock past (in the earlier days, IQ often dropped the "G" bomb—sonic references to Genesis) the band has been dubbed "neo-prog"—a label that has ruffled a few feathers.

"I was only aware of it cropping up in the U.S. in the '90s, when it seemed to be used in a disparaging way, basically criticizing a band for not playing 'legitimate' prog," Nicholls says. "In other words, not having enough Mellotrons onstage and daring to break convention by writing some shorter songs or using more contemporary instruments."

"It's a convenient term that someone has invented," says Orford. "I mean, when we were there with the Marillion guys and Pendragon in London, nobody called it neo-prog. It's quite an insulting term as well, because it carries with it the inference that it's somehow inferior to the proper prog. That's interesting, because none of the guys from the '70s bands that we have played with over the years have made that differentiation. You know, 'No, I'm not playing with you. You're only neo.'"

"I have the same conversations with journalists when we tour," adds Marillion's Steve Rothery. "We've been called progressive, neo-prog, and symphonic rock—whatever the hell that is—and for some [people] it's a compliment. For others, it's the worst possible insult. It implies a regressive, stuck-in-a-'70s-time-warp type of music. In fact, it's music that isn't easy to categorize. Giving it a label, at least in some people's minds, is shutting you up in a little box. I could use Taurus pedals, play in 7/8, use a Minimoog. But who gives a damn, you know? The question should be, 'Is it musically interesting?'"

Acknowledgments

FOR YEARS I'VE KEPT IN MY MIND A STORY JOHN WETTON TOLD ME ABOUT AN ASIA SONG he penned with Geoff Downes in the early 1980s, called "Daylight."

Asia, a progressive pop rock supergroup formed in 1981, had spent a long and gloomy winter toughing it out in the Great White North completing their self-titled debut.

"The big event of our day was looking out the window to see how many moose walked past the lake," Wetton said. "When you've been in Canada for six months in darkness and suddenly the dawn breaks, it's gorgeous. It started to look clear again and that's when I wrote [the song]. I've never been so glad to see daylight in my life."

"Daylight" encapsulates the private thoughts of the songwriter ruminating on the dawning of a new day, but also something much more universal: Wetton, in clear, bold language, imparts illuminating lyrics of survival, revelation, and spiritual transformation.

The song's positive message (and the courage it instilled in me) was one of my motivations for writing this book. Because "Daylight" has been a beacon, I say, thank you, prog rock.

These acknowledgments wouldn't be complete without mentioning some of those who've given me their valuable time and wisdom (ushering in their own form of "daylight") for this work. These include Bill Bruford, the Moody Blues, Ian Anderson, Derek Shulman, Kerry Minnear, Beppe Crovella, Annie Haslam, Greg Lake, Eric Woolfson (R.I.P.), Steve Howe, Jon Anderson, Chris Squire, Gianni Leone, Danny Brill, Ian McDonald, Gustavo Moretto, Hugh Hopper (R.I.P.), Phil Ehart, Eddie Jobson, Jonathan Mover, Paul Northfield, Jordan Rudess, Lori Lousararian, Peter Sinfield, Mel Collins, Ray Bennett, Carol Kaye, Brian Kelleher, Terry Ellis, Lori Hehr, Peter Morticelli, David Hadland, Dan Hanley, Leonardo Pavkovic, Anne Leighton, Patrick Moraz, Billy Sherwood, Pat Mastelotto, David Rohl, Lee Jackson, Keith Emerson, Trey Gunn, Iconic Music, Steven Wilson, Richard Barbieri, Bruce Pilato, Andy Leff, Eileen Craddock, Michael Farley, Lindsey Nutter, Martin Orford, Peter Nicholls, Peter Noble, Graham Smith, Peter Banks, Erika Tooker, Kaitlin Lindsey, Wil Sharpe, Dale Newman, Nick Davis, Michael Lavigne, and the hundreds of other generous interviewees too numerous to name here. I thank you.

I also want to thank my wife and soul mate, Sharon; George and Judy Bailey; my brother, Michael; Tony "Long Distance Runaround" Romano; Jim Kelly; my boyhood neighbor Dave Penna (now a full-time musician and multi-instrumentalist with the band Ad Astra); Vincent Tallarida (remember spinning ELP and King Crimson?); Anthony Bernard (a keyboard whiz and Genesis fan); longtime friend Gary Jansen; Jim Goodin; Polly Watson, this book's excellent copy editor; Marybeth Keating; Carol Flannery; and my patient editor at Backbeat/Hal Leonard, Mike Edison. Thanks for seeing this through to the end.

SELECTED BIBLIOGRAPHY

BOOKS

Ammer, Christine. *The HarperCollins Dictionary of Music*. Second Edition. New York: HarperCollins Perennial, 1987.

Banks, Tony, and Phil Collins, Peter Gabriel, Steve Hackett, and Mike Rutherford. *Genesis: Chapter and Verse*. London: Weidenfeld & Nicolson, 2007.

Bloom, Harold, and Lionel Trilling. *Romantic Poetry and Prose*. New York: Oxford University Press, 1973.

Bruford, Bill. *When in Doubt, Roll!* Cedar Grove, NJ: Modern Drummer Publications, 1988.

Carroll, Lewis. *Alice's Adventures in Wonderland & Through the Looking Glass*. New York: Signet Classic, 2000.

Collins, Jon. *Rush: Chemistry*. London: Helter Skelter, 2005.

Davies, Hunter. *The Beatles*. New York: McGraw-Hill, 1981.

DeCurtis, Anthony, and James Henke with Holly George-Warren, eds. *The Rolling Stone Album Guide*. New York: Random House, 1992.

Di Scala, Spencer M. *Italy: From Revolution to Republic, 1700 to the Present*. Second Edition. Oxford, U.K.: Westview Press, 1998.

Dos Passos, John. *The Big Money*. New York: Signet Classic, 1969.

Elstrott, Kelly. *The Fifth Revelation*. New Orleans: Mighty Messenger Press, 1998.

Emerson, Caryl. *The Life of Musorgsky*. Cambridge, U.K.: Cambridge University Press, 1999.

Emerson, Keith. *Pictures of an Exhibitionist*. London: John Blake Publishing, 2004.

Genesis Anthology. New York: Warner Bros. Publications, no date listed.

Goulding, Phil G. *Classical Music: The 50 Greatest Composers and Their Greatest Works*. New York: Fawcett Books, 2007.

Hamilton, Edith. *Mythology*. Boston: Back Bay Books/Little, Brown and Company, 1998.

Heckstall-Smith, Dick, with Pete Grant. *Blowing the Blues: Fifty Years of Playing the British Blues*. Bath, U.K.: Clear Books, 2004.

Hesse, Hermann. Translated by Hilda Rosner. *Siddhartha*. New York: Bantam, 1971.

Holm-Hudson, Kevin, ed. "Progressive Rock Reconsidered." New York and London: Routledge, 2002.

Jung, C. G. *Memories, Dreams, Reflections*. New York: Vintage Books, 1989.

Laing, R. D. *The Divided Self*. New York: Pelican Books, 1972.

Macan, Edward. *Rocking the Classics: English Progressive Rock and the Counterculture*. New York: Oxford University Press, 1997.

Maltin, Leonard, ed. *Leonard Maltin's 2001 Movie & Video Guide*. New York: Signet, 2001.

Martin, Bill. *Listening to the Future: 1968–1978, the Time of Progressive Rock*. Chicago: Open Court, 1998.

McArthur, Tom, ed. *The Oxford Companion to the English Language*. Oxford, U.K.: Oxford University Press, 1992.

Morse, Tim. *Yesstories: Yes in Their Own Words*. New York: St. Martin's Griffin, 1996.

Poe, Edgar Allan. *Selected Tales*. Oxford, U.K.: Oxford University Press, 1992.

Potter, Keith. *Four Musical Minimalists: La Monte Young, Terry Riley, Steve Reich Philip Glass (Music in the Twentieth Century)*. New York: Cambridge University Press, 2000.

Rosen, Charles. *The Romantic Generation*. Cambridge, MA: Harvard University Press, 1998.

Schuller, Gunther. *Early Jazz: Its Roots and Musical Development*. Oxford, U.K.: Oxford University Press, 1968.

Slavic Myth and Mankind: Forests of the Vampire. New York: Barnes & Noble Books, 2003.

Spitz, Bob. *The Beatles: The Biography*. New York: Little, Brown and Company, 2005.

Stands in Timber, John, and Margot Liberty with the assistance of Robert M. Utley. *Cheyenne Memories*. Lincoln, NE: University of Nebraska Press/Bison Books, 1972.

Tamm, Eric. *Brian Eno: His Music and the Vertical Color of Sound*. Boston: Faber and Faber, 1989.

Thomas, Dylan. *Under Milk Wood*. Fourteenth Edition. New York: New Directions Publishing, 1954.

Warwick, Neil; Jon Kutner; and Tony Brown. *The Complete Book of the British Charts: Singles and Albums*. Third Edition. London: Omnibus Press, 2004.

Well, H. G. (Herbert George). *The Time Machine*. New York: Penguin Classics, 2005.

Wheeler, Bill. *Drum Techniques of Rush.* Secaucus, NJ: Warner Bros. Publications, 1985.

Whitburn, Joel. *The Billboard Book of Top 40 Hits.* New York: Billboard Books; an imprint of Watson-Guptill Publications, 1989.

Yogananda, Paramahansa. *Autobiography of a Yogi.* Thirteenth Edition. Los Angeles: Self-Realization Fellowship, 2002

Zappa, Frank, with Peter Occhiogrosso. *The Real Frank Zappa Book.* New York: Poseidon Press, 1989.

LINER NOTES
Aston, Laurence. *The Transatlantic Story* by various artists. Box set. Castle Communications, 1998.

Fripp, Robert. *Absent Lovers, Live in Montreal, 1984* by King Crimson. Discipline Global Mobile, 1998.

Fripp, Robert. *Exposure* by Robert Fripp. Discipline Global Mobile/Inner Knot, 2006.

Fripp, Robert. *The Great Deceiver* by King Crimson. Box set. Discipline/Virgin/Caroline, 1992.

Fripp, Robert. *Vroom Vroom* by King Crimson. Discipline Global Mobile, 2001.

Genesis Archive 1969–1975 by Genesis (Peter Gabriel announcing his leaving from Genesis (press release reprinted from 1975). Box set. Atlantic Recording Corporation, 1998.

Genesis Archive #2, 1976–1992 by Genesis. Box set. Atlantic Recording Corporation, 2000.

Hammill, Peter. *The Aerosol Grey Machine* by Van der Graaf Generator. Fie!, 1997.

In the Land of Grey and Pink by Caravan. Original sleeve notes. Deram/Decca, 1971.

Lake, Steve. *Drop* by Soft Machine. Moonjune, 2008.

Powell, Mark. *Vital* by Van der Graaf Generator. Charisma/Virgin, 2005.

Reed, John. *On the Threshold of a Dream* by the Moody Blues. Decca, 1997.

Wilson, Brian, and Brad Elliott. *Pet Sounds* by the Beach Boys. Capitol, 1999.

MAGAZINES AND PERIODICALS
Alper, Garth. "Making Sense out of Postmodern Music?" *Popular Music and Society*, 1740–1712, vol. 24, no. 4, Winter 2000.

Blackwell, Mark. "'Out of This World' Production Set for Pink Floyd." *Amusement Business*, January 31, 1994.

Borneman, Ernest. "Creole Echoes." *The Jazz Review*, vol. 2, no. 8, September 1959.

Boucher, Caroline. "Mr. Wright." *Disc and Music Echo*, February 5, 1972.

Brooks, Michael. "Yes: Steve Howe." *Guitar Player*, April 1973.

Browne, David. "Prog's Legs: The Power Pomp of Dream Theater Proves Rumors of Art Rock's Demise Have Been Greatly Exaggerated." *Entertainment Weekly*, February 6, 2002.

Clarke, Steve. "Jethro: Nothing to Get Passionate About." *New Musical Express*, July 21, 1973.

Coryat, Karl. "Geddy Lee: Still Going!" *Bass Player*, December 1993.

Dallas, Karl. "Boy Genius 'Not Broke' Shock." *Melody Maker*, December 29, 1979.

Dallas, Karl. "This Is the Year of the Expanding Man . . ." *Melody Maker*, November 25, 1978.

Diliberto, John. "Zen & the Art of Fripp's Guitar." *Electronic Musician*, June 1987.

DiPerna, Alan. "Mysterious Ways." *Guitar World*, December 2001.

Ditlea, Steve. "Ian Anderson Shows You How to Lose Your Way Through 'Thick as a Brick.'" *Circus*, April 1972.

Farber, Jim. "Jethro Tull Ride the Rock Frontier." *Circus*, June 22, 1978.

Flick, Larry. "Virgin's Ferry on the Joy of Frantic." *Billboard*, May 25, 2002.

Flippo, Chet. "After a Record-Breaking Decade on the Charts, Pink Floyd's David Gilmour Tries a Solo Tour." *People*, March 12, 1984.

Foster, Richard S. "A Nice Morning Drive." *Road & Track*, November 1973.

Gallo, Armando. "PFM/Reading." *New Musical Express*, May 18, 1974.

Garcia, Guy. "Waters Still Runs Deep." *People*, October 26, 1992.

Gibson, John. Pink Floyd Live in Pompeii review. *Melody Maker*, September 16, 1972.

Gilmore, Mikal. "The Madness & Majesty of Pink Floyd." *Rolling Stone*, April 5, 2007.

Gress, Jesse. "A Saucer Full of Secrets: Unscrambling Early Pink Floyd." *Guitar Player*, June 1994.

Hackett, Vernell. "Touring Records Are Broken: Gross Beats 1988 by $45 mil." *Amusement Business*, December 30, 1989.

Hamblett, John. "Rock Against Right-Wing Rock Being Called Fascist." *New Musical Express*, May 5, 1979.

Harris, John. "In the Flesh." *Q* magazine, special edition, Autumn 2004.

Hedges, Dan. "Steve Howe: Renaissance Man of the Guitar." *Guitar Player*, May 1978.

Heining, Duncan. "Soft Machine Way Ahead." *Jazzwise*, August 2003.

Henderson, Peter. "Intelligent vs. Pig-Headed." *Mojo*, March 1998.

Hogan, Richard. "Pink Floyd's Zoo Story: When Pigs Have Wings, 'Animals' Will Rule the Top Ten." *Circus*, April 28, 1977.

Holden, Stephen. A Passion Play review. *Rolling Stone*, August 30, 1973.

Humphries, Stephen. "Meet Marillion, the Band with the Most-devoted Fans." *Christian Science Monitor*, May 18, 2001.

Kordosh, John. "Rush. But Why Are They in Such a Hurry?" *Creem*, June 1981.

Legrand, Emmanuel. "The Indies." *Billboard*, November 6, 2004.

Lewis, John. "Strange Brew." *Uncut*, October 2009.

Marshall, Wolf. "Music Appreciation: Allan Holdsworth: The Early Years." *Guitar for the Practicing Musician*, March 1989.

Miller, William F. "King Crimson's Bill Bruford & Pat Mastelotto . . . A Perfect Pair." *Modern Drummer*, November 1995.

Miller, William F. "Neil Peart." *Modern Drummer*, December 1989.

Miller, William F. "Neil Peart: In Search of the Right Feel." *Modern Drummer*, February 1994.

Miller, William F. "Phil Collins: Drummer to the Core!" *Modern Drummer*, March 1997.

Morris, Mitchell. "Kansas and the Prophetic Tone." *American Music*, vol. 19, no. 1, Spring 2000.

Mulhern, Tom. "Adrian Belew: Sonic Radical." *Guitar Player*, January 1984.

Mulhern, Tom. "Robert Fripp: On the Discipline of Craft & Art." *Guitar Player*, January 1986.

Mulligan, Brian. "Scaling the Dizzy Heights of Success." *Record & Tape Retailer*, October 10, 1970.

Murray, Charles Shaar. "Jethro Tull: The House That Jethro Built." *New Musical Express*, September 1, 1973.

Music Week. "Singles–01.05.04: Marillion." May 1, 2004.

Music Week. "Singles–07.04.07." April 7, 2007.

Music Week. "Single–24.07.04: Marillion." July 24, 2004.

New Musical Express. "Crimson Disband." September 28, 1974.

Nooger, Dan. "Emerson, Lake and Palmer's Grandest Design." *Circus*, April 28, 1977.

Puterbaugh, Parke, and Greg Kot, Anthony DeCurtis, David Fricke, David Thigpen, and Jon Pareles. "The Beatles: Inside the Hit Factory: The Stories Behind the Making of 27 Number One Songs." *Rolling Stone*, March 1, 2001.

Puterbaugh, Parke. "Yes: Happy Together?" *Rolling Stone*, June 27, 1991.

Record Mirror. "King Crimson Have Ceased." October 5, 1974.

Reesman, Bryan. "Marillion: The Long Road to Happiness." *Goldmine*, March 27, 2009

Rosen, Steve. "The Minstrel Boy Calls the Tune." *Sounds*, September 27, 1975.

Rosen, Steve. "Tull's Ian Anderson." *Circus*, December 9, 1975.

Rosen, Steve. "Two Guitars from Kansas: More Than Twin Leads." *Guitar Player*, August 1978.

Schaefer, John. "New Sounds Interview with Mike Oldfield." *New Sounds*, December 1993.

Sciabarra, Chris Matthew. "Rand, Rush and Rock." *The Journal of Ayn Rand Studies*, vol. 4, no. 1, Fall 2002.

Sheppard, R. Z. "Books: The Head Game." *Time*, October 27, 1975.

Sounds. "Jethro Tull Cancel Wembley Gigs." April 28, 1973.

Stud Brothers. "Catch Their Fall." *Melody Maker*, October 14, 1989.
Sutcliffe, Phil. "Coming Back to Life." *Q* magazine, special edition, Autumn 2004.

Sutcliffe, Phil, and Peter Henderson. "The First Men on the Moon." *Mojo*, March 1998.

Tyler, Tony. Genesis interview (no title). *New Musical Express*, September 13, 1975.

White, Timothy. "Ferry's 'Brilliant' Singing Takes Flight." *Billboard*, July 20, 1996.

Welsh, Chris. "Tull: Enough Is Enough." *Melody Maker*, July 21, 1973.

Young, Charles. "Jethro's Magic Pan." *Rolling Stone*, March 10, 1977.

Zappa, Frank. "The Oracle Has It All Psyched Out." *Life*, June 28, 1968.

NEWSPAPERS

"5 British (and Irish) Rock Groups Arrive." *The New York Times*, January 31, 1968.

Associated Press. "Frank Zappa, 52, Wrote Musical Satire." *Albany Times Union*, December 6, 1993.

Bird, Peter. "Obituary: Don Allum." *The Independent*, December 5, 1992.

Blair, Iain. "Step Aside, Punks, Marillion Making '70s-Type of Name for Itself in Britain." *Chicago Tribune*, March 23, 1986.

Branson, Sir Richard. "20 Pounds for Tubular Bells? They'd Better Be Worth It." *The Daily Mail*, April 21, 2007.

Brown, G. "Marillion Thriving in Europe." *Denver Post*, April 10, 1992.

Dove, Ian. "Peter Gabriel Star in Rock by Genesis." *The New York Times*, May 6, 1974.

Dove, Ian. "They Won't Bach Around the Clock." *The New York Times*, December 16, 1973.

Erlich, Nancy. "A Madman Grins." *The New York Times*, August 15, 1971.

Erlich, Nancy. "Classical Rock: What Is It?" *The New York Times*, April 1, 1973.

Goldstein, Richard. "We Still Need the Beatles, but . . ." *The New York Times*, June 18, 1967.

Golemis, Dean. "British Band's U.S. Tour is Computer-Generated." *Chicago Tribune*, September 23, 1997.

Holden, Stephen. "Rock: Asia, a 'Supergroup,' Mixing Art and Hard Styles." *The New York Times*, May 6, 1982.

Holden, Stephen. "Serious Issues Underlie a New Album from Styx." *The New York Times*, March 27, 1983.

Jahn, Mike. "British Bands Take the Fillmore." *The New York Times*, May 2, 1971.

Jahn, Mike. "Visiting Britons Bring Loud Jazz: Colosseum Forsakes Rock Beat—Bass Impresses." *The New York Times*, August 28, 1969.

Knickerbocker, Conrad. "Books of the Times: Variations in Doxology of Terror." *The New York Times*, March 22, 1966.

Lanham, Tom. "Marillion: The Time Is Right for Anachronistic Rock Band." *San Francisco Chronicle*, March 9, 1986.

Lee, Craig. "Fish 'N' Ambition." *Los Angeles Times*, March 9, 1986.

McGregor, Craig. "Zapparap on the Zappaplan." *The New York Times*, November 8, 1970.

Montanelli, Indro. "Italians Have Lost All Faith in Democracy." *The New York Times*, April 21, 1978.

Morse, Steve. "It's Not All Paradise for Styx; Chicago Band Is No. 1 With Fans, but Not with Rock Press." *Boston Globe*, April 23, 1981.

Palmer, Robert. "King Crimson: Despite Upheaval, the Band Plays On." *The New York Times*, May 20, 1984.

Palmer, Robert. "Rock: Kansas, Middle West Energy and Synthesizing Influences." *The New York Times*, August 30, 1979.

Palmer, Robert. "Rock: King Crimson Mixes Its Fare." *The New York Times*, August 3, 1982.

Palmer, Robert. "Trance Music: A Trend of the 1970s." *The New York Times*, January 12, 1975.

Palmer, Robert. "Why Robert Fripp Resurrected King Crimson." *The New York Times*, November 1, 1981.

Pareles, Jon. "Concert: Styx on Tour." *The New York Times*, April 3, 1983.

Perrone, Pierre. "Obituary: John Panozzo." *The Independent*, July 20, 1996.

Racine, Marty. "A Rested Rush Brings Polished Act to Town." *Houston Chronicle*, February 25, 1990.

Reich, Howard. "Can Styx's Dennis DeYoung Find Happiness in Show Tunes?" *Chicago Tribune*, September 25, 1994.

Rockwell, John. "A Pink Floyd Album Marks 10 Years as a Best Seller." *The New York Times*, May 6, 1984.

Rockwell, John. "Emerson, Lake and Palmer + 60 = Rock." *The New York Times*, July 9, 1977.

Rockwell, John. "Gentle Giant Rocks Toward Top Billing." *The New York Times*, November 3, 1974.

Rockwell, John. "Robert Fripp Makes Personal Statement." *The New York Times*, April 27, 1979.

Rockwell, John. "The Pop Life." *The New York Times*, August 5, 1977.

Rockwell, John. "The Pop Life." *The New York Times*, April 7, 1978.

Rockwell, John. "The Pop Life: An Avant-Garde Spirit for Tangerine Dream." *The New York Times*, October 4, 1974.

Rockwell, John. "Two British Bands, New Here, Indicate Evolution in Rock." *The New York Times*, December 15, 1972.

Sandall, Robert. "Quiffs, Riffs and Reinventing Rock." *The Sunday Times*, August 22, 2004.

Selden, Ina Lee. "3 Italian Newsmen Are Victims of Increasing Wave of Violence." *The New York Times*, June 4, 1977.

St. Louis Post-Dispatch, "Jesus Christ Superstar Popular Still." June 1, 1993.

Shelton, Robert. "Pop-Music Recordings Are Now Spinning in Highbrow Orbit." *The New York Times*, April 5, 1968.

Shelton, Robert. "Son of Suzy Creamcheese." *The New York Times*, December 25, 1966.

Shelton, Robert. "The Soft Machine, Trio, in Jazz Series." *The New York Times*, July 12, 1968.

Stelter, Paul. "Zappa Guitarist Subs In." *The Washington Times*. February 9, 2006.

Strauss, Neil. "The Lights! It Must Be Pink Floyd." *The New York Times*, June 8, 1995.

Telecomworldwire. "E-mail Plea Net GBP 100,000 Backing for New Album." August 21, 2000.

The New York Times, "Columbia Installs Nuclear Generator." September 18, 1955.

The New York Times, "Dr. Dvorak's Latest Work." December 17, 1893.

The New York Times, "Literary London's Current Gossip." May 30, 1908.

The New York Times, "Pension for Tramp Poet." July 7, 1911.

Van Matre, Lynn. "Team Player J. Y. Young, a Kid from Styx, Goes Solo with 'City Slicker.'" *Chicago Tribune*, January 30, 1986.

WEB SITES
www.allmovie.com
www.allmusic.com
www.aynrand.org
www.astrology.com
www.babaji.net
www.bancodelmutuosoccorso.it
www.bbc.co.uk/history/british/
   civil_war_revolution/
www.crystalinks.com/cheyenne.html
www.dailymail.co.uk
www.elephant-talk.com
www.elgar.org
www.eloy-legacy.com
www.expose.org/GaryGreen/
   gary_green_complete.htm
(Interview with Gary Green by Jeff
   Melton for Exposé online.)
www.galenet.com
   (biography resource center)
www.gurdjieff.org
www.jacquimcshee.co.uk
jam.canoe.ca
www.johnhelliwell.com
www.kansasband.com
www.kingcounty.gov/environment/
   animalsandplants/noxious-weeds/
   weed-identification/giant-hog-
   weed.aspx
www.liftsounds.com
www.livinglegendsmusic.com
   (Mike Portnoy interview segment,
   "Sex, Drugs and Rock and Roll",
   accessed through YouTube.com)
www.marillion.com
www.masque-studio.com
www.nga.gov
www.oliver-wakeman.co.uk
www.originalasia.com
www.pfmpfm.it
www.riaa.com
www.rwcc.com
www.schott-music.com
www.senate.gov
www.ses-la.com
www.starcityrecording.com
www.steve-walsh.de
www.strawbsweb.co.uk
www.stringdriventhing.com
www.telegraph.co.uk
www.tubular.net
www.williamneal.co.uk
www.zappa.com

DVDS & VIDEOS
Bruford & the Beat. Baltimore, MD: Axis Video, 1982.

Buddy Rich Memorial Scholarship Concert: Tape Four. New York: DCI Music Video, 1991.

King Crimson in concert (videotaped MTV broadcast), 1984.

Neil Peart: A Work in Progress. Paul Siegel and Rob Wallis, producers/directors. Miami: DCI Music Video Productions, 1996.

Pink Floyd Live at Pompeii: The Director's Cut. Adrian Maben, director; Michele Arnaud, Reiner Moritz, associate producers. Santa Monica, CA: Universal Pictures, 2003.

Rush: *Exit Stage . . . Left* video interview with Alex Lifeson, 1981.

Rush *R30: 30th Anniversary World Tour*. Pierre Lamoureux, director; Pierre Lamoureux and Allan Weinrib, producers, 2005.

OTHER DOCUMENTS AND SOURCES
Anderson Bruford Wakeman Howe official tour program, 1989.

Asia tour program, 1983.

Conference guide: "A Day in the Life—Sgt. Pepper's at 40." School of Music, University of Leeds; Simon Warner, director PopuLus, the Centre for the Study of the World's Popular Music, 2007.

Discipline Global Mobile press release, summer 2001.

Genesis: *Genesis Archive 1969–1975*, 1998. Gabriel recounting the story of Rael.

International Council on Monuments and Sites (ICOMOS), World Heritage List identification and nomination, No. 437, prepared by ICOMOS in Paris, May 1987.

Introducing the Mini Moog synthesizer, Model D, product brochure, R. A. Moog, Inc., Trumansburg, NY, 1970.

Porcupine Tree timeline, provided by Lava Records, 2002.

Robert Fripp online diary: September 8, 1999.

Robert Fripp online diary: September 14, 1999.

Robert Fripp online diary: January 13, 2000.

Robert Fripp online diary: July 27, 2000.

Robert Fripp online diary: January 11, 2001.

Robert Fripp online diary: March 11, 2001.

Robert Fripp online diary: March 26, 2004.

Robert Fripp online diary: October 1, 2008.

Rush *Grace Under Pressure* Tour program, essay by Neil Peart, 1984.

Rush *Hemispheres* Tour program, essay by Geoff Barton, 1978.

Rush *Moving Pictures* Tour program, essay by Neil Peart, 1981.

Rush *Permanent Waves* Tour program, essay by Neil Peart, 1980.

Rush *Power Windows* Tour program, essay by Neil Peart, 1985.

Rush *Signals* New World Tour program, essay by Neil Peart, 1982.

Steven Wilson: The Complete Discography, Seventh Edition, compiled by Uwe Häberle, May 2007.

The Official Frank Zappa Discography, provided by the Zappa Family Trust.

Yes North American Tour program, 1984.

DISCOGRAPHY

BRAIN SALAD SURGERIES: 297 ESSENTIAL PROGRESSIVE ROCK LISTENS

This list reflects the author's opinion of what constitutes the 297 essential progressive rock recordings of all time. Rankings were determined based on artistic merit, historical significance, popularity, and importance to the genre. Dates refer to original release.

1. Pink Floyd: *The Dark Side of the Moon* (Capital/EMI Records, CDP 0777 7 46001 2 5), 1973
2. Emerson, Lake and Palmer: *Brain Salad Surgery* (Atlantic, SD 19124), 1973
3. Yes: *Close to the Edge* (Atlantic, SD 19133), 1972
4. King Crimson: *In the Court of the Crimson King* (EG Records/Editions EG/JEM Records, EGKC 1), 1969
5. Camel: *Moonmadness* (Janus Records, JXS-7024), 1976
6. Jethro Tull: *Thick as a Brick* (Chrysalis, F2 21003), 1972
7. Genesis: *Selling England by the Pound* (Yellow Dog Music/Atlantic/Stratton Smith Productions, KSD 19277), 1973
8. King Crimson: *Red* (EG Records/Editions, EG/JEM Records EGKC 8), 1974
9. Pink Floyd: *Meddle* (Capital/EMI Records, CDP 0777 7 46034 2 3), 1971
10. Yes: *Fragile* (Atlantic, SD 7211), 1972
11. Premiata Forneria Marconi: *Storia di Un Minuto* (RCA/Sony, 82876760302), 1972
12. Rick Wakeman: *The Six Wives of Henry VIII* (A&M, SP4361), 1973
13. Genesis: *The Lamb Lies Down on Broadway* (Atlantic, 82677-2), 1974
14. Pink Floyd: *Wish You Were Here* (CBS Records, CK33453), 1975
15. Banco del Mutuo Soccorso: *Io Sono Nato Libero* (Dischi Ricordi, MPCD00206), 1973

16. Emerson, Lake and Palmer: *Tarkus* (Atlantic/EG Records, SD 19121), 1971
17. Jethro Tull: *Songs from the Wood* (Chrysalis, CHR-1132), 1977
18. Magma: *Mekanïk Destruktïw Kommandöh* (A&M, SP-4397), 1973
19. Caravan: *In the Land of Grey and Pink* (Deram/Decca, 8829832), 1971
20. U.K.: s/t (EG Records/Editions EG/JEM Records, EGLP 35), 1978
21. Camel: *Music Inspired by the Snow Goose* (Decca/Universal, 8829302), 1975
22. Utopia: s/t (Warner Bros./Bearsville/Earmark Music BR 6954), 1974
23. The Soft Machine: *Third* (CBS, 66246), 1970
24. Banco del Mutuo Soccorso: *Darwin* (Dischi Ricordi, MPCD00205), 1972
25. Gentle Giant: *Free Hand* (DRT Entertainment, RTE 00350), 1975
26. Kansas: *Song for America* (Kirshner/CBS, AL 33385), 1975
27. The Nice: *Ars Longa Vita Brevis* (Essential, 646), 1968
28. Jethro Tull: *A Passion Play* (Capital/Chrysalis, 72435-81569-0-4), 1973
29. Genesis: *Foxtrot* (Atlantic, 82674-2), 1972
30. King Crimson: *Larks' Tongues in Aspic* (EG Records, Editions EG/JEM Records, EGKC 6), 1973
31. Procol Harum: *Shine On Brightly* (A&M, SP-4151), 1968
32. Yes: *Tales from Topographic Oceans* (Atlantic, SD 2-908), 1973
33. The Moody Blues: *Days of Future Passed* (Deram/Decca, 42284 4767-2), 1967
34. Gentle Giant: *Octopus* (Columbia/Alucard, CK 32022), 1972
35. Emerson, Lake and Palmer: *Pictures at an Exhibition* (Atlantic, SD 19122), 1972
36. New Trolls: *Concerto Grosso Per I* (Warner Fonit/Nuova Fonit Cetra, 3984 26602-2), 1971

37. Refugee: s/t (Time Wave Music, IDVP002CD), 1974
38. Brian Eno: *Here Come the Warm Jets* (EG Records, EGCD 11), 1973
39. Hatfield and the North: s/t (Carol, 1833-2), 1974
40. Pink Floyd: *Animals* (Columbia, JC 34474), 1977
41. Tool: *Lateralus* (Toolshed Music/EMI Music/Volcano Entertainment, 61422-31160-2), 2001
42. The Soft Machine: s/t (Big Beat/MCA, CDWIKD), 1968
43. Yes: *Relayer* (Atlantic, SD 19135), 1974
44. Van der Graaf Generator: *Pawn Hearts* (Virgin/EMI, 07243 474890 2 0), 1971
45. Colosseum: *Valentyne Suite* (Vertigo, VO 1847900 VTY), 1969
46. Styx: *Styx II* (Wooden Nickel, WNS-1012), 1971
47. Triumvirat: *Illusions on a Double Dimple* (Harvest/EMI, 7243 5 35162 2 2), 1973
48. Frank Zappa and the Mothers of Invention: *Freak Out!* (Ryko, RCD 10501), 1966
49. Gong: *Angel's Egg* (Virgin, 8665562), 1973
50. Renaissance: *Ashes Are Burning* (Repertoire Records, REP4575-WY), 1973
51. Premiata Forneria Marconi: *Per Un Amico* (RCA, ND 71784), 1972
52. Henry Cow: *Leg End* (East Side Digital, 80482), 1973
53. Pulsar: *Halloween* (Musea, FGBG 4022.AR), 1977
54. Gentle Giant: *Acquiring the Taste* (Vertigo, 6360 041), 1971
55. Dream Theater: *Scenes from a Memory* (Elektra, 62448-2), 1999
56. Jethro Tull: *Aqualung* (Chrysalis, F2 21044), 1973
57. Marillion: *Misplaced Childhood* (EMI Records, 7243 5 27116 2 8), 2000
58. Steve Hackett: *Voyage of the Acolyte* (Virgin, CASCD 1111), 1975

59. Locanda delle Fate: *Forse le Lucciole Non Si Amano Più* (Polygram Italia, 523688-2) 1977
60. Univers Zero: *Univers Zero (1313)* (Cuneiform, Rune 20), 1977
61. Kansas: *Leftoverture* (Kirshner/CBS, AL 34224), 1976
62. Family: *Music in a Doll's House* (Pucka Music, PUC 1968), 1968
63. The Beatles: *Sgt. Pepper's Lonely Hearts Club Band* (Capital/EMI SMAS-2653), 1967
64. Pink Floyd: *The Piper at the Gates of Dawn* (Capitol/EMI, 46384-2), 1967
65. The Beach Boys: *Pet Sounds* (Capitol, 72435-21241-2-1), 1966
66. Magma: *Köhntarkösz* (A&M, SP-3650), 1974
67. Radiohead: *OK Computer* (Capitol, 55229-2), 1997
68. Arti + Mestieri: *Tilt* (Akarma, 1024), 1974
69. Genesis: *Wind & Wuthering* (Atlantic, SD 36-144), 1976
70. Utopia: *Ra* (Bearsville Records/Earmark Music, BR 6965), 1977
71. Ange: *Par Les Fils de Mandrin* (Philips/Phonogram, 842237-2), 1976
72. Ethos (Ardour): s/t (Capitol, ST 11498), 1975
73. Frank Zappa and the Mothers of Invention: *We're Only In It for the Money* (Ryko, RCD 10503), 1968
74. Pink Floyd: *The Wall* (Columbia, AL 36185), 1979
75. The Nice: *Five Bridges* (Virgin, CASCD 1014), 1970
76. Tangerine Dream: *Phaedra* (Virgin/Atlantic, VR 13-108), 1974
77. Traffic: *John Barleycorn Must Die* (Liberty/UA, UAS 5504), 1970
78. Mike Oldfield: *Tubular Bells* (Virgin/Atlantic, VR 13-105), 1973
79. Stomu Yamash'ta: *Go* (Island Records, ILPS-9387), 1976
80. Yes: *The Yes Album* (Atlantic, SD 19131), 1971

81. Peter Banks: *Two Sides of Peter Banks* (Capitol Records/Sovereign, SMAS-11217), 1973
82. Emerson, Lake and Palmer: s/t (Cotillion/Atlantic/EG, SD 9040), 1970
83. Jethro Tull: *Minstrel in the Gallery* (Five Star Records/EMI, 72435-41572-2-6), 1975
84. Mahavishnu Orchestra: *The Inner Mounting Flame* (Columbia/Sony, CK65523), 1971
85. Curved Air: *Phantasmagoria* (Warner Bros., WPCP-4224), 1972
86. Liquid Tension Experiment: *2* (Magna Carta, MA-9035), 1999
87. Robert Wyatt: *Rock Bottom* (Caroline, CAROL-1634-2), 1974
88. Focus: *Moving Waves* (Red Bullet, RB 66.188), 1971
89. Eloy: *Ocean* (Harvest/EMI, 7243 5 35160 2 4), 1977
90. David Bedford: *The Odyssey* (Virgin, V2070), 1976
91. Marillion: *Afraid of Sunlight* (El Dorado/EMI Records/I.R.S. Records, 7243 8 33874 2 7), 1995
92. Genesis: *A Trick of the Tail* (Atco/Atlantic, SD 38-101), 1976
93. Harmonium: *Si on avait besoin d'une cinquième saison* (Polydor, 8339902), 1975
94. Tool: *Aenima* (Volcano Entertainment, 61422-31087-2), 1996
95. The Mars Volta: *Frances the Mute* (CSL/Strummer Recordings/Universal, B0004129-02), 2005
96. The Strawbs: *Hero and Heroine* (A&M, 540 935-2), 1974
97. Alas: s/t (EMI, 389126), 1976
98. Il Balletto di Bronzo: *Ys* (Polydor, 523 693-2), 1972
99. Styx: *The Grand Illusion* (A&M/Almo, SP-4637), 1977
100. Ange: *Au delà du Délire* (Philips/Phonogram, 842 239-2), 1974
101. Klaus Schulze: *Moondawn* (Magnum Music Group/Virgin, CDTB 093), 1976

102. Ozric Tentacles: *Erpland* (Snapper Music, 55542), 1990
103. Genesis: *Nursery Cryme* (R&M Music/Buddah Records, CAS 1052-B), 1971
104. Yes: *Going for the One* (Atlantic, SD 19106), 1977
105. Eloy: *Dawn* (EMI Electrola, 064-31), 1976
106. Rick Wakeman: *Journey to the Centre of the Earth* (A&M, 75021-3156-2), 1974
107. Banco del Mutuo Soccorso: *Come In Un'Ultima Cena* (Virgin Dischi, MPICD 1001), 1976
108. Patrick Moraz: *The Story of I* (Atlantic, SD 18175), 1976
109. Focus: *3* (Red Bullet, RB 66.189), 1972
110. Neal Morse: *Testimony* (Radiant/Metal Blade 14451), 2003
111. Kevin Ayers: *The Confessions of Dr. Dream* (Island, ILPS 9263), 1974
112. The Alan Parsons Project: *Tales of Mystery and Imagination* (Mercury/PolyGram, 832 820-2), 1976
113. Uriah Heep: *Salisbury* (Mercury/Hit Records Productions, SR-61319), 1971
114. Todd Rundgren: *Initiation* (Warner Bros./Bearsville/Earmark Music, BR 6957), 1975
115. Marillion: *Fugazi* (EMI Records, 7243 8 35271 2 0), 1984
116. Saga: *Images at Twilight* (BonAire, 258158), 1980
117. Mandalaband: *Eye of Wendor: Prophecies* (Chrysalis, CHR 1181), 1978
118. Spock's Beard: *Don't Try This at Home* (Radiant Records/Metal Blade Records 3984-14329-2), 2000
119. IQ: *The Wake* (GEMA/InsideOut Music, IOMACD 2108), 1985
120. Le Orme: *Felona e Sorona* (Philips/Polygram, 842 507-2), 1973
121. Happy the Man: s/t (One Way, 34546), 1977

122. Dream Theater: *Awake* (East/West, 90126-2), 1994
123. Amon Düül: *Yeti* (Warner Music/Liberty Records, 0630 17779-2), 1970
124. The Flower Kings: *Stardust We Are* (InsideOut Music, IOMCD 048), 1999
125. The Band: *Music from Big Pink* (Capitol, C2 46069), 1968
126. Jade Warrior: *Last Autumn's Dream* (Repertoire, 1104), 1972
127. Yes: *The Ladder* (Beyond Music, 63985-78046-2), 1999
128. IQ: *Subterranea* (GEMA/InsideOut Music, 2102), 1997
129. Ange: *Le Cimetière des Arlequins* (Philips Records, 9101 022), 1973
130. Spock's Beard: *The Light* (Radiant Records/Metal Blade Records, 3984-14494-2), 1994
131. Gong: *You* (Virgin/EMI, 66552-2), 1974
132. Porcupine Tree: *In Absentia* (Lava Records, 83604-2), 2002
133. Dixie Dregs: *What If?* (Capricorn Records/No Exit Music/Dregs Music, CPN 0203), 1978
134. Anekdoten: *Vemod* (Arcangelo, ARC-1001), 1993
135. Can: *Future Days* (Mute/Spoon-Music/GEMA, LC 7395), 1973
136. Gentle Giant: *The Power and the Glory* (Alucard, ALU-GG-011), 1974
137. Kayak: *See, See the Sun* (Harvest, 11305), 1973
138. IQ: *Dark Matter* (InsideOut, 60802), 2004
139. Lunatic Soul: s/t (Kscope, 112), 2008
140. Neal Morse: *Sola Scriptura* (Radiant/Metal Blade, 14612), 2007
141. The Tangent: *The World that We Drive Through* (InsideOut, 00392), 2004
142. Spooky Tooth with Pierre Henry: *Ceremony: An Electric Mass* (Island, ILPS-9107), 1970
143. The Flower Kings: *Unfold the Future* (InsideOut Music, IOMCD 112), 2002

144. Marillion: *Clutching at Straws* (EMI Records/Capital Records, CDP 7 46866 2), 1987
145. Amazing Blondel: *Fantasia Lindum* (Island, ILPS-9156), 1971
146. Manuel Göttsching: *New Age of Earth* (Spalax, 14505), 1976
147. Porcupine Tree: *Fear of a Blank Planet* (Atlantic, 2-115900), 2007
148. Coheed and Cambria: *In Keeping Secrets of Silent Earth: 3* (Equal Vision/Columbia, CK92686), 2003
149. Änglagård: *Hybris* (Exergy Music, EX-9), 1992
150. King's X: *Gretchen Goes to Nebraska* (Atlantic, 81997-2), 1989
151. SBB: *Nowy Horyzont* (Metal Mind, 0321), 1975
152. The Soft Machine: *Volume 2* (Big Beat/MCA, CDWIKD), 1969
153. Wigwam: *Being* (Love Records, LRCD 92), 1974
154. Gryphon: *Red Queen to Gryphon Three* (Talking Elephant/Sanctuary Records, TECD112), 1974
155. Hawkwind: *Space Ritual* (EMI Records, 7243 5 30032 2 7), 1973
156. Popol Vuh: *Brüder des Schattens ~ Söhne des Lichts* (Brain, 0060.167), 1978
157. Caravan: *Waterloo Lily* (Decca/Deram, 8829822), 1972
158. Fates Warning: *Perfect Symmetry* (Metal Blade, 14048), 1989
159. White Willow: *Ex Tenebris* (The Laser's Edge, LE1029), 1998
160. Frank Zappa: *Apostrophe (')* (Ryko, RCD 10519), 1974
161. Bruford: *One of a Kind* (EG Records/Winterfold Records, BBWF 004 CD), 1979
162. Eno: *Another Green World* (EG Records, EGCD 21), 1975
163. Can: *Tago Mago* (Spoon/Mute, 9273-2), 1971
164. Opeth: *Blackwater Park* (Koch, KOC-CD-8237), 2001
165. No-Man: *Flowermouth* (K Scope/Snapper Music, KSCOPE111X), 1994

166. Supertramp: *Crime of the Century* (A&M, 3936472), 1974
167. Renaissance: *Turn of the Cards* (BTM Records/Repertoire, REP 4491-WY), 1974
168. Roxy Music: *Stranded* (Virgin/EG Records, 47451 2), 1973
169. Glass Hammer: *The Inconsolable Secret* (Sound Resources, SR1320), 2005
170. The Jimi Hendrix Experience: *Electric Ladyland* (MCA, MCAD 10895), 1968
171. Electric Light Orchestra: *On the Third Day* (United Artists Records/Anne Rachel Music/Yellow Dog Music, UA-LA188-F), 1973
172. Gentle Giant: *In a Glass House* (DRT Entertainment, RTE 00351), 1973
173. Grobschnitt: *Rockpommel's Land* (Universal Music/Revisited Records, SPV 49812 CD), 1977
174. Eloy: *Silent Cries and Mighty Echoes* (Harvest/EMI, 7243 5 63774 2 4), 1978
175. Mutantes: *Tudo Foi Feito Pelo Sol* (Som Livre, 4179-2), 1974
176. The Moody Blues: *On the Threshold of a Dream* (Deram/Decca, 42284 4769-2), 1969
177. Renaissance: *Scheherezade and Other Stories* (BTM Records/Repertoire, REP 4490-WY), 1975
178. 801: *Live* (EG Records, EGCD 26), 1976
179. Rick Wakeman: *The Myths and Legends of King Arthur and the Knights of the Round Table* (Almo Music/A&M Records, SP-4515), 1975
180. Barclay James Harvest: s/t (Harvest, 1C 064-04 372), 1970
181. Van der Graaf Generator: *Godbluff* (Virgin, 00946 311393 2 1), 1975
182. Greenslade: *Spyglass Guest* (Warner Bros./Wounded Bird Records, WOU 8672), 1974

183. Van der Graaf Generator: *Still Life* (Charisma, CAROL 1641-2), 1976
184. Ekseption: *Trinity* (Philips, 6423056), 1973
185. Tonton Macoute: s/t (Neon Records/RCA, NE-4), 1971
186. Barclay James Harvest: *Octoberon* (Universal/Polydor, 80100133), 1976
187. Frank Zappa: *Roxy & Elsewhere* (Ryko RCD 10520), 1974
188. Spring: s/t (Neon Records/Akarma Records/Comet Records, AK 213), 1971
189. Rush: *A Farewell to Kings* (Mercury/Polygram, 822 546-2), 1977
190. Electric Light Orchestra: *ELO II* (Jet Records/CBS, BL 35533), 1973
191. Colosseum: *Those Who Are About to Die Salute You* (Fontana, STL 5510), 1969
192. The Strawbs: *Ghosts* (A&M, 540 937-2), 1975
193. Rush: *Hemispheres* (Mercury, 822 547-2), 1978
194. Caravan: *For Girls Who Grow Plump in the Night* (Decca/Deram, 8829802), 1973
195. Queensrÿche: *Operation: Mindcrime* (EMI/Capitol, 72435-81068-2-4), 1988
196. Captain Beefheart: *Trout Mask Replica* (Reprise, 2027-2), 1970
197. Brian Eno: *Before and After Science* (EG Records, EGCD 32), 1977
198. Transatlantic: *SMPT:E* (Radiant/Metal Blade, 3984-14290-2), 2000
199. Robert Fripp: *Exposure* (EG, EGLP 101/PD-1-6201 (2310 661), 1979
200. Pain of Salvation: *Remedy Lane* (InsideOut Music, 2031), 2002
201. Curved Air: *Air Conditioning* (Warner Bros., K 56004), 1970
202. McDonald and Giles: s/t (Virgin, CDV 2963), 1971
203. Renaissance: s/t (Paradox Music BMI/Collector's Choice Music, CCM-272-2), 1969

204. The Enid: *In the Region of Summer Stars* (BUK Records, BUK INS 3005), 1976
205. Omega: *200 Years After the Last War* (Bellaphon, BAC 2022), 1974
206. OSI: *Office of Strategic Influence* (InsideOut, SPV 089-65400), 2003
207. Roxy Music: s/t (Virgin, 47447), 1972
208. Greenslade: s/t (Warner Music/WEA, 7599-26812-2), 1973
209. Espers: *II* (Drag City, DC310 CD), 2006
210. Spock's Beard: *V* (Radiant, 3984-14335-2), 2000
211. Supersister: *Present from Nancy* (Polydor, 843 231-2), 1970
212. Ash Ra Tempel: *Schwingungen* (Ohr, OMM 556020), 1972
213. Samla Mammas Manna: *Maltid* (Silence, SRSCD 3604), 1973
214. Trance: s/t (Musea, 4144), 1974
215. Between the Buried and Me: *Colors* (Victory Records, VR351), 2007
216. National Health: s/t (Esoteric, 2129), 1977
217. U.K.: *Danger Money* (EG Records/Editions EG/JEM Records, EGLP 39), 1979
218. Symphony X: *The Odyssey* (InsideOut/SPV, 693723 65342 6), 2002
219. Trans-Siberian Orchestra: *Christmas Eve and Other Stories* (Lava/Atlantic, 92736), 1996
220. Focus: *Hamburger Concerto* (ATCO/Atlantic/Radio Tele Music/Canadian Radmus, SD 36-100), 1974
221. Pendragon: *The Masquerade Overture* (Toff Records, PEND7CD), 1996
222. Osanna: *Palepoli* (Warner Fonit, 3984 28279-2), 1973
223. King Crimson: *Discipline* (Warner Bros/EG Records, BSK 3629), 1981
224. Nektar: *A Tab in the Ocean* (Passport Records/ABC/Bellaphon Records, PPSD-98017), 1972

225. Anthony Phillips: *The Geese & the Ghost* (Passport Records/ABC/Run It Music, PP-98020), 1977
226. Il Rovescio della Medaglia: *Contaminazione* (Sony Music, ND 74511), 1973
227. Manfred Mann's Earth Band: *Roaring Silence* (Warner Bros., 3055), 1976
228. Museo Rosenbach: *Zarathustra* (Ricordi, 74321531842), 1973
229. It Bites: *The Big Lad in the Windmill* (Virgin, CDV2378), 1986
230. The Incredible String Band: *The Hangman's Beautiful Daughter* (Elektra, 7559-60835-2), 1968
231. Sylvian/Fripp: *Damage* (Virgin, 7243 8 39905 2 8), 1994
232. Semiramis: *Dedicato a Frazz* (Trident Records, TRI 1004), 1973
233. Fripp & Eno: *Evening Star* (Opal/Inner Knot, DGM0516), 1975
234. Sfinx: *Zalmoxe* (Electrecord, ELCD 135), 1978
235. Various artists: *Peter and the Wolf* (Viceroy, VIC 6006-2), 1976
236. David Bowie: *Low* (Virgin, 52190706), 1977
237. Radiohead: *Kid A* (Capitol, CDP 7243 5 29684), 2000
238. Soft Machine: *Bundles* (Harvest, SHSP4044), 1975
239. Latte e Miele: *Passio Secundum Mattheum* (Polydor, 2448 011), 1972
240. Jan Akkerman: *Tabernakel* (Wounded Bird, WOU 7032), 1974
241. Egg: s/t (Deram, 18039), 1970
242. Steve Hillage: *L* (Caroline/Blue Plate, CAROL 1801-2), 1976
243. Matching Mole: s/t (Sony Music, 618), 1972
244. Henry Cow: *Unrest* (East Side Digital, 80492), 1974
245. Miriodor: *Mekano* (Cuneiform, Rune 148), 2001
246. King Crimson: *Three of a Perfect Pair* (EG/Warner Bros., 1-25071), 1984

247. Umphrey's McGee: *Mantis* (Sci Fidelity, 1117), 2009

248. Echolyn: *As the World* (Sony/550, BK 57623), 1995

249. Phideaux: *Chupacabras* (Bloodfish, zyz-1777), 2005

250. Alamaailman Vasarat: *Maahan* (Nordic Notes, 02911), 2007

251. Upsilon Acrux: *Galapagos Momentum* (Cuneiform, Rune 245), 2007

252. Sigur Rós: *( )* (Fat Cat Records, 22), 2002

253. Don Caballero: *2* (Touch & Go, 143), 1995

254. Godspeed You Black Emperor!: *Lift Yr. Skinny Fists like Antennas to Heaven!* (Krank, 043), 2000

255. Tortoise: *Millions Now Living Will Never Die* (Thrill Jockey, 25), 1996

256. Cynic: *Focus* (Roadrunner, 9169-2), 1993

257. Bo Hansson: *Music Inspired by Lord of the Rings* (Charisma, CAS-1059), 1972

258. Manfred Mann's Earth Band: *Solar Fire* (Bronze, ILPS 9265), 1973

259. Threshold: *Critical Mass* (InsideOut Music, IOMACD 2041), 2002

260. Chris Squire: *Fish out of Water* (Wounded Bird, 8159), 1975

261. Amon Düül: *Tanz der Lemminge* (Warner Music/Liberty Records/Repertoire, 0630 17780-2), 1971

262. Can: *Ege Bamyasi* (Mute, 69056), 1972

263. Espiritu: *Crisalida* (Sony Music, 509130), 1975

264. Asia: *Aura* (Spitfire, 13003), 2001

265. Riverside: *Anno Domini High Definition* (CMA, 310005), 2009

266. Cathedral: *Stained Glass Stories* (Delta Records, DRC 1002), 1978

267. Nektar: *Remember the Future* (Passport Records/Famous Music/Bellaphon Records, PPS-98002), 1973

268. Slapp Happy/Henry Cow: *Desperate Straights* (Vivid Sound, 2081), 1975

269. Coheed and Cambria: *Good Apollo I'm Burning Star IV, Vol. 1: From Fear Through the Eyes of Madness* (Equal Vision/Columbia, 93989), 2005

270. Gilgamesh: *Another Fine Tune You've Got Me Into* (Esoteric, 2126), 1978

271. Jean Michel Jarre: *Oxygene* (Polydor, 800 015-2), 1976

272. Supertramp: *. . . Even in the Quietest of Moments* (A&M, 3297), 1977

273. Frank Zappa: *Hot Rats* (Ryko, RCD 10508), 1969

274. Muse: *The Resistance* (Warner Bros., 521130-2), 2009

275. Henry Cow: *Western Culture* (East Side Digital, 80852), 1979

276. Rush: *Caress of Steel* (Mercury/PolyGram, 822543), 1975

277. Steve Hillage: *Fish Rising* (Virgin, 2031), 1975

278. Hatfield and the North: *The Rotters' Club* (Virgin, CAROL 1834-2), 1975

279. Caravan: *If I Could Do It All Over Again, I'd Do It All Over You* (Mantra, 001), 1970

280. Aphrodite's Child: *666* (One Way, OW 31375), 1972

281. Steve Howe: *The Steve Howe Album* (Topographic Music/Atlantic/WB Music, SD 19243), 1979

282. Emerson, Lake and Palmer: *Trilogy* (Cotillion/Atlantic, SD 9903), 1972

283. Genesis: *Trespass* (MCA, MCAD 1653), 1970

284. Dream Theater: *Six Degrees of Inner Turbulence* (Elektra, 62742), 2002

285. Gentle Giant: *Three Friends* (Columbia/Malibu Records, CK 31649), 1972

286. Camel: *Mirage* (Deram/Decca/Universal, 8829292), 1974

287. Étron Fou Leloublan: *Les Trois Fous Perdégagnent (Au Pays Des . . .)* (Musea, 8660), 1978

288. National Health: *Playtime* (Cuneiform, Rune 145), 2001

289. Fripp & Eno: *(No Pussyfooting)* (Opal/Inner Knot, DGM5007-B), 1973

290. Far Corner: s/t (Cuneiform, Rune 194), 2004

291. Bozzio Levin Stevens: *Situation Dangerous* (Magna Carta, MA-9049), 2000

292. Kansas: *Masque* (Kirshner/CBS, PZ33806), 1975

293. Centipede: *September Energy* (RCA, BGOCD485), 1971

294. Mike Oldfield: *Ommadawn* (Caroline, CAR 1855), 1975

295. Be Bop Deluxe: *Sunburst Finish* (EMI, 7947272), 1976

296. Allan Holdsworth: *Allan Holdsworth, i.o.u.* (Enigma, ST-73252), 1982

297. Area: *Arbeit Macht Frei* (Cramps, CRSLP 5101), 1973